Bakunin

Bakunin
Selected Texts 1868-1875

ANARRES EDITIONS

This collection first published in 2016 by
Anarres Editions, an imprint of
The Merlin Press
99b Wallis Road
London
E9 5LN

www.merlinpress.co.uk
info@merlinpress.co.uk

Translations and notes © A.W. Zurbrugg, 2016

ISBN. 978-0-85036-722-5

Catalogue in publication data is available from the British Library

All rights reserved. No part of this publication may be reproduced, stored in a retrieval system, or transmitted, in any form or by any means, electronic, mechanical, photocopying, recording or otherwise, without the prior permission of the publisher.

Printed in the UK by Imprint Digital, Exeter

CONTENTS

Introduction	1
Chronology	28
The Programme of the International Alliance for Socialist Democracy: October 1868	33
Open Letter from the Central Bureau of the International Fraternity: March 1869	35
Letter to James Guillaume: April 1869	38
Articles in *L'Égalité*:	39
[1] Organisation and the general strike: April 1869	40
[2] Four articles on the politics of the International: August 1869	42
Draft resolution on inheritance	56
On Inheritance. Speech at the Basel congress of the IWA: September 1869	57
On Real Democracy: February 1870	60
Prospects for Socialism: September 1870	71
Letters to Nikolai Ogarev & the Red Poster September-October 1870	90
On Discipline: Winter 1870-71	95
On Democracy and Education: May 1871	96
Socialism and the Paris Commune: June 1871	101
On Leaders and Politics: July 1871	113
On the Alliance: August 1871	142
Letter to the Jura comrades: February-March 1872	170
Letter to Celso Ceretti: March 1872	184
Letter to Tómas González Morago: May 1872	208
The Programme of the Slav section in Zurich: August 1872	217
Writings against Marx: November-December 1872	221

On Lassalle and Marx: August 1873	242
Letter of resignation from the Jura Federation: October 1873	247
Letter to Élisée Reclus: February 1875	251
Notes	253
People, places, organisations, events	284
Sources	293
Subjects discussed by Bakunin	295
General index	296

INTRODUCTION

Mikhail Bakunin was born in 1814, the year that Napoleon was defeated and went into exile in Elba. Nineteenth century radicals saw the great French revolution of 1789 as a landmark, but came to have differing perspectives as to its ongoing significance. Some viewed it as a model from the past but not for the future; others, still confronting monarchies and feudalism, still looked forward to some sort of Jacobin revolution.

Some features of the 1860s may seem familiar: ups and downs in economic cycles and states struggling to maintain creditworthiness. In this era, although new enterprises were developing – railways, textile factories and mines – older forms of traditional and artisan production were still more common. Political and social circumstances were rather different. France was under the heel of an Emperor, Napoleon III. In Eastern and South-eastern Europe the heads of other empires – Austria-Hungary, Russia and Ottoman Turkey – ruled over many diverse peoples. There had been a revolt in Poland in 1863, but it remained divided under the rule of Austria-Hungary, Prussia and Russia. The map of Europe featured Papal States, and a Confederation of Northern German States. Germany and Italy were still emerging as nation-states. This was an era of brief wars with successive Prussian victories in 1864, 1866 and again in 1871 establishing a new German Empire – the most powerful state in continental Europe by far.

Illiteracy, unemployment and underemployment were very common. Schooling as it now exists was almost wholly lacking. Rational scientific thinking was struggling to overcome prejudice – often rooted in reactionary churches. Trade-union rights barely existed, but trade-unions or syndicates were gaining strength in Belgium, Britain, France, Spain and Switzerland. Press freedom and liberal democracy were scarce. Switzerland was unique in Europe as the only republic where liberal 'radicals' were in government and where male nationals had the vote. Women were employed in numbers in some sectors e.g. textiles, but had few rights, either at work or in the home. In this era, travel and communications flowed slowly, letters kept people in touch and newspapers were the key medium for large scale communication.

Bakunin knew poverty in diverse social, economic and political conditions. He was often a fugitive from the law and almost always short of funds. He encountered various forms of popular patriotism amongst many peoples: French, Germans, Italians, Poles, Russians, Scandinavians, Slavs and Swiss.

***

Had Bakunin died in 1868 he might be remembered as a courageous revolutionary in 1848, lucky to have avoided execution after his capture in 1849, famous for his escape from Russia and the author of some interesting writings, but perhaps not more than this. The Bakunin who emerged after 1868 helped define gradually emerging forms of revolutionary, libertarian or anarchist socialism. It was not so much that he invented new ideas, rather he helped organise and shape a new form of political thinking.[1] His ideas evolved in collaboration with revolutionary socialists across Western Europe and drew on the experience of the International Working Men's Association (IWA) in many countries.

This book presents a selection of his texts: letters, a lecture, brief speeches and newspaper articles, both finished and unfinished works. The selection begins in 1868, the year Bakunin moved to Geneva and became a member of the local section of the IWA, and ends in 1875, the year he died. Many of these texts focus on the development of politics in and around the IWA. After its formation in 1864 the IWA had developed with a medley of diverse components: new workplace sections (unions), affiliations of previously organised unions, sections based in particular locations, some organised on the principle of language, and others inspired by particular perspectives; at first some of its bodies resembled political clubs. There were no political parties affiliated to the IWA.

Bakunin's politics

The Basel IWA congress of 1869 debated prospects for workplace organising. Jean-Louis Pindy*[a] proposed a motion concluding that:

> Federations [of workplace unions] should be responsible for the collection of information relative to their particular industries, for shaping common measures that should be taken, for regulating strikes and for working to ensure their success until the time comes for wage-labour to be replaced by a Federation of Free Producers.[2]

Workplace unionism depended for much of its strength on basic labour solidarity – organisation, strike action, preventing strikebreaking and

---

a * indicates a note in the glossary on page 284

stopping the 'importation' of strikebreaking labourers from other parts – such solidarity motivated much of the support for the motion above, which was passed unopposed by the Basel Congress.[3]

This resolution was both defensive and offensive. It suggested necessary struggles in the present and perspectives looking forward to broader change in the future. It also set out a vision of change mediated through participatory democracy, Federations of organised Free Producers and Communes, in the workplace and in the community. It suggested that, for the IWA, the way forward involved the strengthening of its workplace sections, until they could establish a network that might displace current social and political powers. Federations helped build strength, but the basis for that strength lay in the grassroots rather than in some centralising leadership. (*Bakunin discusses these issues in the text below*: 'Leaders and politics'.)

Bakunin shared this participatory and pre-figurative perspective. Was such a vision utopian? Impractical? 'If there is something dreamy and mystical in imagining that the International should contain – in germ in some way – the whole future organisation of human society, then we should have to humbly confess that we were mystics and dreamers. But, firstly let us console ourselves dear friends, we are absolutely not alone in sharing this belief.' In his view working people could not use the organisational forms of exploiting classes: 'The aims that we propose being so different, the means that we propose to the working masses must be essentially different to theirs.' (*See the text below*: 'To the Jura Comrades, 1872')[4] A circular sent by the Jura Federation to other IWA federations concluded:

> Future society should be nothing other than the universalisation of the organisation that the International has provided for itself. We should therefore take care to make our organisation come as close to our ideals – as much *as it may be possible*. How could one hope to have a free and equal society emerge out of an authoritarian body? It is impossible. The International, as the embryo of future human society, is bound to be, from the present, the faithful image of our principles of federation and freedom and should expel from its midst any principles that might tend to dictatorship and authority.[5]

In Bakunin's view the ideals of the French revolution – liberty, equality and fraternity, and a centralised republic – had to be revisited. Working people needed economic rights. The aim of the IWA – that working people should liberate themselves – was something that inspired him. He wrote that those seeking change should 'look for inspiration within the people, and not beyond it'. (*See the text below*: Letter to Celso Ceretti.)

Bakunin looked to a future in which political and economic organisation and choices were made not from the top, but by working people, from the base of society. As he reviewed recent experience of male citizens' suffrage in Switzerland he concluded that the winning of these civil rights was not enough to empower working people. (*See the text below*: On Real Democracy). Another path was needed.

Repression

In 1868-9 the IWA was expanding. It was 'legal' in Britain and Switzerland, but in many other places it was harassed or banned: its press was seized, its offices were raided, leaders imprisoned and strikes attacked by the armed forces of the state. On May 1870 Bakunin noted:

> At the [moment] reaction is complete in France: many of our friends – in Paris ([Malon*] for example), in Lyons (Richard* and many others), in Rouen and Marseilles are still in prison – Varlin* has fled and has taken refuge in Belgium, Bastelica in Spain, some others in Switzerland. Have you also read in the press that the police have descended on the IWA in Brussels and seized all records. They will find nothing I'm sure; it was assuredly France that was pushing and I don't doubt that there is a coalition of all European governments, not accepting the Swiss government, all against the International – it is beginning to really scare them.[6]

Nevertheless there were some rising expectations. The next few months saw many strikes, the destruction of the regime of Napoleon III, an attempted rising in Lyons, then other Communal uprisings. Events in Spain were also encouraging. The monarchy was replaced by a new republic. There was an enthusiastic response to the efforts of one of Bakunin's friends, Fanelli,* to promote the Alliance for Socialist Democracy and the IWA. One phase of repression achieved its zenith in Paris in May 1871, where the new French republic killed some 10,000 rebels. The defeat of the Paris Commune brought a wave of refugees and radical politics to Barcelona, Geneva, London, New York and elsewhere. In Spain local insurrectionary movements emerged in 1872-3. In Italy the new state was somewhat unstable. Riots broke out when new taxes increased the cost of bread. In the years after the defeat of the Commune state power was reasserted and Bakunin acknowledged that revolutionary change was no longer on the cards.

Bakunin recognised that there was a huge diversity in social, economic and political conditions in Europe. Disputes over perspectives for the labour movement reflected, in part, the locations and linkages of particular thinkers. The critique of 'democracy' articulated by Bakunin and his co-thinkers arose from their reflection on the democratic politics of Switzerland and France and led them towards setting out a wider form of participatory politics than that of German Social-Democrats who chose to use the limited 'democracy' allowed by Bismarck. What many Germans radicals saw as a progress – eradicating feudalism, creating a modern, unitary state – was seen elsewhere as an inadequate programme, one that had been tried and that had brought little progress. Perspectives on priorities were influenced by the reference points chosen by map-makers looking for landmarks and paths towards change in the future.

Revolutionary agendas

Bakunin worked with friends and co-thinkers to develop a comprehensive socialist agenda, considering contemporary problems: the corruption of representatives, bureaucratic power, the oppression of rural people and 'progressive nationalism'. In matters of economics Bakunin acknowledged that Marx was on the right track and that his research was invaluable – but Marx's research in the British Museum did not provide him with equal insight into other matters. Most often Bakunin his comrades and co-thinkers preferred to struggle and organise not on the terrain of the bourgeoisie, within the law and the state, but on the terrain of working people: the community and the workplace. For them, the basis of the IWA lay more, but not exclusively, in the solidarity that developed in and across the workplace. They fought for a grassroots and internationalist socialist politics; a politics that flowed from class and that recognised other forms of oppression.

They fought against a Social-Democracy that, so they believed, was subordinating general social progress to the progress of representatives' power. They suspected that this Social-Democracy, whilst working for electoral-party-political representation within the framework of national states, was abandoning internationalism and solidarity, and subordinating general class interests to the interests of prosperous male citizen artisans.

They challenged and condemned the priorities and perspectives of those who thought and wrote that some form of Jacobin democracy could be tantamount to socialism. Back in 1852 Marx had written of Chartism in the circumstances then appertaining that 'universal suffrage is the equivalent for political power for the working class of England'. It would also be a 'more socialistic measure than anything which has been honoured with that name on the Continent. Its *inevitable* result here, is the political supremacy of the working class.'[7] Switzerland experienced several strikes of textile and construction workers in these times, but the universal suffrage that was available to its male citizens did not facilitate any definite working-class influence in government.[8] Bakunin sets out his reasoning as to why, in the circumstances of the day, democracy was a fraud even in 'democratic' states and would not facilitate a transition towards socialism. In April 1870, shortly before a congress of the French-Swiss Romande Federation, he concluded:

> Beyond its local importance the battle that is about to open in La Chaux-de-Fonds will have an immense universal interest. It will be the harbinger and precursor of one that will be waged at the next IWA general congress: Do we want comprehensive universal socialism or the small politics of bourgeois radicals as revised and corrected from the viewpoint of bourgeois workers? Do we seek the abolition of bourgeois homelands and of political States or the advent of a single, universal, socialist State? Do we want the complete emancipation of workers or only the improvement of their lot? Do we want to create a new world or patch up the old one?[9]

Bakunin was sensitive to matters of age, gender, culture and language. He hoped to find some generosity of spirit amongst bourgeois youth:

> Among young people there is energy, a generous, wide-open instinct for justice that counterbalances pernicious influences. They may be corrupted by the ideas and by the example of their fathers, but as yet, bourgeois youth have not been corrupted in everyday practical living ... They are disrespectful: instinctively despising tradition and the principle of authority.[10]

He had less respect for universities in Europe as institutions. Academics, as they began to form a new scientific network, were servicing the needs of the bourgeoisie – much as the Catholic clergy had serviced the nobility and aristocracy in earlier times.[11] Language factors had a particular influence. For example German was the language of the state in the Austro-Hungarian Empire, and Slav speakers might resent labour organisation couched in the language of the state. Immigrants often organised distinct IWA sections by language. At IWA congresses those who spoke the same language might sit together. Bakunin spoke and wrote in several languages and was able to shape a discourse that bypassed London and challenged the influence of German speakers at the centre of the IWA's administration.[12]

Bakunin believed that the peoples of 'Latin' Europe had revolutionary potential.[13] He was often sceptical about prospects for change in Germany (*see the texts below*: 'To the Jura comrades' and 'Prospects for Socialism'). Bakunin noticed that *Volksstaat*, the journal of German Social-Democrats,[14] published sentences saying that with the defeat of Napoleon III the initiative in the labour movement had passed to Germany.[15] He rejected this. Nor did he see any forcible correlation between economic development and the development of revolutionary potential; other human factors were at work in the matter.

Bakunin believed that most German liberalism was little distinguished from German servility.[16] He attacked the alliance between labour and liberals. (*See the text below*: 'Prospects for Socialism' for comments on the Social-Democratic Party.) At the time few saw the new German Empire as a threat to progress.[17] Bakunin however saw Berlin becoming a huge menace and 'the head and the capital of everything reactionary'.[18] In his view, a 'passion for equality and the instinct of freedom' were somewhat lacking amongst German radicals.[19] In the light of subsequent development, between 1870 and 1945, Bakunin's views on Germany may seem somewhat prophetic.[20] While he hoped that German workers would rebel, he saw German Social-Democracy as an expression of the privilege of the urban, male, skilled citizen artisan/worker – as opposed to the wider interests of women and men, skilled and unskilled, citizens and migrants. He stressed that the privileged status of 'bourgeois workers' made them less ready to press for change, as compared with the rascally, tattered workers that he found in Latin Europe (*see the text below*: 'Writings against Marx'). His guess that only some huge war would re-open opportunities closed by the defeat of the revolutionary movements of the early 1870s may also appear far-sighted.

Strategies and perspectives

Bakunin endorsed varied forms of organising, both open and democratic, and clandestine, as circumstances dictated. He advocated democratic forms in mass organisations where there was some degree of freedom, and clandestine forms where repression made open organisation dangerous. It should be remembered that Bakunin wrote for particular audiences in particular circumstances.

In Geneva he worked in a mass IWA organisation largely based on workplace organisation. He repudiated elitist strategy and practice. He deplored 'governmental' IWA leaderships in Geneva and on the General Council, who attempted to rule by opaque, covert, underhand manipulation. Such practices were counter-productive in his view: the shell of the organisation might survive in the form of a leadership, but the content of the organisation would dissipate leaving that shell empty.

He repudiated political strategies that focused on working to influence the state through the building of alliances with elements of the radical or not so radical bourgeoisie. He advocated the priority of building labour and workplace solidarity. This focus on building union-type organisations and solidarity in and around the workplace had been the general practice of the IWA as it grew after 1864. This strategy came to be challenged by a new strategy of building electoral-party-agitation, which became the strategy of Marx and his entourage on the General Council in league with emerging Social-Democratic and Radical Party groupings after 1869.[b] The new policy – the beginnings of an outline of a view of parties, their role, remit and priorities – began to be enunciated in London in 1871 – although the strategy had never been debated by an IWA congress. Bakunin and other critics noted that no proper discussion process had been implemented. Bakunin objected also to the very idea of attempting to impose any political policy on a mass workplace-based network:

> We deny the existence of an official theory, or a single doctrine, be it religious or philosophical, be it sophist or socialist, in the International. Religious or philosophical dogmas would transform the International into a church; socialist or political dogmas would turn it into a state; brought together these two dogmas would establish a unitary state-church along the model proposed by Mazzini. Then the General Council would become some sort of lay collective Pope, whose every opinion, whose every perspective, whose every ex-cathedra speech, repeated in official circulars by secretary-correspondents would have the force of law, and hitherto autonomous sections and the people of the International would become nothing but a heard of sheep, obeying thinking that it not their own – as in every church, in every state, and even in the most democratic of republics. The development of thinking in the International should be entirely free, something that it could not be from the moment it was forced to recognise some official theory.

The miseries that would accompany any attempt to impose a single doctrine in the International can be avoided through a respect for:

---

b In several countries sections and federations disregarded the law of the land to affiliate to the IWA. German Social-Democratic bodies chose to work within the law, neither affiliating nor paying dues.

unavoidable and natural diversity of ideas and tendencies, and by looking within all this diversity, in the conscience of the proletariat of every land, for principles that are common and fundamental for the popular masses of every land, broad enough to unite the proletariat of Europe and America in the same way of thinking and determination. This was the imperishable glory of the first founders of the International, and amongst all, above all – we are happy to acknowledge it – of Comrade Karl Marx; finding and formulating these principles was the glory of our first congress of 1867 [1866!] in Geneva.[21]

Later he would write that it was useful that there should be political discussions in the IWA – but not for there to be *one single official* programme. Other bodies – some sort of political party or organisation – were also helpful for the discussion and elaboration of policy, politics, and other matters. Bakunin wrote in a letter of May 1872:

> The Alliance is the necessary complement to the International. But the International and the Alliance, while having the same ultimate aims, perform different functions. The International endeavours to unify the working masses, the millions of workers, regardless of nationality and national boundaries or religious and political beliefs, into one compact body; the Alliance, on the other hand, tries to give these masses a really revolutionary direction. The programmes of one and the other, without being in any way opposed, differ only in the degree of their revolutionary development. The International contains in germ, but only in germ, the whole programme of the Alliance. The programme of the Alliance represents the fullest unfolding of the International.[22]

Nonetheless, Bakunin did not advocate beginning with the politics of an ideas-based organisation Rather, he argued the opposite: that one should begin through building thorough economic solidarity:

> when it comes to suggesting means to fight these woes, and to improve circumstances, one must at first talk not about those general and revolutionary means, which now form the action programme of the IWA … No, at first one should suggest only means that natural good sense and daily experience cannot misunderstand, means whose utility cannot be rejected. (*See the text below*: 'Leaders and politics'.)

He recognised that if labour organisations were based on programmes then there might be as many programmes as there were organisations. (*See the text below*: 'Writings against Marx'.) So, in his view what mattered most was the energy that sustained the IWA:

> Let us recognise this then: this saintly poverty is a sure proof of the International's sincerity, because if the IWA develops and progresses despite its incontrovertible poverty, despite every machination of the coalition of powers that is against it, then this is because it evidently constitutes a greater historical reality, a reality that is driven forward, not by an artificial combination in a more or less arbitrary [fashion] by some tens, hundreds or even thousands of fanatical, ambitious or interested individuals, but rather because of the fatal social development, the irresistible needs and tendencies of this era, because it contains in itself the future.[23]
>
> Strikes ruin us, yet we can neither prevent them, nor impede them. Never, or almost never, are they the result of some plot, whim, or caprice – they are the forcible result of current economic circumstances. When workers see the sureties of their independence – even of their existence – menaced further and further by the day, they know that to begin a strike is to condemn themselves to unimaginable suffering. But more often than not they have no other means to defend their miserable crumbs of bread, or such shadows of freedom that are left to them by the economic organisation of society. One more step on this path – a path that makes for the prosperity and progress for the wealthy owners of capital, but makes for retrograde disaster for them, will see them changed into serfs or Negro slaves. White slaves! That is the name that workers of the USA, workers of that democracy, that great republic par excellence, now give themselves.[24]

Bakunin looks forward to strikes spreading – becoming more powerful and more universal – and more intense, with IWA members resolved to help each other across frontiers. This was perhaps an anticipation of the call for a general strike.

Authority, discipline
Bakunin recognised that he was not of working-class origins and that new social relations should not depend on him or persons like him:

> I don't care to become a Garibaldi,* or to have any sort of [leading] role. I will die my dear, the worms will eat me, but I want our ideas to win. I want hands that are black and dirty to be really free from all authorities and from all current or future heroes. I want our ideas to triumph, not some more or less dramatic exhibition of my own person. Not my power but *our* power – the power of *our* organisation and *our* collective in collective action. I am ready, I will be the first to abdicate and annihilate my own name and person in favour of that. The time for brilliant and historic individuals is over my dear – and much for the better ...[25]

Bakunin did advocate authority of a sort, and discipline of a sort. When France was defeated in the Franco-Prussian war it remained rich, populous and intelligent, but disorganised; to save itself, it needed 'nothing but the spontaneous organisation an immense popular rising, revolution'.[26] Revolutionary ends implied revolutionary organisational forms – not Jacobin forms, suited to a fake and bourgeois revolution defending property, but voluntary self-discipline and temporary authority (*see the texts below*: 'Prospects for Socialism'. 'On Discipline').

As the regime of Napoleon III fell apart in 1870, Bakunin advocated respect between peasants and townspeople: working people should look towards taking power through their federated communes. There were openings to work for a socialist revolution; the widespread outrage felt by French working people seeing much of their country under occupation by the forces of monarchical German states should be mingled with a radical social agenda. Urban socialist revolutionaries should avoid imposing themselves and should build trust with peasants (*see the text below*: 'Prospects for Socialism'). Failure to do so would kill the revolution.[27] Bakunin might well have recognised similar dangers and patterns in the unfolding of the Russian revolution that began in 1917 when the Russian Empire faced defeat. 'It is the duty of leaders,' he wrote, 'not to impose their own fantasies on the masses, but to go as far as one may, as permitted and commanded by popular wishes and instincts.' (*See the text below*: Letter to Celso Ceretti.) He believed that real change – if it was to empower working people – needed to be rooted in working communities and in their common solidarity. He sought a co-operative form of social life:

> Of all the habits which corrupt social humanity, that of directing others, that of commanding them is the most pernicious; and at the same time the one which it is most difficult to unmake. All honest men recognise as much and need only to consider their own experience, because almost

anyone who exerts, or has exerted some absolute power, in some narrow or not so narrow circle, has only to examine their conscience to find that they have ended up by believing their habit of command is a right inherent to their own persons, implying the negation of other persons' rights and represents thereby the pinnacle of human deparavity.

Respecting the existence and human freedom of another – that is the plenitude of morality; loving them – that is human grace and virtue. Working for one's own complete freedom through the freedom of all, at first through individual and collective revolt, later, through work, science and collective organisation, that is right and duty – on the basis of equality, and without any other impulse but freedom for the one or the many; there is our right and duty.[28]

Bakunin sought egalitarian relations between intellectuals and manual workers. In his view even the brightest inventors did not invent in a vacuum. They stood on past knowledge and achievements and were sustained by others:

As for invention – the isolated work of individual intelligence and all cerebral work – it seems to us that such things should be free and unpaid work (but their application should not be so). And as for these talented persons, these geniuses, what should they live in? Yes, good God! They would live by their collective and manual labour, as others do. *So you wish to compel great intellects to do manual labour, alongside other inferior intellects.* Yes, this is what we seek, and for two reasons: firstly because we are convinced that great intellects – far from losing something – would on the contrary gain much in strength of spirit and bodily well-being, and above all in the spirit of justice and solidarity; and secondly because this is the sole means of humanising and uplifting manual labour, thereby establishing real human equality.[29]

The International Workers' Association
The IWA's federations were each subjected to pressures exerted by particular economies and states. Each state sought to restrict, limit and shape the power of labour. So, varied politics developed in varied contexts. Bakunin wrote:

The unity of the International is founded not on uniformity of an official theory, nor on one single orthodox dogma as in the Church of Mazzini.* It is founded only on the commonality of misery, economic servitude, needs, instincts, and the current aspirations of the proletariat of all lands on the one hand, and [on the other hand] on perfectly free organisation, from bottom to top, rather than top to bottom, through the course of [its] spontaneous federation, across frontiers, of communes, regions, States – of its *practical international solidarity*.[30]

The pace of change could not be forced: 'for the International, what is on the agenda is not the destruction from one day to the next of every state. To endeavour to achieve all that, even to dream it would be madness.' (*See text below*: 'To the Jura Comrades'.) Bakunin warned against ill-prepared coups and attempted risings by small groups of activists. (*See the text below*: Letter to Celso Ceretti.) He criticised Mazzini for attempting to 'transform the entirety of Italian workers into a blind and passive instrument to be used by the Prophet.'[31] Mazzini, he said, would set up an organisation where:

every question of principle would be resolved by a Central Commission – the first sketch of a Mazzinian Church-State. The popular masses, that is to say local associations should neither reflect nor discuss, it should believe and obey. This is life distorted and entirely absorbed by centralisation, paralysed and dead all around …'[32]

Bakunin's reflections on the workings of general assemblies of members of the IWA in Geneva perhaps suggested that the mass meetings held there might provide a forum in which disagreements might be aired and worked through; he also highlighted that smaller meetings – where speech-making was not welcome, and where discussion was more conversational, might encourage people who ordinarily were less ready to express their opinions to speak. (*See the text below*: 'On the Alliance'.)

The fight against Marx
The conflict with Marx absorbed a considerable part of Bakunin's energies between 1870 and 1873. Bakunin, along with Guillaume was expelled from the IWA by a vote at the Congress of The Hague in 1872, but that congress was in turn repudiated by the bulk of the IWA.

Bakunin wrote that Marx and his co-thinkers wanted a revolution driven from the top by engineers, socialist bureaucrats and officious academics. 'His economic ideal is a State that has become the sole owner of land and of every form of capital, cultivating the former through agricultural associations, directed by his civil engineers, well paid, and using others to sponsor all commercial and industrial bodies.' Bakunin looked for change that put workers' associations in charge and organised from the base of society.³³ He warned that if revolutionaries failed to build alliances between town and country, and if instead an urban left sought to impose itself on rural areas, then such an imposition would, in conjunction with a new state, revive new forms of oppression. (*See the texts below*: 'On Lassalle and Marx', 'To the Jura Comrades' and 'Socialism and the Paris Commune'.) 'A revolution that is imposed, either by official decrees, or by force of arms is no longer a revolution but the opposite of a revolution, because it necessarily provokes reaction.'³⁴ In Bakunin's view conditions tended to determine life, and socialists were not immune from the malign influence of privilege. If we were given power and held it even for a few months it might have corrupting effects, 'we would cease to be what we are now':

> As socialists, we are convinced, you and me, that the social environment, status and position, living conditions are more powerful than either intelligence or the will of the most energetic or strongest individual, and it is precisely for this reason that we demand equality: not natural equality but the social equality of the individual, as the precondition and basis for morality and justice, and it is for this reason that we detest power, in every form, just as the people do.³⁵

Bakunin wrote of Marxist socialists:

> It seems to them that life proceeds from thinking that it is the concomitant of a predetermined idea, and beginning there they affirm that thought – of course they mean their own needy thinking – should direct life. They do not understand that, on the contrary, thinking flows from life, and to modify thinking, one must transform life. Give a people a broad and humane life and it will astound you by the profound rationalism of its ideas.³⁶

Bakunin wrote that given the nature of modern society no change could be brought about except by mass popular movements, and those pressing for change needed to respect popular will – the people were not some blank sheet on which revolutionaries could impose their will. He was arguing for a leadership of ideas – not the power of persons; he once wrote:

> [Being] enemies of States and of all state management, we assert – against all positivists and metaphysicians prostrated before the Science Goddess, be they scientists or not – that social and natural life always comes before

thinking; life is never the result of thought, it is only one of its functions. Life develops out of its own inexhaustible depths, through successive events each one different, and not through abstract thinking. Such events engendered by life (not events engendering life) only indicate, like milestones the direction and the various stages of life's natural and real development. In accordance with this conviction, we have neither the intent, nor the least desire, to impose on our own people, or any other foreign people, any scheme of social organisation taken from a book or dreamt up by ourselves. We are convinced that the masses of the people have gathered in themselves, in their instincts (more or less developed by history), in their daily needs and in their conscious or unconscious aspirations, all the elements for their harmonious future social organisation. We seek this ideal in the people themselves. As every State power, every government is placed by its very nature and position above and outside the people and must inevitably work to subordinate the people under rules and for objectives foreign to them, we declare ourselves enemies of every government and state power, of the State system in general. We think that people can be free and happy only when organised from the bottom up, that the people themselves will create their own lives through autonomous associations that are completely free, beyond official paternalism, but never beyond the influence, in equal measure, of diverse but free persons and organisations.[37]

The London Conference of 1871 – which was nothing but a General Council writ large – had been the occasion for Marx and his allies to begin redirecting the IWA. The conference adopted administrative measures to permit the suppression of special interest groups in the IWA. It had bodies like the Alliance in mind. There was nothing even-handed about this measure. Other 'friendly' special interest bodies, such as the London German Communist Workers Association, continued to exercise influence within the IWA.[38] The resolution was symptomatic of the desire of one London-based faction to intimidate enemies challenging its leadership.

On several occasions members of the sub-committee of the General Council sent secret and private communications to push particular perspectives – on General Council letterheads – to select IWA correspondents; leaving others in the dark. The sub-committee cultivated or sidelined contact with corresponding bodies depending on their political viewpoints. IWA resources were used for factional purposes.

Persons with language skills – especially particularly key insiders on the General Council in London – shaped and edited contacts, conversations and

IWA policy without fully disclosing their views to colleagues.[39] The 15 June 1872 issue of the Jura Federation *Bulletin* printed several letters responding to the Marxists' missive on 'Fictional Splits in the IWA'. Bakunin remarked in his letter to the *Bulletin*:

> Nothing better proves the calamitous domination of Mr Marx on the General Council than the current circular. Scan the names of the 47 who have signed it and you will barely find seven or eight who can pass judgement on this business with some knowledge of the matter.[40] All the others – blind and complacent instruments of Marxian anger and politics, in counter-signing this infamous condemnation against us – have neither heard, nor seen us, and yet they have judged and sentenced us without even deigning to address one single question to us! So this is how the General Council in London understands *Morality, Truth* and *Justice*, which – given the 'considering' clauses of our General Statutes, should serve as the basis for all relations be they individual or collective in the IWA? Ah! Mr Karl Marx, it is easier to place such words at the start of a programme than it is to implement them![41]

Marx had accused Bakunin of setting himself up as a dictator in the IWA.[42] Accusations of organisational wrongdoing obstructed recognition of the real 'crime' that Bakunin had committed: posing a political challenge to Marxist politics and Social-Democracy. Accusations and expulsions would serve several purposes – intimidating critics and limiting discussion of the future course of the IWA. Several key collaborators of Marx and Engels broke with them criticising the manner in which they forced through their opinions. Eccarius,* a long-standing member of the General Council, argued that if matters had been properly discussed critics might have been won over.

Bakunin and the press

The most influential journals of the IWA were published by its regional federations in Belgium, Francophone-Switzerland, Italy and Spain. In addition there was *Der Vorbote* – published in Geneva by Johann Philipp Becker.* Becker ran a German language IWA structure and his paper circulated widely, but most especially in Germany. His influence diminished after 1869 as Social-Democratic parties came together and developed their own press.

The IWA press made a small dent in the monopoly of information held by the ruling classes, it kept members in touch, helped build solidarity, facilitated the raising of funds for strikers, and facilitated reflection on socialist politics and the exchange of ideas between regions. The press in these times was the principle means of communication of ideas and opinion: in effect a centre of public and collective leadership.

If Bakunin was able to influence IWA members, that influence was facilitated by a set of journals and printers. Some were somewhat non-partisan – *Il Gazzettino Rosa* (Milan), *La Liberté* and *L'Internationale* (Brussels), others were more sympathetic to him: *Eguaglianza* (Sicily); *La Federación* (Barcelona); *Mirabeau* (Verviers) and the journals supported by the Jura Federation: *Progrès, Solidarité, La Révolution Sociale*, the *Bulletin*, and the annual *Almanach du people*. All of these helped publish, translate and re-publish his writings.[43] Marx, it may be remembered, was asked to contribute to *L'Égalité*, the journal of the Geneva IWA, but declined, excusing himself by saying that his other commitments left him no spare time.[44] Bakunin wrote articles for *L'Égalité* in 1869 addressing the themes to be discussed at the Basel congress of the IWA, not least the potential impact of a general strike. (*See below*: 'Articles in *L'Égalité*'.)

Bakunin had influence but he did not command or control – despite accusations by Marx. (Marx wrote in December 1869: 'This fellow [Bakunin] now has control over four organs of the International (*Égalité, Progrès* [of Le] Locle, *Federación* [of], Barcelona, and *Eguaglianza*, of Naples.'[45])

The Jura *Bulletin* of 15 June 1872 contains several interesting points. It noted: 'when Bakunin became one of our collaborators, as with others, his articles were passed to the editorial committee, which often subjected them to considerable modification to adapt them to the needs of the journal.' The same issue noted as 'simply ridiculous' the accusation that an earlier journal of the federation, *Progrès*, was the personal organ of Bakunin. Over many years the Jura Federation facilitated an ongoing open discussion of labour and IWA policy and politics through its successive organs; an achievement never emulated by IWA organisations in Britain, despite greater resources available to its labour movement and the presence of the General Council in London.

The General Council had been instructed by the IWA congress to publish regular reports on social and economic conflict in various languages. It failed to do so. It was suggested that it should have reports published in the IWA federations' press, but no such reports were prepared.[46] When it sought to have its opinions published in liberal and radical journals, whatever was published was inevitably edited by others. It had no dependable press under its own control. So, in the area of communication, the General Council had a very limited capacity.

Marx – insofar as he could influence the General Council – resented public criticism. The London Conference of 1871 resolved that the General Council should be charged to disavow and denounce all journals of the IWA which might 'follow the example of *Progrès* and *Solidarité*'.[47] A resolution was passed condemning the discussions that had been started in their columns, because these would be open to a bourgeois public, and because, so it was said, such matters should be addressed exclusively within local, federal committees, or the General Council or in private or administrative sessions of federal or general congresses. James Guillaume* replied.[48] He noted that the pro-General Council journal published in Geneva, *L'Égalité*,[49] addressed these controversial matters, so *Solidarité* could not abstain. How, he asked, could *Solidarité* be indicted for the crime of conducting a polemic when *L'Égalité* had set the example? Bakunin commented that it was the arguments of the press of the Jura Federation that were being targeted – the matter of procedure was only a pretence. In his opinion: 'every questions affecting the International should be treated fearlessly and in the full light of day.' (*See the text below*: On the Alliance).

One can see in this 'administrative' fracas a conflict between two forms of process. Bakunin and his co-thinkers were ready and willing to have all matters discussed in public and in the press. The Jura Federation was open to critical perspectives: it recommended the reading of the press of German Social-Democracy, notwithstanding political disagreements. In contrast the London Conference sought to endorse limited discussions behind closed doors, through 'proper channels', restricting public political debate. Where the General Council had influence a hierarchy of insiders and outsiders was created, with the ordinary membership of the IWA having restricted access to their organisation's policy discussions. The hubris of the General Council obstructed the democratic functioning of a network of diverse elements. Its practices begged the question of how an IWA that endorsed the restriction of public discussion could function as a body that would promote the self-liberation of working people?

These conflicts highlighted the weakness of the General Council and its vain attempts to impose its influence. The General Council had little capacity; its reach was hugely restricted as compared with that of particular federations through their press. In the period between the Basel Congress of 1869 and the Congress of The Hague in 1872 it communicated through private and confidential letters – through discreet and conspiratorial methods – to selected individuals. Such methods had only a limited reach, so that the greater influence within the IWA arose not so much out of the General Council with its occasional semi-secret briefings but rather from the regular collective press of the various IWA federations and through their weekly or monthly publications.

Democracy, accountability and solidarity

Were Bakunin and his supporters 'as bad' as Marx and his supporters? Was each 'side' equally manipulative? Consider the internal practice of IWA politics, and the sequence of expulsions and splits: the refusal by the local IWA to accept the Geneva Alliance as a section of the Romande Federation in 1869, the expulsion of Bakunin and friends from the Geneva IWA in August 1870; the expulsion of Paul Robin from the General Council and of Malon and friends from the Geneva IWA in 1871; in 1872 the expulsion of Bakunin and Guillaume at the congress at The Hague, the expulsion of the Jura Federation, and, later in 1873, the expulsion of every other IWA federation by the General Council. In this sequence it was the 'Marxists' and their allies who took the initiative, using administrative sanctions to achieve dominance over the IWA apparatus.

The logic of Marx and Engels was that the IWA should be dominated by their 'correct' leadership, and that the political process of the IWA should be managed to obtain the 'right' results. 'Hostiles' – journals, persons and affiliates – were to be disciplined whilst 'friendlies' were to be supported and funded out of Engels' private purse. In political conflict all means – including lies, slanders and manipulations – were to be used. Engels for one clearly saw his goal as being one of *destroying* Bakunin. If there was never an honest debate between persons close to Bakunin and close to Marx, not the least reason for that was that Marx and Engels worked hard to prevent the political differences at issue from becoming a focus for discussion. To debate political ideas with another person involves recognising them as being worthy of some respect – something that Marx and Engels were loath to do; their letters are replete with invective and disrespect – both for their allies and enemies. Organisational disputes served as pretexts for expulsions and obstructed discussion of the underlying conflicts. Marx and Engels' officious domineering practices were condemned as authoritarian even by persons who had agreed with them on the priority of electoral-party-politics and had collaborated with them over many years. Marx and Engels bequeathed a poisonous intellectual inheritance to followers who uncritically absorbed their sectarian arrogance.

The regular sequence of annual IWA congresses up to 1869 had provided some opportunities for broad discussions of policy – opportunities for meetings, exchanges, debates and disagreements as to the direction of labour movements in varied contexts. The better organised sections and federations prepared reports on organisation and activities. The Basel congress agenda was circulated three months before it met, so that members could discuss issues in their sections and federations before choosing delegates to represent their views. At the congress each delegate was allowed to speak only twice on any subject, and for no longer than fifteen minutes. Each delegate had an equal vote irrespective of the size of the section or federation they might represent.

Egalitarianism had limits. Only those able to pay costs of travel could use opportunities afforded by congresses.[50] In 1872 the General Council was able to fix a congress with a fictitious majority in The Hague, but it could not fix the vast majority of the IWA. Most of the active membership of the IWA considered that the location, attendance and process at The Hague had been fixed and gerrymandered[51] by the General Council. In the winter of 1872-3 these federations condemned and repudiated The Hague congress, its resolutions and the new General Council. Representatives met at a congress in Geneva and condemned everything that had been agreed in The Hague the previous year. Bakunin was not a key player in the ongoing IWA. It was the Belgian and Jura Federations which, through their media and organisations, helped maintain the International after the congress of The Hague.

Given the limited capacity of the IWA to shape policy in a democratic and accountable manner Bakunin's view was that international solidarity was the 'supreme compulsory law', rather than agreement on political policy, tactics and strategy:

> Resolutions of General Congresses are themselves not obligatory for sections, only solidarity is, and any failing in such Solidarity is considered as a crime. If congresses themselves have no right to impose an opinion voted by a majority for the free conscience of autonomous sections, then for even stronger reasons that right cannot be appropriate for a secret conference, one irregularly and arbitrarily[52] composed – chosen and convened arbitrarily by the General Council.

So Bakunin came to the view that there should be some mutual tolerance of conflicting perspectives in the IWA, and no 'official truth'. Where open politics was possible – as in Geneva – Bakunin practiced public struggle, arguing for his politics in mass meetings open to all local IWA members:

> Amongst the means we used against them always the chief one was calling them into this public struggle, in which we fought disdaining personality and personal intrigue and almost always we confounded them ...'[53]

Bakunin had other norms in mind when he discussed prospects for change in Russia. He once wrote that the influence of revolutionary conspirators might amount to some form of secret, collective, ideological 'dictatorship' to promote popular self-determination.[54] The role of revolutionaries would be one of planning and strategizing ways forward, forming a military headquarters maybe, providing a secret and 'dictatorial' leadership-of-ideas. Intimate brother members of a revolutionary network would take no official positions in a new society – they would be self-renouncing. As yet no organised labour movement or IWA section had been formed either in town or country in Russia, so there was no obvious body which might provide a new model for a new society. Until new democratic structures emerged any conspiratorial power might be largely unaccountable. Bakunin was willing to work through narrow conspiratorial networks for change in Russia despite the absence of mass democratic structures. Conspiracy was perceived as indispensable – a necessity given persecution by the state police forces. Bakunin's critics would present these elements – conspiracy and lack of accountability – as evidence of his dictatorial leanings; and it would be alleged that such leanings extended to all his activities. However most IWA members were more impressed and revolted by the authoritarian practices they saw at work in the General Council rather than by Bakunin's supposed commitment to conspiracy and dictatorship.

Socialists have always confronted a fundamental problem in organisation: how to make organisation effective, participatory, accountable and democratic. One of the early watchwords of the IWA was 'No rights without duties, no duties without rights' a formula advocating balance and reciprocity. Bakunin did write that in emergencies some authority might be useful on a temporary basis – to be subjected to review, constrained and restricted, forbidden to lay down ongoing roots and deprived of any privilege. He argued repeatedly for federalism, with autonomy for grassroots bodies (workers' associations or Communes). In the 1870s this was a newish model, opposed to the earlier Jacobin centralist model of organisation (a tradition that looked back to the unitary French Republic of the 1790s, formed at a time when no consciously working class organisations were organised). Federalist organisation was (and is) no cure-all. It started from the premise that there was and would be some forceful impulse towards solidarity. If solidarity was absent, how then might it be nurtured? – Bakunin answered, not by the use of force, but through building dialogue and respect.

After 1873, when anti-authoritarians came to administer the ongoing IWA, they did not follow a similar course in abusing administrative power to restrict discussion and expel 'political' opponents.[55] Bakunin and his co-thinkers sought a structure that was democratically accountable, with responsibility to rooted local organisations – federalist organisation.[56] IWA congresses were defined as venues in which differences could be aired, and harmony sought. The ongoing IWA brought together partisans of various politics – both abstentionists and electoralists – the latter included persons who had worked with Marx but rejected his overbearing manipulative practice. So one might ask: why is it that accusations of preferring conspiratorial forms of politics continue to be put[57] against Bakunin, rather than against Marx and Engels?

Revolutionary and reformist socialism

Bakunin and his co-thinkers were called 'Anarchists',[58] although this was not the term they themselves used most often. Bakunin rejected the bourgeois politicking that he saw in parts of Western Europe: making alliances with non-socialist political parties, prioritising electoral politics,[59] electing unaccountable person to legislatures, collaborating with employers' representatives. Bakunin concluded: 'To conquer political freedom *first* can mean nothing other than conquering it first and *alone* …'[60] (*See the texts below*: Articles in *L'Égalité*.) Electoral prospects were enhanced where softer perspectives were highlighted – civil rights and help for co-operatives. Conversely they were undermined by any talk of overthrowing capital. He argued:

> The International does not reject politics in general, it is forced to be involved so long as it constrained to struggle against the bourgeois class. It rejects only bourgeois politics and religion, because the one established its plundering domination and the other consecrates and sanctifies it.[61]

What alternative form could politics take?

> Beyond the Mazzini system with its State-Republic – there is only one [form] that of the Commune-Republic, the Federation-Republic, the frankly popular and socialist Republic – the [form] of Anarchy. This is the politics of Social Revolution which wants the abolition of the State and fully free economic organisation of the people from bottom to top, through the path of federation.[62]

Bakunin saw mass workplace based organisations as the foundation of labour power. But he also worked with a range of parties – not electoral-party-political parties – but parties of a sort, to organise, make propaganda and plan activities. These political organisations might chose to take on conspiratorial forms in the face of states where any open dissent landed people in prison. (*See the text below*: Letter to Celso Ceretti.) For Bakunin such ideas-based organisational forms – parties of a sort – should adopt forms consonant with participatory socialist politics. (*See the text below*: 'Letter to Tómas González Morago'.) Bakunin advocated gender equality and argued that all young and old people should be educated, trained or sustained. Nevertheless, his focus on economic or workplace organisation and on paid and waged work obstructed consideration of unpaid work and the gendered division of labour.

Bakunin and his co-thinkers were accused by enemies of being 'sectarians', and 'conspirators', seeking to disorganise labour and the organisation of the IWA. There were real and polarised choices: on the one hand to focus on workplace organisation, with ideas-based organisations as bodies ancillary to that broad 'economic' organisation; on the other hand politicking with the bourgeoisie, prioritising electoral politics and subordinating workplace organisation and any form of activity deemed illegal by the state to building some sort of electable electoral alliance.

Bakunin's attempts to intervene in France and Italy did not succeed. But, if one compares workplace and community organisation in various European countries in the early 1870s one might draw the conclusion that the liveliest lands were closer to Bakunin. The Spanish IWA was a huge body as compared with the IWA in Germany. Bakunin judged that all Mazzini's attempted risings failed, yet 'they revived, formed, inspired and built up this patriotic youth …'. (*See the text below*: Letter to Celso Ceretti). Something similar might be said of Bakunin and his accomplishments: he failed, but he inspired.

The same might almost be said of German Social-Democracy. It too was beginning to inspire hope. Political conditions were so depressing towards the end of the 1870s that German Social-Democracy's votes appeared to offer a way forward as against complete passivity. It was seen to attract hundreds of thousands of votes and hopes were raised that voting might facilitate some progress in the future. But there was a difference: in Spain a vast network of community, workplace and cultural counter-institutions were built up; in Germany large numbers of votes were won but there was no equivalent social power in workplaces and communities. Bakunin set out a critique of the programme of German Social-Democracy, but after the autumn of 1873 he withdrew from active political activity and wrote little on its further development.[63] Bakunin did not advise friends to withdraw from standing for election in Italy. One might surmise that in certain periods electoral politics was better than nothing.

These were fluid times: concepts and organisational forms that were to be consolidated, refined and defined in future decades were as yet somewhat vague. The Social-Democratic movement that was beginning to emerge was, as yet, not the mass structures that would be built some twenty or thirty years later. In these times little clarity had emerged in matters relating to the nature, dynamics and goals, inherent to and interacting within and between various types and forms of workplace-based and ideas-based labour organisation.

Measuring Bakunin

How have socialists appreciated Bakunin and his thinking? And what value may he have for the future socialists? Today new circumstances demand new thinking; education, media, new social movements and developments have created a world somewhat different than the one known to Bakunin. René Berthier, someone who has written extensively on Bakunin's writings comments: 'when I try to analyse a phenomenon I never ask myself how Bakunin would have thought things through.'[64]

Some Marxist have been dispassionate. Franz Mehring, in a biography of Marx first published in 1918, wrote the following appreciation of Bakunin:

> With all his mistakes and weaknesses, history will give him a place of honour amongst the pioneers of the international proletariat, though that place may be contested so long as there are Philistines in the world, whether they conceal their long ears under the nightcap of petty-bourgeois respectability or don the lion's skin of a Marx to cloak their trembling limbs.[65]

Mehring – despite coming from another tradition – tried to be fair minded. Other 'Marxists' have been less equitable. For example Marcello Musto has written recently that that only once in all his writing did Bakunin set forth 'positive' ideas and that otherwise he preferred the 'terrain of personal accusations and insults' rather than a reasoned political response.[66] Many years earlier Hal Draper portrayed Bakunin as a covert, conspiratorial authoritarian, defined by 'the conspiratorial putschism of the left-Jacobin tradition plus a Russian-accented terroristic nihilism'.[67] So Bakunin was to be condemned for promoting demonstrative propaganda and for ghostly networks of conspirators – in effect icons of terror – notwithstanding the use of this technique, earlier and famously, by the Mr Marx who had announced that 'the sceptre of communism was haunting Europe'!

Errico Malatesta wrote the following in 1926:

Some fifty years ago I saw him for the last time in Lugano – already mortally afflicted and reduced to a shadow of himself. He said to me, half seriously, half ironically: 'My dear, I am playing a part in my dissolution'. Nonetheless, his thinking had such an effect, that it warmed my heart and filled me with youthful enthusiasm.

That above all was Bakunin's quality: he inspired sacrifice, faith and feverish activity in everyone lucky enough to have met him. He himself had a habit of saying that he had a 'devil inside him'. And that was really so, the rebellious Satan of mythology was in his mind and body, he knew neither God nor Master; his struggle against everything that hampered thought and action never stopped.

Like every comrade of my generation I was a Bakuninist. Alas, those day are long gone. Today, and for many years since, I would not describe myself as such. My ideas have evolved and developed. Today I find too much of the Marxist in Bakunin – in matters of political economy and historical interpretation. I find that his philosophy constrained in a contradiction between a mechanical conception of the universe and faith in the efficacy of will on persons and human destiny, without finding a way out. But that matters little. Theories are uncertain and impermanent concepts. Philosophy generally makes hypothesis based in the clouds; it has little or no substantial influence on life. So this is why Bakunin remains our great inspiration and example, over and above possible disagreements.

The radical critique of the principle of authority and of the State, which he incarnates, is very much alive. Also alive is his struggle against deceitful politics, the critique of those two forms through which the masses are oppressed and exploited: dictatorship and democracy. The reputation of that false socialism which he called sleep-inducing is still alive, and consciously or not, it tends to consolidate the domination of privilege, singing workers to sleep with the lullaby of vain hope. And, above all intense hatred against everything that humiliates and degrades humanity coupled with infinite love of freedom, every freedom – all this is very much alive.

Let comrades consider Bakunin's life – full of practical and ideal struggles – as an example of devotion to the cause of revolution. Let them – and us too – seek to follow in his glorious footsteps, however distant they may be – each in accordance with his potential and strength![68]

Malatesta recognised that Bakunin and his friends had attempted to push for their opinions in the IWA. He did not imply that underhand means were used, but he did seem to suggest that some restraint might have been better.

Paul Avrich wrote of Bakunin's personal qualities: broad magnanimity and childlike enthusiasm, his 'volcanic onslaughts against privilege and injustice, all gave him enormous human appeal in libertarian circles' – something that Marx could not rival. Kropotkin wrote that his influence came not so much from intellectual authority but more from his moral personality.[69] James Guillaume did more than anyone to promote Bakunin's ideas. After the last congress of the IWA in Verviers in 1877 he took up residence in Paris. His three volume history of the International (*L'Internationale: documents et souvenirs*) and his six volume collection of Bakunin writings resonated widely within anarchist and syndicalist organisations.[70]

Bakunin had defects: he was not a disciplined writer.[71] James Guillaume once noted 'As an author he had no vanity [amour-propre] he said of himself that "he completely lacked the talent of an architect in literature" and that when he "built his house" he needed a friend "to put in the doors and windows"'[72] His writings often contains digressions, turning from one subject to another, but, as Paul Avrich notes, despite their fragmentary nature, his writing abounds in 'flashes of insight'.[73] Max Nettlau, when he wrote an introduction to a collection of Bakunin's writings, asked why so many Bakunin texts were unfinished? 'Because immediate demands constantly distracted him from theoretical work absorbed his energies and re-directed him elsewhere.'[74]

Earlier English-language editions of Bakunin's works have been presented in various ways: as anthologies with or without a theme, or in the form of short quotations. The texts presented here are organised in chronological order, chosen to illustrate Bakunin's thinking on a number of themes. Hopefully a chronological order may facilitate understanding of changes in Bakunin's thinking, and the relation between text and context. The source of each text is given along with other annotation. Many titles of the texts below are my own. A list of works cited, titles and dates, is to be found on page 293.

I have used some of Bakunin's terms – e.g. Marxian and Socialist Democrat – rather than the more familiar Marxist and Social-Democrat. The word 'section' is widely used for the basic (union) branches, locals or groupings of the IWA. I have refashioned some terms. I have rendered phrases on economic rights as workplace rights and have often preferred un-gendered plural terms in place of the male terms used in the texts in the French.

The initials JG or AL indicate notes brought forward from the texts of earlier editors of Bakunin's writings: James Guillaume or Arthur Lehning. MB indicates a note written by Bakunin. Other notes and matter in square brackets has been introduced by the translator. The italics and emphasis are largely taken from earlier editions and texts.

CHRONOLOGY

1814: Mikhail Aleksandrovich Bakunin born at Premukhino, Tver province, Russia.

1840: Bakunin moves to Berlin.

1848: Bakunin participates in insurrections in Germany and in a Pan-Slav congress in Prague. He writes 'An Appeal to the Slavs'. A paper edited by Marx, *Neue Rheinische Zeitung*, accuses Bakunin of being an agent of the Russian Tsar.

1849: Bakunin helps organise defence of Dresden against Prussia army. He is arrested, sentenced to death in Saxony, handed over to the Austrians and eventually to the Russian police and imprisoned. His health suffers and he loses all his teeth.

1857: Bakunin is sent to Siberia and marries Antonia Kwiatkowska.

1861: Bakunin escapes, travelling via Japan and USA to London. He contacts Herzen and Ogarev, the editors of the Russian radical journal *Kolokol* [The Bell]. He translates Marx & Engels' *Communist Manifesto* into Russian.

1863: Bakunin travels to Denmark and Sweden to take part in an insurrectionary movement in Poland and meets up with his wife. German General Workers' Association founded in Leipzig, led by Ferdinand Lassalle (Lassalle dies 1864).

1864: Founding of the International Working-Men's Association (IWA). Schleswig war, Denmark defeated.

1865: IWA Conference in London. American civil war ends.

1866: Bakunin travels to Italy and settles in Naples. Geneva: First IWA Congress. Austrian Empire defeated in war with Prussia and Italy.

1867: Lausanne: Second IWA Congress 64 delegates. Bakunin is one of 6,000 delegates who attend congress of the League for Peace and Freedom in Geneva, and is a member of its central committee. *Belgium* – Miners' strike defeated, soldiers kill three workers. *France* – many internationalists arrested. Riots in Lille. *Italy* – Antonia Kwiatkowska and Carlo Gambuzzi become lovers.

1868: Brussels: Third IWA Congress 99 delegates. Bakunin moves to Geneva and joins the local IWA central section. September: Second congress of the League for Peace and Freedom in Bern. Bakunin proposes a socialist manifesto, he and a minority around him withdraw; these friends found the International Alliance for Socialist Democracy in Geneva and apply for membership of the IWA. December: General Council rejects this application. *Belgium* – March, army breaks up a 3,000 strong miners' occupation in Charleroi, six killed. *Cuba* – beginnings of independence movement. *France* – IWA officials imprisoned. Government announces toleration of unions; membership mushrooms. *Spain* – military revolt, Queen Isabella deposed. *Switzerland* – Geneva, strike of some 2,500 building workers; November crushing defeat of Social Democrats (Parti de la République démocratique et sociale) in elections in Geneva, defeated candidates resolve to stand in future as radicals rather than as socialists; IWA members: P. Coullery and J. Frey elected to local government. First issue of *L'Egalité* published (it runs to 1872), replacing P. Coullery's *La Voix de l'Avenir*.

1869: February: the Alliance – as an International body with its own Central Bureau is dissolved, its Geneva section applies for IWA membership. Bakunin meets Nechaev. June: Bakunin fills in as editor of *L'Égalité*, the paper of the Romande Federation until September. July: Eccarius writes to say that the General Council of the IWA has admitted the Geneva Alliance section. September: Basel, Fourth IWA Congress, 78 delegates – Bakunin has a mandate from sections in Lyons and Naples; General Council motion on inheritance defeated; unions defined as basis for a new labour-run society, discussion of electoral politics not prioritised. Liebknecht is condemned for his attacks on Bakunin and apologises. After this congress Bakunin moves to the Ticino. *Belgium* – violent strike conflicts in Seraing and in the Borinage. *France* – elections show decline in support for the government, army kills 14 miners, widespread strike wave. *Germany* – Borkheim, a friend of Marx, calls Bakunin a Russian agent in the Berlin *Zukunft*. August, Eisenach, foundation of the Social-Democratic Workers' Party. *Italy* – first IWA section organised; publication of *L'Eguaglianza*. Riots against tax on grain, 47 killed. *Spain* – Fanelli, a confidante of Bakunin travels to Spain and instigates the formation of IWA sections. *Switzerland* – January: Francophone-Swiss regional IWA federation created (It adopts a set of regulations from a draft prepared by Bakunin); February onward: Bakunin visits Jura, wins sympathy of the local IWA sections; strikes in Basel, Geneva and Lausanne. August: Brosset, President of the Romande Federation, resigns.

1870: January: death of Herzen. February: Bakunin writes 'The Bears of Bern and the Bear of Saint-Petersburg' against extradition of Nechaev, and helps Ogarev edit a new series of *Kolokol*. March: Bakunin in Milan; Marx sends an IWA *Confidential Communication* to German Social-Democrats vilifying Bakunin, saying that 25,000 francs a year were being paid to him to conduct pan-Slav propaganda. June-July: Bakunin breaks off relations with Nechaev. *France* – March-April: IWA mass meeting in Lyons (6,000 persons), local federation constituted with some thirty sections. July: Franco-Prussian War. Bakunin writes 'Letters of a Frenchman'. September: Napoleon III defeated at Sedan, fall of the Third Empire, communes declared in Lyons and Marseilles. IWA Congress due to meet in Paris is cancelled. September: Bakunin hopes for popular rising in France against German occupation of northern France. He travels to Lyons (14-15th) and joins a local, insurrectionary Commune committee. The insurrection failed. Bakunin is arrested, escapes and returns to the Ticino via Marseilles and Genoa. *Italy* – repression of Naples IWA (leaders imprisoned). *Spain* – June, first Spanish IWA congress in Barcelona, 90 delegates representing 40,000 workers. November, Amadeo of Savoy becomes King. *Switzerland* – March: Becker resigns from the Geneva Alliance. April: La Chaux-de-Fonds, split in the Romande IWA Federation, two rival federations emerge: one based in the Jura, the other based in Geneva. Utin attacks Bakunin and threatens to kill him. August: Geneva IWA expels Bakunin and his allies.

1871: January: armistice suspends Franco-Prussian war. March: Bakunin visits Florence. 12 August: Alliance section of Geneva dissolved. Shortly afterwards former members, and refugees from the Paris Commune constitute a Section for Socialist Revolutionary action and propaganda. Bakunin writes on the politics and activities of the Alliance in anticipation of an IWA conference or congress. September: Private IWA Conference held in London with selected participants: it endorses political parties and votes itself extended powers. Utin is instructed to collect information that will incriminate Bakunin. November: Jura congress rejects London conference resolutions, and sends Sonvilier circular (*Circulaire à toutes les Fédérations de l'AIT*) to IWA federations. Bakunin begins to write texts later known as 'Knouto-Germanic Empire and the Social Revolution', 'God and the State', and 'Statism and Anarchy'. *France* – February: elections, two IWA members elected. March: Paris Commune formed in revolt against republic based in Versailles. May: Commune vanquished – some 10,000 are shot, more deported; IWA banned; June: France invites other governments to supress the IWA. Communard refugees spread radical influences. *Germany* – Bebel and Liebknecht imprisoned. *Italy* – Mazzini attacks the Commune; Bakunin writes: 'Reply of an Internationalist to Giuseppe Mazzini', ('Risposta d'un Internazionale a Giuseppe Mazzini; (Milan, August 1871), 'The Socialism of Giuseppe Mazzini'; IWA sections dissolved by the police. Cafiero acts for Engels. November, Rome, Mazzini camp organise a labour congress. *Spain* – June: Spanish federation office moves to Lisbon to escape persecution. Strike wave, defeat in Cartagena. Valencia – IWA congress.

1872: Marx circulated a confidential circular accusing members of the Alliance of wishing to 'disorganise the International'. Bakunin replies: the circular was 'the habitual weapon of Marx, a heap of filth'. August: Nechaev arrested in Zurich. Fifth IWA congress, 2-7 September, in The Hague with some 61 delegates attending (of which 21 are members of the General Council). Bakunin and Guillaume are expelled and the General Council is relocated to New York. 15-16 September, Extraordinary Saint-Imier IWA congress, fifteen delegates repudiate the decisions taken in The Hague. November: followers of Blanqui leave the IWA. *Belgium* – December: repudiation of decisions of The Hague by Belgian congress meeting in Brussels. *France* – March: new law bans organisations promoting strikes, prohibits affiliation to the IWA (repealed 1901). November: 22 out of 23 delegates at a French IWA meeting support electoral abstention. *Italy* – June, Cafiero, who had hitherto acted for Engels in Italy, announces his support for anti-authoritarians. August: Rimini IWA conference, Italian federation breaks with General Council (no delegates are sent to The Hague). November: policy to 'prevent disorder' announced in parliament. *Spain* – January: IWA banned; December: congress of Cordoba, (up to 45,000 workers represented by 44 delegates) repudiates decisions of The Hague congress.

1873: May: New York General Council declares that all the IWA bodies that have rejected the resolutions of The Hague have 'placed themselves outside' the IWA. 1-6 September: Geneva, Sixth IWA Congress – attended by some 24 persons representatives from the Belgian, Dutch, English, Italian, Jura, and Spanish federations and others. Marx is criticised by former colleagues. A week later the final, shambolic, General-Council-IWA Congress is organised by Becker. October: Bakunin resigns from the Jura Federation. *France* – a list of IWA members is revealed to the police, two (of three) delegates of the General Council are exposed as turn coats; ongoing persecutions, labour organisation is banned. Anti-authoritarians organize a congress in Lyons and publish *La solidarité révolutionnaire*. *Italy* – March: Bologna, second federal congress; planning for a rising disrupted by state repression. December: Italian Committee for Social Revolution founded to prepare insurrectionary movement. *Spain* – January: IWA congress in Cordoba; February: Amadeo resigns, republic proclaimed. June-July: cantonalist regional movements and risings – influenced by IWA in some places e.g. Alcoy, Sanlúcar de Barrameda (Cadiz).

1874: March, Lugano conference, Italian federations' plans for insurrection not supported by other IWA bodies. July: Bakunin travels to Bologna to take part in a planned insurrection there, little comes of it. Brussels, Seventh IWA congress. *France* – April: Lyons, 26 labour activists imprisoned or deported in a mass trial. *Germany* – January: Socialists win 350,000 votes (6.8%) in national elections; *Italy* – attempted insurrection in Romagna, Castel del Monte; IWA banned. *Spain* – January: defeat of last rebel administration in Cartagena; military dominate state; June, (clandestine) 4th congress in Madrid; IWA banned.

1875: Annual IWA international congress unable to meet. *Italy* – trials of IWA members – antipathy towards government secures acquittal. *Spain* – monarchy restored.

1876: 1 July, Bakunin dies and is buried in Bern two days later. 15 July: Dissolution of the General-Council-IWA. October: Bern, Eighth IWA congress, 28 delegates. *Italy* – October: Florence, third Italian IWA federal congress.

1877: Russian-Turkish war. Most Belgian IWA supporters rally to support Social-Democracy; final IWA congress in Verviers. *Italy* – attempted insurrection in Matese.

PROGRAMME OF THE INTERNATIONAL ALLIANCE FOR SOCIALIST DEMOCRACY

[October 1868][1]

In the 1860s Geneva was Switzerland's largest city, it was also a refuge for radicals from France, Germany, Italy, Russia, Spain and elsewhere. Bakunin became a member of two IWA bodies when he moved to Geneva: a local central section and the Alliance for Socialist Democracy.

The Alliance was set up as a political club. It organised open, public debates on issues of current interest. Bakunin and Johann Philipp Becker* were elected as its president and vice-president. Many members had been active previously in the League for Peace and Freedom,* and had resigned from that body, others were key figures in the Geneva IWA.

The text below was most likely drafted by Bakunin, before being discussed and accepted by a public meeting of the Alliance.[2]

The Alliance's membership documents included both its programme and the statutes of the IWA. At the congress in The Hague in 1872, it was said that the Alliance had goals incompatible with those of the IWA, even though this programme above had been submitted to the General Council and amended in the light of its comments.

Two texts below – *On Leaders and Politics*, and *On the Alliance*, set out Bakunin's views on politics in Geneva and on the subsequent development of the Alliance.

***

1. The Alliance declares itself atheist; it seeks the abolition of [religious] cults, the substitution of science for faith, human justice rather than divine justice.

2. Above all it wants a full and final abolition of classes and the political, economic and social levelling of individuals of both sexes, and to obtain this goal, it demands above all the abolition of the right of inheritance, so that in future all should enjoy their productivity equally, and so that, in conformity with the decision taken at the last workers' [IWA] Congress in

Brussels, instruments of labour, land and all forms of capital should become the collective property of society as a whole, and should be used only by workers, that is to say by industrial and agricultural associations.

3. It wants equal means of development for children of either sex, from birth and for life – i.e. support, education, and training to the fullest extent allowed by industry, science and the arts – being convinced that this equality, if at first it is only economic and social, will result more and more in the greater natural equality of individuals, eliminating every sort of artificial inequality that is a consequence of social organisation and a past history that was both false and iniquitous.

4. Above all it rejects any political action that does not have as its immediate and direct objective the triumph of the cause of workers over capital. Being the enemy of all despotism, it rejects absolutely every reactionary alliance and recognises, as a political form, only the republican form.

5. It recognises that all actually existing political and authoritarian States of every land should disappear. Once they are minimised, with their public services' activities becoming ever more simple administrative functions they should disappear within a universal union of Free Associations: both industrial and agricultural.

6. The Alliance rejects any politics based on rivalry between nations and so-called patriotism, because a real and definite solution to the social question can be found only on the basis of an international solidarity of workers of every land.

7. It desires a universal Association, freely formed, out of all local associations.

OPEN LETTER FROM THE CENTRAL BUREAU OF THE INTERNATIONAL FRATERNITY

[March 1869] [1]

From 1864 to 1867, whilst living in Italy, Bakunin had been an active leader of a secret network of political activists a 'Fraternity' with national and international brothers, including: Giuseppe Fanelli,* Saverio Friscia,* Nikolaï Ivanovitch Joukovsky,* Benoît Malon,* Charles Perron,* Élie Reclus* and Élisée Reclus,* and several freemasons.[2]

Bakunin feared that revolutionary and working-class interests might be subordinated to bourgeois republican politics. This letter was sent out from Geneva in March 1869. Names were encoded to prevent police persecution.

***

Citizens,

Former members of the International Fraternity, in agreement with its Central Bureau declare the institution dissolved.

This announcement has been carefully considered. It arises out of the obvious ineffectiveness of this organisation – with men who, for the most part, were so little committed to this International Fraternity that they thought they had the right to act in ways contrary to the statutes and principles which are incumbent on each brother. This constituted a flagrant injustice towards loyal brothers and placed them in an untenable position.

We wish to avoid any useless recriminations, but nonetheless we think that taking such a serious decision needs some explanation. You will be aware that the International Fraternity took upon itself the immense task of working for a radical and wholesale transformation of the current social, political and economic situation in Europe. You know that the first commitment made by each brother was not only *not* to take part in bourgeois half-revolutions, nor to take part in any bourgeois enterprises – be they economic or political – but also to fight such things as contrary to the interests of the popular masses; also *not to engage in any political activity that did not have as its direct and immediate goal the full emancipation of labour and of labourers through the destruction of every political state, with their frontiers, powers and institutions;* the immediate suppression of all private and public debt; through universal immolation [auto-da-fé] of civil and legal regulation [actes]. [Such a programme was to be achieved through] the abolition of the right of inheritance – that social foundation of every political system and law, the ongoing source of inequality – and lastly through the creation of collective property, the absolute precondition for real, universal equality, for freedom, justice and meaningful fraternity.

Brothers had committed everything – interests, personal sympathies, etc. – to this supreme goal. The most absolute secrecy – in respect of our existence and our every activity – was also necessary. Unfortunately this is not how things always turned out. Some of our brothers travelled to Spain, and instead of working to organise socialist elements (which, as we have material proof and know – are already quite [well] developed in urban places as well as in the rural areas of that country), they engaged in a great deal of radicalism and a little bourgeois socialism. In our times overtly socialist movements (in a non-bourgeois and widely popular sense), have as their real objective the takeover of all social capital, be it in land or other forms, for the benefit of those forms of ownership that alone are legitimate – ownership by labour associations. All other politics is, from the viewpoint of the liberation of labour, reactionary in its direction and goals: this is what these brothers forgot. Forgetful of the goals they were working for, which they were supposed to have been pursuing, they embraced the cause of that poor bourgeois republicanism, a cause shaking Spain with much noise and impotence. They have defended it in the press – both in France and in Spain – and have pushed onwards, with disdain for our principles, to the point of working towards tentatively reconciling themselves, at need, with Espartero, and even with Prim[3] himself.

So you can see how far all this is removed, not only from the principles and solemn commitments of our International Fraternity, but even from the principles loudly promoted by workers throughout Europe by that magnificent organisation the IWA, which alone provides a real foundation for the liberation of every people, as none can deny. Citizens, you will understand that we cannot accept such solidarity, something so contrary to the programme of Labour.

These facts alone would be enough to show how lightweight our fraternal organisation [has become], even if, they were not accompanied by something more, that cannot be disregarded, something that makes any hesitation as to the timeliness of our dissolution impossible: the secrecy of our work has been compromised. Strangers gossip about us. Our activity is strong only when it is secret. So our Fraternity, even if its programme and regulations have been faithfully observed by many of its members, has become not just useless, but ridiculous.

For these reasons above all, our fraternity, which might have rendered such great service to Revolution, has had to be dissolved. No one is more pained than us by this dissolution, but you will agree dear citizen, that given what has happened we no longer have a reason to go on.

[a]For the Central Bureau: 1/16; 2/16; 1/19; 1/13.
Through 7/12 – 6/12.

---

a These fractions – 1/16; 2/16 and so on – designated particular individuals; the code was used to help protect them from the police.

LETTER TO JAMES GUILLAUME, 21 APRIL 1869[4]

Although many members of the IWA were influenced by Proudhon,* they did not act together as one party. Bakunin and his co-thinkers supported collective forms of property ownership, whereas other Proudhonians supported individual ownership of property. These trends came into conflict at the Basel Congress of the IWA and some months later.

***

I am waiting impatiently for you and Papa Meuron.* As for the protests of Paris communists against Tolain,* Chemallé and others, I am amazed by your amazement. They are socialists you say, but there is socialism and socialism. They are Proudhon-ians of the second and bad sort; they are doubly in error – they want individual property and, full of conceit, they want to debate with and parade along with the bourgeoisie – all of which is a waste of time. It can only provide them with some enjoyment, and vainglory for their stunted spirits, and can only lead to some sort of rotten entente with bourgeois socialists. All at a time when we need to separate them from ourselves and marshal our own forces.

We'll talk about all this in Geneva.
I'm waiting for you and Papa Meuron impatiently.
Your devoted, MB.

ARTICLES IN L'ÉGALITÉ

L'Égalité was an organ of the Francophone Swiss Federation[1] of the IWA published in Geneva. Bakunin wrote for it and for a short time became its editor. He was in touch with the Belgian IWA and was much influenced by its theory and practice.

Building workers in Geneva had won an important strike in the spring of 1868 and the local IWA had expanded its membership. The Geneva IWA had become a mass organisation. In a city of some 60,000 it had 3,000 members in 1868 and 4,000 in 1869, organised in 32 trade groupings.[2] Many foreigners worked there, perhaps as many as three or four out of ten in waged work. This high proportion of non-citizens had a great bearing on the political strategies that might be adopted by the IWA. Another building workers strike broke out in March 1869.[3]

The word 'equality' was often highlighted in Bakunin's polemics. It was one of the key motifs of the Great French Revolution, a key reference point for thinking about change. Bakunin stressed the limitations of the French revolution; he wrote: 'This is what the great heroes of the revolution of 1793, Danton, Robespierre, and Saint Just never understood. They wanted only political liberty and equality, not economic and social equality. And this is why the liberty and equality that they created set up on a new basis the domination of the bourgeoisie over the people.'[4]

The IWA challenged older labour traditions, such as the Grütli association.* At leadership level the latter worked alongside the Radical Party for the development of a modern unitary Swiss nation-state, for the separation of church and state, and for labour regulation.[5] In 1843 the Grütli defined itself as an association promoting patriotic national democratic interests above cantonal peculiarities. Membership was restricted to Swiss citizens.[6] It sought to promote reform in co-operation with employers, and for the most part it refused to collaborate with the International.[7] (Some of the first workers' organisations had been formed by Germans living in Switzerland, so the Grütli's rule excluding the non-Swiss was no small matter.) Even so, despite hostility from its national leadership, some Grütli grass-roots bodies were more open to foreign influences, and some helped the non-Swiss. Bakunin defined patriotism as follows:

The state has always been the patrimony of one or another class: the clerical class, the noble class, the bourgeois class, and in the end, when every other class has been used up, the bureaucratic class. The state rises and falls, turn and turn again, as if it were a machine, but for the survival of the state it is absolutely necessary that one privileged class should have an interest in its preservation. What passes for *patriotism* is precisely the common interest of that privileged class.[8]

The Radical Party was a powerful force in local government in Geneva. An ephemeral Social Democratic Party stood for election in November 1868 but broke up after being defeated. There was some debate as to socialists' and radicals' future course. Should socialists act independently or ally themselves with radicals? Was it better to focus on another form of politics? How could various forms of conservatism – in conservative and radical parties, in the labour movement (Grütli) and in rural areas – be overcome? Although for a short time the IWA had won a mass base in Geneva, it had not changed society as a whole.

***

Organisation and the General Strike[9]
[*L'Égalité*, 3 April 1869][10]

Workers, stay very calm. If your sufferings are great, be heroic, and put up with them a little longer. Read carefully what is written in the journal *L'Internationale*[11] for the workers of Charleroi. This is all good for us to learn. Listen indeed to the wise advice of our brothers from Belgium:

Let our Swiss brothers be patient a little longer! They like us are obliged to wait for the signal for social confrontation to arise from a major country – England, France or Germany. While we wait, let us continue to organise all the strength of the proletariat in sections (union branches); let us do our best to help each other against the tribulations imposed on us by the current state of things, and, above all let us study solutions to the great economic problems which will arise on the morrow of victory; let us seek out, as best we may, ways to promote the liquidation of the old society and the constitution of a new one.

Be patient: 'the day of justice will come'. Meanwhile, reinforce your ranks and build your organisation.

News of the European labour movement can be summed up in one word: strikes. A typesetters' strike in many Belgian towns, a spinners' strike in Ghent, a decorators' strike in Bruges; in England a strike is imminent in the manufacturing areas; in Prussia a zinc miners' strike; in Paris a strike of painters and plasterers; in Switzerland strikes in Basel and Geneva.

As we advance strikes spread. What does this mean? That the struggle of labour against capital is growing ever stronger, that economic anarchy is becoming stronger day-by-day, and that we are advancing at a great pace towards Social Revolution – the final confrontation at the end of this [period of] anarchy. Certainly, if the bourgeoisie wanted to have a night of 4 August,[12] and if it were to renounce its privileges: the right of capital to draw benefits from labour, then the emancipation of the proletariat might be accomplished without any upheaval. But – so inveterate and blind is bourgeois egoism – one would have to be a real optimist to hope to see this sort of solution to the social problem – a bipartisan entente between the privileged and the disinherited. So it is more likely that a new social order may arise out of further excesses of the current [economic] anarchy.

As strikes spread and as neighbours learn about them the general strike comes ever closer. These days, with the idea of liberation so current amongst the proletariat, a general strike can result only in a great cataclysm, giving society a new skin. We have not got there yet, but no doubt everything is leading us there. And the people need to be ready, they must not allow themselves to be cheated again by talkers and dreamers as in [18]48; they need to be seriously and strongly organised.

Given that strikes are coming along so quickly, one after another, should we not be afraid that the cataclysm might arrive before an adequate proletarian organisation? We do not believe so, because first of all strikes already indicate a certain amount of collective strength, a certain understanding between workers and furthermore because each strike becomes a starting point for further new organisation. The necessities of struggle push workers to support each other; from one country to another and from one trade to another; thus as struggles becomes ever more active, so too does the federated organisation of the proletariat become broader and stronger. And then there are the narrow-minded economists – accusing this workers' federation, represented by the IWA, of instigating strikes and creating anarchy! This is a simple matter of taking causes for effects. It is not the International that creates the war between the exploited and the exploiter, but the necessities of war that have created the International.[13]

§

Bakunin wrote prolifically for *L'Egalité, Le Progrès* and other journals throughout much of 1869. He produced a series of nine articles on patriotism for *Le Progrès*. He wrote more for *L'Egalité*. Between February and August, in addition to the articles below, he wrote: 'On *Fraternité*' (a journal of 'bourgeois socialism'), 'A reply to Mrs André Léo', 'On the Double Strike in Geneva', 'On Russia', 'On the International Labour Movement', a series of articles – 'The Sedators' (Les Endormeurs) – also on bourgeois socialism; 'The Agitation of the Socialist Democratic Party in Austria', several articles judging and condemning Mr Coullery and his paper *La Montagne*, and a series of articles on Integral Education.

The four articles below consider the Politics of the International. The first one begins with a quotation from Pierre Coullery.* Bakunin wrote that Coullery helped to create new IWA sections but wanted them 'only as an instrument of reaction, making of them a platform for his own use'.[14]

Coullery defended individual property rights. He repudiated the resolutions of the Brussels IWA congress of 1868 looking forward to new forms of collective property. He fell out with the local Radical Party, then in office in Neuchâtel, and formed an alliance with local conservatives to secure his election to the cantonal legislature. As a consequence of this alliance he was repudiated by the local IWA.[15]

Bakunin had attacked Coullery in *L'Égalité*, writing: 'Mr Coullery professes a fanatic cult for this [Jacobin revolutionary] society, for this divine liberty. This is a lovely passion, we might give him ample praise and might ask to share it, except that we know that *this freedom* – the cause for which he nominates himself as the sole champion – is, in reality, only privilege for the few and slavery for the many. This is the liberty of the *Journal de Genève*, the liberty supported by every bourgeois [manager], one that arranges things so that their workers are under police surveillance.'[16] Bakunin begins with a quotation from Coullery's new paper, *La Montagne*.

The Politics of the International
[I, *L'Égalité*, 7 August 1869][17]

'We have believed hitherto', says *La Montagne*, 'that the quality of a member of the International was independent of their religious and political opinions, and it is on this terrain that we have placed ourselves'.

We might think that Mr Coullery is right, at first sight. Because, in truth, when the International accepts a new member, it does not ask whether this or that person belongs to a political party or whether they are religious or atheist. It asks just this: are you a worker, or if you are not, do you wish, do you feel the strength and desire to fully and faithfully embrace the workers' cause, to identify with it, to the exclusion of all other interests which may oppose it?

Do you realise that workers today – the sole producers of all the world's wealth, the creators of civilization and the ones who have conquered every freedom for the bourgeoisie – are condemned to slavery, ignorance and misery? Have you understood that the principal cause of all the evils endured by workers is misery and poverty, and that this poverty, which is the lot of all workers throughout the world, is a necessary consequence of the current economic order of society, and especially of the servitude of labour – the proletariat – under the yoke of capital, that is to say, of the bourgeoisie?

Have you understood that there is an irreconcilable antagonism between the proletariat and the bourgeoisie and that this is the inevitable consequence of their respective economic positions? That the prosperity of the bourgeois class is incompatible with workers' freedom and well-being, because the particular wealth of the bourgeoisie exists and can be based only on the exploitation and servitude of labour; and that for this reason, the prosperity and the human dignity of the working masses demands the abolition of the bourgeoisie as a distinct class. And that in consequence the war between the bourgeoisie and the proletariat is a matter of life and death, and it can end only with the destruction of the former?

Have you understood that no worker, however intelligent or energetic, is able to fight alone, against the well-organised power of the bourgeoisie, a power represented and sustained by the organisation of the state, of every state? That to empower yourselves, you need to join, not the company of bourgeois [managers] – which would be foolish and criminal, because every bourgeois is, as a bourgeois, an irreconcilable enemy; nor of disloyal workers, persons who will be so scared that they will go and beg for smiles and approval of the bourgeoisie – but of honest and energetic workers, who truly desire the same things as you?

Have you understood that no isolated local or national workers' association, even one based in the largest of European countries, can ever triumph in the face of a formidable coalition of every privileged class, of every wealthy capitalist, and of every state in the world? And that faced with that coalition, to stand up to it, and to achieve supremacy, what is needed is nothing less than the unity of all local and national bodies coming together in one universal association – the great *International Workers' Association of every land*?

If you recognise and understand this thoroughly and truly; if you want all this, come to us and you will be welcomed, irrespective of your national loyalties and religious beliefs. But, to be accepted, you must first pledge:

1. To subordinate your personal interests, even those of your family, as well as your political and religious beliefs to our association's supreme interest: the struggle of labour against capital, to the economic struggle of workers against the bourgeoisie;

2. Never to compromise with the bourgeoisie for your personal gain;
3. Never to promote yourself individually, for your own interests, above the mass of workers; doing so would make you immediately into a bourgeois, an enemy and an exploiter of the proletariat, because the whole difference between the bourgeois and the worker lies in this, that the former seeks success outside the collective; while the latter seeks and strives to achieve it in solidarity with everyone who works and is exploited by bourgeois capital;
4. Always to remain loyal to the solidarity of labour, because the least betrayal of solidarity is considered by the International as the greatest infamy and crime that a worker can commit – in a word you must fully and frankly accept our general statutes, and pledge yourself faithfully to live and act by them.

We think that the founders of the IWA, in eliminating from the first moment all religious and political questions from the IWA programme, showed great wisdom. Doubtless they were themselves not lacking in poignant anti-religious opinions, or in political opinions, but they deliberately refrained from putting them forward in its programme because their main concern was above all to unite the oppressed and the exploited workers of the civilized world in one common practice. By necessity they had to look for a common starting point, a set of elementary principles on which workers – as long as they were serious, suffering and harshly exploited – might and should agree, whatever their political and economic divergences.

The inclusion of an anti-religious or political programme, far from uniting the workers of Europe, would have further divided them. A mass of false ideas has been spread amongst the working masses facilitated by workers' ignorance, and aided by the eminently corrupting and self-interested propaganda of priests, governments, and all bourgeois parties – not excepting those that are the most red. Moreover the blind masses are still too often passionately enamoured of these lies, the sole purpose of which is to make them serve – voluntarily and stupidly – the interests of the privileged class, to the detriment of their own.

Besides, today, differences are still too great in the level of moral, political, and industrial development of the working masses in various lands for it to be possible to unite them on the basis of one identical, political and anti-religious programme. To present such a programme for the IWA, to make it an absolute condition for membership of this International, would be to wish to organise a sect, not a universal association; it would only kill it.

There is now – apparently at least, and only apparently – yet another important reason to eliminate all political tendencies. From the start of history until now there has never yet been a true politics of the people, and by 'people' we mean the low people, the 'rabble,' whose toil sustains the world. There has only been the politics of the privileged classes, those who have used the physical strength of the people to dethrone one another, to replace each other. The people in turn have taken for one or other of these opposing sides, only in the vague hope that in at least one of these political revolutions (none of which were made for it, and none of which could have been made without it) there would be some alleviation of its misery and secular slavery. It was deceived – always. Even the great French Revolution deceived it; it killed the nobility, only to replace it with the bourgeoisie. The people are no longer called serfs or slaves, the law calls them born free, but reality shows that their misery and slavery is still the same.

And so they always will remain, so long as the popular masses continue to serve as a tool of bourgeois politics, whether that politics –however it is called – is radical, progressive, liberal or conservative and whatever garb it may adopt, even the most perfectly revolutionary in the whole world. All bourgeois politics – whatever its name or colour – can have but one single, fundamental purpose: to perpetuate the domination of the bourgeoisie; with the domination of the bourgeoisie meaning slavery for the proletariat.

So, what was the International to do? It had first to separate the working masses from all bourgeois politics, it had to expunge from its programme every bourgeois political programme. But at the time it was first organised, the only politics was that of the church, the monarchy, the aristocracy, or the bourgeoisie. The latter, particularly that of the radical bourgeoisie was assuredly more liberal and humane than the others, but equally they were all based on the exploitation of the working masses; and they had in reality, as their sole purpose, to fight amongst themselves over who should organise, and monopolise, exploitation. So the International had to begin by clearing the ground. Since all politics as far as the emancipation of labour was concerned was sullied by reactionary elements, it had first to eject from its midst all known political systems, to build the politics of the International, the true politics of workers, on the ruins of the bourgeois world

[II, *L'Égalité*, 14 August 1869]

The founders of the International acted with even greater wisdom in avoiding philosophical and political questions being placed as the basis of that association, and in giving it, in the first place – as its sole foundation – only the economic struggle of the workers against capital. They were certain that the moment workers set foot on this terrain and engaged with fellow workers in struggle, in common solidarity against exploitation by the bourgeoisie, their confidence – in their just cause and numerical strength – would grow. In the course of things and through the development of that struggle, they would recognise every philosophical, socialist and political principle of the International; principles which are indeed nothing other than a fair explanation of its starting point and goal.

We have set out these principles in earlier issues [of this journal].[18] From a social and political angle, their necessary consequence is the abolition of class, [also] in consequence the abolition of the bourgeoisie, which is the dominant class today; the abolition of every territorial state and of every political homeland, and, on their ruins, the establishment of a great International Federation of all local and national producer groups. From a philosophical viewpoint – insofar as it seeks nothing less than the achievement of human ideals, of human well-being, justice, equality and freedom on earth – thereby it renders superfluous every aspiration for an alternative, better, heavenly world; necessarily coming too with all this will be the abolition of cults and religious systems.

If you were to announce these two aims to ignorant workers, persons poisoned, demoralised and crushed by daily toil – one might say knowingly perverted by doctrines of governments in concert with privileged casts, bourgeois, nobles, priests; if you were you to hand them out freely, you would terrify them. They would perhaps repel you, not realising that all these ideas are nothing but the truest expression of their own interests, that these aims have, within them, the potential to achieve their most cherished wishes and, contrariwise, that the political and religious prejudices in whose name they might perhaps spurn you, are the immediate cause of the perpetuation of their misery and slavery.

One should distinguish clearly between the prejudices of the popular masses and those of the privileged classes. As we have just said, the prejudices of the masses are founded only on their ignorance and are quite in opposition to their interests; while those of the bourgeoisie are based precisely on their class interests and they are preserved, against the corrosive effects of bourgeois science itself, only through collective bourgeois egoism. The people want, but do not know. The bourgeoisie know, but do not want. Of the two, who is incurable? Without doubt the bourgeoisie.

A general rule: you can convince only those who – by instinct or because of the misery of circumstances within or around them – already feel the need for everything that you might want to give – but never those who feel no need for any change, nor even those who may desire to escape from circumstances in which they are discontented, but by virtue of their social, intellectual, and moral habits, are impelled to seek out change in a world of ideas that is not yours.

Try to win over to socialism a noble who loves wealth, or a bourgeois who wishes to be ennobled, or a worker whose heart and soul is bent on becoming a bourgeois! Try again to convince an aristocrat of the intellect – a real one, or one who imagines themself to be one, an expert or one who is half, a quarter, a tenth or just one per cent of an expert, one who is full of scientific pretention, often because they have just had the good fortune to have understood, more or less, a few books, and are full of arrogant contempt for the illiterate masses, imagining themselves called on to form, with others like them, a new dominant, i.e. exploiting, caste – no amount of reasoning or agitation could suffice to convert these unhappy people. Only one thing would do to convert them – the real destruction of their privileged positions, of every form of exploitation and domination. So, social revolution, as it sweeps away every inequality in the world, will give them morality, compelling them to seek their happiness in solidarity and equality.

Things are different with serious workers. By serious workers, we mean all who are crushed beneath the weight of work; all those whose position is so precarious or miserable that not one of them (except through extraordinary circumstances) could ever hope to think of obtaining *for themselves* – and only for themselves – a better place in the current economic or social order; becoming in turn, for example, a boss, or a state councillor. Naturally in this category we also rank those rare and generous workers who, although they have the opportunity to raise themselves individually above the working class, do not wish to take up that opportunity, preferring to suffer bourgeois exploitation a little longer in solidarity with their comrades-in-misery, rather than becoming exploiters in turn themselves. Such workers need no conversion, they are pure socialists.

We speak of the great mass of workers, who are miserable and ignorant – exhausted by work day-in and day-out. The awareness and conscience of this mass – whatever attempts are made, and which may even partially succeed, in influencing it with religious and political prejudice – is *socialist without knowing it*. It is seriously, more really socialist than every bourgeois and scientific socialist lumped together; it is so from the depth of its instincts and through the pressure of its condition. It is so through every circumstance of its material existence, through every impulse of its being, whereas the latter are so only by virtue of the imperatives of their thinking; and in real life, the necessities of life exert an ever greater strength than those of thought, thinking being here, as always and everywhere, the expression of life, the reflection of the successive evolution, but never its principle.

What workers lack is neither reality, nor an awareness of the necessity of socialist aspirations but only socialist thinking. What every worker aspires to, from the depth of his being, is a fully human life: i.e. material well-being and intellectual development, both based on justice – that is to say on the equality and freedom of each in work – this instinctive ideal of everyone, who lives only through work, this ideal can evidently not be realised under present social and political conditions, based on the injustice and cynical exploitation of the working masses. Only through the overthrow of the existing social order can workers' emancipation be achieved, and so in every serious worker there is of necessity a revolutionary socialist. Either the organisation of this injustice must perish – and with it its entire apparatus of iniquitous law and institutional privilege – or the working masses will remain condemned to eternal slavery. So this is socialist thought – its germs are to be found in the instinct of each serious worker. The aim then is to make them fully conscious of their desires, to awaken thinking in them that corresponds to their instincts; because, from the moment that workers' thought is raised to the level of their instinct their resolution will be set and their power will become irresistible.

What is it then that prevents a more rapid development of this salutary thinking amongst the working masses? Ignorance, and in large part, religious and political prejudice – it is through these that interested parties continue to work even today, clouding workers' consciousness and natural intelligence. How then to dissipate this ignorance, how to root out these malicious prejudices? Through education and propaganda?

These means are doubtless substantial and wonderful, but things being as they are, they are insufficient. The isolated worker crushed by work and daily worries lacks sufficient time for education. And then, who would carry out this propaganda? Would it be the few sincere socialists emerging from the bourgeoisie, who are full of generosity no doubt, but who are too few in number to carry out propaganda as fully as it is needed; moreover belonging to another world, they lack sufficient grasp of the world of workers, and may excite some distrust – to some extent a legitimate distrust – amongst those workers?

The preamble of the statutes of the International states: 'The emancipation of the workers is the task of the workers themselves' – it is absolutely right; this is the fundamental basis of our great association. But the world of workers is generally an ignorant place, as yet it is wholly lacking in theory. So only one method remains, *liberation through practical action*. What then should be this practice?

There is one only. It is workers' struggle and solidarity against their bosses, *the organisation and the federation of resistance funds* [strike funds].

[III, *L'Égalité*, 21 August 1869]

It was not because of indifference that the International was at first forbearing towards the conservative or reactionary ideas, in religion or politics, of workers who joined it. It cannot be said that it was indifferent because, as we have shown in earlier articles, it detested and rejected every reactionary idea with every breath of its body, because such ideas would throw over the very principles of the International.

This moderation, we repeat, was inspired by great wisdom. It counted on workers' collective experience – something that a worker could not fail to acquire within the International; it knew perfectly well that, given their miserable situation every serious worker must be a socialist out of necessity. If a worker had some reactionary ideas these were only the effect of ignorance, and more than anything else it relied on the collective struggle of workers against management to deliver them [from such prejudices].

So, one could be sure that workers would soon abandon any heavenly concerns. From the moment they came to believe in the possibility of a future radical transformation of their economic situation, and along with their comrades began a real struggle to reduce hours of work and increase pay, and from the moment that they began to take a lively interest in this very material struggle – they would then, voluntarily, renounce heavenly assistance. Relying on workers' collective strength more and more, they would voluntarily renounce the aid of heaven. In their thinking socialism would take the place of religion.

As for reactionary politics – things will go the same way. As workers' consciousness is liberated from religious oppression it will lose its principal support. From another viewpoint, economic struggle, as it develops and spreads more widely, as it develops further, through collective action and practice – which is always necessarily more instructive and profound than isolated experience – will lead workers to realise that their real enemies are the privileged classes, including the clergy, bourgeoisie, nobility and the state. The latter is only there to preserve every class privilege, and always and forcibly it takes their side against the proletariat.

Workers, once engaged in struggle, will necessarily end up understanding that there is an irreconcilable antagonism between the accomplices of reaction and their own dearest human concerns, and at this point, having arrived and realised this, they will not fail to squarely take sides, and will see themselves as a revolutionary socialists.

This is not the way of things with the bourgeoisie. In heart and mind they repel the great act of liberation and justice which we call social revolution. Their every interest is opposed to the economic transformation of society. If their ideas are also opposed, if their ideas are reactionary, or to use a polite term if they are today called 'moderate'; if they are horrified by real social equality, or by what one might call equality – one that is at one and the same time economic, social and political; if in the depths of their soul they wish to keep for themselves, for their children or for their class one single privilege, be it only intelligence, as many bourgeois socialists do today; if they do not detest the current order of things – not only with every part of their thinking and logic, but also with all the power of their passion – then one can be sure that they will remain reactionaries and enemies of the workers' cause throughout their lives. They must be kept away from the International and kept at a distance, because they can enter it only to demoralise it, and to make it deviate away from its [proper] path. There is also an infallible sign by which workers can recognise if there is good faith – without a shadow of hypocrisy and without the least detrimental reservation – in the bourgeois who seeks membership in their ranks. This sign consists of the relations that such a person maintains vis-à-vis the bourgeois world.

The antagonism that exists between the workers' world, and that of the bourgeoisie is taking on ever more pronounced features. Everyone who thinks seriously, whose thinking and imagination is not affected by the often unconscious influence of self-interested sophisms must understand that today no reconciliation is possible between them. Workers want equality and the bourgeois want to preserve inequality. Evidently one destroys the other. And the great majority of bourgeois capitalists and landlords have the courage to frankly admit what they desire. They display their horror of the current working-class movement with equal courage and sincerity. It is good that we should recognise them as resolute and sincere enemies.

But there is another type of bourgeois who lacks both sincerity and courage. Enemies of social liquidation, of what we call, with all our strength, a great act of justice (the necessary starting point, and the indispensable base of a rational and egalitarian organisation), they wish, like other bourgeois to preserve economic inequality, that eternal source of every other inequality. And, at the same time, they pretend to desire, like us, the complete liberation of work and workers. They maintain against us, with a passion worthy of the most reactionary bourgeois, that very cause of the slavery of the proletariat, the division between labour and property (capitalist or landed property), represented today by two different classes. And yet they pose as apostles for the deliverance of the working class from the heel of property and capital!

Are they deceiving us or themselves? Some of them are deceiving themselves in good faith; many are deceiving themselves and deceiving us at the same time; all belong to that category of radical bourgeois and bourgeois socialists who founded the *League of Peace and Freedom*.* Is this League socialist? In the beginning, and in the first year of its life, it was horrified by socialism and rejected it, as I have said before on occasion. Last year, at its congress in Bern, it triumphantly rejected the principle of economic equality. Today, feeling itself near death, and wishing to survive a little longer; understanding, at last, that political life is no longer possible beyond the social question, it calls itself socialist, it has become bourgeois socialist, which means that it would like to resolve every social question on the basis of *economic inequality*. It seeks and is impelled to preserve the interest of capitalists, and land rents, and pretends that thereby workers can be emancipated. It attempts to add substance to nonsense.

Why does it do so? What made it undertake such a sterile and incongruous task? It isn't difficult to understand. A large part of the bourgeoisie is tired of the reign of Caesars and of the militarism that it itself inaugurated in 1848, out of fear of the proletariat. Remember the June days*, the forerunners of the December days*; remember that [French] National Assembly which, after the June days with one exception insulted and slandered unanimously that illustrious and one might say heroic socialist, Proudhon,[19] who alone had the courage to throw down the challenge of socialism in the face of that enraged herd of bourgeois radicals, liberals and conservatives. And it should not be forgotten that amongst those who insulted Proudhon,* there are many citizens still alive [today], who are more militant than before, who, having been baptised by the persecutions of December, have subsequently become martyrs for freedom.

So there can be no doubt that it was the entire bourgeoisie, including the radical bourgeoisie that created the Caesarean and military despotism whose effects it now deplores. Having made use of it against the proletariat, it now seeks to be delivered from it. Nothing is more natural – the regime ruins and humiliates it. But how is it to obtain its deliverance? In earlier times it was courageous and powerful, it had the strength of its conquests. Today it is scared and debilitated, it is afflicted by the impotence of old age. It knows its weakness only too well; it knows that it can do nothing alone. It needs help. Help can come only from the proletariat, so the proletariat must be won over.

How to win it over? Through promises of political equality and freedom? These are words that do not touch workers. They have learnt to their cost, through bitter experience; they have come to understood that such words mean nothing for them, just ongoing economic slavery, often harder than ever. If then you want to touch the heart of every miserable slave of labour, speak to them of economic emancipation. There are no workers left who do not now know that, for them today, this is the only serious, single and real basis for all other forms of liberation. So to them one must talk of the economic reform of society.

'So,' said these members of the League of Peace and Freedom, 'let us discuss all this, let us call ourselves socialists too. Let us promise workers social and economic reforms, but always on condition that they respect the basis of civilisation and bourgeois omnipotence – individual and hereditary property, capitalist interest and land rent. Let us persuade them that it is only on these conditions – which however guarantee our domination and workers' slavery – that workers may be freed.' 'Let us further persuade them that, to achieve these social reforms, a fine political revolution is needed; an exclusively political one, one as red as you please from a political viewpoint, with many heads cut off, if that should be needed – but one with the greatest respect for the sanctity of property; a very Jacobin* revolution in a word, one which will make us the masters of the situation; and, once we are the masters, we will give workers what we can and what we want to give them.'

Workers can recognise a phoney socialist, or a bourgeois socialist by a sign that is infallible – if in talking to them of revolution, (or if you wish of social transformation), he says that political transformation must precede economic transformation; if he denies that both should be made at the same time, or [if he says] that the political revolution should be something less than the immediate and direct act of full and complete social liquidation – let them turn their back on him, he is either an idiot, or a hypocritical exploiter.

[IV, *L'Égalité*, 28 August 1869]

The IWA, if it is to remain true to its principles, if it is not to go astray from the only path that might lead it to safety, must above all be forewarned and forearmed against the influence of two sorts of *bourgeois socialists:* the advocates of *bourgeois politics, including bourgeois revolutionaries,* and the so-called *'practical men'* of *bourgeois cooperation.*

Let us consider the former first. As we said in the last issue, economic emancipation is the basis of every other form of liberation. In these words we have summed up the entire politics of the International. Thus we read, in the 'considering' clauses of our general statutes, the following declaration:

[T]*hat the subjugation of labour to capital is the source of all material, moral and political servitude,* and that for this reason the economic emancipation of workers is the great objective to which every political movement must be subordinated …

It is clear that every political movement, if its objective is not the *direct and immediate* economic emancipation of workers – *definitive and complete* – and which does not clearly and unmistakably proclaim on its banner in a clear and whole-hearted manner the principle of *economic equality*, i.e. the *wholesale restitution of capital to labour*, or [in other words] *social liquidation* – that all such political movements are bourgeois, and as such must be excluded from the International.[20]

In consequence the politics of bourgeois democrats or bourgeois socialists must be excluded without pity, a politics which as it declares that political liberty is the *precondition* for economic liberation, can understand, through these words, only this: 'political reforms, or political revolution should *precede* economic reforms or economic revolution; in consequence workers should ally themselves with the more or less radical bourgeoisie to achieve firstly the former with them, only achieving the latter thereafter against them.'

We protest vociferously against this dire theory, which for workers can only result in making them serve once again as instruments against themselves, delivering them once again, into exploitation by the bourgeoisie. To conquer political freedom *first* can mean nothing other than conquering it *first and alone*; leaving, at least in the first days, social and economic relations in their existing condition – so misery for the workers, and insolent wealth for the landlords and capitalists.

But we are be told, political liberty, once conquered, will serve workers, as an instrument to win, later, *equality* and *economic justice*. Freedom is, of course, a magnificent and powerful instrument. Everything depends on knowing if workers can really use it, if it might become something they own, or whether – as it has always been the case hitherto – their *political freedom* will be a fraudulent facade, a fiction? Workers, in their current economic circumstances, if one came to talk to them of *political freedom*, might they not respond using the refrain of the popular song: 'Do not talk of freedom, poverty is slavery!'[21]

Indeed, one would have to be in love with illusions to dream that workers, in the face of current social and economic conditions, could really take advantage of their political freedoms and really make serious use of them. They lack two little things to do so – leisure and material means.

Besides, what did we see in France the day after the 1848 revolution, from a political viewpoint the most radical revolution that might be desired? The French workers were certainly neither indifferent nor unintelligent, yet though they had the widest universal suffrage* they had to leave things to the bourgeoisie to do what they liked. Why? Because they lacked the material means that would be needed, to make political liberty a reality; because, driven by hunger, they remained slaves of toil. Things were not like this for the liberal and radical bourgeois, or even the conservatives – some latterly republicans, some converted subsequently. They could come and go, they could conspire freely, some benefiting from rents, or from lucrative bourgeois positions, others being able to draw on the state and its finances, which they naturally preserved. They entrenched themselves and made themselves stronger than ever. We know the results: firstly the June days, later, as a necessary consequence, the days of December.

But, it will be said, workers will be made wiser by their very experience and instead of electing a bourgeois to constituent or legislative assemblies they will send simple workers. Poor as they may be, they can yet afford the upkeep of their deputies. Do you know what will happen? These worker-deputies, transplanted into a bourgeois environment, into a political atmosphere of wholly bourgeois political ideas, will cease to be actual workers and will become statesmen, they will become bourgeois, and perhaps more bourgeois than the bourgeoisie. Because people do not make circumstances; no, on the contrary circumstances make people. And we know from experience that *bourgeois workers* are often no less egotistical than bourgeois exploiters, no less disastrous for the IWA than the bourgeois socialists, and no less vain and ridiculous than the bourgeois who has become a noble.

Whatever is said or done, so long as workers remain saddled with the current state of things, no freedom is possible as far as they are concerned. Those who urge workers to win political freedom without dealing first with the burning question of socialism, without pronouncing the word that makes the bourgeoisie grow pale – *social liquidation* – they are saying simply: 'Conquer political liberty for us, so that later we can use it against you.'

But, it will be said, are they not well intentioned and sincere these bourgeois. But good intentions and sincerity do not hold out against the influence of circumstances. We have said that even workers once in this position will forcibly become bourgeois, and all the more so will the bourgeois who remain in this situation, remain bourgeois.

If bourgeois people, inspired by a great passion for humanity, equality and justice seriously wish to work for proletarian emancipation let them first break off all social and political links, all relations of mind and interest, of heart and soul with other bourgeois. Let them understand that

---

* Male suffrage.

no reconciliation is possible between the proletariat and this class, which depending only on the exploitation of others, is the natural enemy of the proletariat.

Having turned their back on the bourgeois world once and for all, let them take their place beneath the workers' banner, whereon is inscribed 'Justice, Equality and Freedom for all. Abolition of classes through universal economic equalisation [Levelling]. Social Liquidation.' They will be welcome. As for bourgeois socialists and bourgeois workers,[22] who come to us with talk of conciliation between bourgeois politics and the socialism of workers; we have only one word of advice to give: turn your back on them.

Since today bourgeois socialists are using socialism as bait and are working hard to organise a formidable workers' agitation to win political liberty – a liberty which as we have seen will only profit the bourgeoisie – since the mass of workers, having come to understand their situation, and enlightened and shaped by the principles of the International, are organising themselves effectively and begin to form a true power, one that is not national, but international; carrying out not the business of the bourgeoisie but rather their own agenda; and since even to achieve that bourgeois ideal of complete political freedom with republican institutions a revolution is needed, and since no revolution can triumph except through the power of the people, what is needed is for this [people] power to cease pulling the chestnuts out of the fire for the benefit of bourgeois gentlemen. Henceforth this power should work only for the victory of the people's cause: the cause of all who work, against all who exploit labour.

The International Workers' Association will, in keeping with its principles, never endorse political agitation which does not have as its direct and immediate goal the *complete economic emancipation of the worker*, that is to say the abolition of the bourgeoisie as a class economically separate from the great mass of the people. Nor [will it support] any revolution which fails to write on its banner, from the first day, from the first moment, *social liquidation.*

However revolutions are not improvised. They are not made arbitrarily, nor by individuals, nor even by the most powerful associations. They are always brought about by the natural force of things, independent of every will or conspiracy. They can be foreseen, sometimes one can sense them approaching, but one cannot accelerate their explosion. Convinced of this truth, we pose the question: What policy should the International pursue in the interval – however long it may be – which separate us from the terrible social revolution which everyone expects?'

Disregarding all local and national politics, as its statutes enjoin, the

International will give an essentially *economic character* to workers' agitation in every land; setting as its goal the reduction of working hours and higher wages. [It will advocate] as means *the organisation of the mass of workers* and *the creation of resistance* [strike] funds. It will develop propaganda for its principles. These principles, being the expression of the most pure collective interest of workers of the entire world, are their soul; they constitute the vital energy of the Association. It will carry out this propaganda extensively, without respect for bourgeois susceptibilities, so that all workers, escaping from the moral and intellectual torpor in which they are constrained, can understand their situation, know what they should like to accomplish and understand the conditions through which they may conquer their human rights.

The propaganda that it promotes will be made with greater sincerity and energy, even if we may often encounter in the International itself those influences that attempt to disrespect its principles, seek to pass them off as useless theories, and attempt to push workers back, to coral them within the bourgeoisie's religious, economic and political catechism. The International will grow and organise strongly across the frontiers of every land. And when that revolution breaks out – brought on by force of circumstance – it will find its real strength, one that knows how to act, and so capable of taking things in hand and capable of giving them a sense of direction that will be really salutary for the people; a serious international organisation of workers' associations of every country. It will have the capacity to replace the political world of the state, and the departing bourgeois.

We end this faithful exposition of the politics of the International by reproducing the last paragraph of the considering clauses of its general statutes:

The movement that is developing amongst workers in the most industrious countries of Europe, as it nurtures new hopes, sets out a solemn warning never to fall back into old errors.

§

Draft resolution on inheritance

L'Égalité, of 28 August 1869 also carried a draft resolution concluding a report on the commission on inheritance, nominated by an IWA general assembly in Geneva, in preparation for the Basel IWA congress.[23]

Considering that the right of inheritance is one of the principal causes of prevailing political, social and economic inequality; that without equality, there can be neither justice nor freedom, and that there will always be oppression and exploitation, slavery and misery for the proletariat, with riches and domination for those who exploit the labour of the people; Congress recognise the necessity of the full and complete abolition of inheritance, with this abolition being achieved, in consequence of events, either by the path of reform or through revolution.

§

On Inheritance

[Speeches at the Basel congress of the IWA, September 1869][24]

At the Basel congress of 1869 the debates on property marked out some of the divisions within the IWA. In the debate about property-in-land a majority came together calling for land to be made common property. The matter had been debated at the previous congress, but those defeated there – persons attached to a mutualist or individualistic strain of Proudhonist thinking – wanted and were allowed a second debate on the matter.[25] They were defeated by those who advocated a 'pushed to the limit Proudhonism'[26] – Bakunin and co-thinkers, and supporters of the General Council.

Revolutionaries and reformers[27] parted company over the question of other forms of property. The latter worked to maintain alliances with radical bourgeois parties – abolishing inheritance would have undermined their alliance.

Revolutionaries said that it would be illogical to advocate collective ownership of land and not to advocate collective ownership of other property.[28] Bakunin considered the demand for the abolition of inheritance of fundamental importance. Coupled with demands for social and collective property it announced Labour's project of overthrowing capitalism. It served to undermine family relations insofar as men and women would not be tied by property. Children he envisaged would not be the property of their parents. Both children and older people would be educated and looked after by Communes and workers' collectives; in this respect Bakunin was in favour of communism.

Abolishing inheritance might have some effect in facilitating not the dispossession of peasants from their land, but rather allowing new arrangements to evolve once collective and common ownership was instituted and individual inheritance rights curtailed.

The General Council's views on inheritance were decisively rejected by congress but they were nevertheless reproduced in the official English-language congress report. The motion sponsored by the Council was rejected by a vote of 37 against, 19 for, and 6 abstentions. A motion in favour of abolishing inheritance won a plurality of votes (23 against, 32 for, with 13 abstentions) but was not reproduced.[29] The report, as edited, prevented English speakers from knowing what had been debated and concealed the fact that the General Council's views had been rejected by congress.

Critics of the General Council came to see a pattern here: such editing was characteristic of the practice of the General Council's executive sub-committee. It was just one example of the deliberate and repeated misrepresentation of discussion and manipulation of records, for partisan ends.

***

Between the collectivists who find it *not useful* to vote for the abolition of rights of inheritance and the collectivists who see it as both useful and *necessary* to vote for it, there is a different point of view. The first take the future as the starting point, [collective property in land and in the instruments of labour] as something already accomplished; whereas we, we take the present as our starting point, that is to say individual hereditary property in full flower. We see the right of inheritance as an obstacle in our way on our path towards collective property. We believe that it should be overthrown and abolished.

In the report made by [Eccarius]*[30] on behalf of the General Council it has been said that law is only a consequence of realities, and that once the reality of individual property is abolished, the right of inheritance will fall away by itself. Certainly, in history, all legal and political rights have always preceded law, and are an expression and product, of an existing system.

But it is also incontestable that having been an effect of prior events and acts, law has in turn become the cause of further developments; it has itself becomes a real fact, the cause of subsequent effects, a very powerful reality, which has to be overturned if one seeks to come to an order of things that is different to that which now exists. In this way the right to inherit, having been a natural consequence of the violent appropriation of natural and social wealth, has become a basis for, and a principle condition for individual property, in so far as it is guaranteed by the state. So we must vote for its abolition.

It has been said that this abolition will in no way be practical, because when workers are sufficiently powerful to abolish inheritance, they would take advantage of this power to proclaim and accomplish social liquidation. But it is in the name of practicality that I recommend above all the abolition of inheritance.

We have discussed what difficulties there will be concerning the dispossession of peasants. Doubtless, if one wanted to dispossess peasants by decree, millions of small landowners would be driven towards reaction, and force would have to be used to make them submit to revolution, in other words reaction.

So they would be left as de facto possessors of parcels of land of which today they are the owners. But if the law of inheritance was not abolished, what would happen? They would transmit their title to their children with the sanction of the state, with the title of property. You would preserve and perpetuate individual property, the abolition of which you have voted as being necessary, having in mind transformation into collective property.

But on the contrary, if you proclaim the liquidation of the legal and political State and abolish rights of inheritance at the same time as you accomplish the social liquidation, in that case what would peasants be left with? Only the reality of their possession would remain, and that fact, being no longer protected by the power of the state, will be reversed and transformed easily, by the pressure of events and revolutionary forces.

§

Bakunin made a second brief speech in which he said that although there were no representatives for small landowners at the congress, it should nevertheless support the resolution to abolish inheritance. He concluded:

As for organisation in the future, I consider that all productive work is necessarily a collective endeavour and that labour that is erroneously called 'individual' is actually collective labour, because it is made possible only because of the collective labour of both past and current generations.

I conclude and agree with the majority of the commission,[31] calling for the common-and-in-solidarity organisation of communes, and I do so that much more willingly because this solidarity implies the organisation of society from bottom to top, whereas the minority project speaks to us of state [organisation]. I am a resolute opponent of the state, and of every bourgeois and state-centred politics. I demand the abolition of every territorial and national state and, on their ruins, the foundation of an international state of workers.

ON REAL DEMOCRACY

[Extract from: 'The Bears of Bern and the Bear of St. Petersburg', March, 1870][1]

Switzerland in 1870 was a confederation[2] composed of 22 cantons. Agriculture dominated much of the economy, but there was a luxury sector too producing clocks, watches and jewellery; and a modern sector: textiles, construction and railways. Bakunin wrote that economic centralisation was a precondition for civilization and created freedom, but political centralisation destroyed spontaneous popular action and benefited rulers and the ruling classes.

Switzerland had suffered a brief civil war in 1847, resulting in the defeat of the more conservative and catholic cantons, and the emergence of a new form of government dominated by the Radical Party. A new constitution reinforced confederal powers. Bakunin commented on the changes brought in since 1848 that: 'The centralisation that was created by the Radical Party, in the name of freedom, has killed freedom.' He did not oppose suffrage:

> Is this to say that we revolutionary socialists do not want universal suffrage, and that we prefer either a limited suffrage or the despotism of one person alone? Not at all. What we affirm, is that universal suffrage, on its own, and working in a society founded on social and economic inequality, will never be anything other than a trap; that on the part of bourgeois democrats, it will never be anything other than an odious deception, the surest means to consolidate, with a façade of justice and liberalism the eternal domination of the owning and exploiting classes, to the detriment of popular liberties and interests.[3]

Bakunin's sceptical survey of the process of Swiss male suffrage contrasts with those of the Friedrich Engels who wrote that with democratic rights 'the proletariat will thereby also acquire all the weapons it needs for its ultimate victory. With freedom of the press and the right of assembly and association it will win universal suffrage, and with universal, direct suffrage, in conjunction with the above tools of agitation, it will win everything else.'[4]

Switzerland provided a haven for radicals fleeing from repressive governments but that freedom was always under threat from more powerful neighbours. Mazzini* was ordered away from cantons bordering Italy. Bakunin developed an infatuation for Nechaev,* a 'boy' who talked of revolution in Russia. Nechaev was being sought by the Russian police. Bakunin was aware that the government of Wurttemberg had surrendered a Russian prisoner just six months earlier; and very recently a Russian student had been arrested in Vienna. He feared that Nechaev's arrest might follow. Bakunin severed relations with Nechaev in July 1870, but he continued to campaign against his rendition to the Russian government.[5] James Guillaume* began to publish protests against extradition, notably an article from Bakunin in the Le Locle journal *Le Progrès* on 19 February 1870.

People such as Nechaev, Bakunin wrote, were commonly accused of being assassins or forgers. Anyone who displeased the Russian government might be falsely accused: 'They are neither assassins, nor forgers; the Russian government knows that best, and other countries' governments know it too. But face is saved and services are rendered.' Nechaev, said Bakunin, had made the mistake of believing the legend of William Tell and thinking that an act of revolt against oppression arouses sympathy. Such attitudes, he wrote, were legends from the past, but in the present revolt was neither useful nor lucrative; and the Swiss state feared being overrun. Nevertheless such legends still influenced people's minds and some believed that Swiss dignity still lived. So, to justify extradition, victims were slandered.

Posing as a 'desperate and humiliated Swiss citizen', Bakunin portrayed extradition as a facet of the solidarity that existed between all governments. He attacked the press: 'Our so-called liberal newspapers – dedicated to the task of defending freedom against the encroachment of [excessive] democracy – feels no obligation to defend it against despotic violence. They fear and slander forces from below, but scream and bless any use of force by those on high.'

Bakunin's concerns begged wider questions: just how different were liberal and conservative states? Could democracy empower working people to control the state? In his view what was needed was another form of social organisation: 'the abolition of all political states – be they federal or cantonal – and the transformation of the political federation into a national and international economic federation.'[6]

***

It will be easy to show that nowhere in Europe is there real popular control. Here we will confine ourselves to reviewing Swiss practice, firstly because it is close to us, also because Switzerland is the sole democratic republic in Europe. After a fashion, it has achieved the ideal of popular sovereignty, and good sense would suggest that whatever is true as far as it is concerned, should also be true for other countries.

In the 1830s the most advanced Swiss cantons sought to assure freedom through universal suffrage – a wholly legitimate project. So long as differences existed in electoral rights, between town and countryside,[7] and between [urban] patricians and the people, so long as our legislative Councils were nominated only by one class of privileged citizens, the executive power nominated by these Councils, and the laws elaborated within their midst could result only in assuring and regulating the domination of the aristocracy over the nation. So, in the interest of popular freedom, it seemed necessary to overturn these regimes, replacing them with popular sovereignty.

It was thought that popular freedom would be assured once universal suffrage was established. Well this was a grand delusion, and one can say that awareness of this delusion led to the defeat of the Radical Party in several cantons, and today, to the flagrant demoralisation of that party everywhere. As our so-called liberal press assures us, the Radicals did not wish to deceive the people, but they did deceive themselves. They really were convinced when they promised the people freedom through the means of universal suffrage. They were fully convinced that they had the power to energise the people and to overthrow established aristocratic governments. Today, having learned from experience and the exercise of power, they have lost faith in their own principles and in themselves and so have been entirely corrupted and beaten.

And indeed things appeared so simple and natural: once legislative and executive powers emanated directly from popular elections, shouldn't they become a pure expression of the popular will – and how could this will engender anything other than general prosperity and freedom?

As far as the representative system is concerned the entire deception depends on this fiction – that the power or the legislative assembly that arises out of a popular election, really should, or can represent the real will of the people. The people, in Switzerland, as elsewhere, necessarily and instinctively desires two things: the greatest possible material prosperity, and, to the greatest extent, freedom to live and space to move and do things for themselves; in other words, the best organisation of their economic interests and the complete absence of any power, of any political organisation, because all political organisation has fatal consequences leading to the negation of its freedom. Such is the basis of every popular instinct; the instincts of governors who make law and exercise executive power are – arising out of their exceptional position – diametrically opposed.

Given the heights in which they are situated and irrespective of their ideas or democratic intentions, they can only view society as a tutor views a pupil. But there can be no equality between a pupil and a tutor. On the one side there is a feeling of superiority, necessarily inspired by elevated positions; on the other side are feelings of inferiority resulting from tutors' superiority, and the exercise of legislative or executive power. Whoever speaks of politics, speaks of domination; and wherever domination exists, there must necessarily be a smaller or greater part of society that is dominated, and those who are dominated naturally hate those who dominate them, whereas those who dominate must necessarily repress and consequently oppress those who are subjected to their domination.

This is the eternal history of political power, ever since that power was established in this world. This too explains how and why men – those who are the reddest of democrats, the most determined of rebels when they were amongst the mass of the governed – become excessively moderate conservatives as soon as they rise to power. Ordinarily such changes of opinion are attributed to betrayal. This is an error; the principal cause of such things is a change of position and perspective. Let us never forget that circumstance and the forces that they impose are always more powerful than the hatred or ill will of an individual.

Being entirely persuaded of this truth, I would have no fear in expressing the conviction that if tomorrow a parliament, a legislature or a government were established, composed exclusively of workers; those workers, today firm Socialist Democrats – would become determined aristocrats, later timid or bold lovers of principles of authority, oppression and exploitation. My conclusion is the following: *one should completely abolish, both in reality and in principle, everything that calls itself political power; because so long as political power exists, there will be persons who dominate and persons dominated, masters and slaves, exploiters and the exploited. Once political power is abolished, it needs replacing by the organisation of productive forces and economic services.*

Coming back to Switzerland – there is amongst us, as everywhere else, a class of rulers that is quite different and completely separated from the mass of the governed. In Switzerland, as elsewhere, however egalitarian political constitutions may be, it is the bourgeoisie that rules, and it is working people, peasants included, who obey its law. The people has neither the leisure, nor the necessary education to spend time on governmental matters.

The bourgeoisie has both – not in law – but in reality, and it has exclusive privilege. So political equality in Switzerland as elsewhere, is nothing but a puerile fiction and a lie.

How can the bourgeoisie accomplish the will of the people, its ideas or feelings, in its legislation and government, being separated from the people by every aspect of its social and economic life? It is impossible. In legislation and in government, the bourgeoisie is little concerned with the interests and instincts of the people, and is shaped in the main by its own interests and instincts; reality, daily experience proves as much.

It is true that our legislators, as well as all the members of our cantonal governments are elected, either directly, or indirectly, by the people. It is true that on election days, the proudest bourgeois, if they are ambitious, are compelled to play court to the Majesty of the Sovereign People. They come to it cap in hand, and appear to have no will, other than the People's will. But this is just an inconvenient quarter of an hour and it soon passes. Once the elections are finished everyone returns to their everyday occupation: the people to their work, and the bourgeoisie to their political intrigues and lucrative enterprises. They barely meet each other, or know each other. How can the people, crushed by work and ignorant of most of the matters that are being discussed, control the political activities of those it has elected? And is it not obvious that the control exercised by electors over their representatives is nothing but pure fiction? And, since popular control is the one and only guarantee of popular freedom in a representative system, it is obvious that this freedom too is nothing but fiction.

To avoid this inconvenience, the Radical democrats of the Canton Zurich have secured a new political system – *the referendum* – or direct legislation by the people. But *the referendum* too is only a palliative means, a new illusion, a lie. To vote with full knowledge of whys and wherefores and with complete freedom such legislation as is proposed or which one oneself seeks to propose, it would be necessary for the people to have the necessary education and the time to discuss, consider, and study such things; it would need to transform itself into some immense open air parliament. Such things are possible only on grand or rare occasions, when a law being proposed excites attention and touches everyone's interests. Such cases are excessively rare. Most of the time draft laws appear to have only a narrow purpose and to understand their real significance one must be used to thinking in the abstract terminology of law and politics. Naturally their meaning and significance escapes the attention or understanding of the people, who vote blindly, trusting their favourite orators. Each of these laws seems too insignificant – if taken one by one – to attract much popular interest, but taken together they form a net that chains down the people down. And so with, or despite the *referendum*, government in the name of the Sovereign People remains the very humble servant and instrument of the bourgeoisie.

So it may be seen that in the representative system – even one corrected by the *referendum* – popular control does not exist, and, since there can be no real or serious freedom without such control, we conclude that our popular freedom, the government of ourselves by ourselves, is a lie.

Day by day events in every Swiss canton confirm our unhappy conviction. Where is the canton where the people can intervene really or directly over issues raised by an executive or on legislation fabricated by a legislature? Where is the fictional Sovereign that has *not* been treated as an eternal child by those it has elected? Is there anywhere where that Sovereign has not been compelled to obey orders from on high; without knowing – much of the time – either the purpose or the reason why?

The greater part of business and legislation – including much that is important, relating directly with the well-being and material interest of communes – takes place over their heads, without the people being involved or concerned, without them knowing anything. The people are compromised, bound and sometimes ruined – all unawares. They lack the habit and the time to study; they allow those they elect to get on with things. Naturally, the latter serve not the world of the people but their own world and their own class interests. Their greatest achievement is to present their measures and laws in the most popular and anodyne of ways. The system of democratic representation is a perpetual deceit and hypocrisy. It requires the stupidity of the people, and thereby arises its every success.

However patient or indifferent the people of our cantons may appear, they nevertheless have certain ideas, and instincts for independence, justice and freedom with which it is best not to meddle, and which a crafty government will be careful not to disturb. When popular sentiment feels itself under attack, on matters that, one might say, constitute their *holy of holies* affecting the full political awareness of the Swiss nation, they awake from their customary torpor and revolt, and then their revolt can sweep everything before it: the constitution and the government, the legislature and the executive. Before 1848 the entire Swiss progressive movement went through a series of cantonal revolutions. These revolutions, the ever present possibility of popular uprisings, the salutary fear that they inspire, still today these constitute the single form of control that actually exists in Switzerland, they are the one barrier that arrests the spread of our rulers' passions, self-interest and ambition.

Revolution was the mighty weapon used by our Radical Party to upset aristocratic constitutions and governments. Having used it once so happily, it destroyed the weapon, so that no other party would have a chance to use it against them. How did it destroy that weapon? Through the destruction of cantonal autonomy, through the subordination of cantonal governments to federal power. Henceforth cantonal revolutions – *the one means that people in each canton had to exert real and serious control over their governments, to check the despotic tendencies inherent in each government,* these popular uprisings of salutary indignation – have become impossible. They are shattered by federal intervention.

Imagine if the people of a canton, at the end of their patience, rose up against their government, what would happen? According to the constitution of 1848, the Federal Council [national executive] has not only the right, but the duty to send federal troops from other cantons – as many as may be needed – to re-establish public order and to enforce the law and constitution of that canton. Such troops would not depart from that canton until legal and constitutional order was perfectly re-established; that is to say – to speak more frankly – not before *men, ideas, and a regime that enjoyed the sympathy of the Federal Council had entirely triumphed.* This was the outcome in the Canton of Geneva in the last insurrection of 1864.[8]

Radicals are now able to appreciate for themselves the consequences of the centralised system they introduced in 1848. Because of this system, the republican peoples of [various] cantons now have federal power as an all-powerful sovereign. To safeguard their freedom they need to control that power and even, should need arise, overturn it. It would be easy for me to prove that, failing entirely extraordinary circumstances – unless a powerful and unanimous passion enflames the entire Swiss nation, and every canton simultaneously – neither control, nor revolution will ever be possible.

Let us consider how federal power is constituted? It comprises a federal legislature [the Federal Assembly] and a Federal Council – the executive. The legislature has two chambers – one the *National Chamber* [representatives] directly elected by the people of each canton, and [secondly] the *Chamber of States*, composed of two members for each canton, elected almost everywhere by the cantonal legislatures. Both chambers of the legislature elect the seven members of the executive Federal Council.

Of these elected bodies, the *National Chamber*, because it is nominated directly by the people, is obviously the body that is more democratic and more frankly popular.[9] But, the *National Chamber* has these democratic attributes to a much smaller extent, if at all, compared with the legislating bodies of the cantons. I trust none will contest this. It is so for a very simple reason. The force of economic circumstance, now working on the people, make them indifferent and ignorant. People know properly only those matters that affect them most closely. They understand well their everyday interests. Beyond these there begins the uncertain, the unknown, and the danger of political mystification. Being possessed of a healthy dose of practical instinct – they rarely make mistakes in elections for a locality or a Commune.[10] They know the business of their own Commune pretty well – and take a great interest in its affairs. They know how to choose among their own the best and most capable men who can conduct things well. In these matters control is indeed possible, because matters are conducted under the eyes of the electors and concern the closest interests of their everyday life. This is why elections for Communes are always and everywhere the best ones, most in keeping with feelings, interests and popular will.

Cantonal legislatures and executive bodies – where the people elect the latter directly[11] – are already much less perfect. The good conduct and solution of administrative, legal and political matters, which constitutes the principal business of these councils, are things most often unknown to the people; they are beyond the limit of their daily experience, almost always they escape their control. The people have to rely on men who live in a sphere that is almost entirely separated from themselves, men more or less unknown to them. They are known, if at all, only through speeches, not through their private lives. Speechmaking can mislead people, however, especially when it has as its goal winning over popular esteem, and when the speeches concern matters largely or wholly unknown.

It follows that cantonal executives are already, and necessarily must be much further removed from popular awareness than councils of the communes. However one cannot say that they are absolutely estranged from each other. By virtue of a lengthy practice of freedom, and the people's habit of reading newspapers, the Swiss population is at least aware of cantonal affairs in general terms and take some interest in it. On the other hand they are completely unaware of federal affairs and attach no interest to national matters. In consequence, as regards the national Federal Assembly, they are entirely indifferent as to who might represent them there, or what their delegates[12] might decide. The Chamber of States being composed of members elected by each cantonal legislature[13] is thereby further from the people than the lower house, which at least results from direct popular elections. It represents the double quintessence of bourgeois parliamentarianism. Our governmental classes, their exclusive interests and political abstraction dominate there.

The Federal Council [national executive] is in turn elected by the Federal Assembly [both houses of the legislature]. As a body, it is forcibly not just a stranger, but also an enemy to every independent instinct, and to the justice and freedom that inspires our peoples. In respect of very delicate Swiss affairs, matters that are important, very little distinguishes it from authoritarian European governments other than the undiminished republican forms which conceal its power; there is no control over it other than that of the Federal Assembly. It sympathises with those governments and shares almost all their oppressive passions. If exercise of popular control over cantonal matters is excessively difficult, in national and federal affairs it is quite impossible. These affairs are conducted exclusively in the most elevated official locations, over and above the head of our people, such that most often, they are completely unaware of them.

Were the Swiss people consulted – in the case of the extradition treaty concluded recently with Imperial [Napoleonic] France, in the case of the expulsion of Mazzini,* over the violent treatment of Princess Obolensky,[14] in the case of the threatened extradition of Mrs Limousin,[15] or in the search of cantonal police forces for Mr Nechaev – as ordered by the Federal Council;[16] matters that closely affect our national dignity and rights, even our national independence?

And, if it had been consulted, would it have given its consent to measures so opposed to our traditions of hospitality and freedom, and so disastrous for our honour? Certainly not. How can it be that such measures are ordered by the Federal power, and executed by our cantonal police forces, all in a country that calls itself a democratic republic, and that has the air of self-government?

They will say it is the fault of the press: a press whose only task is to call the attention of the Swiss people to anything that might interest it: its well-being, freedom and national independence. In all these matters it has not fulfilled its duties. It is true – the conduct of the press has been deplorable. But why so? Because the entire Swiss press – be it radical or aristocratic – is bourgeois, and because with exception of a few papers edited by labour bodies, no real, proper, popular press exists as yet. There was a time when the radical press was proud to represent popular aspirations. That time is long gone. The radical press, as much as the party whose name it shares, today represents only the individual ambition of its leaders. In line with the dictum: 'Leave this place and let us replace you', it seeks to take over seats and jobs that others have occupied before. As for the rest, for many years since, radicalism has renounced revolutionary extravagances; much as the conservative or aristocratic party has renounced all its former aspirations for its part. Properly speaking there is practically no difference between the two parties, and soon we will see them merge into one single party for bourgeois domination and conservation, putting up desperate resistance to popular revolutionary and socialist aspirations. So, all in all, should one be astonished that the radical press has failed to fulfil what it no longer considers as its duty? Or, should we not be thankful that, so far, it has not overtly sided with government?

Supposing – in one canton or in many – that through one means or another, through the press, or by some other means, the attention of the people was attracted to some unpopular measure ordered by the Federal Council and implemented by cantonal governments. What could they do to stop such a measure? Nothing. Would they overturn the government? Federal troops would intervene and would suffice to obstruct them. Might they protest in popular assemblies? Yes, but the Federal Council has nothing to do with popular assemblies, the only limit that it recognises to its power consists of orders issued by the Federal legislature; and for the latter to embrace the party of dissent, it would need be that this dissent had taken hold of at least half the Swiss cantons. A national revolution of Switzerland as a whole would be needed to overturn Federal power – the Federal Council and the legislature together – not just an uprising of a few cantons.

One can clearly see that popular control of Federal power does not exist. The creation of this power placed a crown on the governmental edifice of the republic, [it marked] the death of Swiss freedom. And what do we see? In every canton the conservative or aristocratic party had waged a war to the death against the system of political centralisation created in 1848 by the Radical Party; but now it has gone over quite openly to support it. Today, in the matter of Mrs Limousin, it warmly embraces the camp of the Federal Council against the council of Canton Fribourg. What does this mean?

It proves simply that the aristocratic party, having learnt from experience, has come to understand that the Radical Party, being much more conservative and governmentalist than itself, has elevated Federal power above cantonal autonomy, and has created a magnificent instrument, not for freedom [but] for government – an all-powerful means to consolidate the domination of the rich bourgeoisie of every canton, and the building of a salutary barrier against the menacing aspirations of the proletariat.

But, if this system of political centralisation, instead of increasing the amount of freedom that Switzerland might enjoy, has tended on the contrary to destroy it entirely, did it at least strengthen and increase the independence of the Helvetic Republic vis-à-vis foreign powers? No, it has diminished it considerably. So long as each canton was autonomous, federal power, even if it wished to win over the good graces of some foreign power – through some ignoble compromise – had neither the right nor the opportunity to do so. It could neither conclude extradition treaties, nor order cantonal police forces to search out political refugees, nor compel cantons to deliver them to despots. It would have neither dared to force Canton Ticino to expel Mazzini, nor Canton Fribourg to extradite Mrs Limousin. The Federal Government, in so far as on the one hand it exercised only limited power over cantonal governments, did not have to answer to foreign powers for their acts, and, when the latter demanded things from that Federal power, it commonly took refuge behind its constitutional powerlessness. Cantons were autonomous, and it had no power to order them about. Representatives of [foreign] powers had to deal directly with cantonal governments, and if the matter concerned a political refugee, it was enough for that person to move to a neighbouring canton, to force a foreign minister to begin the process once again. Such things had no end: tiring of the conflict the diplomats most often abandoned their pursuit. The right of asylum in Switzerland, a sacred tradition, remained intact, and no foreign government had the right to complain to the Federal government, which, precisely because it was impotent, had strength to face them all. Today, Federal power is overwhelming.

PROSPECTS FOR SOCIALISM

[Extract from: 'Letters to a Frenchman', August-September 1870]¹

Bakunin hoped to see the regime of Napoleon III defeated in the war against Prussia that commenced in July 1870, and, once Napoleon was gone he hoped that the Prussians would, in turn, encounter 'every possible distress'.² In *Solidarité** of 20 August he wrote that he had no wish to see the Second Empire* win a new lease of life through a reinforcement of its monstrous state machine:

> This is why – I don't know if you share my feelings in this matter – this is why, I keenly wish that the French are once again defeated, despite all the hatred I have for the Prussian squires, for their insufferable bluster for German unity, and for Bismarck and his King.³

Shortly afterwards German victories brought an end to Napoleon III's Second Empire. On 23 August Bakunin wrote: 'if in ten days there is no popular uprising France will be lost.' Patriotism could promote universal liberty. German armies occupied much of northern France. A new French state – the Third Republic – was born on 4 September 1870 and a new Prussian-led Imperial Germany.

The occupation of northern France by German troops was characterised by Bakunin as 'a military, monarchical and aristocratic, invasion. The five of six hundred thousand German soldiers now throttling France are obedient subjects, slaves of a despot infatuated with his divine rights. They are directed, commanded, and pushed about like automats, by officers and generals drawn from the most insolent nobility of the entire world, they are – ask your brothers German workers – the most ferocious enemies of the proletariat.'[4] The occupation opened opportunities for a popular national and revolutionary rising – a repeat of the events of 1792-3. Bakunin would define prospects in terms of Social Revolution or Military Dictatorship.[5]

On 5 September *Solidarité*, published a Manifesto, declaring: 'Republican France represents European freedom, monarchical Germany represents reaction and despotism. Republicans everywhere should rise up and march to the defence of the French republic.' ... 'Long live the universal Social Republic! Guillaume,* the editor of *Solidarité* narrowly escaped prosecution and the paper was suppressed. Perhaps it was for this reason that *Letters to a Frenchman* was published without an author or editor being named.

On 7 September 1870, Eugène Dupont, correspondent for France on the IWA's General Council wrote a letter from London to Albert Richard* and other French contacts advising: 'In these circumstances the role, or rather the duty, of workers is to let the bourgeois vermin make peace with the Prussians. One should use every freedom that circumstances allow to organise every strength of the working class.'

Two or three days later the Paris IWA Federation[6] sent advice to its contacts: firstly that they should excite patriotism by all means possible, to save revolutionary France and secondly that energetic measures be taken against Bonapartist and bourgeois reaction, pushing broadly for the acceptance of broad measures for defence, through the organisation of republican committees, as the first elements of future revolutionary Communes. 'Our own revolution has not yet been accomplished, and we will carry it through when, having rid ourselves of invasion, we will set out through revolution the foundations of the egalitarian society that we all desire.'

Bakunin believed that the cause of revolution, and France itself, might be saved if revolutions took hold of the major provincial cities – Lyons, Marseilles, Rouen, and St Etienne. 'Today only the workers of the provincial cities can save France.' Paris – given its situation enveloped by German troops, was in no position to launch the revolutionary rising that was needed to release energies to defeat the armies of German autocracy.

For his knowledge of events Bakunin depended on newspapers that were two or three days old. The text below was written in Locarno, shortly before Bakunin left to participate in an attempt to set up a popular Commune in Lyons (he arrived there on the night of the 14-15 September, see the letters below). That insurrection failed, but it was followed by others, most notably by the insurrectionary Paris Commune some five months later. In 1917 similar dynamics were at work when the Russian empire faced defeat in the First World War. The fall of each imperial regime opened a new era; new political forms emerged and working people, being liberated from constraints, struggled to assert themselves.

In this text Bakunin sets out his views on prospects for change. He analyses the programme of the Socialist-Democratic Workers' Party (SDWP). This text begins with questions: What were the likely consequences for socialism of recent events – both for France and for Europe as a whole? What might happen if France was to accept a peace dictated by Bismarck?[7] Bakunin speculated that any French government that signed a peace with Bismarck (shortly to become the Imperial Chancellor of the new German Reich) would find itself detested, and indebted to Bismarck for its survival.[8] Being widely hated, it would try to use administrative force to maintain its power. Tax rises were likely. The economy would be disrupted. The bourgeoisie might not be happy, but it would not be disruptive; the new regime would only feel threatened by the urban proletariat.

Changes were also occurring in Italy. On 20 September 1870, ten days after this letter was written, the army of the Kingdom of Italy occupied Rome. The runt papal state[9] was swept away.

Bakunin was concerned that working people in rural areas should be attracted to revolt. Today, he wrote, in almost all of Europe,[10] 'the security and power of each State depends on the peasants, they constitute its principle and almost its only base'.[11] Nonetheless, if urban workers revolted, and came to rural workers as brothers – imposing nothing but provoking the burning of official papers and relief from debt – the peasantry would understand and would also revolt.[12] This small extract from Bakunin's text continues:

Generally speaking one can see two opposite processes at work in historical development – I like to compare these with the rise and fall of the tide. Sometimes – often before great historic events – in periods of great human triumph, everything seems to develop at a great pace; there is energy everywhere – there is new thinking, will and ambition. Everything works together, and advances to conquer new horizons. At such times even people who are widely separated are brought together. It is as if an electric current had affected an entire society and people are touched with similar feelings. People with most disparate ideas come to have the same way of thinking and all are driven by the same concerns.

At such times everyone is full of courage and confidence, feeling themselves carried along by common feelings. If we confine ourselves to modern history, such was the case at the end of the 18th century on the eve of the great [French] revolution. Things were similar – but to a much lesser degree – in the years leading up to the 1848 revolution. And this is how I see things now, presaging events which may surpass those of 1789 and 1793 in grandeur. So, now we feel and see great and potent times ahead; can we not compare these times to those of rising tides?

There are however other times – fatal, sombre and desperate times – when everything is coloured by death, prostration and decadence, when private and public conscience appears to have been truly eclipsed. These are periods of ebb and retreat, following great historical catastrophes. Such was the era of the First Empire and the Restoration.[13] Such was the case for the nineteen or twenty years that followed the catastrophe of June 1848.[14] And, if popular France was to be conquered by the armies of the Prussian despot, if it turns out that the French workers and people are spineless, if France is abandoned, then such times may return – worse than ever – for twenty or thirty long years.[15]

Such historic cowardliness would prove that Germany's gentlemen professors and the colonels of the King of Prussia[16] were right when they said that France's role in the development of humanity's social destiny was finished, that the guiding light of modern times, that splendid French intelligence, had been eclipsed now and forever; that it had nothing further to say to Europe, that it was dead. And worse, that France's great and noble national character, its heroism, its audacity – which through the immortal revolution of 1793 had demolished the infamous prison of the middle ages, and opened a new world of liberty, equality and fraternity, for all nations – that all this was over. Now, on the threshold of this [new] world French people might be so overwhelmed and might become so incapable – unable to will, to dare, to struggle, to live – that they would resign themselves to being slaves, under the boots of a Prussian minister.

There is no nationalism in me. To my very last breath, I will detest the so-called principles of race and nationality, set out by the likes of Napoleon III, Bismarck and the Emperors of Russia, invoked only to facilitate the destruction of every nation's freedom. Bourgeois patriotism is to my eyes a very shabby, very narrow, above all very selfish, and fundamentally anti-human passion; its object is the power and preservation of the national state, i.e. upholding, in the national context, every exploitative privilege. When the popular masses are patriotic, they are stupid – and such is the case today with *some* of Germany's popular masses, who allow themselves to be killed in tens of thousands, with such stupid enthusiasm, for the victory of that great unity and for the constitution of that German Empire which, if it is ever constituted, on the ruins of a conquered France, will become the grave of every hope for the future. So, I am not concerned at this moment with the salvation of France as a great political power, or state, or an imperial or royal France, or even a French republic.

What I would deplore as an immense disaster for all of humanity would be the downfall and death of France as a great national personality; the death of a great national character, of French spirit, of generous and heroic instincts, and of the revolutionary audacity which, when it was charging forward, would demolish every authority that history had fortified and consecrated, every power in heaven and earth. An immense void would open up in the world if, in this hour, that great historic personality, France, left us; if it disappeared from the world scene, or, what would be much worse if this intelligent and generous nation suddenly fell – from the sublime heights to which it had risen through the travails and heroic spirit of past generations – into the mud, and continued to live as a slave to Bismarck. That would be more than a national catastrophe, it would be a miserable, universal disaster.

All of us have assumed – even today we continue to assume – that [every] initiative for Social Revolution [will come] from this France; who could imagine Prussia or Bismarck's Germany, in the place of the France of 1793!

All of us are habituated to following France's initiative. We are always expecting to see it move forward audaciously – even today, when it seems lost and crushed by innumerable armies, betrayed by the obvious stupidity and powerlessness of bourgeois republicans as much as by its every authority. Even though the world and every European nation is astonished, disquieted and dismayed by its apparent downfall, still all look to France for their salvation. They wait for its example, for its watchwords, for it to signal their deliverance. All eyes turn, not to [the army Generals] Mac-Mahon or Bazaine, but to Paris, Lyons and Marseilles. Europe's revolutionaries will move when France moves.

This great German nation appears in this hour to have sent the children of its bourgeoisie and nobility to invade popular France; but as for the Socialist-Democratic Workers' Party,* (SDWP) we have to give justice where justice is due. Since the very start of the war – in the midst of the bellicose enthusiasm of the whole of bourgeois and noble Germany, this party has courageously protested against the invasion of France and waits with trepidation, with passionate impatience, for a French revolutionary movement, a signal for a universal revolution.[17] Every German socialist newspaper asks French workers to quickly proclaim a Social and Democratic Republic, not the *poor positivist, rational Republic, duly and carefully announced,* and often recommended by that poor Mr Gambetta,* but the great Republic, the universal Republic of the proletariat, so that they may at last proudly protest, in words and deeds with the true German people, against the bellicose politics of Germany's privileged classes and with no suspicion of pleading the cause of imperial France, of the France of a Napoleon III. Today then – despite all misfortunes and maybe because of these terrible misfortunes, (very well merited moreover) – this is once again, and more so than before, the general position of revolutionary France. The world looks for salvation from forces audaciously assembled, from a banner triumphantly raised.

And who will take up that banner? The bourgeoisie? I believe I have said enough to prove irrefutably that the bourgeoisie of today, even when it is very red and republican, has become cowardly, stupid and impotent. Symbols of revolutionary France – left in their hands – would fall into the mud. The French proletariat, town workers and rural peasantry united, but above all the former, are the only ones whose powerful hands can raise that banner, for the salvation of the world.

Such then is its great mission. If the proletariat accomplishes it, it will emancipate the whole of Europe. If it falters, it will be lost and defeated. Along with the proletariat of Europe they will be sentenced to at least fifty years of slavery. They will be lost. If today they gave their consent to submit to the Prussian yoke one cannot imagine that later they will be able to find the strength, will, and intelligence, needed to accomplish a Social Revolution. The situation of French workers after such a shameful catastrophe, would be a thousand times worse than that of their predecessors, after the catastrophes of June* and December*. A few rare workers might preserve intelligence and revolutionary will, but they would have no faith in revolution, because such faith is possible only when an individual feels and receives feedback, an echo of support from the instincts and the unanimous will of the masses. But such feedback, such support will no longer be there amongst the masses: the masses would be completely demoralised, crushed, disorganised and decapitated.

Yes, disorganised and decapitated, because the new government, this vice-royalty or vice-empire as it might be installed, protected and led from Berlin, by the great chancellor of the German Empire, Count Bismarck, will not refrain from using against the proletariat, and on a much larger scale, measures for public safety which were first so successful for General Cavaignac,[18] the dictator of the Republic, and then for that infamous Robert Macaire,[19] who under his dual title of Prince President and Emperor of the French calmly murdered, pillaged, and dishonoured France over 25 fatal years.

What might these measures be? They are very simple. Above all to completely disorganise the labouring masses. Rights of association [trade union organisation] would be abolished. The target would be not just the great, much feared and much detested International [Workers'] Association. No, beyond the workplace – where they would be subject to the most severe discipline – French workers would be forbidden any form of organisation. Their spirit would be killed in such ways, along with all hope of forming any sort of collective will amongst themselves (through discussion or mutual education, that being the only current means of getting enlightenment). As after December, workers would find themselves reduced to complete moral and intellectual isolation and would be condemned thereby to unremitting impotence.

At the same time, to decapitate the labouring masses, some hundreds or thousands of the most energetic, intelligent, convinced and devoted [activists] would be arrested and transported to Cayenne – as was done in 1848 and in 1851.[20] What would be the plight of the disorganised and decapitated labouring masses? Consumed by hunger, eating grass they would work frantically to enrich their bosses. Just wait for a revolution of the popular masses reduced to such a position!

But despite its miserable position the proletariat might revolt if it was roused – moved by despair or led on by that French energy that does not easily resign itself to death. Oh! to reinstate 'reason', cannon and guns would then be doubled up; and against their terrible argument, the opposing forces would have neither collective will nor organisation, nor direction, but only despair, they would be ten or a hundred times more impotent than before. And then? Then French socialism would have ceased to count among the active forces pushing forward for the development, emancipation and solidarity of the European proletariat. There may still be socialist writers, doctrines, books and socialist newspapers in France, if the new government and the German chancellor Count Bismarck wished to allow such things. But neither writers, nor philosophers, nor their books, nor socialist journals, would reconstitute a socialism that was alive and vigorous. It is only through enlightened revolutionary instincts, through collective will and through the real organisation of the working masses themselves that the latter has a real existence, and when instinct, will and organisation are lacking the best books in the world will be nothing more than empty theories and powerless dreams.

So, it is obvious then that if at this terrible moment – when its entire future is in question – France submits to Prussia, all will be lost. If it does not prefer the death of its children, the destruction of its wealth, the burning of its villages and towns, of every house, to slavery under the Prussian yoke, if, through the power of a revolutionary and popular uprising it does not break the power of the innumerable German armies – thus far victorious at every point – threatening its dignity, freedom and even its existence, if it fails to provide cemeteries for all these 600,000 soldiers of German despotism, if it does not oppose them with the only means it can use to defeat and destroy them in current circumstances, if it does not respond to this insolent invasion through Social Revolution – one that is no less pitiless and a thousand times more threatening – in my view it is certain that in such a case France will be lost. Its working masses will become slaves, and French socialism will cease to exist. And, in such a case what would be the prospects for socialism, what opportunities would there be for the emancipation of labour in the rest of Europe? In which lands, beyond France, has socialism become a real power? In *Germany, Belgium, Britain and Spain.*

In Italy socialism is as yet still in its infancy. The militant part of the working classes, above all in northern Italy, is as yet insufficiently distinguished from the exclusive preoccupations of political patriotism inspired by the powerful influence of Giuseppe Mazzini – the great Italian patriot and agitator, the true creator of Italian unity. Italian workers are revolutionary and socialist through their instinct and situation, as indeed are all workers throughout the world. But Italian workers are still surrounded by a quasi-absolute ignorance as to the true origins of their miserable circumstances, and misunderstand – one might say – the real sources of their own instincts. They are worn out by work, which barely feeds them, their wives or their children. They are misused and misled, they die of hunger; they are pushed, shoved, and led on blindly by the liberal and radical bourgeoisie. They talk of marching on Rome, as if the building blocks of the Coliseum or the Vatican could offer them bread, freedom or leisure. They are now organising meetings in every city to force *their king* to send *his soldiers* against the Pope; as if the king and his soldiers, as well as the bourgeoisie that pushes them on – the first two official forces of protection, and the latter the main exploiter of property rights – were not the main and immediate causes of their misery and slavery! Their exclusively patriotic and political preoccupations are without doubt very generous, but truth be told, they are also very stupid.

Insofar as the eternal city remains a capital of moral and intellectual despotism and the residence of the infallible Pope there is however one perspective which to some extent justifies this tendency of Italian workers to march on Rome. Over the centuries, good sense dictated that every Italian city should consider Papal and Catholic activity and power as one of the ongoing and fundamental reasons for their misery and slavery, and they want to be done with it. This is one of those overwhelming historical tendencies against which no reasoning – however correct it might be – can prevail. Perhaps Italian workers need another historical experience another bitter disillusion to open their eyes so that they might understand that by sending a royal [Italian] army against the papal power, they will be delivered neither from soldiers, nor from the king, nor from the Pope. Armies, kings and popes are only a consequence, a consecration and a necessary guarantor – to demolish all of them in one go, along with property, and the exploitation of the bourgeoisie and the nobles, only one means will do: to initiate revolt in one's own city, and simultaneously to incite a good Social Revolution in every city. Because nothing – neither popes, nor kings, nor soldiers, nor nobles, nor the bourgeoisie – could withstand such a revolution breaking out simultaneously in every city and in every rural area.

When it comes to Social Revolution in Italy one may say that the countryside is more advanced than the town. Remaining outside every movement and every historical development – so far they have only paid the bill for these – the Italian countryside has neither patriotism, nor political tendencies. These areas have been kept in a terrible misery and ignorance by the successive governments of various parts of Italy. They have never shared the passions of the towns. Delivered up in their entirety to the influence of priests they are superstitious, and, at the same time, only to a very small extent religious. Priestly power in the countryside is therefore very ephemeral, it is real only when it is in accord with the instinctive hated of the peasant for the rich landlord, the bourgeois and the town. But, just stir awake the profoundly socialist instinct which sleep half-conscious in the heart of every Italian peasant; only renew throughout Italy – with revolutionary goals – the propaganda that Cardinal Ruffo had initiated in Calabria, at the end of the last century,[21] just raise the call – *Land to those that work it – with their own hands!* – and you would see how every Italian peasant might rise up to make a Social Revolution. And if priests opposed it, priests would be killed.

The very spontaneous movement of Italian peasants last year, a movement provoked by a law imposing a tax on the milling of grain, showed the extent of the natural revolutionary socialism of the Italian peasant. Detachments of regular troops were beaten, and, when peasants came to town in their masses they began always by burning whatever official papers fell into their hands.

No one can doubt that Italy is on the threshold of revolution. The government of Victor Emmanuel and his successive cabinets, each more thieving, more cowardly and more shabby than the last, have governed it so well that today it has been reduced to a completely impossible political and financial state. The credit of the government, of parliament, of the state, of every element of its official body, is in ruins. Industry and commerce are ruined. Ever increasing taxes are crushing the land, without being able to remedy the ever growing deficit. Bankruptcy is knocking at the door of the state. Embezzlement of every sort is common, political and civil disrepute reigns and subdues society. There is neither faith, nor good faith. Victor-Emmanuel feels himself dragged into the abyss by his overlord Napoleon III. Italy waits on France for the signal to begin revolution, for French revolutionary initiative.

How this revolution might begin matters little. Probably through that eternal Roman question. But any Italian revolution, whatever the occasion or the issue that might prompt it, will soon and of necessity turn into an immense Social Revolution, because the real, gaping, dominating question, the question hidden behind everything else, is that of the horrible misery and slavery of the proletariat. All this is well known by everyone, by both the government and by every Italian political party. And it is for this very reason that Italian liberals and republicans hesitate. They fear this Social Revolution that threatens to engulf them. And yet, I have not rated Italy at all amongst the nations in which socialism is aware of itself and organised. Consciousness and organisation – even more organisation – are completely lacking amongst workers and naturally even more so amongst Italian peasants. Their socialism takes after something in Molière's *Le bourgeois gentilhomme* – they construct prose – but without knowing it. In consequence, the initiative for a socialist revolution cannot come from them. They will have to receive it from somewhere else.

I will say nothing of Switzerland. If the human race was about to die it would not be Switzerland that would revive it. Let us move on.

In Germany socialism has already begun to be a veritable power. The three largest workers' organisations are: the General German Workers' Union – the old organisation of Lassalle* – *Allgemeiner deutscher Arbeiter-Verein*; the Socialist Democratic Workers' Party – *Sozial-demokratische Arbeiter-Partei* – with *Volksstaat* as its organ; and the many Workers' Associations for mutual education – *Arbeiter Bildungs-Vereine*; together they embrace at least 500,000 workers. They are divided not by questions of principle but much more by intrigue and by questions of personal influence. The first two are outspokenly socialist and revolutionary. The third, which remains the most numerous, continues in part to suffer the influence of liberalism and bourgeois socialism. Yet this influence appears to be diminishing, and one might hope that in a short time, above all through the effect of current events, the workers of this third organisation will pass over, en masse and join the Socialist-Democratic Workers' Party (SDWP), (a party born barely a year ago, following a struggle between Lassallian worker and members of the Arbeiter-Bildungs Vereine and a partial fusion of the two).

Today the SDWP is without doubt the dominant organisation. It is, insofar as current German law allows, in direct contact with the International [IWA]. These laws are naturally very severe, oppressive and restrictive, having as their main aim placing all sorts of difficulties in the way of the development of the power of labour. They forbid and incriminate – as a crime of high treason – not only any organised alliance of organised German workers with associations in foreign countries, but also, and despite that *grand idea* of German unity – in whose name the King of Prussia has just launched the united armies of Germany against poor France – they prohibit the workers' associations of each particular German state from collaborating and joining a unitary body with those of other states of this [would-be] united Germany.[a]

Nonetheless the strength and élan of German workers is too great for it to be restricted by such laws, and currently we can see a real organisation unifying labour associations of every German land and holding out a hand of friendship to workers' associations of all parts of western Europe and the USA.

The [Eisenacher] SDWP* and the General Association of German Workers, founded by Lassalle,* are both frankly socialist, in the sense that they want a socialist reform of the relations between labour and capital; and the Lassallians as much as the Eisenacher party are unanimous on the point that to obtain this reform, it *first* [and as a precondition] *has to reform the state*, and, if the state will not agree to be reformed in quiet and voluntary fashion following on from a grand but quiet and legal labour agitation it will have to be reformed by force, i.e. by a political revolution. In the almost unanimous view of German socialists the *political revolution must precede the Social Revolution*, and this is a great and fatal error in my view, because every political revolution carried through *before* and in consequence outside and beyond a Social Revolution, will of necessity be a bourgeois revolution, and a bourgeois revolution can serve only to produce – at most – a bourgeois socialism; i.e. it will infallibly end up with a new [form of] exploitation of the proletariat by the bourgeoisie, one more hypocritical and scholarly perhaps, but no less oppressive.

a Bakunin was writing in September 1870. The German Reich would be formed in the following year, uniting the individual states of southern Germany with the North German confederation dominated by Prussia.

This unfortunate idea, as German socialists say, of a political revolution having to precede a Social Revolution opens wide the entrance door not so much to socialists but to every exclusively political radical democrat in Germany to join the SDWP. So, on various occasions the SDWP, has been led on – not by its own instincts (which are much more popular and socialist) – but by the ideas of these leaders and has fraternised and mixed in with the bourgeois Peoples' Democratic Party (Volkspartei), an exclusively political party, which is not only a stranger, but is also directly hostile to all serious forms of socialism. Moreover all this was proved in a startling manner, as much by the passionately bourgeois and patriotic speeches of its representatives in the memorable popular assembly held in Vienna in July or August 1868, and by the rabid attacks of its papers against the revolutionary socialist workers of Vienna, who in the name of humane and universal democracy, came to disturb their patriotic and bourgeois concert. Those speeches and passionate attacks on socialism, as an eternal kill-joy and hindrance, resulted in the condemnation of bourgeois radicalism and in the world of German labour one that one might say was unanimous, placing men like Mr Liebknecht* in a very difficult and delicate position, because whilst they wished to remain at the head of labour associations, they had no wish to fall out or break their political relations with friends in the bourgeois *Volkspartei*. The leaders of that party soon realised that they had committed a great error, because despite the *energy, active strength and revolutionary audacity of these bourgeois people* – now proven and much better known – they nevertheless had no hope of being able to promote a revolution (or even of constituting the mere shadow of a serious force), alone or without a little help from the proletariat. Indeed it has never been the pattern of the bourgeoisie to make a revolution on their own. Their ingenuity always led them to adopt the following course: use the people's strong arms to make the revolution, but stuff any profit in your own pockets. So the radical bourgeoisie of the *Volkspartei* was forced to explain itself, so to speak; to make some honest reparation and to proclaim that it too was equally socialist. Their new socialism, announced moreover with a great deal of nice phrases and speeches, naturally did not go beyond innocent dreams of bourgeois cooperation.

For an entire year from August 1868 to August 1869, there were diplomatic negotiations between the main representatives of the two parties, labour and bourgeois, and these negotiations resulted in the famous programme of the Eisenach congress (7, 8 and 9 August 1869), which finally constituted the SDWP. Its programme was a true compromise between the revolutionary and socialist programme of the IWA, clearly set out by the congresses of Brussels and Basel, and the well-known programme of bourgeois democracy.

These are the first three articles, which perfectly characterise the economic and political character of the programme of the new Workers' Party of Socialist Democracy:

Article 1. The SDWP (Die Sozial-demokratische Arbeiter-Partei) in Germany works to constitute a *free popular State* (*die Einrichtung eines freien Volksstaats*).

Article 2. Members of the Workers' Party of Socialist Democracy accept the responsibility of working by all means for the following principles:

1. Current political and social conditions are unjust to the highest degree and so must be most energetically rejected.

2. The struggle for workers' emancipation is in no way a struggle to institute new class privileges, but for the equality of rights and obligations and for the abolition of all class domination.

3. The dependency in which workers are placed vis-à-vis capitalists is the principle basis of every form of servitude. The SDWP works to win the entire product of their work for workers through the means of abolishing the current system of production.

4. *Political liberty* is *the most urgent precondition* (*die unentbehrlichste Vorbedingung*) of the economic emancipation of the working classes. In consequence the social question is inseparable from the political question. *Only in a democratic state is a solution possible.*

5. Considering that the economic and political emancipation of the working class is possible only on the condition that all workers are united around the same goals, the SDWP adopts a unitary organisation,[22] one which however allows members to exert their influence for the common good.

6. Considering that the emancipation of labour is in no way a local question, nor even a national one; that it is a social question which affects every land in which conditions have been achieved *for a modern society* (in denen es moderne Gesellschaft gibt), the Workers' Party of Socialist Democracy, as much as laws of association permits, considers itself *to be a branch of the IWA*, and sharing its projects. The Party committee (Vorstand) will in consequence have official relations with the General Council [of the IWA].

Article 3. *The first objectives to be achieved* (*die nächsten Förderungen*) by the agitation of the SDWP are as follows:

1. The right to a direct and secret vote for all men over the age of twenty in the election of deputies to the federal Parliament, to Parliaments of the

various states,[23] and to provincial, communal and all other representative bodies.

2. Direct legislation by the people, and the right to propose and reject laws.

3. Abolition of all privileges, of class, property, birth and religion.

4. The institution of a national [recruit based] army replacing the professional army.

5. Separation of church and state; separation of schools from the church.

6. Compulsory education in popular schools. Education without charge in all public educational establishments.

7. Judicial independence, public trials, the jury system.

8. Abolition of all laws limiting freedom of assembly, of association and of mutual support; complete press freedom. Fixing norms for the working-day [limited working hours]. Prohibition of child labour. Limitations on [hours of] work for women in industrial concerns.

9. Abolition of all indirect taxations, direct taxation of incomes.

10. State support for workers' cooperation, State credit for all producers.

These three articles, in their unfolding express perfectly, not the fullness of the revolutionary and socialist aspirations and instincts of the workers' who are members of this new organisation of Socialist Democracy in Germany, but the projects of the leaders who conceived and now lead the party.

The first article, right at the beginning highlights a complete disagreement with the spirit and text of the fundamental programme of the IWA. The SDWP wants the creation of a *free popular state*. The two words *free and popular* sound well, but the word 'state' must sound badly in the ears of any true revolutionary socialist, or for a sincere and resolute enemy of all bourgeois institutions without exception. There is a flagrant contradiction here with the goals of the IWA, the word 'state' entirely destroys the sense of the words 'free' and 'popular'.

Whoever speaks of the *International Workers' Association* speaks of the negation of the state – every state has to be of necessity a *national state*. Do the authors of the programme have in mind either an *international state* (a universal state) or perhaps something smaller and restricted? Perhaps Western Europe, where there exists, (I will make use of a favourite expression of German socialists) 'a society where this is a modern civilisation', i.e. a society in which capital has been concentrated in the hands of a class promoted by the state, and has become the sole force shaping labour. Here, by virtue of this concentration, the bourgeoisie has reduced workers to misery and slavery. Are they thinking of a state that would encompass all this area? Would the leaders of the SDWP propose the creation of a state that would encompass all of Western Europe: Britain, France, Germany, the whole of Scandinavia, the Slav lands dominated by Austria, Belgium, the Netherlands, Switzerland, Italy, Spain and Portugal?[24] No, their imagination and political appetite did not include both at one and the same time. What they sought with a passion, and what they did not seek to disguise, was the organisation of a *German homeland*, and greater German unity.

It was the creation of an *exclusively German state* that was posed in the first article of their programme as the main and supreme aim of the SDWP. They are above all political patriots.[25]

So then, what is left of Internationality? What would these *German patriots* contribute to the international fraternity of workers of every land? Nothing but socialist words, with no hope of these being achieved because the first and principle basis of their programme – a Germanic state – being exclusively political, destroys the meaning of those words.

Indeed from the moment workers in Germany are *bound* to desire and serve the creation of a Germanic state above all else, the solidarity which *ought to bind them* – from a social and economic viewpoint, to unite and to go so far as to fuse them together with their brothers – the exploited workers of the whole world, and which ought to be, in my view, the principle and single basis for labour associations of every land; that international solidarity is of necessity sacrificed to patriotism, to national, political passion. And it may well happen that workers of one country being divided between these two homes, between these two contradictory projects – *socialist solidarity of labour* and *patriotism for their national state*, (sacrificing to it as they ought to, if they were to obey the first article of the programme of the SDWP) – sacrifice, I say, the international solidarity of labour to patriotism, and so find themselves in the miserable position of being *united with their bourgeois compatriots against workers of a foreign country*. This is exactly what has happened today to workers in Germany.

At the beginning of the war it was interesting to see the spectacle of struggle that broke out within the working classes of Germany, between principles of German patriotism, as imposed on them by the programme of their party, and their profoundly socialist instincts. One might at first have thought that their patriotism might overcome their socialism, and fear that they would allow themselves to be dragged along by warlike enthusiasm and hatred of the French with the immense majority of Germany's bourgeoisie.[26]

In a great labour meeting of the of the SDWP held in Brunswick in early July many speeches were tainted by pure patriotism, but at the same time, and as an effect of that patriotism, almost wholly lacked feelings for justice and international fraternity.

To the really fraternal, generous and frankly socialist addresses of the workers of the International of Paris and other French cities a response was composed of invective against Napoleon III, as if there was something in common between that criminal and miserable fraudster, who for twenty years had taken on the title of Emperor of the French, and the workers of France. It went hand in hand with *sarcastic* advice – to overthrow their tyrant as quickly as possible, *in order to deserve the sympathies of European democrats*. Reading these speeches one might have believed that one was listening to free men, proud of their liberties, and speaking to slaves. Experiencing proud German indignation inveighing against the dishonest tyranny of Napoleon III, one might have imagined that the dream of socialist democracy, a free and popular state, had been achieved already in Germany and that German workers would have good reason to be satisfied with their own governments!

Is there any greater difference – between the policies of Napoleon III and that of the great German chancellor, the count of Bismarck – except that the policies of one have succeeded whereas the policies of the other failed? At base, they were entirely the same: immoral, despotic, rapacious and disrespecting human rights. Or were German workers so naïve that they thought that Bismarck *as a political leader* was more moral than Napoleon III, and that he will stop himself before engaging any in sort of immorality, whenever there is some possibility of accomplishing a particular political goal? If they really thought so, it would be because they have not paid any attention to the policies of the great Chancellor, especially in recent years, since the last insurrection in Poland, during which he played the role of henchman for Moscow's slave-drivers ... [27]

... it is clear that they [the SDWP] will always continue to sacrifice popular freedom to State grandeur, socialism to politicking, and international fraternity and justice to patriotism. It is clear that their own economic emancipation will be nothing but a lovely dream – relegated eternally to a distant future.

It is impossible to achieve at the same time two contradictory aims. Socialism and Social revolution imply the destruction of the state, it is evident that whoever supports the state-system must renounce socialism, and must sacrifice the masses' economic emancipation to the political power of one or another chosen party. The SDWP has to sacrifice economic emancipation, and so in consequence the political emancipation of the proletariat, or rather its liberation from politics to the ambition and the triumph of bourgeois democracy. This follows clearly from the second and third articles of its programme.

The first three paragraphs of article II are quite in conformity with the socialist principles of the IWA and they copy the text of its programme. But the fourth paragraph of that article, which declares that political liberty is the precondition for economic emancipation, completely destroys the practical value of this acknowledgement of principle. It can only mean this: Workers, you are slaves, victims of capital and property. You wish to liberate yourselves from your economic yoke. That's fine, and your wishes are perfectly legitimate. But to achieve them *you must first help us make a political revolution. Later we will help you carry through a social revolution.* Let us first establish a democratic state, a good bourgeois democracy as in Switzerland, and then... then we will give you equal well-being such as workers enjoy in Switzerland. (Remember strikes in Basel and Geneva.)

To be convinced that this incredible aberration expresses perfectly the spirit and tendencies of the German Socialist-Democratic party – in respect of its programme, not in respect of the aspirations of the German workers who compose it – one has only to study carefully article III, in which are listed all the first and immediate demands (die nächsten Förderungen) which should be promoted by the party's peaceful and legal agitation. All of these demands (except the tenth, one which was not even proposed by the authors of the programme but added later in the middle of discussion, following proposals made by a member of the Eisenach congress) have an exclusively political character. Every point recommended as *main objects for immediate party activity* constitutes nothing but the well-known programme of bourgeois democracy: universal suffrage, with direct legislation by the people; abolition of all political privilege; national armament; separation of Church and State, separation of schooling and State; compulsory and free education; press freedom, freedom of association, assembly and coalition; transformation of all indirect taxes into one single progressive direct tax on revenue.

This then is the true object, the real goal of this party: an exclusively political reform of the State, of the States' institutions and laws. Am I not right to say that this programme is socialist only in its dreams of some far away future, but the reality is that it is a purely bourgeois and political programme; so bourgeois that none of our former colleagues of the League for Peace and Freedom would have hesitated to sign it? Am I not right to say that, if this German SDWP was judged by its programme – something that I would not allow myself to do – knowing that the real aspirations of these workers goes much beyond this programme, one would have the right to think that this party institution has its goal nothing more than to use the working masses as a blind and sacrificial instrument to achieve the political projects of Germany's bourgeois democracy?

In this programme there are only two points not to the taste of the bourgeoisie. The first of these is contained in the second half of the eighth paragraph of article III, where there is a demand for a ruling on a norm for the working day, the abolition of child labour, and a limitation on women's work – all of these things that always make the bourgeoisie shudder, because being passionate lovers of every sort of liberty that helps turn a profit, they vigorously demand that the proletariat should have the freedom to be exploited, crushed, and stunned without the state interfering. Yet times have become so hard for the poor bourgeois, that they have had to consent to state intervention – even in Britain – into current social organisation, which, as far as I know, is in no way socialist.

The other point, one much more important, and with a more explicit socialist aspect is contained in the tenth paragraph of article III, a paragraph which as I have noted already was proposed not by the drafters of the programme, but arose on the initiative of a member of the Eisenach congress and suggested during discussion of the programme. This point demands *State support, protection (die Förderung) and credit for workers' co-operation* and above all for associations of producers, with every desirable guarantee of freedom.

This is a point that no bourgeois democrat will accept happily, because it absolutely contradicts what bourgeois democracy and bourgeois socialism call freedom. Indeed freedom for the exploitation of the proletariat's labour – which *forcibly* has to be sold to capital at the lowest possible price, constrained not by any civil or political law but by the economic position which labour has to endure, through fear and the apprehension of hunger; this freedom – I say – does not fear competition from labour associations – be they for consumption, mutual credit, or production – for the simple reason that labour associations, with their own limited means, will never be in a fit state to create sufficient capital to be able to struggle against bourgeois capital. But if labour associations are supported by state power and its immense credit, they might not only be able to struggle, but in the long term they will finally be able to overcome bourgeois commercial and industrial enterprise founded solely on private capital, or the capital of associates brought together in capitalist companies, since the state is naturally the most powerful company of all.

Labour commissioned by the State that is the fundamental principle of *authoritarian communism*, of State socialism. *The State that has become the sole proprietor*, at the end of some transition period that will be needed to allow society to change, without excessive political and economic shocks, from the current regime of bourgeois privilege to a future organisation where there is an official equality of all, with the State as the single capitalist, banker, financier, organiser, the director of all national work and the distributor of every product. This is the ideal, the fundamental principle of modern communism.

LETTERS TO NIKOLAI OGAREV & THE RED POSTER

Alexander Herzen* and Nicholas Ogarev* had published a stream of subversive literature – notably *Vestnik* and *Kolokol* – seeking to promote revolution in Russia. Bakunin, although he spent most of the last fifteen years of his life in Western Europe, never forgot his commitment to work for the overthrow of Tsarism. The correspondence between these three witnesses to their common interests and ongoing friendship.

When new opportunities opened in September 1870, with the defeat of Napoleon III and his regime, Bakunin looked first to Lyons – France's second city some seventy miles from Geneva – where the IWA had been very active, and where he had close friends. Women textile workers had won a strike there in 1869. It was they who had given Bakunin one of his mandates for the Basel IWA congress. In March 1870 a meeting of 6,000 people had been organised there, the biggest assembly ever organised by the French IWA. Bakunin did not attend that meeting but he sent a letter urging working people to build their own power and to count only on themselves. He advised:

> To constitute a real force they need organisation, and so that that organisation should be appropriate for its base and for its aims, it should not take in any foreign elements. You should distance yourselves from anything that belongs to the culture, and the social, political and legal structures of the bourgeoisie. [Keep them away] Even when bourgeois politics is as red as blood or as hot as molten steel, if it does not accept as a direct and immediate aim the destruction of legal property and the political State – the two forts on which all bourgeois domination relies – their triumph could only be a fatal disaster for the cause of the proletariat.[1]

An anti-war demonstration was organised in Lyons in July 1870. On 4 September 1870 a crowd gathered at the City Hall, proclaimed a republic, and set up a red flag. The Lyons protestors faced opposition from local officials but an attempt to disperse them was thwarted when troops refused to open fire. A Central Committee for the Safety of France (Comité Central du Salut de la France) was set up on the 17th.[2]

Letter to Nikolai Ogarev, 1

[25 September 1870, Lyons]

My dear friend,

I am sending you our proclamation in which we appeal to the people to overthrow every authority that continues to stand in its way. Tonight we will arrest our main enemies, tomorrow our ultimate struggle and, we hope, success.

Send Henry [Sutherland] to Lindecker. Probably Guillaume has had the pamphlet[3] delivered. If not ask Lindecker to bring it to you immediately once he gets it. And as soon as you get it, hurry it along to Lyons at once, with our friend the brave colonel – don't lose a moment; have the colonel take it directly to Palix's house, 41 cours Vittou, through 20 rue Massena, first floor. Here the pamphlet is indispensable, we are all waiting for it.

Your M. B.

[date unclear]

As for the title *Central Committee for the Safety of France* don't let this title – narrowly national in appearance – scare you. Our committee 'for France's Safety' is a revolutionary socialist committee in the widest sense of the word. Well! Dear friend, help us and soon we will help you; we will be building serious resources here and work with you for the cause of revolution in Russia.[4] Depend on my passion, my honour, my head even.

Your M. B.

PS. Tell Henry that if we have the money now we would have called on him [to come] at once to Lyons. If he has some, even just fifty francs, let him come. If not let him wait a little. We will have him come.

On 26 September, at a meeting in Lyons attended by 6,000 persons it was agreed that urgent action was needed – including the removal of officers, the local prefect Challemel-Lacour and the city council. The poster below was read out and acclaimed; later it was pasted up all over the city; this Red Poster (Affiche Rouge) called for a Revolutionary Federation of Communes, and was signed by several IWA members, including André

Bastellica, Bakunin, Gaspard Blanc, Louis Palix* and Albert Richard*.

Bakunin refers to it as 'our proclamation' and he probably helped draft it. James Guillaume comments that Bakunin thought it was his duty to sign it, even though he was a foreigner. It served to outline a path towards revolution, rather than to decree a new form of state.

Some months later, when the Paris Commune was isolated, Varlin* advised radicals to try to promote risings where they were, rather than coming to Paris. New insurrections were attempted in Limoges, Narbonne, and Saint-Etienne. The isolation of the Paris Commune greatly facilitated its defeat.

The National Guard drawn from bourgeois areas suppressed the Lyons insurrection. Bakunin was arrested but escaped. The last letter below was written while he was in hiding. Later he was able to leave France via Marseilles and Genoa. Twenty or so leading members of the IWA were arrested and the Lyons Federation was shattered.

§

The Red Poster

[Lyons, 26 September 1870 (l'Affiche rouge)⁵]

FRENCH REPUBLIC
REVOLUTIONARY FEDERATION OF **COMMUNES**

The disastrous situation in which the country finds itself, the powerlessness of official authorities and the indifference of the privileged classes have brought the French nation to the edge of the abyss.

If people do not hasten to act, if popular revolutionary organisation fails, the future will be lost, the revolution will be lost, all will be lost. Inspired by the immensity of the danger, and considering that desperate popular action should not be delayed for an instant, the delegates of the Federated Committees for the Safety of France, united in a Central Committee propose the immediate adoption of the following resolutions:

- The [existing] governmental and administrative state machine, having become powerless, is abolished.

- All civil and criminal tribunals are suspended and replaced by Popular Justice.

- The payment of loans and taxes is suspended and replaced by levies for Federated Communes, raised on the rich classes, in proportion to the needs of France's safety.

- The State, being defeated, can no longer intervene for the payment of private debts.

- All existing municipal organisations are cancelled and replaced in every Commune, by Committees for the Safety of France, exercising every power under the immediate control of the People.

- Committees from every departmental town shall send two delegates to a Revolutionary Convention for the Safety of France.

- This Convention is to meet at the City Hall in Lyons, it being the second city of France and the place best suited to promote the energetic defence of the country.

With the support of the entire people this Convention will save France.
To Arms!

Lyons, 26 September 1870.
Declaration signed by 26 names, including:
Albert Richard, Michael Bakunin, Gustave Blanc, E-B. Saignes, Louis Palix (from Lyons), Rajon (from Tarare), A. Bastellica (from Marseilles).

§

Letter to Nikolai Ogarev, 2

[16 October 1870, near Lyons.[6]]

Well old man! Day by day everything is getting worse. I have just received a letter from Lyons telling me that Blanc[7] and Valence have not only been arrested but that the latter was also carrying a dictionary [of codes] containing not just the names of our friends, but also very compromising words such as assassination, pillage, fire, etc. It is very bad and it exposes them to very great danger. The people remain quiet, scared by official Republican terrorism. Orders were given to arrest anyone named on the list. As yet I do not know how many arrests have been carried out. The police certainly arrest everyone who falls into their hands. It seems that the news of the arrest of Blanc and Valence is correct. The police went to Palix's home; but seeing him ill and in bed let him be. Bastelica was also named on the list, as well as Combe. I have already written to you that an order came from Tours[8] to arrest Bastelica, but Esquiroce and the Lyons state prefect refused to carry it out fearing that it would provoke a great reaction among the people and maybe even an explosion. Hell! Following the revelation of that damned dictionary, things may change and perhaps he [Bastelica] may well be arrested too. So I will soon be forced to leave here. But I haven't even a cent. So, my dear friends – help me out. Club together to raise the sum of a hundred francs for me – it is absolutely necessary – and send it to Mrs Bastelica, 32, boulevard des Dames, with a letter signed in the name of Eulalie Berthier, asking her to pass it on to Mrs Lise. I will be very sad to leave here, but it becomes indispensable, and with as little delay as possible. Where should I go? I don't know as yet – Barcelona or Genoa – to travel onwards to Locarno. What do you advise dear friends? Of course if things work out to force me to leave here – I will do so only as a last resort. Reply at once to the address of Mrs Bastelica (for Michael). Put that latter on the inside envelope, and not on the outside one.

M. B.

ON DISCIPLINE [9]

[Extract from a text written in the winter 1870-1] [10]

Bakunin was reflecting on the form of a new society and on socialist strategy when he wrote this text; he took issue with those who might seek to impose discipline to empower themselves in a hierarchical Jacobin state, and set out other forms of authority and discipline.

***

Being wholly an enemy of what is called discipline in France I recognise nevertheless one particular form of discipline – one not automatic, but thoughtful and voluntary and, perfectly in accord with individual liberty – one form that is and will remain always necessary, whenever many individuals, are freely united and undertake some collective act, or labour, together. In such cases this discipline is nothing but the thoughtful and voluntary harmonious agreement of every individual effort in favour of a common goal. In times of activity, in the middle of struggle, roles divide up naturally, following the aptitudes of each person, as appreciated and judged by the whole collective: some direct and command, others execute orders. But no functions are petrified, or fixed; nor do they remain irrevocably attached to any one person. Hierarchical promotion and order does not exist – one day's commander may be the next day's subordinate. No one is placed above another, and if someone does rise ahead, it is only to fall back a moment later, like the tides of the sea, always returning to the salutary level of equality.

In this system, real power has ceased to exist. Power melts away into a collective, and it becomes a sincere expression of each person's freedom, the serious and faithful realisation of general will, because the orders of the commander-of-the-day are only what everyone would want themselves all obey. This is truly human discipline, a discipline that is needed for the organisation of freedom. This is not the discipline promoted by your republican statesmen.

ON DEMOCRACY AND EDUCATION[1]

Second lecture to the workers of the Saint-Imier valley

Bakunin spent some weeks in the Jura in April and May 1871 hoping to participate with local internationalists in an expedition to support the Paris Commune. On 21 May the Commune was defeated and the project abandoned. Meanwhile Bakunin had delivered three lectures surveying current history.

In the first lecture he reflected on the Reformation, on the weakening of feudal society and on peasant revolt; serfdom and slavery still persisted in parts of Germany. The bourgeoisie had been a force for change, but it was so no longer, recent events – the invasion of France – showed that it preferred the Prussians to popular revolution. In his third lecture he considered the great French revolution. He contrasted the courage of Babeuf, Robespierre, Saint-Just and others with the cowardliness of the bourgeoisie in current times. In economic terms the bourgeoisie was dominant and had been so since 1830; but in terms of political influence and control of state power their influence was limited in some areas, particularly in Germany, Scandinavia, Italy, Spain and Portugal. Progress could now come only from the action and solidarity of working people. Revolution was on the agenda.

Bakunin began his second lecture with a review of the great French revolution of 1789. He asserted that the revolution had benefited the middle classes exclusively; it created political rather than social change. He cited the saying that 'poverty is slavery'. Poverty impacted on both bodies and minds – depriving the poor of knowledge and education. Freedom is impossible for a solitary individual; it develops only in society and was incompatible with inequality. He continues:

***

My dear friends, you all know from experience, that so-called political equality, divorced from social and economic equality, is a great fraud. For example, in a largely democratic state, all adults, if not encumbered with a criminal conviction, have the right, and, it is also said, the duty to exercise political rights and to take on any function with which they may be entrusted by their fellow citizens. The last man of the people, the poorest and the most ignorant, can and must exercise all his rights and accept his duties. Could one imagine a fuller equality? Yes, he has the right, in terms of law; he has the capacity, but the thing is impossible in reality. For men of the popular masses this power is only a notion, it cannot become a reality, unless there is a radical transformation at the economic base of society, let us use the word: a social revolution. So political rights supposedly enjoyed by the people are nothing but idle notions.

We are weary of these fabrications – be they religious or political. The people are tired of being fed fables and phantoms. On such a diet one can never be satisfied. Today, it is reality that is called for. Consider, is there any substance to their enjoyment of political rights?

To have some real capacity to take on positions in the state, especially higher responsibilities, a high level of education is needed. But the people are wholly deprived of such education. Are they at fault? No, the problem lies with the institutions. It would be a major responsibility of really democratic states to spread education widely among the people. But has any state done as much? No need to speak of monarchical states, which are not interested in disseminating education for the masses, but only a poisonous Christian catechism. Consider instead democratic and republican states, such as the USA and Switzerland. Certainly, one must recognise that these states have done more than others in popular education. But notwithstanding their good intentions, what have they achieved? Have they been able to educate every child born amidst them, equally and without distinction? No, it was impossible. For the children of the bourgeois, extended education; for the children of the people only primary education and on rare occasions, a little secondary schooling. Why the difference? For the simple reason that the people – workers of urban and rural areas – do not have the means to support – feed, clothe, house – their children for the entire length of their studies. To have a scientific education one has to study to the age of 21 or on occasion to 25. I ask you, where are the workers so well off that they can support their children that long? Given that they have no capital or property, given that they live from day to day, and their wages barely suffice to support their numerous families, such sacrifices are beyond their strength.

Moreover, one has to say, dear comrades workers of the Jura that you are comparatively pretty happy, in a trade that capitalist production, i.e. the exploitation of big capital, has thus far not been able to absorb.[2] Working in small groups in your workshops, often in your own house, you earn much more than is paid in larger industrial establishments with hundreds of workers. You work is artistic and intelligent, it does not brutalise you, as machines do. Your skill and intelligence has a value. And you have more leisure and relatively greater freedom; and so you are freer and happier, and have a better education than others. In large factories, created, directed and driven by big capital, where machines rather than persons dominate, workers necessarily become miserable slaves, so poor that most often they are compelled to condemn their poor little children – some barely eight years old – to work twelve, fourteen or sixteen hours a day for a few miserable cents. And they do so out of necessity, not out of greed. Only through such means can a family can get by.

So that is the education that they can give. Dear comrades, there is no need for me to waste more words to prove to you – who know such things through experience – that, *as long as the people work to enrich the owners of property and capital, rather than for themselves,* the education on offer for the children of the people will always be infinitely inferior to that given to the children of the bourgeois class.

So then, there is gross and baleful social inequality at the very base of the organisation of the state, a forcibly ignorant mass and a privileged minority, which even if is not always very intelligent is at least comparatively well educated. One can easily conclude that the educated minority will always govern the ignorant masses. It is not just the case of natural inequalities among individuals, that is inequality that we are forced to accept. One person or another may have a happier disposition, one may be born with a natural faculty of intelligence and/or drive greater than another. But I hasten to add, these differences are not as great as some might say. From a natural viewpoint people are more or less equal, for the most part their qualities and defects more or less cancel each other out. There are two exceptions to this natural law of equality – the genius and the idiot. But exceptions do not follow the rule, and in general one can say that all human beings are of equal worth and that if there are enormous differences between individuals in society today, these originate in the monstrous educational inequality and not in nature.

Children gifted with great talents but born to poor families, in families of workers living from one day to the next by their rude daily labour, are condemned to ignorance, which kills off their natural faculties rather than developing them; they will be compelled to act as workers, labourers, providers and helpers for bourgeois persons who are by their nature much more stupid than themselves. The children of the bourgeoisie and the rich, on the contrary, however stupid they may be naturally, will receive education necessary to develop their limited faculties as far as possible: they will become exploiters of labour – masters, bosses, legislators, and governors – gentlemen. However stupid they might be, they will make law for the people, against the people, and they will govern the popular masses.

They say, only good people will be chosen [elected] in a democratic state. But how can one know who will be a good person? They have neither the necessary education to distinguish good and bad, nor the leisure needed, to get to know the men who put themselves up for election. Moreover these men live in a society different to their own: they doff caps to their Majesties the Sovereign People only at election time, and once elected they turn their backs on them. Also, given that they belong to a privileged class, an exploiting class, however excellent they may be as members of a family or neighbours, they will always be bad for the people, because quite naturally they will desire the preservation of their privilege which sustains the basis of their social existence, and which condemns the people to eternal slavery.

And why doesn't the people send its own men, men of the people to legislative bodies and governments? Firstly because men of the people, having to live from their own labour, do not have the time to devote themselves exclusively to politics. Also they are not able to do so, being for the most part uninformed of the economic and political matters that are to be discussed in these lofty circles; almost always they would be duped by lawyers and bourgeois politicians. Furthermore, for such men of the people, for the most part it is sufficient for them to join a government for them to become bourgeois too. Sometimes they become even more disdainful of and detestable to the people they leave behind than those who are born bourgeois.

So, as you can see, political equality is a lie even in the most democratic of states. The same is true of legal equality and of equality in the law courts. Law is made by the bourgeoisie, for the bourgeoisie; it is exercised by the bourgeoisie against the people. The state and the law that it expresses exist only to prolong the slavery of the people for the benefit of the bourgeoisie. Moreover as you know, when you and your interests are endangered, or when your honour or rights are at issue, and when you want to go to trial, in order to do so you first have to prove that you can pay the costs, that you have access to certain resources. If you do not have funds you cannot go to trial. But do the people, the majority of workers, have the funds to pledge for a court hearing? Most of the time no, so the rich can attack and insult you as they wish, because for the people there is no justice.

Political equality will be a lie so long as there is no social and economic equality – so long as any minority of any sort can become rich, proprietors, capitalists not through their own work, but through inheritance. Do you know what the true definition of hereditary property is? It is the hereditary ability to exploit the collective labour of the people and to enslave the masses. This is what all the greatest heroes of the revolution of 1793 – Danton, Robespierre, or Saint Just – never understood. The equality and liberty that they desired was political, but not social and economic. This is why the equality and liberty that they founded constituted and set up on a new base the domination of the bourgeoisie over the people.

They thought to disguise this contradiction by placing a third term in the formula of revolution – *fraternity*. Another lie! How is fraternity possible between the exploiter and the exploited, between the oppressor and the oppressed? All day long I will make you sweat and suffer, in the evening when I have gathered in the fruit of your suffering and sweat, I will leave you a little, (enough for you to live on, i.e. to survive, to sweat and suffer again tomorrow for my benefit), and at night I will tell you, let us embrace, we are brothers! Such is the fraternity of a bourgeois revolution.

My dear friends, we too want that noble Liberty, that salutary Equality and that saintly Fraternity, and we want such things, such great things, not as fiction, as lies, but as truths that develop and constitute reality! This is the sense and the goal of what we call the Social Revolution.

It can be summarised in few words. It seeks and we seek to ensure that all who are born on this earth become fully human in the fullest sense of the word, that all should have not just the right but the means necessary to develop their faculties, to be free and happy, in equality and through fraternity! This is what we want and we are all ready to die to achieve this goal. Dear friends, I ask for one third and last session to allow me to fully express my thinking.

SOCIALISM AND THE PARIS COMMUNE

[Extract from: Préambule pour la seconde livraison de *L'Empire Knouto-germanique*. June 1871][1]

The Paris Commune was the greatest in a series of insurrections that began in Lyons in September 1870 and came to an end with revolts in Spain and Italy, in 1873 and 1874. Many of the few texts that Bakunin wrote on the Commune arose as activity beckoned.

He believed that revolutions could not be led from on high as in 1793:

> We who are real revolutionaries let us act in the opposite way. Let us talk little of revolution but let us act much. For now, let us leave to others the burden of a theoretical development of revolutionary principles; let us content ourselves with applying them widely, incarnating them in reality. Amongst our friends and allies those who know me well may be astonished that I should now speak so, I who have done so much theory, I who has always been such a fierce and jealous watchdog in matters of principles. Ah but times have changed! [...]
>
> What should revolutionary authorities do – let us work so that there are as few of them as possible – what should they do to spread and organise the revolution? They should provoke the masses, but they should not do things themselves, through decrees; they should not impose things on the masses. They should not impose any organisation but should facilitate the masses' autonomous organisation from bottom to top, supporting them quietly through individual influence on the most intelligent individuals in each locality, so that organisation should be in conformity with our principles. All the secret of success lies there. Who can doubt that such activity will meet with immense difficulties? Should one imagine that our work for the triumph of the revolution will not face innumerable problems? That it might be a children's game? Today's socialist revolutionaries can imitate very little, or nothing, from the Jacobin revolution of 1793. They have to work with actual life, they have to create everything. Revolutionary routine would be fatal.[2]

James Guillaume set out aspects of the organisational form of a Commune revolution in an article in *Solidarité*,* 12 April 1871.

> Federalism in the sense that was given it by the Paris Commune, and by that great socialist Proudhon many years earlier – he being the first to develop its scientific theory – federalism is above all the negation of the nation and of the state.
>
> In the mind-set of federalism there is no longer a *nation*; there is no more national or territorial unity. There is only an agglomeration of federated communes, an agglomeration which has no other determining principles other than those of the contracting bodies, and in consequence has no regard for questions of territory or nationalism.
>
> Equally there is no longer a state – no central power superior to bodies imposing its authority on them; there is only collective force that emanates from that federation of groups, and this collective force, works to guarantee and maintain its federal contract – a true contract, one that is at last *reciprocal and synallagmatic*, and is set out individually by each of its [contracting] bodies, this collective force, as we define it, can never become something preceding and above federated bodies, something analogous to the state of today in its relations to communes and society. Since the national and centralised state no longer exists, and with Communes enjoying full independence, there is a true anarchy, an absence of central authority.
>
> But one should not believe that having supressed the State and nationalism, that federalism should end up with complete individualism, in isolation or in egoism. No, federalism is socialist, that is to say that it is itself for a *solidarity* that is inseparable from *freedom*. Communes – while they remain wholly autonomous – feel themselves, by the force of things, in solidarity with each other, and, without giving up any of their freedom, or, to put it better, to better assure that freedom, unite closely through federations and contracts. In these they stipulate everything that touches on their common interests: major public services, the exchange of production, guarantees of individual rights, mutual assistance whenever any attack is threatened.[3]

Bakunin took an active part in events in Lyons in September 1870. He wrote the text below – an unfinished text – on 30 May 1871, a few days after the destruction of the Commune by forces acting for the Versailles* government. He never made a fuller analysis of the Commune's internal dynamics.[4]

Subsequently Italy attracted much of Bakunin's attention. He defended the Commune against attacks from Mazzini* and Pope Pius IX. The latter had little sympathy for the tens of thousands deported, imprisoned and killed by the new republic: Pius denounced the Communards as 'enemies of God', and reproached the Swiss for providing a sanctuary for IWA supporters. Some refugees from the Commune, notably Jean-Louis Pindy* and the Reclus brothers,* had some long term influence on the ongoing work of the Jura IWA Federation.

Bakunin wrote that one had only to compare the numbers of those killed by the repressive forces that put down the Commune – including women and children – with the numbers killed by the revolution to see who was on the side of humanity. Bakunin reproduced these arguments in his polemics with Mazzini.

He also wrote: 'We all wish for a peaceful solution, since we are not Jacobins* and we do not love the shedding of human blood, even that of our most bitter enemies.'[5] On another occasion he wrote that the first demand of the Commune was comprehensive education, the institution of excellent primary schools for boys and girls, rationalist, run humanely, and without priests.[6]

The extract below[7] follows on from 'Prospects for Socialism' (Letters to Frenchman). Like that text it was 'born in events' and as an explanation of events.

***

The task that I have set myself is not an easy one. I am aware of this – and I might be accused of some presumption, if I brought to this work the least personal pretension. I can assure the reader, there is nothing of that here. I am neither an academic, nor a philosopher, nor even a professional writer. I have written very little in the course of life, and I have become a writer only to defend myself, and only when passionate conviction compelled me to overcome my instinctive revulsion towards making an exhibition of myself in public.

What am I then? What pushed me on towards publishing this work? I am a passionate seeker after *truth*. I am, in equal or greater measure, an implacable enemy of the malevolent inventions of the *Party of Order*, that official, self-interested, protected representative of every turpitude – social, economic, juridical, political, metaphysical or religious – of the past or the present, which seeks to use such things, even today, to stupefy and enslave the world.

I am a fanatical lover of freedom, it is only in this environment that happiness, human dignity and intelligence can develop and grow. I do not mean official freedom – regimented, measured or bestowed by the State, an eternal lie representing in reality nothing but the privilege of the few and based on the enslavement the many. Nor do I mean that individualistic, artificial, malicious or egotistical freedom that is promoted by the school of J.-J. Rousseau, and by every other school of bourgeois liberalism. They consider the State – representing the so-called rights of everyone – as the be-all, and end-all of individual rights, always and inevitably leading to the reduction of individual rights to nothing.

No, I mean the only freedom which is really worthy of the name, the freedom that relies on the fullest development, the moral, intellectual and material attributes of all, and is found in latent form in the capabilities of every person. I mean the freedom that accepts as restrictions only things set out by our own natural law, things that properly speaking are not restrictions, since they are not laws imposed on us by some legislator from the outside, living besides or above us – but things that are immanent and inherent within us, moral, intellectual and material things that constitute the very basis of our every being. Instead of regarding such things as barriers we should consider them as the real basis of, and condition for, our freedom.

I mean the freedom of each, which, far from stopping as if before a border when it encounters the freedom of another, instead finds therein both its own confirmation and its extension into infinity. It finds the unlimited freedom of each through the freedom of all; freedom in equality, freedom through solidarity; freedom triumphing over brute force and the principle of authority – which was never anything but the idealised expression of that force. This is the freedom which, when it has overthrown all heavenly and earthly idols, will build and organise a new world of human solidarity on the ruins of every church and state.

I am a convinced supporter of *social and economic equality*, because I know that freedom, justice, human dignity, morality, the well-being of individuals and the prosperity of nations will never be anything but lies in the absence of that equality. But while I am a partisan of freedom, that precondition for humanity, I believe that equality must be established in the world through the spontaneous organisation of work, through the collective property of producer associations, through communes freely organised and federated, and through the equally spontaneous federation of these communes – and not by the overbearing tutelage of the state.

This is the principle factor dividing collectivists or revolutionary socialists from authoritarian communists – partisans of the unlimited initiative of the State. The goals of both parties are the same: both equally desire the creation of a new social order, based solely on the organisation of collective work, an order inevitably imposed on each person and on all by the force of development, with economic conditions that are equal for all, and through the collective appropriation of the instruments of labour. But communists imagine they will be able to achieve things through the development, organisation and power of the working classes in politics, principally of the urban proletariat, with the help of bourgeois radicalism; while revolutionary socialists think the other way, being enemies of every equivocal alliance or merger, they look to achieve their goals only through the development and organisation of [another sort of] power – not power in politics, but the social and, in consequence, anti-political power of the working masses of both town and country, taking in all men of good will from the upper classes, persons who sincerely wish to join them, breaking with their past and wholly accepting the programme of labour.

Two different methods flow from this. Communists believe they should organise the workers' forces to take over the political power of the state for themselves. Revolutionary socialists organise with a view to the destruction, or, if one wants a more polite word, the liquidation of the state. Communists are supporters of the practice and principle of authority; revolutionary socialists place their confidence in freedom alone. Both are equally in favour of science – to replace faith and destroy superstition. The former wish to impose it and the latter strive to disseminate it, so that human groups, convinced of its truth, may organise and come together in federated organisations – spontaneously, freely, from the bottom up – through their own momentum and in conformity with their real interests, and never according to some plan pre-prepared and imposed by some superior intellectuals on the *ignorant masses.*

Revolutionary socialists think that there is much more practical sense and character in the instinctive aspirations and real needs of the popular masses than in the deep intelligence of all these doctors and teachers of humanity who, after so many failed attempts to make people happy, still want to have their own projects tried out. Revolutionary socialists on the contrary think that humanity has allowed itself to be governed long enough, too long, and that the source of its woes resides not in one or another form of government but in the reality and very principle of government, of whatever kind it may be.

Lastly, there is the contradiction – one that has already taken on historic proportions – that exists between, on the one hand, the communism scientifically[8] developed by the German school and partially accepted by the English and American socialists, and on the other the widely developed and pushed to the limit Proudhonism accepted by the proletariat of the Latin countries.[9]

Revolutionary socialism has just attempted a first demonstration, one both practical and stunning, in the *Paris Commune*. I am a supporter of the Paris Commune. It became all the more evocative and powerful in the heart and mind of the European proletariat, precisely because it was massacred and drowned in blood by the thugs of clerical and monarchic reaction. Above all I support it because it was a clearly expressed, bold negation of the state.

It is a huge and historical fact that this negation of the state should have occurred in France in particular, hitherto the country of political centralisation par excellence. Also that it should have been precisely in Paris, the historical source of a great French civilisation, that the initiative was taken. To give life and freedom – to France, to Europe, to the whole world – un-crowned Paris enthusiastically proclaimed its own abstention! Paris once more affirmed its historic ability to take the lead – to all enslaved peoples (and where are there popular masses that are not slaves in some way?). It showed the way, the one way, towards salvation and emancipation! Paris struck a mortal blow against the political traditions of bourgeois radicalism and gave revolutionary socialism a real basis! Once again Paris earned the curses of every reactionary in France and Europe! Paris, buried itself in ruins to show solemn defiance to overbearing reaction. Through its afflictions it saved France's future and its honour. Some human consolation has been proved: the proletariat has energetically preserved morality and intelligence, and life in its full potential, while these are now lacking amongst the upper classes! Paris inaugurated the new era, for the complete and final emancipation of the popular masses and for their solidarity – henceforth a very real solidarity, across and despite state frontiers. Paris has destroyed patriotism and built a humanitarian religion on its ruins! Paris has proclaimed itself atheist and humanist: it replaced divine fiction with faith in science and the great realities of social life. The lies and inequalities of legal, political and religious morality have been replaced by the principles of fraternity, equality, justice, and freedom – the eternal foundations of all human morality! Heroic inspired, rational Paris, affirming its energetic belief in human destiny even in its glorious ruin and death, bequeathed liveliness and greater energy to future generations! This Paris – drowned in the blood of its most generous-hearted children – was humanity crucified by a European coalition of international reaction, under the immediate inspiration of the Pope, the high priest of iniquity and every Christian church. But the next revolution – one that is international and built through popular solidarity – will be Paris's resurrection.

This is the real meaning, and the immense and beneficial consequence, of the two months of life – and death – of the ever to be remembered Paris Commune. The Paris Commune lasted for too short a time. Its internal development was restricted too greatly by the struggle to the death that it had to wage against the reactionaries of Versailles, for it to have been able to elaborate in theory – I do not even say to apply – its socialist programme. Also, it must be recognised that the majority of the members of the Commune were not really socialists and if they appeared to be so, it was because they were swept along irresistibly by the force of events, by circumstance, and by the necessities of their position and not by personal conviction. The socialists, at the head of whom was naturally our friend Varlin,* formed only a tiny minority of the Commune. At the very most they were only some fourteen or fifteen members. The remainder were Jacobins. But, let it be understood, there are Jacobins and Jacobins. There are Jacobin doctrinaires and lawyers, like Mr Gambetta: his *positivist* republicanism[10] is formalistic, despotic and presumptuous; it has repudiated old, Jacobin revolutionary beliefs and has preserved only the cult of unity and authority; it has delivered popular France to the Prussians, and later to indigenous forces of reaction. Then there are frankly revolutionary Jacobins; heroes, the last sincere representatives of the democratic beliefs of 1793, able to sacrifice their love of authority and unity to the necessities of the Revolution, rather than surrendering conscience to the insolence of reaction. These broad-hearted Jacobins – headed naturally by Delescluze,* a man of great character and spirit – wanted above all the victory of the revolution. And as a revolution without the popular masses is an impossibility, and since the masses today have pre-eminently socialist instincts and can only make a social and economic revolution, Jacobins of good faith, letting themselves to be drawn ever forward by the logic of the revolutionary movement, will end up – despite themselves – becoming socialists.

That was the exact position of the Jacobins in the Paris Commune: Delescluze and many others around him who signed proclamations and programmes; their promises and their general spirit was positively socialist. But since in spite of all their good faith and intentions they were socialists more because of external pressure, rather because of their own convictions, and, since they had neither the capacity nor the time to overcome or suppress a mass of bourgeois prejudices in themselves, which were in contradiction with their recently come by socialism, one can understand that, paralysed by this internal conflict, they could never get beyond generalities, nor take those further decisive steps that might have definitely broken their solidarity and every connection with the bourgeois world.

This was a great misfortune both for themselves and for the Commune; they were paralysed, and they paralysed the Commune; but all this neither amounted to a failing nor something with which they might be reproached. Men do not change their natures or habits as they might wish, they do not transform themselves from one day to next. In letting themselves be killed for the Commune they proved their sincerity. Who dares ask for more?

Moreover they should be excused because the people of Paris, under whose influence they thought and acted, were themselves socialist much more by instinct, rather than in ideas or in well-considered conviction. All their aspirations are exclusively and to the highest degree socialist; but their ideas, or rather the traditional formulations of their ideas, are still far from reaching these heights. There are many Jacobin prejudices still, many dictatorial and governmental ideas in the proletariat of France's large cities and even among workers of Paris. So far the cult of authority – the fatal product of religious education and that historic source of all evil, of every popular servility and depravity – has not been completely uprooted from among them. So true is this that even the most intelligent children of the people, the most convinced socialists, have not yet entirely succeeded in liberating themselves from all this. Rummage in their consciousness and you will find tucked away in a dark corner a fan of Jacobin government; true to say they have become rather modest, but such thinking is not entirely dead.

The small number of convinced socialists who formed part of the Commune were furthermore in an extremely difficult position. The IWA organisation was itself very imperfect, scarcely numbering a few thousand persons. They had to keep up a daily struggle against the Jacobin majority, and moreover, they did not feel sufficient support from the great mass of the people of Paris. And in the middle of such circumstances! They had to give bread and work to some hundreds of thousands of workers, organise them, and arm them. And at the same time they had to keep an eye on the reactionary plots in Paris, a huge besieged city, threatened with starvation. They were exposed – facing every dirty trick that could be formed, developed and hatched by the forces of reaction based in and growing out of Versailles, and sanctioned *by the grace of the Prussians*. They had to oppose the government and army of Versailles with a revolutionary army and government. So to say, to combat clerical and monarchic reaction, they themselves had to organise a Jacobin *reaction*, sacrificing or forgetting the first conditions of revolutionary socialism.

Was it not natural that in such circumstances the Jacobins should have had immense advantages over the socialists: they were the strongest, since they constituted the majority in the Commune and moreover they possessed to an infinitely higher degree a practice of governmental organisation, traditions and political instincts? What is astonishing is that they did not take a greater advantage than they did, that they did not give an exclusively Jacobin character to the Paris insurrection, and that on the contrary, they let themselves be drawn along amidst a social revolution.

I know many socialists – with very consistent theory – who reproach our Paris friends for not demonstrating sufficiently their socialism in their revolutionary action, while all the barking bourgeois press accuses them on the contrary of having followed their socialist programme only too loyally. Let us for the moment leave aside these ignoble press denunciators. I would have those severe theoreticians of the emancipation of the proletariat note that they are unjust to our Paris brothers. Between the most exacting theory and its implementation there is an immense distance, which cannot be resolved in a few days. For example whoever was happy enough to have known Varlin – to name just one who is certainly dead – knows how deep, considered and passionate his socialist convictions were – and those of his friends too. These were men whose ardent zeal, devotion and good faith could never be doubted by anyone who approached them. But precisely because they were men of good faith, who had devoted their life and thinking to that immense task, they also lacked all confidence in themselves: they placed so little value on themselves! Moreover they were convinced that in the Social Revolution – diametrically opposed in this, as in everything else to the Political Revolution – individual acts mattered almost not all and spontaneous mass activity was everything. All that individuals can do is to develop, clarify and promote ideas that correspond to popular instinct, and, in addition, through ceaseless effort to contribute to the natural power of the masses and their revolutionary organisation, but nothing more than that – nothing else should be, nor can be done – except by the people themselves. Otherwise, one would be led through paths that are logical but divergent to re-establish economic, social and political slavery over the popular masses; one would end up with a political dictatorship, that is to say, the reconstruction of the state, of privilege, injustice and all sorts of state oppression.

Varlin, like all his friends, like all other sincere socialists, like all workers born and bred among the people, entirely shared this perfectly legitimate apprehension: a foreboding against the ongoing power of initiative becoming fixed and lodged with the same persons, against domination being exerted by uppity individuals. Being above all even-handed, he and others kept in mind this misgiving, this forestalling, against themselves as much as against anyone else.

Contrary to authoritarian communist thinking – quite wrong in my view – that a Social Revolution can be organised and decreed by a constituent assembly arising out of a political revolution, or by a dictatorship, our friends the socialists of Paris thought that it could be made and fully developed only through the continuous and spontaneous activity of popular associations, groups and masses. Our friends in Paris were a thousand times right. If one considers the infinite diversity and multiplicity of needs; the will, aspirations and real interests which, all together, constitute the collective will of a people, where is the head, however great, with such a vast and powerful brain that could embrace all this? Or if one wishes to speak of collective dictatorship, even one formed of hundreds of persons, where are there the superior mental faculties that might invent a social organisation to satisfy everybody? Such an organisation would nothing but the bed of a Procrustes,[a] on which the force of the state would used, with a lesser or greater level of violence, to ensure the subjugation of an unhappy society. That is how things have been done hitherto and it is precisely this antiquated model of forcible organisation that should be put aside; the Social Revolution should return complete freedom to associations, communes, groups, and the masses, even individuals, and should destroy once and for all the historic cause of all violence, the very existence and power of the state. The juridical law with all its inequity, and the lies of various religions are also to be swept away, along with the destruction of the state. Law and religion have never been anything but an obligatory ritual blessing, in ideals and in reality, of every violence represented, guaranteed and protected by the state.

It is clear that freedom will never be regained by humanity until the state is no more, only then will real satisfaction be found for the real interests of all who make up society: all local organisations, groups, as well as all individuals. Clearly all the so-called general social interests, which the state allegedly represents, are in reality nothing but an ongoing, general negation of the positive interests of associations, communes, regions, and most individuals subjected to the state. Together all this constitute an abstraction, a fiction, a lie. The state is like one great slaughter-house, a huge cemetery. All real aspirations, all the life force of every land is drawn into its shade; there, beneath its artificial pretence, they allow themselves be sacrificed and buried, in blissful ignorance.

Just as no abstract entity can exist by itself, or for itself – having no

---

a A man who having a bed of limited dimensions cut off the legs of travellers to make them fit that bed. From Greek mythology.

legs to walk on, no arms to make things, no stomach to direct the mass of victims that are given it to devour – so it is clear that as much with heavenly and religious abstraction, 'God' in reality represents very active interests, the very real interests of a privileged class, the clergy. As for its earthly compliment, that political abstract entity, the state, it represents interests that are equally real and tangible – those of the main or sole exploiting class of today (moreover a class that tends to envelop every other class) – the bourgeoisie.

And just as the clergy has always divided itself up – and is doing so all the more today – into a very powerful, very rich minority and a majority which is pretty miserable and subjugated, so the bourgeoisie and its diverse political and social organisations in industry, agriculture, banking and commerce, as well as in the military, police, university, State finance and administration tends to sub-divide progressively day by day, into an actually dominant oligarchy and a mass of innumerable creatures of lesser or greater vanity and dilapidation, living in perpetual illusion. Being progressively pushed towards the proletariat by irresistible force, the force of actual economic development, the latter are reduced into being the blind instruments of this all-powerful oligarchy.

The abolition of church and state must be primary, indispensable conditions for the real emancipation of society; thereafter it should and must organise in another manner. Not from top to bottom according to some ideal plan, dreamt up by scientists or sages, nor following the decree set out by a dictatorship, or even by a national assembly elected by universal suffrage. Such a system, as I have said before, would unavoidably lead to the creation of a new state, and in consequence to the formation of a governmental aristocracy, that is to say an entire class of persons having nothing in common with the mass of the people, and it would be a certainty that this class would recommence subjugation and exploitation, either on the pretext of common well-being or to save the state.

The future social organisation should be made from bottom to top, through the free association and federation of workers, in unions [association] at first, then in communes, followed by regions, nations and lastly in one grand international and universal federation.

In 1872 Bakunin also commented:

So great was its [the Commune's] impact everywhere that the Marxians themselves, whose ideas were reversed by this insurrection, found themselves obliged to doff their hats to it. They did more – reversing simple logic and their real feelings – they proclaimed that its goals and programme were their own. This was a comic travesty – one they were forced to adopt. They were forced to do so, failing which they would have been overwhelmed, and abandoned by all – so powerful was the passion that this revolution provoked in everyone.[11]

ON LEADERS AND POLITICS[1]

[Protestation de l'alliance, July 1871]

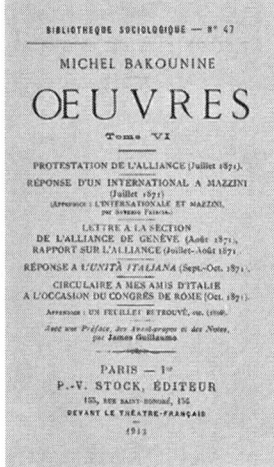

Volume 6 of James Guillaume's edition of Bakunin's works

In this text Bakunin sets out his views on labour and political organisation in the Geneva IWA.

In this era much of the city population – some 60,000 – and most members of the IWA were non-citizens. Bakunin describes the workings of the local IWA, and the particular roles and attributes of its complex structures in the community and workplace.

The first or foundation IWA Geneva section, a *'central section'*, or a *'section of initiative'*, was, after a fashion, a political section formed to discuss ideas and politics and to initiate and promote the IWA's development. There was also a 'ladies' section. Most sections organised around trades or workplaces. In addition to sections there was a general assembly and a Geneva-wide committee. This committee (Bakunin calls it a *central committee*) was somewhat akin to a trades' council, with delegates from each section. Mass assemblies open to all local members met occasionally to debate policies and problems.

The Romande* Federation included organisations from Geneva and from all over French-speaking Switzerland, with a committee elected by an annual regional delegates' meeting; Bakunin had helped draw up the regulations of this federation, and for a short while helped edit its journal, *L'Egalité*.

Older Swiss labour organisation had excluded non-Swiss members, but the local IWA had a diverse membership. Most of its members were non-voters. (Only male citizens of Canton Geneva could vote in elections for that canton; women, male citizens of other cantons, and the non-Swiss had no vote.) The citizen-members of the IWA who tended to dominate the central section were courted by the Radical Party. It wanted IWA votes and presented the prospect of one or two IWA members being elected onto a Geneva legislature. There was some common feeling between a layer of skilled workers, (workers in luxury trades and watch and clock-making) called the Fabrique, and local artisans supporting the Radical Party. Other IWA members – many of them manual workers with precarious jobs or ill-paid work might have viewed an alliance with a bourgeois party – a party that also represented employers – as a betrayal of class solidarity.

As we have seen, an Alliance for Socialist Democracy section was formed in 1868, and was admitted into the IWA by the General Council. It was in fashion akin to the central section, attracting members wanting to talk politics. It had begun as a political club, but as it organised it came to challenge Geneva-centric electoralist politics. This set the stage for political conflict. It should be noted that various IWA structures often had overlapping memberships, their struggles were complex and involved disputes over affiliations, membership and majorities in particular structures.

Marx and Engels encouraged a campaign against Bakunin through their agent[2] Utin.* They had resolved to destroy Bakunin and the Alliance section. The political war was first fully revealed in April 1870, at a congress of the regional Romande Federation at La Chaux-de-Fonds. Among the delegates attending the congress the majority was formed from IWA members in the Jura region and from the Alliance for Socialist Democracy. The minority drew support from the central Geneva IWA section, the Fabrique and its allies.

The ostensible policy difference concerned the *usefulness* of electoral work – whether it was a *useful* means of propaganda. On both sides resolutions set out a rejection of a 'parliamentary road to socialism'. The resolution of the 'abstentionists' called for the renunciation of 'national political reforms' and declared: 'This Federation is the real representative of labour, its place is completely outside political governments.'

The opposing resolution – for the Fabrique and its allies – condemned abstentionism; it argued that '*all political agitation* is subordinated to the socialist movement, and serves *only* as a means ... representing labour'.[3] However, the electoralist minority had signalled their actual and real priorities before the congress by re-forging links with Pierre Coullery, and through their ongoing support for an electoral alliance with the Radical Party in Geneva.

After the congress *L'Egalité* came under the editorial direction of Utin. Utin argued that the consequence of not voting progressively would be reaction: for example educational reforms would be abandoned, and public roads and works would be neglected. Such public polemics suggested that there was *only one* possible form of politics, electoral politics, and to abstain from that implied facilitating reaction.[4] This polar choice – either reaction or progress – both denied that other choices were possible and skated over distinct and separate agendas as between 'progress' and 'socialism', and their distinct interests. The electoral abstentionists wrote that one did not have to engage in electoral politics to oppose reaction.

The Fabrique dominated central section soon rid itself of its abstentionist minority, expelling four members – Bakunin, Perron*, Joukovsky* and Henry Sutherland – in August 1870. By that time Bakunin had left Geneva and his former ally and friend Becker* had become his enemy. The expulsions were part of an ongoing campaign against the Alliance and its politics. Later, enemies of the Alliance alleged it had never been admitted into the IWA and that letters from the London-based General Council, purporting to recognise it, were forgeries. The matter was eventually raised, and refuted, on 25 July 1871; with some reluctance the London General Council was forced to admit that it had indeed been properly recognised as an IWA section.[5]

Hermann Jung, the General Council's correspondent for Switzerland, had set out, in a private letter on General Council notepaper that the Jura IWA had no right to decide to abstain from 'politics'.[6] Jung argued that past IWA congresses had already asserted the need for 'politics'. Jung disregarded the Basel IWA congress, which had demonstrated an unresolved conflict of perspective. His argument did not recognise that the Basel congress had refused to give electoral matters any priority in its deliberations. Jung's reaction highlighted the General Council's disinclination to facilitate a non-partisan process and its lack of empathy for 'Latin' members. Subsequent actions manifested the partisan intentions of the General Council's leading members, and their resolve to use covert and underhand means to marginalise and undermine those who did not agree with their electoral line. So democratic 'electoral' politics were to be imposed through a manipulated undemocratic process! Jung cut lines of communication with the Jura IWA – and thereby set the stage for a conflict over direction of the IWA as a whole – would IWA congresses, or the General Council set the direction of travel of the IWA as a whole?

James Guillaume* thought that disagreements might have been forgotten and peace should have re-established in the face of the tragic events of 1870-1871 – the siege of Paris and the Commune – but this was not to be. The situation of the labour movement deteriorated as trade was disrupted with the Franco-Prussian war. Some Swiss workers were mobilised into the army. One might guess that the non-Swiss were particularly hard hit by unemployment. These then were the circumstances[7] when Bakunin began to write this text in July 1871. An IWA congress was due. Bakunin was concerned to explain the political differences that underlined the conflict in the Francophone-Swiss IWA and elsewhere.

In this text Bakunin sets out the view that the split in the Romande Federation had its roots in the composition, consciousness and politics of different layers of working people. These layers might push and pull in opposing fashion, with distinct and sometimes opposing priorities. He believed that the Geneva labour aristocracy – the Fabrique – had interests that ran against those of the IWA as a whole. This layer were mainly natives and citizens. They lived in the city centre, had some education, and social and political influence. They dressed and behaved as gentlemen. Being tied to the production of luxury goods, their prosperity would have been endangered by a social revolution. Their organisation pre-dated the IWA and was nationalistic – in a Swiss-republican fashion. Bakunin wrote that they were – in their souls – bourgeois.[8] Hermann Jung conceded that almost all of them were indeed individualists.[9]

Another much larger layer of working people laboured in the building trades. They were largely non-citizens, they commanded poorer wages, they were less educated (some were Italians and had poor French language skills) and they lived further away from the city centre. Being less skilled, and dependent on irregular or seasonal work they were a 'precariat'.

Bakunin noted that change depended on mass movements, rather than action by committees and the small central section. He considered the development and interaction of social and political ideas. Bakunin accused the representatives of the Fabrique of discussing policy in an authoritarian and governmental spirit, in small, closed meetings of the central section, using the mass of IWA members as blind instruments. He saw solidarity as the glue that kept the IWA together and gave it purpose. He recognised that unions might take various forms and some of them had little or no radical content. For example, a note in his text 'Rapport sur l'Alliance' (*On the Alliance*) recalls a report in *l'Egalité* of 30 October 1869 concerning a meeting on the 27th. Utin was reported as saying that British trade unions were models of solidarity, resistance and good organisation. Bakunin observed that 'the goals of trade unions were much less radical than those of the International, the former wanted only improvements in the situation of workers within existing conditions, the latter worked for complete social transformation and the suppression of waged-work and management'.[10]

Bakunin wrote little about the Alliance in this text, but in a subsequent document (See *On the Alliance*) he does write on the specific role played by that organisation. Marx was working to cast Bakunin as a nothing but a conspirator: 'This damned Muscovite has succeeded to call forth a great public scandal within our ranks, to make his personality a watchword, to infect our Working Men's Association with the poison of sectarianism, and to paralyse our action by secret intrigue.'[11] There was more truth in the opposite perspective: 'the most democratic guise in the world masks absolute power' – as Bakunin puts it in the text below. His critique of committee-autocracy threatened and obstructed the particular politics and the sway of committee leaders in Geneva and London.

The initial pages of this manuscript, 'Protestation de l'alliance', have been lost – Guillaume surmises that they discussed the development of IWA activity in and around Geneva and the dynamics and governmental habits emerging around IWA sections. The extracts below presents about a third of the manuscript. Bakunin went on to discuss arrangements for the organisation of strike funds and considered the role of central sections and members' assemblies.

***

… what they might think or desire has been thought and desired by sections, even to the extent that they do not need to consult with others to know what they should decide, or do, in their name.

Every aspect of this invention and illusion is unfortunate. It is greatly improper – in the first place – for the social morality of the leaders themselves, insofar as it habituates them to think of themselves as absolute masters of a certain mass of men, as permanent leaders – whose power is legitimate both to the extent that they had provided services and because of the length of time that this power has endured. The best of men are easily corruptible, especially when the environment itself provokes a corruption of individuals, through the lack of some ongoing opposition and serious control. In the International it cannot be a matter of mercenary corruption, because the association is as yet too poor to provide funds or even fair compensation to any of its leaders. In contrast to the situation in the world of the bourgeoisie, self-interested calculation and embezzlement is very rare and appears only exceptionally. But another sort of corruption does exist, unfortunately one not unknown in the International Workers' Association [IWA]: vanity and ambition.

There is a natural instinct for order which firstly arises in all men as a basic fact of life, in that no individual can protect his life and existence, nor assure the respect of his rights except through struggle. This struggle between men began with cannibalism; then, continuing through the centuries under various religious banners, it developed progressively. It became, very slowly, little by little, more humane – on occasion seeming to fall back into primitive barbarism – through all sorts of servitude and slavery. Today it is manifested in a twofold fashion, through the exploitation of waged work by capital and through [many forms and varieties of] state oppression – political, legal, civil, military and police – and through the various official churches of the state. All these continue to arouse amongst individuals born in this society the desire, the need, sometimes even the necessity of ordering others and exploiting them.

It is obvious that the instinct to order people about, in its primitive essence, is a carnivorous instinct, one that is quite bestial and savage. Under the influence of human intellectual development, it grows somewhat more towards the ideal, its forms are ennobled, it shapes itself as an organ of intelligence and as the devoted servant of the abstraction or political invention called the public good; but at base it remains and becomes ever more malevolent as it uses science and its inventions to extend and empower its grasp. If there is one devil in all of human history, it is the principle of command. Alone, and in conjunction with stupidity and mass ignorance – this has been its foundation and without such things it could not exist – it alone has produced every misery, every crime, and every infamy in history.

And this damnable and fatal principle can be found as a natural instinct in all people, even the best. Everyone carries this germ within them, and like every germ – as a fundamental law of life – it grows and develops whenever it finds the right conditions. In human society these conditions are stupidity, ignorance, apathetic indifference and the habit of mass servility; so that one might be right in saying that the masses themselves produce their exploiters, their oppressors, their despots and their executioners – with humanity as victim. When the masses sleep, when they patiently tolerate abjection and slavery, the best of men born amongst them, the most intelligent and energetic, the very ones who in other circumstances might render immense services to humanity, forcibly become despots. Often they become so in self-deceit and whilst believing that they are working for those whom they oppress. On the other hand, in an intelligent society, one that is attentive, jealous of its freedom and ready to defend its rights, the most egotistical individuals, those who are most malicious, turn out well. Such is the power of society, a thousand times greater than that of the strongest individual.

Thus it is clear that the absence of opposition and ongoing control inevitably becomes a source of depravity for every individual invested with some sort of social power; and that those amongst them who take to heart the preservation of personal morality should take care never to hold on to power too long and should be careful – first, next and as long as they do hold power – to arouse against themselves some salutary control and opposition.

This is what the committee members in Geneva – doubtless in ignorance of the dangers they were running, as regards their own social morality – generally neglected to do. Lacking sufficient devotion and self-sacrifice they made out of leadership a cosy habit, and through some sort of natural and almost inevitable hallucination – one that affects all who keep power in their hands for too long, they ended up imagining that they were indispensable. So it was, imperceptibly, that some sort of governmental aristocracy formed amongst the frankly popular building worker sections. In a moment we will show what disastrous consequences ensued for the IWA organisation in Geneva.

Is there any need to say how damaging this state of things is for the sections themselves? More and more it reduces them to a purely nominal state; they only exist on paper, or in a state of atrophy. Along with the growing authority of the committees, there naturally develops ignorance and indifference in the sections – for every matter, except those concerning strikes and the payment of dues, (payments moreover that are raised with ever greater difficulty and with great irregularity). This is a natural consequence of the moral and intellectual apathy in the sections; while the apathy in the sections is in turn the very inevitable result of the mechanical subordination fostered within them by the authoritarianism of the committees.

With the exception of strikes and dues, on all other points the sections of building workers have quite given up on all decision making, deliberation, and intervention; they concern themselves simply with their committees' decisions. 'We have elected our committee, it is for them to decide things.' This is how building workers often reply to those who make an effort to find out their opinion on some matter. They have come to a state of having none – like a blank sheet of paper on which their committees can write whatever they want. So long as their committees refrain from asking them for too much money, and do not press for arrears, they can decide and act with impunity, without consulting members and doing whatever seems best in their name.

Such things are very convenient for the committees, but it is not at all good for the moral, intellectual and social development of sections, nor for the real development or the collective power of the IWA. Because in reality all that remains from this way of doing things is committees alone, and, as all governments do by slight of hand they invent and proclaim their own will and thinking in place of that of their respective sections, whereas in reality the latter – as far as most issues are concerned – no longer have either a mind or a will. And the committees are only capable of developing the illusion of power, rather than one that is real and genuine, because they represent only themselves, and behind them they have only an indifferent and ignorant mass.

This illusory power is an inevitable and detestable consequence of authoritarianism, once that was brought into the organisation of IWA sections, and their organisation. It is all too prone to promote every sort of intrigue, vanity, ambition and personal interest – it may indeed be efficacious in inspiring an infantile self-satisfaction and a ridiculous, fatal and false sense of security in the proletariat, and equally in scaring the imagination of the bourgeoisie – but, when it comes to the life and death struggle that must be waged by the Europe-wide proletariat against the all too real power of the bourgeois world, it will be wholly ineffective.

This ever increasing indifference to general matters, this laziness of spirit which leads building workers to leave all matters to committees to decide, this habit of blind and automatic subordination that ensues as a natural consequence, all this entails that within these very committees the majority of the members end up becoming either the unthinking instruments of the will and thinking of twos and threes, or even on occasion of just one comrade; one who is more intelligent, energetic, determined and active than the rest. The consequence is that the most democratic guise in the world masks absolute power. So most sections only consist of a mass that is governed, serving the will either of an oligarchy, or of some single individual dictator.

Given this state of things those who wanted to take over the leadership of the entire Geneva IWA, and of the building workers especially, had just one thing to do – to win over, by one means or another, the few most influential leaders in the various sections, some twenty or thirty individuals at the outside. Once they were won over and properly subordinated as vassals the entire range of building workers' sections came into their hands. It was exactly these means that were used successfully by the crafty leaders of the Geneva Fabrique.

The summit of the fully and characteristically 'Genevan' organisation is the Central Committee of the Geneva IWA. Each section sends two delegates, so that at its meetings, now that the local IWA has some ...

sections, some ... members should be convened, given two per section.[a] Rarely does the number of those actually attending [regular] sessions of the Central Committee amount to as many as a third of the potential total.

The Central Committee is without doubt the highest authority in the Geneva International. Given the power it possesses and its direct relations with every section – it is moreover the immediate personification of those sections – it is their constitutional representative and after a fashion a standing Parliament. So, in Geneva, this Central Committee is certainly more powerful than the Federal Committee itself.[12] The latter is the higher and exclusive representative of the collective will, thinking, aspirations and interests of every section in Romande Swiss Federation, both vis-à-vis the IWA General Council and other national IWA organisations of various lands. In this capacity it is only subordinated to, firstly the General Council, (and it may appeal against the latter to a General [i.e. international] Congress) and secondly and more immediately to the Federal Congress of sections of Romande Switzerland, which has not only the right to supervise it and to impose on it its definitive resolutions, but also the right to throw it over, and replace it with a new Federal Committee.[13]

Moreover the Federal Committee has overall responsibility for the IWA's [local] journal [*L'Egalité*, then *Progrès*]. Editors, are indeed nominated by the Romande Congress; but the Federal Committee has a right to supervise, and undoubtedly the right to impose its spirit there. If it knew how to use this instrument, the latter might give it a great influence, because, through speaking directly to members of the International, it might contribute effectively to the promotion of a collective strategy.

These then are the main prerogatives of the Federal Committee. One should add that it has the right and the important responsibility of taking in hand the leadership of strikes, from the moment a strike passes from being a local dispute and calls for active co-operation, or even moral and material support from every other section of the Romande Federation, or from sections from other countries.

In addition to such very extensive rights it also has a right to supervise, control, arbitrate, and – where needed – remind others of the basic and fundamental principles of the IWA, as formulated by General Congresses. It has no other duties, other than acting as a regular intermediary between the General Council and local organisations. In those places where there is a

---

a   Here, and in the line above, Bakunin left numbers blank. In the margin he wrote the note below, to friends in Geneva who were to read the manuscript: 'My Geneva friends should insert current numbers, which I don't know. In any case there are over thirty sections, and so sixty members of the Central Committee.' JG

Central Committee,[b] or a local parliament of sections, the Federal Committee has no right to address the latter directly; it may do so only through the intermediary Central Committee, which is the natural safeguard of freedom and local autonomy against any encroachment of [superior] authority. In consequence the Federal Committee cannot exercise immediate or direct influence on the activity of sections: that right is reserved exclusively for a Central Committees which has much greater local influence than the Federal Committee.

The authority of a Central Committee is subordinated to the Federal Committee but without doubt the latter exercises only a formal rather than a real oversight. More seriously, a Central Committee might be susceptible to the criticism of the journal [*L'Egalité*], if only the Federal Committee could find the courage, when necessary, to use it against a Central Committee. But in its administration of local and internal affairs, this authority has no real restraint, except that a Central Committee might encounter a challenge [to its authority] from [the action] of each autonomous section or from a general assembly, such assemblies being local congresses. The latter are truly popular rather than representative, in the sense that all current IWA members may participate. Local congresses, according to the statutes agreed by the first Romande Congress held in Geneva in January 1869, have the right to reverse all resolutions of local Central Committees and can even impose their will on them, and the latter can only appeal to the Federal Committee or to a Romande Congress. However, such appeals might be made only if a resolution of a General Assembly was contrary to the basic principles of the IWA.

Where sections really exist, their autonomy – as against any arbitrary behaviour of a Central Committee – is very substantial. And the Central Committee of Geneva has always shown [great] respect for the Fabrique sections and their rights. Not only did their solid organisation precede the existence of the IWA, as we have already observed,[14] but it was also, in many respects inappropriate, if not to say entirely opposed, to the spirit and principles of that Association most positively expressed.

Things are quite different as regards the sections of building workers. Their organisation – being very imperfect and being often, as we have already seen, concentrated exclusively in their committees – fails to impress, or command respect from the Central Committee. The latter needs only to advise a recalcitrant section committee of their views for their resistance to be broken; indeed such a case has scarcely ever arisen. So, the only means by which building workers could defend their rights and independence

---

b 'Central Committees' might more properly be called local committees. JG

was through a General Assembly. And, it must be said, nothing was more disliked by a Central Committee than these truly popular assemblies; it was always working to replace these with *meetings of section committees*, i.e. with a governmental aristocracy.

We shall return to this important point. Here we must explain the interest that the Central Committee – seemingly the representative not of a clique, but of all sections – had in replacing popular meetings with governmental meetings. Was not the Central Committee some sort of popular Parliament born out of the universal suffrage of every section? In theory yes, in practice, no. In theory it represented everyone. But in reality, after struggles lasting several months, it ended up representing only local, Geneva-centric domination.

We shall now outline, as briefly as we can, the main phases of this struggle, which explain how a Central Committee, having been a purely democratic and popular institution, became little by little an aristocratic, Geneva-centric, governmental institution.

In the Geneva IWA, there were more branches and sections of building workers and intermediate workers (print workers, typographers, tailors, shoemakers, etc.), than sections of the Fabrique, and each section, however many members it might have, had only two delegates to represent it on the Central Committee. The result should have been a majority of non-Geneva members on the committee and a minority of members from the Geneva area. But things did not always work out like that, for the simple reason that many intermediary sections, and even sections of building workers, although composed of foreigners for the most part, were accustomed to send comrades from Geneva as delegates to the Central Committee, and these delegates – being loyal to their patriotic inspiration – almost always voted with [the representatives of] the Fabrique.

So, right from the start, the voice of the properly Geneva delegates predominated – even when they were in the minority within the Central Committee. This was so for a number of reasons: firstly because, on the whole, workers from Geneva were better educated and had much greater political experience, and they knew infinitely better than building workers how to make a speech. Secondly the Fabrique sections always nominated their most intelligent and distinguished members, often their key leaders, as delegates to the Central Committee, persons who had their full confidence, persons who, in conformity with the duties of all delegates vis-à-vis their respective sections – as defined in statutes – regularly reported back to their colleagues everything that they proposed and supported in the Central Committee, asking instructions for their future course, so that the Fabrique sections could and can say that they are really represented in that Central Committee; whereas most of the time the representation of building workers' sections on Central Committee was entirely notional.

The strength of building workers – as we have already said[15] – depended not so much on the development of their political or scientific thinking, but rather on their correct and deep instinct, and on their natural good sense; almost always this led them toward the right course, just so long as they did not allow themselves to be distracted by the sophism of some speech-maker or by the lies of some malign conspirator, which unfortunately was too often the case. There were some educated men amongst them, men used to public speaking and debate, and with experience of organisation and administration. They keep these more able comrades on their section committees, and often they sent some of their less able or less committed persons as delegates to the Central Committee. Such delegates, understanding little or nothing of the importance of their responsibilities, often missed committee meetings and lacked the habit of reporting back to their sections on resolutions and votes; frequently, when they were present, the form of their participation was limited to being passive and uncritical.

So one can understand how – in the face of such a majority – the hold of the properly local and Geneva minority was so strong. Well, this weight – one moreover that was growing – was restrained for a time by one man alone, by Comrade *Brosset*,* a locksmith. We have no need to say what sort of man Brosset was.[c] He brought together real goodwill, great simplicity of manner, and a character that was proud, ardent and energetic; he was intelligent, full of talent and spirit. He instinctively understood things that he had neither the leisure, nor the means to recognise or consider through scientific study. He was a true tribune of the people, passionately devoted to the proletarian cause, exceedingly jealous of popular rights and, as such, a bitter enemy of anything that was pretentious or authoritarian. Inordinately loved and appreciated by all building workers, he became after a fashion their natural leader, and as such, he alone, or almost alone, resisted the Fabrique in their Central Committee, in the governmental meetings of committees, and in popular assemblies.

c Bakunin wrote in this way because, in 1871, within the sections of the IWA in Romande Switzerland everyone knew this locksmith, a national of Savoy, who for some time appeared to personify the aspirations and revolutionary temperament of the building workers in Geneva. At the time of the great strike of April 1868, François Brosset was the principle 'leader'. In January 1869, when the Romande Federation was founded, he was elected president of the Romande Federal committee, and retained these duties for seven months. Later, disgusted by the attacks he faced from leaders of the Fabrique, and downhearted by the death of his brave wife, he retired from struggle. JG

He remained in the front line for several months, notably after the end of the great strike of April 1868, until his election by the first Romande Congress to the presidency of the Federal Committee of the Romande Swiss IWA, in January 1869.[16] It was a heroic period of IWA activity. In the Central Committee and in the meetings of committees, he alone was a real fighter; very often he prevailed despite the powerful local and Geneva coalition – supported by every reactionary element in these committees. You can only guess how much he was hated by the leaders of the Fabrique.

§

The principal matter under discussion was this: should the International in Geneva organise according to the true and fully international principles of the IWA; or, while retaining the great name of the International, should it become a narrowly, exclusively Geneva-centric institution? Everything the 'properly' Genevan workers did worked naturally towards this aim. As far as the masses were concerned such things arose, no doubt, without their being aware of what was happening. But their leaders were fully aware of all these things and of their whys and wherefores. They knew full well that in their hands the International could not fail to quickly become a very powerful tool for a triumphant intervention in the local politics of the Canton Geneva, for the benefit of the Radical Party, rather than socialism.

In the Geneva International this was the beginning of an unending debate between the proletariat's revolutionary socialism and bourgeois radicalism: a debate which, being then only in its initial stages, was naturally swathed in uncertainty, conducted by both opposing parties and influenced by instinctive aspirations rather than by a reasoned knowledge of aims. It was fully clarified only later, in 1869, under the influence of *L'Egalité* and of the propaganda of the *Alliance section*.

Comrades,[17] we do not need to explain to you how much those who defended the party of revolutionary socialism were in the right, and how much those who wanted to make use of the International as an instrument of bourgeois radicalism were in the wrong; how much the latter were working, no doubt without knowing or wanting it, for the total destruction of the spirit, consistency and even the future of the International Association.

You are well aware that this very debate was rehearsed at the last General Congress of the IWA, held in Basel in September 1869. And whatever our political enemies may say, the party of bourgeois radicalism – or rather the party of equivocal conciliation of workers' socialism with the politics of bourgeois radicalism – was tacitly rejected by the majority of that Congress. The majority of delegates from German Switzerland, together with the two delegates of the Geneva Fabrique,[18] and with them almost all German delegates, sought in vain to obtain a discussion of that famous question of the *referendum* or of direct legislation by the people. Designated as the last question [on the congress agenda], it was eliminated for lack of time, and indeed because the majority in the Congress was opposed to it.[19]

For you, as for us, it is clear [firstly] that the revolutionary socialist part of the proletariat can never ally itself with any fraction, however advanced, of bourgeois politics without becoming, against itself, the instrument of that politics; and [secondly] that the programme of the *Socialist-Democratic Workers' Party* (SDWP),[20] voted by the congress of that party in August 1869, in declaring that the *conquest of political rights was the* precondition *for the emancipation of the proletariat*, flagrantly contradicted the basic principles of the International Association. Today, very happily, this programme has had to be modified because of weighty events. We say that this programme can result only in placing the proletarian socialist movement in hock to, and tailing behind, bourgeois radicalism. A politics such as this – one that makes bourgeois politics into the foundation of socialism (because every sort of *prerequisite* politics, i.e. a politics that precedes socialism, can develop only outside of the proletariat, which means against itself) – can only be exclusively bourgeois.

For you, as for us, it is clear that bourgeois and political radicalism (however red and however revolutionary it may say it is, or might be in practice) could never seek, either now or in the future, the full economic emancipation of the proletariat, because it is unnatural that any real person, individual or organisation should desire the destruction of the very basis of their own existence. And so in consequence, bourgeois radicalism, *nolens volens*,[d] consciously or unconsciously, will always betray any workers who are stupid enough to place their trust in its sincerity, socialist aspirations and intentions.

Radicals demand nothing more than to once again use the strong arms and votes of the proletariat to achieve their exclusively political aims, but they will never wish or be able to serve the latter as an instrument for the conquest of social and economic rights. We are [all] equally convinced, are we not, that there would be a twofold swindle on the part of the proletariat, if it were to ally itself with bourgeois radicalism? Firstly because the latter tends towards aims that have nothing in common with those of the proletariat and which are diametrically opposed to its own. And secondly because bourgeois radicalism no longer has real power. There can be no possibility of mistake, it is obvious that it is worn out, so flagrant is its utter

d Willingly or unwillingly.

exhaustion all over Europe today. It no longer believes in its own principles, it has doubts, even about its very existence, and it has a thousand reasons to doubt because it really no longer has any reason to exist. Only two realities remain today: either the party of the past, of reaction, taking in every class of privilege and wealth, today sheltering more or less openly under the banner of military dictatorship and state authority; or the party of the future, of fully human emancipation, the party of revolutionary socialism, the party of the proletariat.

Out there in the middle, are some platonic people, pale phantoms of liberal and radical republicanism. They are lamentable, wayward shadows, who would like to adhere to something real and alive, to give themselves some reason to exist. Thrown by reactionaries into the party of the people, they would like to take over its leadership. They would paralyse, distort, and impede its development, giving it nothing back, neither the shadow of real, material power, nor a single fruitful idea.

The Socialist-Democrats of Germany have experienced all this. Is there anything that have they *not* done, since 1867, in an effort to contract an alliance – one that was patriotic, pan-Germanic – for offense and defence – with the famous democratic, republican, radical and firmly bourgeois party, which used to be called People's Party (*Volkspartei*)? A party formed in southern Germany, in opposition to Bismarck's Prusso-Germanic politics, having its main centre in Stuttgart, in the capital of those good Swabians; it was one of the main supporters and creators of that no less famous League of Peace and Freedom.* Failing to understand that the People's Party was nothing but an impotent phantom, the SDWP offered it every possible concession – and even impossible concessions – to descend to its level; they actually emasculated themselves to facilitate an ongoing alliance. We can now see how useless and damaging these concessions were. The People's Party was blown away like empty smoke by the triumphant Prusso-Germanic brutality of Emperor William. Now it no longer exists, while the SDWP can be neither dispersed nor destroyed, because it is a party not of the bourgeoisie but of the German proletariat, and it must reshape and expand its programme, to give itself ideas, aims and a soul more in keeping with its bodily strength.

Because we energetically repelled any collusion or alliance with even the most radical of bourgeois politics, it has been alleged – foolishly and injuriously – that we were indifferent to the great questions of freedom, that we were siding with reaction, that we considered only the economic or material side of the social question. A German delegate even dared to declare, at the Basel congress, that whoever did not recognise the programme of the

German Socialist-Democrats – 'that the conquest of political rights was a precondition for social emancipation' – *or put another way that in order to deliver the proletariat from bourgeois and capitalist tyranny, one should first make an alliance with that tyranny to accomplish either reform or a political revolution* – was becoming, consciously or unconsciously, an ally of the Caesars [Emperors].[21]

These gentlemen are greatly mistaken, and, consciously or unconsciously, they work to mislead the public about us. We love freedom more than they do, we love it so much that we want it whole and entire; we want it not as an idea but as a reality; and it is for this reason that we reject absolutely any bourgeois alliance, being convinced that all liberty conquered with the aid of bourgeois politics, through the means and the arms of the bourgeoisie, or by an alliance of dupes with it, might be very real and profitable for those bourgeois gentlemen, but would be nothing but make-believe for the people.

When it comes to earning money through the ever more extensive exploitation of popular labour, the politics of all these bourgeois gentlemen, of all parties – and even of the most advanced parties, however cosmopolitan they may be – is equally fervent and fanatical, patriotically loyal to the state. Their patriotism is, in reality, nothing but a passion for and the cult of the national State, as Mr Thiers – the illustrious assassin of the proletariat of Paris and the current saviour of France – has clearly said. Whoever says state says domination, and whoever says domination says exploitation, proving that the word *Volksstaat* [popular state], having unfortunately become and remained today the slogan of the SDWP, is a ridiculous contradiction, a fiction, a lie (no doubt an unconscious lie for those who adopt it), and a very dangerous snare for the proletariat. The state, however popular it might be made or shaped, will always be an institution for domination and exploitation, and so in consequence for the popular masses an ongoing source of slavery and misery. So, there is no means to promote the political and economic emancipation of the people, of giving them at one and the same time both well-being and freedom, other than abolishing the state, every state, thereby killing once and for all what hitherto has been called *politics*; politics that has been precisely nothing other than the functioning, the internal and external manifestation of State activity, that is to say the practice, the art and the science of dominating and exploiting the masses for the benefit of the privileged classes.

It is therefore incorrect to say that we gloss over or ignore politics. We do not do so – because we have a positive longing to kill off politics. Here, at this turning point, we separate ourselves wholly and absolutely from radical, bourgeois socialists and from such politics. Their politics consists of the use, reform and transformation of politics and the state, whereas our own politics, the only politics we accept, consists of the complete *abolition* of the state and with it the politics which it inevitably inspires.

And it is only because we frankly desire this abolition that we believe that we have the right to call ourselves internationalists and revolutionary socialists. Moreover because those who wish to pursue politics in another fashion and not as we do, because those who unlike us do not want the abolition of politics will of necessity pursue a politics of the State, one that is patriotic and bourgeois. That is to say that in reality they will, in the name of some large or small national State, renege on human solidarity with peoples outside their borders, as well as the social and economic emancipation of the masses within them

As for the negation of human solidarity in the name of egoism and patriotic vanity, or, to speak more politely, in the name of national glory and grandeur, we have a sad example precisely in the SDWP, or rather in the programme and politics of its party leaders. Before the last war, this party appeared to have adopted in its entirety the pan-Germanic programme of the party of the radical bourgeois, the so-called popular party, or *Volkspartei*. Like the leaders of this party of shadows – German shadows rather than Chinese shadows – the leaders of the SDWP also travelled to Vienna, to further [encourage] the nationalisation and pan-Germanisation of the proletariat of Austria, which was, in their view, too cosmopolitan, too humanely open in its socialist aspirations. [They sought] to inspire tendencies and ideas that were more narrowly patriotic and political: in sum to discipline and transform that proletariat into a great national party, one that should be exclusively Germanic. The logic of this false position, of this patent, patriotic and political betrayal of international socialism and its principles, even pushed them to attempt a rapprochement with what is called in Austria the German Party – a semi-liberal and semi-radical party – an eminently bourgeois and official party which wants nothing but the subjugation of all non-German peoples, of the Slav peoples above all, under the exclusive domination of the German minority, by means of the state. And, apparently, while very sensibly they were attempting to criticise Mr Schweitzer* for paying court illicitly to the Knouto-Prussian Pan-Germanism of Mr Bismarck, they themselves were paying court indirectly to the pan-Germanism of the quasi-liberal ministers of the Austrian Empire. So their astonishment was very great, and their anger very comic, when they saw these liberals, these Austrian radicals and official patriots clamp down on workers' associations.[22] And yet, logic was not on their side but on that of the ministers. The ministers, as faithful and intelligent servants of the state, had a thousand reasons to crack down on Socialist workers. If anything was extraordinary in all this it was the naiveté of the leaders of the SDWP. They disregarded the essential basis of the state (of every state) and were greatly indignant and astonished when persecutions that might easily have been predicted, actually followed.

We are telling a very old story here. Great and terrible events have happened since, in Germany and elsewhere, changing the face of Europe, and one hopes that the SDWP is now cured, once and for all, of their traditional naiveté and all their patriotic, political and national leanings. Their truly admirable conduct during and after the war, their energetic protests against the crimes of official Germany and against the cowardliness of bourgeois Germany, including the radicals of the *Volkspartei*, the truly heroic homage that they rendered courageously to the revolution and to the sublime death of the Paris Commune – all this proves that the SDWP, today encompassing the immense majority of Germany's proletariat, has at last broken all the old chains that bound it hitherto to the patriotic, bourgeois politics of the State; to serve henceforth only and exclusively the greater calling of International emancipation, the only one that can lead the proletariat to well-being and freedom.

This is what the so-called socialists of the Geneva Fabrique have not understood as yet. They have worked from the first to bring their local and Geneva-centric politics into the International, to transform it into a tool for their politics. For the International of Geneva this made even less sense than for the SDWP. In Germany at least – we will not speak of Austria* – all workers were Germans; whereas at this time, in the International in Geneva, the majority of the membership were foreigners, which imbued the organisation with a doubly international character. It was international not only in its programme and intentions, but also by circumstance and in reality, because the greater part of its members were condemned, by reason of their various nationalities, to remain on the outside, beyond local and Geneva-based interests and politics. To make of the International a tool for Geneva-centric politics, was this not to force the mass of workers – French, Italian, Savoyard, or even Swiss from other cantons,[23] to play a ridiculous game of soldiers on manoeuvres, for a cause which was entirely foreign to them, for the exclusive profit – and under the immediate command – of the leaders of the sections of citizen-workers of Geneva and for their grand or not so grand ambition?

It was precisely this decisive argument that was used against them. They were told: 'Since you are Geneva-citizens, do what you like in Genevan politics, outside the International: that is your right, and perhaps even your duty, but in any case such things do not matter much to us. We do not recognise your right to bring over your local intrigues, preoccupations and struggles into our International Association, which, as its name alone indicates, must seek out aims that are very different, greater and more interesting than all these patriotic declarations of bourgeois radicalism and personal ambition.'

Moreover it must be said that at this point – the second half of 1868 – after the great building workers strike showed the bourgeois politicians of Geneva that the International could, and should, become a great power, the Radical Party had not yet been able to get its hooks firmly in place in its flesh. On the contrary, the citizen-workers of Geneva, having become members of the International, allowed themselves to be guided by comrades Ph. Becker,* Serno-Solovievitch,* Charles Perron,* to form a new Socialist Democratic Party under the presidency of Mr Adolphe Catalan, a young man whose ambition was such that he could easily adapt his programme to fit the needs of the moment, a man who, having been repudiated by the Radical Party, hoped for a time that he might make use of the growing power of the International as his footstool, although he did even belong to it, and although he had barely finished fighting against it. At that moment his calculations demonstrated great flexibility, generosity of conscience and levity, but naturally they had no effect in practice. The young Socialist Democratic Party of Geneva – whose programme moreover encompassed many excellent things, but things impossible to achieve so long as bourgeois domination continued to exist, i.e. so long as States existed – showed itself to be unviable. The infant, barely two or three months old, died, strangled and buried with and by the opposition or rather the almost complete indifference of the electors of Canton Geneva.[24] However, he rendered a great service to the moderate conservative party, otherwise known as the 'independents', prolonging their reign by two years. Since then the worker-citizens of the International in Geneva, after hesitating for some months, began to form ranks beneath the banner of the Radical Party. As for Mr Catalan – he sought a new path for his youthful ambition. He sought to create a Socialist-Conservative party, akin to that of citizen Coullery, a party that had served as the medium in which that all too famous man had drowned himself.[25]

§

Another point which divided the two parties in the International in Geneva was the question of *co-operative work*. You know there are two sorts of co-operation: bourgeois co-operation, which tends to create a privileged class – some sort of new collective bourgeoisie, organised as a limited partnership;

and real socialist co-operation, that of the future and which, for this very reason, is more or less unachievable in the present. You will guess that the main orators of the properly Geneva sections defended this first option with passion.

Lastly there is a third question, one of great importance from the viewpoint of the practical organisation of the International and of proletarian struggle against the arbitrary action of bosses and capitalists: that of *caisses de resistance* [strike funds]. How should they be organised? Should each section have its own distinct funds, or should they be shared? [...][26]

There was another terrain on which matters might be debated with greater freedom – in monthly meetings, and on occasion in extraordinary meetings of the *central section*.

The *central section*, as we have said, was the first IWA body organised in Geneva; it should have continued as its ongoing centre for propaganda, its inspiration and soul. In this sense, no doubt, it was often called the 'Section of Initiative'. It created the International in Geneva, it should have preserved and developed its spirit. Every other section was 'corporative' [tied to a workplace]; in them workers were organised and united not by ideas but by facts, by having the same needs and identical work. This economic reality of a specific industry with a particular type of industrial exploitation by capital, the solidarity and particular intimacy of aspirations, circumstance, sufferings, needs and interests between workers in a workplace section – all this constituted the real basis of their connection. Ideas come afterwards, an expression or explanation, in proportion to the measure and development of a real collective conscience.

Workers need no great intellectual preparation to become members of a workplace section that represents their trade. Quite naturally, even before they know it, they are already members. They need to know that in striving and wearing themselves out at work, labour is killing them, it suffices barely to feed their families and to renew their lost strength. It enriches their bosses – and in consequence the latter are their pitiless exploiters, their indefatigable oppressors, their enemies, their masters; slaves owe masters nothing but hatred and revolt. Only later, only when they are defeated, can bosses be allowed the fraternity and justice of free men.

They also need to know – something not difficult to understand – that alone each person is powerless in the face of a boss, and that, to avoid being crushed by them, they must organise with their workplace comrades and keep faith with them in every workplace struggle against this boss. They need to know also that the unity of workers in one workplace is not enough, what is needed is that all workers in the same trade, working in the same area, should unite. Once they know this – and unless one is very stupid daily experience will soon make them appreciate it – they consciously become devoted members of their workplace section. The latter is already constituted as a reality, but as yet it lacks an international conscience, as yet it is only a very local reality. The same now *collective* experience, does not long delay the eclipse of a narrow or exclusively local solidarity – even among the least intelligent workers. A crisis or a strike breaks out. Workers in the same trade, in one or another location, make common cause, they demand a wage rise from their boss, or a reduction in working hours. Management does not agree and – as they cannot do without workers – they attract others from some other locality or province of the country, or even from another country. But in those countries workers labour for a smaller wage; so management can sell products with a better margin, and thereby, as they compete with products from countries where workers earn more, with less sweat, they force management in those countries to reduce wages and to increase the work of their labour; and the consequence of this is that the relatively more bearable situation of labour in one country can be maintained only on condition that its prevails equally in every other country. Such things are repeated so frequently that they cannot escape being noticed by even the simplest of workers. So they end up understanding that to protect themselves from management's ever growing exploitative oppression it is not enough to organise just local solidarity, they must work to bring together a solidarity that encompasses every worker in a trade, not just those who work in the same province or country, but in all countries, and most especially those linked particularly by ties of industry and commerce. So, for one trade, what is developed is not just local, nor just national, but a real *international* organisation.

But all this is not yet a general workers' organisation, this is only an International organisation of one trade. If uneducated workers are to recognise the real solidarity that necessarily exists between all trades, in every land throughout the world, other workers with greater understanding, with some notions of economic science, need to help them out. It is not that daily experience is lacking in this area, but because the economic phenomena – through which this undoubted solidarity is manifested – are infinitely more complicated, so that their real meaning may escape, and often does escape less educated workers.

If international solidarity has been perfectly established in one trade, but not in others, the inevitable result is that in this industry workers' wages will be higher and working hours lower as compared with other industries. And, as has been proved, in consequence of the competition among management and capitalists, their real profitability depends only on the low level of wages and the greater length of the working day. It is clear that, in an industry in which workers have organised international solidarity, management and capitalists earn less. It follows that, little by little, management and capitalists will relocate their funds, credits and exploitative activity to those industries [in which workers] are little or not at all organised. But this will have the necessary consequence of reducing – in that industry where workers are organised internationally – demand for workers, and this will naturally worsen the circumstances of those workers, who will be compelled, so as not to die of hunger, to work more, and to content themselves with a reduced wage. So, the condition of labour in any particular industry cannot be made better or worse without workers of other industries soon feeling the effects, without it being felt that every trade union is really and indissolubly in solidarity.

This solidarity is demonstrated by experience and theory [science]; theory being moreover nothing but universal experience made plain, compared, systematised and properly explained. But, in the world of labour, this solidarity is made manifest through passionate and profound mutual sympathy. It makes itself felt ever more strongly in the heart of the entire proletariat, growing and becoming ever more intense as economic reality develops, with political and social consequences that become ever more bitter for workers in every trade. Workers are informed of the moral and material support that they receive from every trade, and every other land in times of struggle. On the other side they learn more in consequence of the censure and hateful, systematic opposition that they encounter, not only from their own management, but also from the bosses of industries situated very far away, from the entire bourgeoisie. They come to a perfect awareness of their circumstances and of the essential conditions of their deliverance.

They see that a social world that is actually divided into three principle categories: firstly innumerable millions of exploited proletarians; secondly a few hundred thousand of second or even third rank exploiters; and thirdly a few thousand great predators, well fattened capitalists, who, as they exploit the second lot directly, and through them the first lot indirectly, absorb into their immense pockets at least half of the income of the organised labour of humanity as a whole.

Workers, from the moment that they are able to appreciate such ongoing, distinct realities, and however limited their understanding may be, cannot fail to understand soon that, if there is one means of salvation for the struggle against bourgeois exploitation, that means can be nothing other than the creation and organisation of the closest practical solidarity between workers throughout the world, of whatever land or industry.

So this is where the roots of the great IWA are to be found. They emerge not from the head or the thinking of some profound thinker, but out of the actual development of economic realities, from the hard trials that the working masses are forced to endure, and from the reflection and thinking that makes them arise quite naturally among them. For the IWA to be founded, it was necessary for every essential element to be present: economic realities, experience, aspirations and proletarian thinking, and that these should have developed to a sufficiently elevated level that a solid base could be formed. What was already needed among the proletariat was workers' groups or associations, scattered in every land, sufficiently advanced to be ready to take up the challenge of a great movement for the emancipation of the proletariat. What came next was the personal initiative of some intelligent individuals devoted to the cause of the people. We seize this opportunity to pay homage to the illustrious leaders of the party of German communists, to citizens Marx[27] and Engels above all, also to citizen Ph. Becker*, our one-time friend, now our implacable adversary, who were, *insofar as individuals are able to create things*, the true creators of the IWA. We do so with great pleasure, even though we will soon be compelled to fight them. Our esteem for them is sincere and profound, but it does not go so far as to turn to idolatry, nor will we ever allow ourselves to be enslaved by them. And, while we will continue to render them full justice for the immense services they have given, and even today give to the IWA, yet we will fight relentlessly against their false and authoritarian theories, against their dictatorial propensities, and that mania for covert intrigue, vain grudges, miserable personal animosities and dirty and infamous insults – things that characterise the political struggles of almost all Germans – which, unhappily, they have brought with them into the IWA.[28]

For their liberation it is not sufficient that masses of workers should come to understand that only the means of international proletarian solidarity would do; what was also needed was a faith in its real, unfailing efficacy as a means of their deliverance, and that they should believe in the prospect of their coming emancipation. Such faith is a matter of temperament, of inner disposition and of collective spirit. Such things develop by themselves, through history, as nature endows different peoples with faith and temperament. The collective disposition of the proletariat has a twofold origin, it arises firstly out of prior events and secondly out of current social and economic circumstances.

§

[...]²⁹ These individuals, brought together on the occasion of a political issue of the greatest interest in London in 1864 – the issue of Poland (a matter quite foreign to the international solidarity of workers and Labour), under the initial influence of the first founder-members of the IWA, formed the first kernel of this great association. Then, having returned home – in France, Belgium, Germany and Switzerland – they each formed corresponding groups.ᵉ This is how the first *Central Sections* in every land were created.

Since central sections draw together the most advanced workers of every trade they do not represent particular trades. What then do they represent? The very idea of the International. What is their mission? The development and propaganda of that idea. And what is that idea? The idea of emancipating workers not just in one or another trade or land, but of all trades in every land throughout the world – a general emancipation of everyone in this world, who earns a miserable living day-by-day, of all who labour in one form or another, doing productive work under duress, of anyone who is economically exploited and politically oppressed by capital, or rather by landlords and the privileged intermediaries of capital. This is the revolutionary, combative and negative force or the ideal. And the positive force? That is something based on a new social world, something that is self-creating, founded entirely on emancipated labour, on the ruins of the old world, through an organisation and federation of labour associations that is freely accomplished, liberated from the political and economic yoke of the privileged classes.

These two sides of the question – the negative and the positive – are inseparable. Without having at least some long-term imagination, true or false, as to the order of things which in their view should succeed what now exists, no one can want their destruction. The closer they approach the truth, (that is to say the better their imagination fits what is required by developments in the current social world), the more the effects of this imagination becomes more useful and salutary. As imagination becomes livelier, its destructive strength grows and becomes greater. Because destructive action is always determined, not just in its essence and in the

---

e Bakunin is in error here. In the meeting at St Martin's Hall on 27 September 1864, no Belgian, German or Swiss representatives were present, who might have 'returned home' to create sections. The Germans and Swiss who were present – such as Eccarius, Lessner, Jung – (there were no Belgians we believe), were living in London. It was only the workers of Paris who sent delegates to this meeting: Tolain the mason, Perrachon the bronze metal worker and A. Limousin the lacemaker. JG

degree of its intensity, but also in its form, in its path and in the means that it adopts, by the positive ideal, which constitutes its first inspiration and soul.

It is most remarkable – and this has been observed and noticed by very many writers of very diverse tendencies – that today only the proletariat has a positive ideal towards which it strives so passionately; in its being it is still pretty much a virgin. It sees before it a star, a sun. Faith warms and inspires it already, at least in its imagination, it lights up its path, whereas at the same time every allegedly enlightened, privileged class is wretched and frightened, afflicted with blindness. It sees nothing in front of it, it aspires to nothing and believes nothing; it wishes only the eternal conservation of the *status quo*, whilst recognising that the *status quo* is worthless. Nothing better proves that these classes are condemned to die, that the future belongs to the proletariat. It is the 'barbarians' (proletarians) who today represent faith in human destiny and the future of civilisation, whereas the 'civilised' find their salvation only in barbarism: the massacre of Communards and the return of the Papacy. Both of them represent the last word in a civilisation of privilege.

Central sections are the living and active centres where a new faith is preserved, nurtured and explained. Those who join them do not do so as a particular worker, having in mind the interests of a particular trade; all join as workers in general, looking forward to a new social world based on the general organisation and emancipation of labour everywhere. Those who join, whatever their particularities, leave their real or special attributes as real or special workers at the door and take on the attributes of workers 'in general'. Workers in what? Workers of ideas, propaganda, organisation; workers for the militant and economic power of the International – workers for Social Revolution.

Central sections, as one can see, take on a character very different to that of trades' (workplace) sections, even one that is diametrically opposed. Whereas the latter follow a path of natural development, beginning with realities to get to ideas, central sections on the contrary follow the path of developing ideas and abstractions, they begin with ideas in order to get to realities. Evidently in contrast with the entirely positive or realistic method of the trades' sections the method of the central sections appears artificial and abstract. This manner of proceeding, from ideas to facts, is precisely the method used by metaphysicians, theologians and idealists of every school, whose eventual powerlessness has been noted by historians. The secret of this powerlessness lies in the absolute impossibility of thinking that one can begin from abstract ideas to come to actual concrete realities.

If there were only central sections in the IWA, they alone would doubtless not have built even one per cent of the very serious power that it can now boast. Central sections would have been so many labour academies in which workers would be eternally debating every social question, naturally including that of work organisation, but without the least serious possibility – indeed without any possibility – of achieving anything, and all this for the very simple reason that work 'in general' is only an abstract idea, one that achieves 'reality' only in an immense diversity of particular industries. The special character of each of these industries is unique, each has its own particular reality and these conditions cannot be explained, or even less determined by abstract thinking. Only reality, manifested in the facts of actual development, can determine particular forms of equilibrium, their relations and their place within the general organisation of work. This organisation is akin to other general matters – it must be the ongoing ever reiterated result of real and living combinations of every particular industry; it is not the result of abstract principles, or something that doctrine imposes with violence, as German communists, partisans of a *Popular State*, desire.

The International, if it had only central sections, might well have been able to shape popular conspiracies to upset the current order of things: conspiracies of intent, but it would be too powerless to achieve their aims, being unable to draw in and receive more than a small number of workers – those who are most intelligent, energetic, convinced and devoted. The immense majority, the proletarian millions, would remain outside them, and to overthrow and destroy the current social and public politics, such as that which crushes us today, the support of millions is needed.

Only some individuals, only a very small number of individuals, allow themselves to be shaped by pure or abstract ideals. The masses and the millions – not just of the proletariat but also of the enlightened and privileged classes – are always more or less in the dark. They allow themselves to be drawn on only by the logic and power of 'reality', and mostly they consider and understand only their immediate interests or their momentary passions. So, to draw in and interest the whole proletariat in the work of the International, what was, and is needed, is that they should be approached, not with abstract or general ideas, but with a real and lively understanding of their real ills. These everyday ills, while they may well appear to thinkers as having general characteristics, and while they are in reality the particular effects of general and ongoing causes, are infinitely diverse, and take on a multitude of different aspects, the consequence of a multitude of passing and partial causes. This is the daily reality of these troubles. The mass of the proletariat are people forced to live from day to day, with scarcely a moment's leisure to ever consider their future. They can grasp troubles and sufferings only and precisely in this [everyday] reality which afflicts them everlastingly and never, or almost never, in their generality.

So, to touch the heart, and to win the confidence, consent, membership and support of uninformed proletarians – and the immense majority of the proletariat is unfortunately still numbered amongst this mass – one must begin talking with them not about the general troubles of the entire international proletariat, nor of general causes which underlie these, but of particular everyday, very private troubles. One must speak about their own trades and working conditions – precisely in the area where they live – of the harshness of daily work, of excessively long working hours, of inadequate wages, of the wickedness of that management, of the high price of food and the impossibility of feeding and nurturing their family properly.

And, when it comes to suggesting means to fight these woes, and to improve circumstances, one must at first talk not about those general and revolutionary means, which now form the action programme of the IWA – such as the abolition of individual or hereditary property and the creation of collective property; the abolition of the law and of the State, or of their replacement by the organisation and Federation of Free Producer Associations – probably such means would be misunderstood. Indeed one should not be surprised if anger and mistrust shaped responses to some imprudent propagandist using such arguments to make converts – because he or she might well meet the influence of social, political and religious ideas which priests and governments strive to inculcate. No, at first one should suggest only means that natural good sense and daily experience cannot misunderstand, means whose utility cannot be rejected. These initial means are – as we have often said – the development of a thorough solidarity, for resistance and defence, with all their workmates, against the boss or master of them all; and subsequently the extension of that solidarity among all workers in a trade, against managers in that area, that is to say formal active membership for solidarity in a trade section, a section affiliated to the IWA.

New members learn many things once they join a section. They are taught that the same solidarity which exists between every member of one section is established equally between every section, or between every trade union (corps de metiers) in a locality; that the organisation of this wider solidarity, embracing without distinction workers of every trade, has become necessary because the bosses of every trade have come to an understanding amongst themselves to make conditions ever more miserable for all who are forced to earn a living from work. One explains next that this twofold solidarity, firstly with workers in the same trade, then of workers of all trades – or of all trades organised in various different sections – is not limited to one place only, but rather extends much further, across all frontiers, encompassing the workers of the entire world, the proletariat of every land, building a powerful unity to fight and defend against bourgeois exploitation.

From the moment that new members join a section of the International, they soon recognise all such things from their own personal experience which is better than the explanations given by comrades. Henceforth they are in solidarity with every other member of their section and inseparable from it. A trade organisation, pushed to excess by the greed and harshness of management, begins a strike. For workers who have only a wage to depend on, every strike is an excessively painful trial. They earn nothing, but their family, children and their own stomachs continue to demand their daily bread, and they have nothing in reserve. Strike funds (caisse de resistance) gathered with great pain, are not enough for all, over many days, or weeks even. They would die of hunger or would soon be forced to submit to the harshest conditions that their bosses – full of rapacity and insolence – might wish to impose, if they received no help from others. But who would offer such support? Doubtless not the bourgeoisie, who are in league against workers; help can come only from workers of other trades and lands. And, indeed, help would come: sent or brought by other IWA sections in the area or from further afield. Better than any speeches such oft repeated experience demonstrates the wholesome power of international solidarity in the world of labour.

If a worker joins a section to take advantage of this solidarity one does not ask, what religious or political principles do you have? No, there is only one thing to ask: if you take the benefits of the IWA will you also accept every duty and consequence – however painful they may be? Will you remain faithful to your section through every twist and turn of a struggle that is exclusively economic in the first instance? Will you always act henceforth in conformity with the majority and its resolutions, insofar as these resolutions have a direct or indirect relation to the struggle against management? In a word, the very solidarity which is offered as a benefit, and which at the same time is imposed as a duty, is – in the widest sense of the word – *economic solidarity*. But this solidarity, once it is seriously accepted and well established, produces everything else, every principle of the International – the most sublime and the most subversive; those most destructive for religion, law and the state, for all authority be it human or divine, the most revolutionary in a word, from a socialist viewpoint – being nothing but the natural and necessary development of that economic solidarity. And the immense practical advantage of trades' sections over central sections consists precisely in this, that these development and principles are demonstrated to workers not through theoretical reasoning, but through tragic and living experience of a struggle that daily becomes ever broader, more profound, more terrible: such that even the least informed workers – ones who are least thoughtful and most malleable, being drawn on by the very consequences of this struggle, end up by recognising themselves as atheists, anarchists and revolutionaries, without their knowing how they became so.

It is clear that only trades sections can provide members with this practical education, and in consequence that only they can bring the mass of the proletariat into the International, and without this powerful support the triumph of the social revolution would never be possible. If the International had only central sections, they would be souls without bodies, magnificent dreams, quite unable to achieve reality.

ON THE ALLIANCE

[Rapport sur l'alliance, August 1871]¹

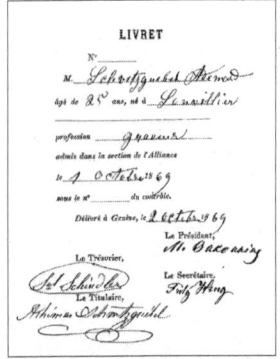

A membership card for the Alliance, signed by Bakunin and Heng

This text provides a portrait of the development, structure and activities of the Alliance for Socialist Democracy.

As noted in the introduction to the previous text, the Alliance, had obtained proof from the General Council that it had been properly recognised as a section of the IWA, countering allegations made by opponents in Geneva that correspondence had been forged. Alliance members in Geneva decided to dissolve the organisation on 6 August 1871 without consulting Bakunin. They believed that they would facilitate reconciliation and were hoping to win support from supporters of the Commune who had taken refuge in the city. Guillaume wrote that although they had no obligation to consult Bakunin they might have consulted him before acting. He was certainly put out.²

Refugees from the Commune were not much impressed by what they saw of the IWA in Geneva.³ They were to make common cause with former members of the Alliance and set up a new Agitational and Propaganda section (Section de propagande et d'action revolutionnaire socialiste) that soon aroused the ire of the leaders of the central section. Past history repeated itself with leaders of the Fabrique* expelling Benoît Malon,* Antoine Perrare, Charles Ostyn* and Gustave Lefrançais*.⁴

The text below was written by Bakunin to explain and defend the activities of the Alliance and its supporters in Geneva and in the Jura; he wanted it sent out to other IWA federations to explain how and why conflict had arisen in Geneva. Here he focuses expressly on the history of the Alliance for Socialist Democracy. He began writing this text towards the end of July, shortly after receiving news from James Guillaume* that the annual congress of the IWA had been cancelled, that a private conference would be taking place in London instead, and that it would consider the controversies that had split the Romande* Federation. Bakunin presented the Alliance as an active and lively catalyst, working fully in the light of day, and energising many who had not previously expressed their political feelings. He hoped that the radical thinking and practice of the Alliance would help undermine local, ethnocentric privilege.

James Guillaume published extracts of this text in 1872 in the Jura Federation's *Mémoire présenté*.[5] Some forty years later, when he came to publish a larger selection of Bakunin's writings he compared what had been published earlier with Bakunin's original texts. Some of his notes commented on differences between the two texts.[6] Other notes corrected imprecise dates and numbers in Bakunin's text. The first 28 pages of this Mss were lost. Guillaume writes that they described the foundation of the Alliance in October 1868.

***

The first cause [of their hostility towards the Alliance][7] was this: the most influential members, the leaders and key men of the Fabrique sections and others, considered our new organisation and propaganda with indifference, and even with a certain degree of goodwill, so long as they believed the Alliance might be some sort of [airy] academy where purely theoretical questions would be debated in theoretical terms. But then they realised that the Alliance group was little concerned with carrying out purely theoretical work for its own sake. They realised it had taken on itself – as its main aim – a review of the actual organisation and principles of the International. In the Alliance's view, the practice of socialism might be summed up in the principles that were being reviewed.

Soon they [the Fabrique sections' leaders] began to develop suspicions about the very legitimate and moreover completely public and open action of the Alliance group; above all when they saw the Alliance beginning to exert some particular attraction on building workers. The Alliance was tending to give them ideas about collective organisation, ideas that they had not had hitherto, and ideas about forms of organisation founded wholly on the principles of the International and inspired by its spirit alone. So, inevitably, it followed that these ideas helped make building workers more clear sighted and more independent, firstly vis-à-vis their [the Fabrique's] committees which were turning more and more towards deceiving them in an excessively authoritarian fashion, and – last of all – vis-à-vis the leaders of the Fabrique.

The latter were not satisfied with forming a governmental clique amongst themselves. They began to work ostentatiously through building workers' committees – to promote the domination of the Fabrique over the sections of building workers.

The entire activity of the Alliance boiled down to this: it gave the large mass of building workers the means to define their instincts, and to translate and express their thinking. Such critical reflection had become impossible – within the Circle[8] and in the general assemblies of the International – because of the control of organised Fabrique workers. The Circle had become, little by little, a purely Genevan institution, administered and governed only by [indigenous] Genevans, in which the building workers, most of them foreigners, were considered – and ended up considering themselves – as foreigners. Often, too often, the Geneva citizens belonging to the Fabrique made them listen to such words as: 'Here we are at home, you are just our guests.' The well-known spirit of Geneva – a bourgeois-radical and excessively narrow spirit – ended up completely dominating everything: no space for international fraternity, no space for international thinking. The result was that, little by little, building workers, growing tired of being subordinated, ended up no longer attending the Circle, which has become today an exclusively Genevan institution.

No serious or thorough discussion of matters affecting the International was possible in general assemblies. In the first place they were quite rare events at the time, and they met only to discuss special matters, principally strikes. There were two opposing tendencies present at the time in the International in Geneva, each was represented in general assemblies, and they came in conflict regularly. There was bourgeois socialism and Radicalism, represented by the Fabrique, and revolutionary socialism, upheld by the just instincts of the building workers. Most often it should be noted it was the latter tendency that prevailed, by virtue of the building workers being in a majority, supported by a small minority from the Fabrique. Furthermore the leaders of the Fabrique had no liking for general assemblies, assemblies which might, sometimes in an hour or two, put an end to intrigues that had taken them weeks to hatch. They were always trying to replace general assemblies – which were popular and public – with secret meetings of committees, through which they managed to establish their complete domination.

The mass of workers remained silent in general assemblies. It was always the same orators from the two conflicting parties who went up to the speakers' platform, repeating more or less stereotypical speeches. Every question was skated over. Happily, or not so happily, the dramatic or sentimental side of things was addressed, while the real and deeper problems were not addressed. Often there were dazzling fireworks, but people were left totally in the dark, without explanations or sustenance.

As for the meetings of the central section, in the beginning it was a huge section, in which building workers, who were the first founders of the section, were equally [numerous], if not in the majority, and it was something of a popular assembly organised as a propaganda section. That section should have become what in practice the Alliance section proposed to become; and if it had really fulfilled its mission, the Alliance section would doubtless have had no reason to exist.

As you know, the central section was initially the first and single section in Geneva, the founding section of the International. It was for the most part made up of all sorts of building workers, irrespective of their particular trade, with a very small number of workers from the Fabrique who had joined it as individuals. So, for some considerable time, it was the frank and instinctive socialism of the building workers which prevailed. It was a very united section. Its fraternity was real, it had not become an empty phrase, as it became later. The section was inspired by a really international spirit; the preoccupations and political struggles of the radical and conservative citizens of Geneva were things quite foreign to it.

In the spring of 1868, after the great building workers' strike, a strike that ended in a stunning success thanks to energetic and generous support of Fabrique workers, citizens of Geneva, the latter joined the central section en masse and naturally brought with them their radical, political and Genevan bourgeois spirit. Thereafter the central section was split into two camps, into two parties, the same as those that were present at general assemblies.

The Genevans were in a minority in the central section at first; but they were organised, whereas building workers were completely unorganised. Moreover the Genevan workers were used to speaking in public and had experience in political struggles. They had experience and skill – against these the building workers could oppose only their deep and truthful revolutionary socialist instinct. Moreover, when conflicts arose, the latter were paralysed by the *gratitude* that they owed to the citizen workers of the Geneva Fabrique for the effective support that the latter had given them when they were on strike.

In conclusion, for some time the two parties balanced each other out, in the monthly meetings of the central section – as in the general assemblies. Later, as time went by, and as trades' sections were formed, the building workers, being too poor to pay dues twice – to a trade section and to the central section – drifted away little by little. So the central section tended to become more and more clearly what it has now become completely – a section for the various united trades of the Fabrique: a section composed exclusively of Genevan citizens. We know now only too well the spirit that inspires them.

So, for the building workers, only trades' sections remained, for them to carry out serious propaganda for the principles of the International, and for the very necessary work of organising people with honest determination. But these sections met just once a month, meeting only to approve monthly accounts, or to elect committee members. In such meetings there was no place for discussion of principles; and what was worse, little by little the trades' sections became accustomed to restricting their role to one of simply checking spending. They would leave everything else to the care of their committees, which became more or less permanent and omnipotent, with the natural outcome that the committees became all powerful and sections became empty cyphers.

The committees for the most part were made up always of the same persons; they ended up thinking of themselves as so many collective dictators in the International. They decided everything, except for money matters, without going to the trouble of checking with their sections; and since all their sessions were held behind closed doors, they ended up, as they came together under the overwhelming influence of the Fabrique committees, in forming a secret, invisible government, one that was more or less unaccountable to the whole Geneva International. This government, so long as it was following the Genevan line of thinking, was bound to be opposed to the very goals and principles of the International. The Alliance group concluded that it should fight this state of things, which could only end up by making the International into a political instrument of bourgeois radicalism in Geneva, as we see now all too plainly.

The Alliance group never had recourse to intrigue to achieve its goals, as the Genevan intriguers later dared allege. Its every 'intrigue' was carried out with full publicity and through public discussion of the International and its principles. The group called all to its debates and discussions, to meetings held once a week. It worked precisely to facilitate things so that those who were always silent – in general assemblies and meetings of the central section – should speak. It was agreed as a law that in its sessions there should be talk, but no speech making. Anyone, both members and non-members, could speak. Such egalitarian habits displeased the majority of Fabrique workers, such that after having taken part in large numbers at first, they drew away from it little by little; so much so that, in effect the Alliance section became a section-in-general for all sorts of building workers. It gave them the means – doubtless much to the displeasure of the Fabrique – to formulate their thinking and to express their concerns. It did more, it gave them a means to understand themselves, such that in a short time the Alliance section formed a small group of convinced workers, all really united together.

The second reason for [the feelings] of the leaders of Fabrique for the Alliance section, resentment at first turning later to clear antipathy, was that the Alliance, through its programme as much as through its every development later elaborated through its programme, expressed itself decidedly against any adulterous marriage of proletarian revolutionary socialism with bourgeois radicalism. It took the abolition of the state as a basic principle – with every legal and political consequence that it might entail.

Such things would not do for the calculating, radical, bourgeois gentleman of Geneva. Soon after encountering a fiasco in the elections of November 1868 they had begun to think of using the International as an instrument for their struggle. Nor would such things do for the leaders of the Fabrique of Geneva; they were aiming higher – aspiring to achieve power with the aid of the International – nothing less. These were the two main reasons for Geneva Fabrique chiefs' hatred of the Alliance section. But these reasons, as much as the hatred they produced, were manifested fully only later, after June 1869.

To return to my earlier narrative, I want to recapitulate the services that the Alliance group rendered to the socialist cause throughout the winter of 1868-1869, both in Geneva and elsewhere.

Let us begin with foreign lands. It was members of the Alliance who founded the first sections of the International in two great countries where hitherto the Association had been completely unknown: Gambuzzi in Naples and all around Naples, Friscia in Sicily, and Fanelli in Madrid and Barcelona. The programme of the Alliance was accepted in Lyons, Marseilles, and Paris. And, note well, all these comrades, far from wanting to organise separate sections, either foreign or hostile to the International, strictly obeyed the statutes of the International. In the interest of organising workers' power everywhere they recommended, even more than was demanded by these statutes, the most punctilious subordination of these new sections to the central leadership of the General Council based in London.

In Geneva it was under the express inspiration of the Alliance and its principles that the first ever frankly revolutionary socialist address was proclaimed in Geneva. I refer to the Address of the Geneva Central Committee to workers in Spain, a letter edited by Perron,* and signed by its president Brosset* and H. Perret,* its secretary.⁹ It was this influence and these same principles and tendencies that went to work in the Romande [Federation] congress, held in Geneva in January 1869. It promoted both a majority on the Federal* committee from outside Geneva and the election of Brosset – the tribune of the building workers and the bête noire of the Fabrique – to the Federal presidency. All this [was achieved] despite the manifestly organised intrigue and opposition of the leaders of the Geneva Fabrique.

The journal *L'Égalité* was the first frankly revolutionary socialist organ in the Romande area; and it owed its nurturing, development, title, programme and editing to the influence which later also helped the change in the programme of the journal *le Progrès*, of Le Locle. In a word, one might say without any exaggeration that it was through the real activities of the Alliance that the first expression of a frankly revolutionary socialist programme arose in Geneva, creating an abyss between the proletariat and the bourgeoisie, one that the International's plotters will never be able to overcome.

Now I should say a few words on the official practice of the Alliance group.¹⁰ The group already had over a hundred members by November 1868, but could only formally set itself up as a branch or section of the International when it was recognised by the General Council of the IWA. Naturally it was the task of the Central Bureau of the Alliance¹¹ to request admission. Citizen J.-Philippe Becker,* a member of the Bureau and a personal friend of the more or less influential members of the General Council, was unanimously made responsible by the other Bureau members (Brosset, Bakunin, Perron, Guétat,* Duval'* and the secretary Zagorski*) for writing to London. He agreed to take on the task, certain, he said, that his request would be well received and adding that the General Council *would have no right to refuse us*, and would necessarily understand after the explanations that he would offer that the Alliance would be immensely useful.

We relied wholly on the promises and assurances of Ph. Becker, confident in the word of a man considered to be a socialist veteran. We knew him only very poorly at the time, and I not at all. Experience had not, as yet, enlightened us. We had not appreciated that this man, a diplomat above all, was bringing together speech that was very lively and a character that was no less versatile. He was always very happy when friends compromised themselves, but he was very careful never to allow himself to be compromised. He always preserved a line of retreat as he pushed others forward. The fact is that, notwithstanding all his promises, he wrote nothing to London, or wrote something else entirely, not what he told us.[12]

At the same time as these negotiations were taking place, or were supposed to be taking place – because none of us knew what letters Becker sent or received[13] – other members of the group, notably Ch. Perron and our prominent current enemy Henri Perret, took it on themselves to request our recognition as a section of the Geneva Federation from the Central Committee of the Geneva [IWA]. Not having all my papers to hand, I cannot say exactly in which month – November or December – this first request was made to the Central Committee. The Central Committee was poorly attended on the day this request was presented and at least two thirds of its members were absent. Nothing was decided; or rather it was agreed that a decision should be postponed until the following meeting of the Congress of Romande sections which was due to be held in Geneva in early January [1869] when the Federation of Romande sections was to be properly constituted.

Indeed, the Geneva group of the Alliance had renewed its request in January and was waiting for a decision of the Central Committee, when the Central Bureau of the Alliance received the following resolution[14] – firstly from friends in Italy and later directly – with the London General Council's resolutions relative to the Alliance (Pièce justificative n° 5):

The General Council of the IWA to the International Alliance of Socialist Democracy

About a month ago, a certain number of citizens in Geneva formed the Central Initiating Committee of a new international society named the *International Alliance of Socialist Democracy*, stating that it was their 'special mission to study political and philosophical questions on the basis of the grand principles of ... equality, 'etc.

The programme and regulations printed that this Initiating Committee had had printed were only communicated to the General Council of the IWA on 15 December 1868. According to these documents, the said International Alliance is 'established entirely within the IWA', [while] at the same time it was established entirely outside of the Association.

Alongside the General Council of the International Association, elected at the Geneva, Lausanne, and Brussels IWA congresses, there would be, in line with the initial regulations, another General Council in Geneva, one that would be self-appointed. Alongside local IWA groups there would be local groups of the International Alliance, which through the intermediary national bureaus working outside the national bureaus of the IWA 'would ask the Central Bureau of the Alliance to have them admitted to the IWA';

the Alliance Central Committee thereby gives itself the right to admit [sections] to the IWA. Lastly, the General Congress of the IWA has a duplicate, a General Congress of the International Alliance, for, as the initial regulations say, 'At the annual IWA Congress, the delegation of the Alliance of Socialist Democracy, as a branch of the IWA, would hold public meetings at a separate location.'

Considering,

That the presence of a second international body operating within and outside the IWA will be the most infallible means of its disruption;

That any other group of individuals, living in one place or another, might have the right to imitate the Geneva initiating group and, for more or less particular pretexts, might bring other international associations into the IWA with other 'special missions';

That the IWA might thereby soon become a plaything for intriguers of any nationality or party;

Moreover that the Rules of the IWA anyway admit only local and national branches into the Association (see Articles 1 and 6 of the Rules);

That sections of the IWA are forbidden to give themselves rules or administrative regulations contrary to the General Rules and Administrative Regulations of the IWA (see Article 12 of the Administrative Regulations);

That the Rules and Administrative Regulations of the IWA may be revised only by the General Congress in which two-thirds of the delegates present vote in favour of such a revision (see Article 13 of the Administrative Regulations);

That the matter has been addressed before in resolutions [agreed] against the League for Peace [and Freedom]* adopted unanimously by the IWA General Congress of Brussels,[15] and that in these resolutions the [IWA] congress declared that the League for Peace had no reason to exist since, according to its recent declarations, its aims were identical to those of the IWA, and that several members of the Alliance initiating group, having been present in Brussels as congress delegates, had voted for these resolutions.[16]

The General Council of the IWA unanimously agreed at its meeting of 22 December 1868, that:

1. All articles of the rules of the International Alliance of Socialist Democracy, defining its relations with the International Working Men's Association, are declared null and void;

2. The International Alliance of Socialist Democracy is not admitted as a branch of the IWA.

G. Odger, Chairman of the meeting; R. Shaw, General Secretary. 22 December 1868.

When this resolution became known we were naturally obliged to withdraw our request to the Geneva Central Committee. Having received the General Council's notice of excommunication we had to work first of all to have ourselves accepted by that body. When their resolution was read out to the Bureau of the Alliance, no voice was raised against it with such loud vehemence as that of fiery old J. Philippe Becker. First of all he told us that these resolutions were entirely illegal and contrary to the letter and spirit of the International's statutes, adding that we had the right and duty to disregard them, describing the General Council as so many idiots who, not knowing how to achieve anything themselves, wished only to prevent others from doing anything. Perron and Bakunin were the two members who resisted Becker most firmly, speaking for the necessity of coming to terms with the General Council. Both of them recognised that the declarations of the General Council against the regulations of the Alliance were entirely correct, since – according to these regulations – the Alliance would have formed within the IWA a new international association, independent of the IWA.[17] Note, in these resolutions, the only ones that the General Council had thus far taken and published against the Alliance, it was only the regulations that were attacked. Nothing was raised about the programme, which was plainly later reproduced in the statutes of the Alliance section – and which was unanimously approved by the General Council.

After a long debate, it was decided unanimously that Perron should contact the London General Council on their behalf. Following this decision, comrade Ch. Perron wrote a letter to either citizen Eccarius, or citizen Jung, and after expressing frankly the situation and the true aims of the Alliance and having described what members of the Alliance had done already for the workers' cause in Italy, France, Spain, as well as in Geneva, he begged the General Council in London to accept the following proposition on behalf of the Central Bureau of the Alliance: the Alliance should dissolve itself as an international organisation; its Central Bureau, representing its internationality, would cease to exist. [He asked that] the General Council recognise sections founded by members of the Alliance in France, Italy, Spain and Switzerland – with the programme of the Alliance – as regular sections of the International, henceforth preserving no other common link other than their programme, but renouncing any international organisation or solidarity other than that which they would find in the greater IWA. On these conditions the Bureau promised to spare no effort to persuade those Alliance sections that were already established in various lands to renounce everything in their constitutions that was contrary to the statutes of the International.[18]

So without wasting time the Central Bureau wrote along these lines to all sections of the Alliance, advising them to recognise the justice of the General Council's resolutions. I should note here that the strongest opposition encountered by this proposal of the Central Bureau, came from the members of Geneva group – Becker, Guétat, Duval, H. Perret – and many others too, most of all persons who today malign us and relentlessly oppose us, I recall their faces if not their names. The greatest recalcitrant was Becker. On several occasions he declared that in Geneva the Alliance alone represented the true International. The General Council, in refusing us had failed to meet its obligations; it was failing to act appropriately and this proved only one thing – its incurable stupidity. Apart from Becker, Guétat and Duval were the most violent. They always had a little stereotypical speech on revolution in their pockets. Mr H[enri] Perret showed more prudence, but he shared their views. In the end the Geneva group also decided that we should wait for a definitive reply from the General Council.

I cannot say exactly how much time went by between Perron sending his letter and a reply coming from London. A month more or less. Throughout this time the Central Bureau continued its provisional role as a representative of the Alliance's international dimension. It met regularly, once a week, at the Bakunin home. Since it had been provisionally elected for one year by the founder members of the International Alliance, and not by the Geneva group, it had no report to make to the latter, and from its correspondence with other Alliance groups of other countries it passed on whatever could be said in public without compromising anyone. Prudence was a necessity: those freedoms and personal security which one might become accustomed to in Geneva were not even remotely present in France and Italy. It is most likely that this half-secrecy allowed Mssrs Duval and Guétat to conclude that they had become members of some secret society.[19] They were in error. These meetings were confidential but not secret. Confidentiality was enjoined on us out of respect for men who, as they spread subversive propaganda, ran the risk of being imprisoned – in both France and Italy But there was no other organisation except the one established by the regulations of the Alliance, and so little were these regulations secret, that we published them ourselves.

Here let me state a dilemma. Either Mssrs Guétat and Duval, who insulted us so strongly at the congress of la Chaux-de-Fonds, were really so stupid that they believed they were part of a secret society, or they asserted all this in the congress only to damage us, without believing it. In the latter case they were slanderers, but in the first case what were they? Traitors. One doesn't join a secret society without solemnly promising to [preserve] secrets. And a person who betrays sworn secrets, or promises made on their honour, isn't such a person called a traitor? So little were we a secret society that we did not ask anyone to swear an oath, either on their honour or by their religion. But, amongst all of us, it was understood that correspondence beyond the borders should not be divulged if it might compromise friends disseminating propaganda in foreign countries.

It was in a meeting of the Central Bureau held at Bakunin's place that the question of women's membership of the Bureau was once discussed. The proposition was suggested by certain friends, devoted founder members of the Alliance, but – no doubt – persons who, when they put this proposition, were acting as unconscious instruments of Utin's* intrigue. Whoever knows the way in which this little Jew[20] acts knows that women are one of the main targets of his activity. He insinuates himself everywhere through women and today, they say, he does so even within the General Council in London. Through the intermediary of women he had hoped to plant the little flag of his intriguing ego within the Alliance.[21]

This was one of the reasons for my absolute opposition to women becoming members of our Bureau. But I also opposed it on principle. I, as much as anyone, favour the complete emancipation of women and their social equality with men; but it does not follow that this question of women should shoved everywhere, or into places where it is not moot. What is most strange, was that when I raised the matter with Guétat, he was amazed, astonished and quite disgusted, saying that he would immediately quit a Bureau in which women were present; and thereafter at the congress of La Chaux-de-Fonds, he told a story in front of Duval – who had been present when this conversation took place, that Becker and I had talked in such immodest terms about the admission of women to the Bureau that his modesty was offended.[22] But let us leave such a miserable matter and return to our history.[23]

I am very annoyed that I cannot find London's reply to Perron in my papers, so that I can quote the [exact] date, nor can I say with certainty whether this letter was from citizen Eccarius* or Citizen Jung*. Probably the former; as far as I can remember it was Perron who had written to citizen Eccarius. In general terms these were the points of this response:

The General Council, having considered the letter of Perron written on behalf of the Alliance's Central Bureau, addressed to one of its members, declares that its resolution against the Alliance was only on account of its regulations which had the pretence to create an organisation independent of the International within the International, and it did not [so resolve] on account of the Alliance's programme, with which it was perfectly in accord, except on one point, *the equalisation of classes*, whereas the International sought the abolition of classes. Moreover it adds that this very point, judging by the spirit of the programme as a whole, could only be a lapse of terminology, and not an error in principle. Lastly then, as soon as the Alliance – as an international organisation, with its Central International Bureau – might be dissolved, the General Council would recognise all the sections of the Alliance, with the programme of the Alliance, as regular sections of the International.'[24]

As soon as the Central Bureau of the Alliance received this reply, and moreover having received approval and unlimited sanction to proceed from [Alliance] sections in other countries as well as from the Geneva group, the Bureau voted its own dissolution, and so informed every other section of the Alliance, inviting them to set themselves up as regular sections of the International, whilst preserving their programme, and having themselves recognised as such by the General Council in London.

Thus it was that Mssrs Guétat and Duval ceased to be members of a terrible secret society which had worked on their poor imagination with such dire effects. A secret society existed only in their minds. The Central Bureau had indeed had a real existence up to that point, but from that day on it ceased to exist.

With the Alliance's Central Bureau having ceased to exist, our official and regular relations with sections established by the Alliance in various countries were interrupted, such that I can only describe in very general terms what became of these sections after the act of dissolution. The Alliance section of Naples, was dissolved after an existence of some months, and the greater part of its members joined the International as individuals. The Madrid section transformed itself into a section of the International, while preserving the programme of the Alliance. Sections of the Alliance in Paris and Lyons acted likewise.

Thus, through a voluntary death, died the *International* Alliance of Socialist Democracy. Desiring above all the success of the great cause of the proletariat, and considering the IWA as the unique means of achieving its goal, it immolated itself, not through some spirit of concession, but rather in a spirit of fraternity, and because it was convinced of the complete justice of the resolutions agreed by the General Council in London in December 1868, that had been published[25] against itself.[26]

From this point on it is quite another Alliance that I discuss: no longer is it an *international* organisation, [rather] it is *a very local and solitary section*, the *Geneva Alliance for Socialist Democracy* recognised by the General Council as a regular section of the IWA in July 1869. On the collective proposition of Perron,* Bakunin, and Becker,* and supported by some other members of the Geneva Alliance group, the latter resolved to submit to the decision of the General Council in London. It decided unanimously to transform itself into a regular section of the International. The first thing it had to do in this regard was to give itself statutes fully in conformity, on every point, with the statutes of the IWA. Citizen Bakunin was given the task of drafting them. It was understood that the programme would be preserved in its entirety, save the replacement, in a second article, of the clumsy phrase: 'It (the Alliance) desires above all the social, economic and political equalisation of classes and individuals', by one that was clearer: 'It desires above all the final abolition of classes and the social, economic and political equalisation of individuals.' But the regulations had to be completely redrafted.

The Alliance Section met once week, always with a very good number present; it debated conscientiously – over some two months – each clause in the new rules as proposed by Bakunin.[27] And it was not just a discussion between a few individuals who usually did all the talking; everyone participated, and those who were at first silent were invited by others to express their opinion. This long and conscientious discussion helped greatly to clarify ideas and to shape the instinct of all the members of the section. In the end, after a lengthy discussion, the new statutes were adopted unanimously in the second half of June 1869. Allow me to cite the first of the Articles of the new regulations. This will be the best reply to those who slander us, who dare to allege that we are seeking the dissolution of the IWA.

Rules and Regulations of the section of the Alliance of Socialist Democracy in Geneva

Articles:
1. The Geneva group of the Alliance of Socialist Democracy, wishing to belong exclusively to the greater IWA, constitutes a section of the International under the name the *Alliance of Socialist Democracy*, but without any other organisation, bureau, committee or congress than those of the IWA.
2. This section adopts, as its particular task, the development of the principles embodied in its programme, the study of the means that may facilitate propaganda and accelerate the final emancipation of workers and of labour.
3. Membership is reserved for those who accept all our principles wholly and sincerely. Founding members are enjoined and subsequent

members should promise to promote around themselves the most active propaganda, through word and deed – as much as their strength allows.
4. Every member has a responsibility to understand the general statutes of the IWA and of the resolutions of its Congresses, which must be considered as compulsory for all.
5. *The relentless, real activity of practical solidarity, between workers of all trades, naturally including those who cultivate the earth*, is the principal down payment towards their coming liberation. *The practice of this solidarity in the life of workers and in their private and public experience, and in workers' struggle against bourgeois capital, must be considered the supreme duty of each member of the section of the Alliance of Socialist Democracy. Any member who has failed in this duty will be excluded immediately.*[28]
6. In addition to the principal questions relating to workers' complete and final emancipation, through *the abolition of rights of inheritance and of political states*, and through the organisation of collective property and production, as well as other paths that may be indicated subsequently by [IWA] congresses, the Alliance section will also begin the study and will try to apply every palliative or provisional means that may lighten – even partially – workers' current circumstances.
7. The strength of the IWA's organisation, one and indivisible across every state frontier, irrespective of every difference of nationality, and also without any respect for patriotism, for interests, or for the politics of one or another state, this is the single means, the most certain down payment to ensure the solidarity and success of the cause of workers and of Labour and in every land. Convinced of this truth, all members of the Alliance solemnly commit themselves to contribute their every effort to build the power and solidarity of this organisation. In consequence of which, they commit themselves to uphold, in every trades body to which they belong, or may have some influence, first, *the resolutions of IWA congresses and the power of the General Council, as well as* that of the [Romande*] *Federal Council, and of the Geneva Central Committee, insofar as this power is legitimated, chosen and established by the [IWA's] statutes.*[29]

So, you can judge just how ridiculous and hateful were the accusations[30] of our enemies!

The day after the Alliance of Socialist Democracy's new statutes were unanimously agreed, Perron, the secretary of the section, hastened to send the new statutes to the General Council in London.³¹ At the same time he informed them of the final dissolution of the former international organisation of the Central Bureau of the Alliance, and he requested that they should recognise the new Geneva section as a regular section of the International. This is his letter:

> Geneva, 22 June 1869
> The Section of the Alliance of Socialist Democracy of Geneva to the General Council in London.
> Citizens,
> In line with what was agreed between your Council and the Central Committee of the Alliance of Socialist Democracy, we have submitted to the various groups of the Alliance the matter of its dissolution – as an organisation distinct from that of the IWA – communicating to them the exchange of letters between the General Council of the IWA and the Central Committee of the Alliance.
> We have the pleasure of informing you that the great majority of groups agreed with the advice of the Central Committee in favour of resolving on the dissolution of the International Alliance of Socialist Democracy.
> Today this dissolution has been resolved.
> As we informed various Alliance groups of this decision we invited them to form, as we did, sections of the IWA and to proceed to obtain recognition – either from you or from the Federal Associations of their respective country. Today, in submitting the statutes of our section, we are requesting official recognition of the section as part of the IWA, confirming the letter that you addressed to the former Central Committee of the Alliance. We send our very fraternal greetings and trust that you will wish to reply promptly,
> On behalf of the Alliance section,
> The provisional secretary,
> Ch. Perron.*³²

Towards the end of July, Perron received the following reply from London:

> General Council of the IWA, 256, High Holborn, London W. C, 28 July 1869.
> To the Alliance of Socialist Democracy section in Geneva.
> Citizens,
> It is my honour to tell you that your letters and declarations as well

as your programme[33] and regulations have been received by the General Council and your membership as a section was unanimously agreed.

On behalf of the General Council.

The General Secretary, J.-G. Eccarius*.

Immediately after this letter was received the Alliance section was definitively constituted. It nominated its committee, which immediately sent the annual section dues to London.[34]

Here is another letter from London acknowledging receipt:

To citizen Heng, secretary of the section of the Alliance of Socialist Democracy, in Geneva.

Citizen,

I have finally received your letter and the sum of 10fr. 40c, representing dues for 104 members for the year 68-69. To avoid in the future the long delays that affected this letter, you would do better to address all correspondence to my address... In the hope that you will practice actively the principles of our Association, dear citizen Heng and friends, receive my fraternal greetings.

H. Jung, Secretary for Switzerland for the General Council. 25 August 1869.

Here then are, I hope, sufficient proofs to show our most determined adversaries, if they are conscientious, that the Alliance section of Socialist Democracy of Geneva, with its programme – atheist, anti-juridical and anti-political – was a quite regular section of the IWA, and was recognised as such not just by General Council but by the Basel congress, to which, in conformity with its rights and obligations, it sent as its delegate citizen Gaspar Sentiñon, a doctor, the delegate of [both] the Alliance section of Geneva and of the Federal Centre of workers' associations of Barcelona.[35]

Messrs Utin,* Perret,* Becker,* Duval,* Guétat* and Co. needed both cynicism and bad faith to challenge the bona fides of our section, as a regular section of the International. Leaving aside [Utin] the little Jew, by nature an intriguer and a liar, let me add that none of the gentlemen had any possibility of feigning ignorance on this point, since it may be observed through the minutes of the Alliance and by dozens of witnesses (several I guess), that Becker and Duval had knowledge of the letters of Eccarius and Jung; that these letters were produced in August 1869, at [a meeting of the] Cantonal Committee of Geneva, and in September after the Basel Congress at [a meeting of the] committee of the Romande* Federation, of which Perret and Guétat were members; these two honourable citizens were present when Duval and Fritz Heng, two other members of that council, and also at one and the same time members of the Alliance section, presented these letters to the Federal* Committee.

Given all this, what can one say about the honesty of such people, people who dared declare in the last but one Federal Congress in Geneva and published in their *L'Égalité* the amazing assertion: 'that they never heard it said that the Alliance section had been recognised by the General Council, that they were unaware of it until now, and that they had just written to the General Council to check the facts!'

The Alliance section, once it was known that had been accepted and properly recognised as a regular IWA section by the General Council in London, charged its committee with the task of asking the Central Committee (of Canton) Geneva to admit it into the Geneva Federation,[36] reserving the request to the Federal Committee for its admission into the Romande Federation to a later date. On this occasion the Cantonal Committee, being already wholly dominated and subjugated by the leaders of the Fabrique, replied with a clear refusal in a session [16 August 1869] at which – as was customary – barely a dozen members were present, although already at this point the committee was formed of over sixty members.[37]

We had expected this rejection and made the application only for form's sake, so that it could not be said that we were rejecting solidarity with Geneva sections; we expected such a refusal because were not unaware of the intrigues and miserable slanders which certain people were already raising against us, people who thereafter dispensed with such subterfuge.

[*Part of the original Mss was lost. Bakunin reverted to a discussion of conflict between the building workers and their leader* Brosset.*]

… who became the target for the jealousies and hatred of the leaders of the of the Geneva Fabrique,* who after having him expelled from the 'Cercle', devoted their every effort to have him expelled from the International. They openly treated Serno-Soloviévitch,* as a Russian spy – although they now speak of him with crocodile tears in their eyes – he having been certainly one of the most devoted members of the International in Geneva. Lastly Perron – a man who was unselfish and had high principles, although at this point they were somewhat loosely formed, because of his profound friendship for Serno-Soloviévitch, a man whom he defended nobly, also attracted the hatred of these Geneva co-citizens. But above all, it was towards the end of 1868, after the Brussels Congress, when he became the founder and the principle editor of *L'Égalité* that he became the scapegoat of the good people of Geneva. No doubt without knowing it, he had had the bad luck of attracting the formidable hatred of Mr Crosset, having wounded his vanity and prejudiced his interests. Mr Crosset, a ferocious typographer,[38] became the centre of a group and a definite party, although for the most part anonymous (Mr Henri Perret and many other of the leaders of the Fabrique were part of it); they showered Perron with slander. Being bound in friendship with Perron, and coming loudly to his defence, I attracted my first enemies in the IWA at this time.

The mere name of *L'Égalité* – over and above these personal matters – was enough to lead us towards major battles. It may be recalled that it was shortly after the Brussels Congress that the question of revolution and socialism were squarely posed for the first time. The resolution in favour of collective property, the condemnation of bourgeois socialism, the obvious breech with bourgeois radicalism, as shown in the rejection of the approaches made by the League for Peace and Freedom,* all these things had greatly annoyed and worried the leaders of the Geneva Fabrique. They feared seeing the International in Geneva adopt a direction that was too socialist, too revolutionary; to see it set off on a wider ocean where they felt unable to follow. Being attached – as bourgeois, and as patriots – to the flowery banks of their [own] Lake Geneva they wanted an International that was not world-wide, but agreeably Geneva-centric, with a socialism that was anodyne and philanthropical, leading directly to a fools' reconciliation with the bourgeois radicalism of their city. All their patriotic dreams, all their ambitious hopes – so much more poignant because undeclared, felt upset and alarmed by that terrible word: *equality*.

All the grand citizens of Geneva then came up with charming explanations, yes, they understood and adored equality; if it was just up to them they would have voted for it with both hands. But that word would not be understood by the crowd, by the rascals in the International; it might offend the aristocratic susceptibilities of the building workers! That at least is what was said by Waehry, the speaker for this coterie, that poor Parisian tailor, a one-time Icarian[39] communist, a man full of devotion, but also of venom and recycled vanity. He always had the unhappy knack of professing the most advanced principles in theory, whilst voting for the most reactionary resolutions in practice. Whilst he lived he was the Benjamin and the prophet of the Geneva Fabrique.

Always we supported the title *Égalité*, and later we succeeded in creating an editorial committee in which the great majority at least were frankly devoted to the principles contained in that very name. These struggles and moreover the ongoing publication of issues of *L'Égalité*, week by week, more socialist and more revolutionary, contributed greatly to the shaping of relations between the two parties present henceforth in the International in Geneva – relations of little friendship. On the one side were the closed and well organised ranks of the Fabrique, with their bourgeois radicalism, with their platonic dreams of narrow and privileged cooperation, with leaders aspiring – in their heart of hearts – to have a seat on the local government executive (Conseil d'État),[40] – working vainly and noisily with their petty Geneva-centric patriotism to transform the International into a plainly Geneva-based body, a pedestal for their local ambitions. On the other side were a mass of more or less disorganised building workers, rich in revolutionary instincts, socialists by natural tendency as much by circumstance, always, or almost always, supporting through their votes the true principles of revolutionary socialism.

Citizens Becker, Guétat and Duval still voted with us at this time; they had thus far not sampled the tasty fruit of reactionary intrigue. But against us we had citizens Grosselin,* Weyermann, Waehry, Crosset, and many other representatives of the Fabrique, or workers of other trades allied with them. Mr Henri Perret, like the great God of Frederick the Great, strove to keep himself always in the middle, voting always with the majority, always on the side of the big battalions. One should note that, in general, the majority of committee members of trades' sections' committees, even those of building trades, as well as those of the city or cantonal committee, voted with the reactionaries, which was natural, because they were a part of that dominant oligarchy, of that secret government, with its evident tendency to muzzle the International and its people.

Our own tendency – one moreover fully in conformity with the statutes of the Romande Federation – was for breaking this authority, this nascent despotism of committees. We sought, as best we could, to subordinate the committees to the popular will of general assemblies. One can imagine that the most ambitious members of these committees could find no pleasure in those assemblies. They even dared on several occasions to support the idea that meetings of committee members should take precedence over popular assemblies. It was not difficult to prove their error, with the statutes of the Romande Federation in hand; the mass membership of the International confirmed that we, rather than they, were in the right.

In this period the Alliance section actively pursued its propaganda work in keeping with its goals. It held its meetings regularly each Saturday. Doubtless not all the 104 members that it comprised at the time of its definitive constitution regularly took part in each meeting, but there were always twenty of thirty members present, and they formed the real kernel of the Alliance. With much regret, I have to say that Perron was not one of them. Fickle, moody, capricious, for some reason that I am not aware of he took against the Alliance and made only brief appearances. His instincts – more or less for Geneva – drew him always towards the Central section, a section which, having been widely international at first, became almost exclusively composed of local people from Geneva. Brosset* also neglected us. He was president of the Federal committee, doubtless he thought it politic not to show himself too openly as a partisan of a section that had become a bête noire for a powerful fraction of the International, with whom, being the political man that he was, he found himself in relations of mutual cosiness. Lastly Guétat,* who had been recommended to us, (the fault of Perron) also abandoned us. After becoming both a member and the Vice-president of the Federal committee, he had his poor head turned by talk of honours. He became entirely ridiculous, full of stupid self-importance. He ended up withholding his usual, stereotypical speech on revolution. Henceforth, both in general assemblies and in the Federal committee, he voted always with the reactionaries.

Among the consistent members of the Alliance were both that versatile patriarch Becker – both Perron and I were to blame for him – and, on the other side – and my fault – that joker Duval. Duval, who was also a member of the Federal committee, came to tell us all the ideas put forward by the Perret brothers, whom he appeared to detest, and Guétat, whom he feigned to despise. It was through him, and also through another member of the Alliance, Fritz Heng, that we came to know everything that was said concerning our section at the Federal committee. Becker now swore only by the Alliance; he repeated many times, at almost every session, that the true International was not over there in the [huge] Temple-Unique,* but rather in the small Alliance section. Mr Henri Perret no longer showed himself amongst us. He was not present on the day of the definitive constitution of our section [26 June 1869], and, after failing to reply to two or three enquiries, he was removed from our [membership] list.

The Alliance became a truly friendly section, we talked there quite freely, full of mutual confidence, in a way that was not done in the Temple-Unique. Often, greatly scandalising Brosset, we talked about the real situation of the International in Geneva, of the reactionary spirit and the excellent organisation of the Fabrique, of the excellent spirit but deplorable organisation of the building workers. Brosset, as president of the Federal committee and as a diplomat, did not wish us to discuss such touchy matters, things that were sacred and official. According to him, such things should be talked of at most only among ones and twos, sotto voce, because decorum should be preserved in relation to the majestic creation that was the International.

This is just how they all think – all governments and all governmental figures. All partisans of obsolete institutions reason like this. No one should be allowed to approach obsolete institutions or examine them too closely; such things are, they say, are all too sacred. They adore them all in the abstract, fearing very rightly that their inanity might be exposed and manifested by indiscrete enquiries or ill-considered words.

This was the general spirit that reigned in the International in Geneva. Wherever there was talk, there was lying. Everyone, or nearly everyone said things that they knew were untrue. In every relationship – of individuals and organisations – some sort of Chinese ceremony prevailed. One was supposed to be, but one was not; belief was assumed but was lacking; determination was assumed, but was missing. Artificiality, officiousness and lying killed the spirit of the International in Geneva. The entire institution ended up as a lie. This was the reason that it could be so easily taken over by such people as Perret, Dupleix, Guétat, Duval and Utin.

The International is not an obsolete or bourgeois institution sustaining itself only by artificial means. It is entirely young, entirely open to the future. So it must allow criticism. Its development can be facilitated only by truth, by openness and fearlessness, in word and deed and by ongoing control – exerted from itself and over itself. It is not an association that should be organised from top to bottom through authoritarian means or through committee despotism. Rather it can organise itself only from bottom to top through popular means, through a free and spontaneous mass movement. The masses need to know everything – there should be no governmental secrets as far as they are concerned; they should never take appearances or stories as reality. They should above all always have an understanding of their real situation, an awareness of the goals and methods that draw them onward and forward. For that reason, every questions affecting the International should be treated fearlessly and in the full light of day. Its institutions and the real state of its organisation should be matters open to frank and public discussion, not governmental secrets.

Is it not remarkable that our adversaries should have dared accuse us of secret leadership when it was they who really created a sort of secret and dominant oligarchy, an occult government, one conducive to their every ambition and personal intrigue in the Geneva International? As for us, our entire politics consisted always of forcing them to come and place matters before general assemblies, in resolutions – something that in our view, and also in conformity with the statutes of the Romande Federation, should have been a compulsory practice for every committee of the International in Geneva.

Amongst the means we used against them always the chief one was calling them into this public struggle in which, disdaining personality and personal intrigue, we fought and almost always confounded them through the power of principle alone. Against this, as befits some governmental coterie, they waged an underground war full of intrigue and personal slander. Almost always many building workers – although not [Alliance] members – came to and took part in the discussions of the Alliance section, brought there by friends and section members. The meetings had some great influence on the spirit of the building workers, much to the chagrin of the heads of the reactionary coterie of the International in Geneva.

Day-by-day an abyss opened up between the Party of Revolution and that of Reaction, it became ever more pronounced from the middle of June 1869 onwards, when Perron on account of his work was forced to abandon the editing of *L'Égalité*, and placed it in the hands of Bakunin. The latter used the opportunity to develop the principles of the International widely and frankly, in every practical application, to its truest and fullest extent. He began his editorial work with an open attack on the Jesuitism of that Jesus Christ of La Chaux-de-Fonds, Coullery,* who – differing from the internationalist reactionaries in Geneva – wanted to convert the International into a pedestal for priestly and aristocratic reactionaries. In contrast, in Geneva, his allies, defenders and friends, the Perret brothers, Grosselin and company, were content to see it used as a tool by bourgeois radicals alone. Bakunin fought and unmasked both groupings, and worked to make plain the unbridgeable abyss which henceforth separated the proletarian cause from that of the bourgeoisie of every shading.

Putting things in this way did not serve the interests of the ambitious leaders of the Fabrique of Geneva. It was at this precise moment that the Geneva Radical Party made incredible efforts to approach and take over the International. Many former members, persons who had separated themselves from the International, known agents of the Radical Party, now returned to it. So sure of success were the radical citizens of the International that one might say they carried out their plot in the full light of day. We fought them openly, as much through our journal, through meetings of the Alliance, and in general assemblies.

All this necessarily earned us the increasing hatred of the leaders of the Fabrique. On one side were the frankly revolutionary and socialist principles promoted so unceremoniously by *L'Égalité*: abolition of states and of political and patriotic frontiers, abolition of the right of inheritance, the collective and free organisation of work and property from bottom to top. All of this, being diametrically opposed to their goal of building a bridge to unite into one single party the Radical bourgeoisie and the bourgeois internationalists of Geneva, was of no use to them. So the entire city Radical Party of Fazy, Vautier, Garleret, Cambessédès and allies was rancorously set against us. They contributed greatly towards fermenting, increasing and organising the hatred and persecutions that targeted us; henceforth exercising a direct influence on the leaders of the Fabrique in the International: Grosselin, Weyermann, Perret and many others.

Although for the most part the sections knew nothing of it, the Fabrique committees sent protests on their behalf to the Federal Committee, against the editorial line of *L'Égalité*. These plots came to nothing so long as Brosset* remained president of the Federal committee. But being excessively vulnerable he was forced to abandon his position through a succession of organised provocations which he failed to counter with the contempt that they deserved. Guétat became president instead [in August 1869], and from that point on the Federal committee stepped into the reactionary camp. Fortunately an article in the statutes of the Romande Federation – which made it somewhat independent of the Federal committee – safeguarded the editorial committee from any arbitrary control.[41]

So the International in Geneva was fully at war: on the one side the Fabrique carefully disciplined, led and blinkered but its leaders; and on the other side the mass of building workers informed by *L'Égalité*, and getting itself organised, little by little, under the influence of the Alliance. In the middle were intermediary trades' sections: shoemakers, tailors, typesetters, etc., whose committees largely sided, true to say, with reaction, but whose members had more sympathy for revolution.

A decisive battle became inevitable. It was waged in the second half of August on the occasion of the election of delegates for the Basel congress.

The Electoral Struggle

This was a memorable battle and one that should be described by a better historian than me. I will limit myself to recalling its main phases.

Amongst the five items set by the General Council for the agenda of the congress which was to meet in Basel in September 1869, there were two that touched on the very basis of the social question: *the abolition of inheritance and the organisation of collective property*, two questions which at all times had the facility of inspiring the ill-temper of the stars and leaders of the Fabrique of Geneva. They had been excessively displeased earlier, when the latter question had been discussed at the Brussels congress: 'Such things are utopian, they said, we should concern ourselves with practical matters.'

So on this occasion they were resolved to eliminate these two matters from the agenda of the Basel congress. Their political position made this a necessity. It was more than a matter of heart or mind: they had come to a definitive understanding and alliance with the radical bourgeoisie of Geneva. All the properly Genevan sections – i.e. those of the citizen-workers of the Fabrique – were working to gather round the Radical [Party] banner for the coming elections, due in November. But to enable an alliance between the bourgeoisie and the citizen-workers, it was essential that the latter should remove from their programme everything that might contradict the fundamental principles, or shock the delicate sensibilities, of their new allies the radical bourgeoisie of Geneva.

The tactics of the Geneva coterie, were quite simple. They directed and inspired the (Cantonal) Central Committee to do their will, and through this intermediary they chose the agenda of general assemblies. They had commissions nominated by general assemblies to prepare and propose reports on all the other questions, but they forgot, [and] neglected to have commissions nominated for these two touchy questions. If things had gone as they wished this is what might have happened – by the eve of congress there would have been no commissions nominated for these agenda items, no reports would have been prepared, and in consequence these two matters would in effect have been eliminated.

We spoilt their ploy in a popular assembly; we recalled that there were still two matters that the Central Committee appeared to have forgotten, and that it was urgent that two more commissions should be immediately be nominated to study and present reports in good time. So then the storm erupted; all the great orators of the Fabrique and their reactionary allies – Grosselin first of all; Weyermann; Crosset; Waehry; Patru; Crosset's typesetters; Dupleix; father Reymond (blind, a Saint-Simonian, the Jesus Christ of the International in Geneva) Paillard, the particular enemy of Robin* a mason from Geneva, a great character, a lover of disputes; Guétat; and many others came in turns to the rostrum to say that it was a scandal, a useless waste of time, a subversive activity, to propose such questions to workers. One should deal with practical and achievable matters, for example bourgeois co-operation, etc., etc. We replied. They were beaten. The general assembly – the Temple-Unique* was full, and building workers, carefully convened by our allies over the past day were present en masse – decided with their immense majority that commissions should be nominated at once to consider these two unwanted questions: Bakunin was elected onto the commission on the question of inheritance, Robin for the one concerned with collective property.

At the next general assembly another matter had to be decided. The general statutes set out that each section had a right to send a delegate to congress. So the International in Geneva would have been allowed to send over thirty.[42] This would have been unaffordable. For this reason all the International sections of Geneva had come together a year earlier to share in common the costs of sending four delegates to Brussels. On this occasion, as the number of sections had increased, it was decided to send five. Sending them collectively was obviously in the interest of the sections of building workers, their sections being much less wealthy than the sections of the Fabrique. The Fabrique workers, inspired and directed by their leaders, naturally took advantage of these circumstances to propose a fix. Their orators came to the tribune to declare, in the name of all their comrades, that the Fabrique sections would agree to sending delegates collectively only if they were placated by the elimination of these two matters of inheritance and property. This was the signal for a second storm.

We went up to the rostrum to explain to the building workers that in the making of such a proposition they were being insulted, their rights and their freedom of conscience were being attacked; that it would be better to send just one delegate, or none, rather than to send five or more on the basis of the unacceptable conditions that would be imposed on them on behalf of the Fabrique sections. The orators of reaction then returned to the tribune singing that eternal refrain of unity that was so necessary, if the power of the working class was to be built; building workers were reminded that they owed eternal gratitude to the Genevan citizens of the Fabrique for the support that they had been given during the great strike in the spring. They warned them against certain 'foreigners', who had come to sow division in the International in Geneva. Brosset, Robin, Bakunin and others replied: there could be no 'foreigners' in the International. Gratitude and unity were no doubt very fine things, but such things should not create servitude; and that it would be better to separate, rather than to become a slave. On this occasion too, victory was ours. There was an immense majority in favour of keeping these issues and for commissions [to prepare discussions].[43]

Two or three days later, in the Temple-Unique, there was a special meeting of all the Fabrique sections. Mr Grosselin facing no opposition, surpassed himself with his eloquence. He made a thunderous speech against Brosset, Robin and Bakunin, transparently designed to stigmatise them as disturbers of the peace, of unity and of the public order of the International in Geneva. 'What are these foreigners doing among us! He said with such excitement that he forgot that he was speaking, not in a meeting of citizens of Geneva, but among workers of Geneva who were members of the International, and that the International did not recognise narrow-minded patriotism. Others

– Crosset and Waehry – came to supplement the eloquence of mighty Grosselin, the future statesman of Geneva: the one adding grand words, the other his bile.

In the end the Fabrique sections decided that they should act separately and together and they named just one delegate, Mr Henri Perret*, the secretary of the Federal committee, with a mandate to abstain from voting on the two questions repudiated by the Fabrique.[44] They did not name Grosselin as their second delegate, firstly to save money, and secondly in the hope that building workers might nominate him. His allies, friends of the Fabrique, Crosset, Waehry, the two Paillard brothers, Guétat, Rossetti, Patru, worked at a distance on the building workers for this goal. So the division became a fait accompli, the Fabrique sent just one delegate. The building workers together with cutters and shoemakers decided on sending three, nominating Heng, Brosset, and Grosselin.[45] Meanwhile Robin and Bakunin made their reports, the one on the organisation of collective property, the other on the abolition of the right of inheritance, both of them naturally in a very positive sense. Their conclusions were praised and voted for almost unanimously.

The commission responsible for reviewing the question of integral education also reported. Here a very strange thing happened. It was not the commission that made the report, but Mr Cambessédès, one of the stars of the bourgeois Radical Party, a statesman but not a member of the International. At the time he had the office of Chief Inspector of all schools in Geneva (if I am not mistaken). Naturally his report was made in an eminently bourgeois spirit. He supported the separation of schools for the two classes, under the charming and touching pretext that the bourgeoisie would never consent to sending children to schools that took in the children of the [common] people. All the rest of the report was equally engaging, such that our friend Fritz Heng, a member of that commission, who had taken on the task of reading it (not having known of its contents earlier) stopped in the middle of his reading and naively declared that this report was useless and was inappropriate as far as the International was concerned. How was it that one of Geneva's bourgeois radicals should have had his work accepted by a commission of the International? That is a secret that only the Fabrique and Mr Crosset, the ally of the Fabrique's leaders and a member of this commission, might have explained.

When the nomination of Grosselin as the third delegate of the building workers was announced[46] the latter declared and voted unanimously that he should be given the task of representing them at the Basel congress only if he promised to vote for the collective organisation of property and for the abolition of the right of inheritance. This placed him in a singular position. He had been the principle promoter of propositions that would have removed these two matters as utopian, untimely and harmful, and of the division that resulted, and now he had to promise to vote in favour of both at the Basel congress!

At the last general assembly before the congress, he attempted to find a way out of this ridiculous situation by a novel means: he posed a personal question, appealing to personal feeling: 'I love you and you love me, you know I have always been your friend; why then do you mistrust me, imposing conditions that neither my dignity, nor my conscience would allow me accept?' It was not difficult to reply that this was not a matter of personality, nor of sympathy, nor of personal distrust; that he was much loved and esteemed, but that principles and collective rights could not be sacrificed for him. Almost unanimously the general assembly expressed itself in favour of collective property and for the abolition of rights of inheritance and he had to reply categorically to this question: would he and could he vote and speak in conscience for these two propositions?

Following our proposal the meeting again resolved that this vote was entirely obligatory for its delegates and imposed a firm mandate on them. So in front of the meeting Grosselin was forced to resign. But this is what occurred next. On the eve of or on the very day when delegates were due to leave for Basel, the [Cantonal] Central Committee met, and gave itself rights – which it could not have – since the statutes of the Romande Federation expressly subordinated all its decisions to those of the general assembly. This committee had even less right to act as it did, as on this occasion as it was a matter of a delegate not of every section of the International, but only of building workers, who paid out of their own pockets.[47] But the [Cantonal] Central Committee, on this occasion composed almost entirely of those members of the Fabrique who had all come to this meeting and with the majority of members of other sections absent, decided that the instructions for Grosselin should be overruled and that he should go to Basel as a delegate of the building workers but *free of the firm mandate that the assembled building workers' sections had imposed on him.* So he attended and, being an inseparable comrade of Mr Perret, the Fabrique delegate, he voted like him on every matter.[48]

Here ends my historical narrative. One can now understand the terrible hatred targeting us – Perron,[49] Brosset, Robin and me – directed by all the main leaders of the Fabrique and by many of their people who, as a result of all sorts of vile slanders, were passionately aroused against us.[50]

LETTER TO THE JURA COMRADES

[Aux Compagnons de la Fédération des Sections internationales de Jura, February-March 1872][1]

The formation of the IWA and its early years coincided with a series of wars. The Brussels IWA Congress of 1868 urged working people[2] to resist militarism and war by ceasing work.[3]

Bakunin saw a contradiction between Marx's patriotism and internationalism. He refers to the *Inaugural Address*[4] drafted by Marx on behalf of the provisional leadership of the IWA and asks why it highlighted only criticism of Russian expansion.[5] Bakunin wrote: 'Every political power, every state is necessarily barbarous in its conquests and repression.'[6]

On relations between particular homelands and the International Bakunin wrote: 'The International does not destroy nationalities or nations; without supressing any one of them it embraces them all. It cannot do otherwise, because the broadest freedom is its fundamental principle. The International does not war against natural homelands, it wars only against political homelands – states …'[7]

Bakunin, praised Bebel* and Liebknecht* for their refusal to support the ongoing war against France,[8] but was at odds with German Social-Democrats who saw 'civilised' Germany as a progressive nation to be defended against 'barbaric' Russia. A unitary German republic had been presented as a force for progress and civilisation.[9] In this view there were 'two powers on the continent of Europe – Russia and Absolutism, the Revolution and Democracy'.[10] Bakunin knew that Marx and Engels had written that victory in the recent war with France would facilitate progress.[11]

Bakunin posed questions to German socialists: would they respect other peoples' rights, and renounce claims to areas peopled by non-Germans (e.g. northern Schleswig, Posen, Bohemia)? He had written that peoples, associations, communes and individuals should always have a right of secession – subject to conditions.[12]

In Bakunin's view Imperial Germany was becoming the leading centre of reaction; he feared that Social-Democracy was failing to confront German nationalism. He accused it of viewing Slav lands as part of Germany's hereditary patrimony.[13] 'So long as the propaganda of German workers begins with [a demand] for their state, they can be certain to meet – from all Slav peoples without exception – enemies rather than brothers.'[14]

Bakunin wrote that currently: 'Their [Germans'] relations vis-a-vis the Slavs are absolutely the same as those of the English towards the Irish people.'[15] But he expected the British to become more liberal and suggested that they would allow the Irish autonomy by way of reparation for past oppressions. In contrast he criticised the politics of all German parties – of the right and left, Social-Democrats included – who confused cosmopolitanism with pan-Germanism and looked towards the dissolution of Slav identity in a pan-German states.[16]

Bakunin called on the General Council of the IWA, which had recently recognised the right of Irish people for automomy from the British, to work to extend that principle and advise their German supporters to adopt the same policy vis-à-vis Slav peoples. He went on to say:

> If they do not do so, that would prove that, being directed for the most part by Germans, they understand humanity and justice only when the latter is not in opposition to vain and over-large German ambition, that it [the General Council] too, like the leaders of the party of Socialist-Democracy, in relation to the Slav race at least, confuses cosmopolitanism with pan-Germanism, a deplorable confusion, one entirely contrary to the most fundamental principles of the IWA and can only benefit Reaction.[17]

German patriotism came from pride in being the top nation: 'I may be a slave but my Emperor is the most powerful Sovereign of them all, he holds me by the throat and will strangle you all.'[18] In the text below,[19] and others, he asked if there was any difference between pan-German and Russian domination? He answered yes, insofar as German domination used science and, 'from the point of view of brutality, insolence and cruelty, I really do believe that the Germans are on top; [in the recent war in France] they surpassed everything done by the Russians in Poland; [but] we must admit that they in turn were overtaken by the patriotic Versailles* army.'[20]

In 1914 many 'socialists' went to war against each other, fighting in the armies of their particular states, all believing they were defending progress, rights and liberties. Later in the 20th century it was argued that defence of the Soviet Union was the litmus test of socialism. Here again, one state was viewed as qualitatively more progressive than another, such that working people had a duty to take sides. Strategies and choices were driven by particular evaluations of what 'progress' and 'socialism' did – or did not – entail. Who was to judge? Bakunin came to a general conclusion: no people could have freedom – a freedom with solidarity – in the humane sense of that word, so long as the whole of humanity was not equally free.[21]

These are a short extracts from a long text written in February-March 1872.

***

And today, with all this, the Russian army is immense, much more numerous, better organised, armed and officered than ever before. It is not as strong as Russian and foreign statisticians make out, but nonetheless it constitutes a very respectable force. It would be unable to wage offensive war on its own against Germany, but it would be able to inflict serious injury, if it could find some powerful European ally, such as France. It might become powerful again if it roused racial and national passions, and nurtured a pan-Slav banner – as Prussia did in recent times when it raised up the pan-German banner against France, and in proclaiming Imperial unity in Versailles. In such a case Russia would find allies: friends and brothers even in the very heart of the Empire – entire peoples even.

But that might be by virtue of some heroic method – one that the Russia Empire might doubtless resort to – perhaps in some distant future. Hitherto at least it has preferred the more regular and less perilous path of diplomatic alliances, and the greater part of its expansion westwards has been by virtue of its very crafty diplomacy, rather than by force of arms. Being uninterested in most of the internal questions which weary and divide Western Europe, like Achilles in this respect, it shows but one vulnerable point: Social Revolution. (A peasant revolution above all – much more than the revolution of urban factory workers, which in Russia forms merely a drop of water in the popular ocean.) Russian diplomacy meddles in every Western question, and never lets an opportunity pass to fish in troubled waters, naturally taking the part of the bad against the good, for reaction against revolution.

So it is on this account that German patriots censure Russia so bitterly, and in this they are in error. Russia, in acting as it does, both now and in the future, will obey its own particular nature as a despotic and military Empire. Such compulsions are inherent in a state, and let us be clear, in any state, be it monarchical or republican. By what right do Germans demand virtues of a Russian government that they have never had from their own?

Have the rulers and cabinets of Berlin and Vienna ever embraced the party of revolution against reaction in Europe?

So, in 1852, did we not see liberal Britain – represented by both its government and by the larger part of it bourgeoisie and nobility – greet Napoleon III with joy as he came to the imperial throne in France? Lastly, today, is not that great republic the USA in a close alliance with the two greatest despotic powers of Europe – Russia and Germany?

Why then demand from a government called barbarous such virtues that are not to be found in the most civilised of governments? Is this German justice? As they know Imperial Russia has neither invented nor provoked reaction in Europe. It has neither the need nor the means of creating reaction. Reaction emerged and grew all by itself, like some magnificent native plant – its [past] history, theology, politics, law, bureaucracy, military depended on the aristocracy, and presently depends on the bourgeoisie. Imperial Russia found the latter all-powerful in Europe, and made it its ally, for its own use. Where is the European state that would have not acted in the same way? Lastly Russian diplomacy has always found European allies, and will always find allies as long as states continue. And this is what makes German patriots always despair. Innocent dreamers, they pray for an alliance of all European states against Imperial Russia.[22] This is absurd. Where states exist they necessarily entail ongoing conflict, latent war or blatant war. Is it inconceivable that Russia might find some more or less powerful ally in Europe, today Germany, tomorrow France, and who knows – sometime later – Britain perhaps?

Russian diplomacy is vastly malicious, perfidious, shrewd, and roguish, say the Germans. No doubt; but where is the diplomacy which practices some more proper or more honourable arts? If Russians diplomats have such 'exquisite' manners – certainly one might not reproach them for lacking such 'manners', they are indeed the most brutish in the entire world – one might well ask where then are there European diplomats who do not exhibit, or do not try to exhibit, these very qualities? Politics, never having any goal other than exploitation and domination, can be entirely summed up in two words: deception and brutality.[23] When it is not engaged in the one, it is necessarily engaged in the other, and too often it works in both ways together. When one looks at these matters more closely one comes to the conclusion that among the various reproaches that might be raised against the Empire of all the Russias there is not a single one that might not be *equally* – and sometimes with greater reason – addressed to every other government of one of the greater European states, and particularly to the current government of the German Empire.

But, say the Germans, what makes Russian despotism so dangerous is that it commands a race of slaves used to obeying the least wish of their masters like robots, whereas in Germany ... ah! In Germany, no doubt, you will only find people who are free, proud, and in revolt! The nobility, is it not both servile and arrogant? And the bourgeoisie is it in not a body of lackeys? Do peasants disobey the law – do they refuse to pay taxes or to deliver their sons for military servitude? So, to conclude, is it not the case that all of Germany is prostrated before its terrible Emperor?

Only the German proletariat is standing on its feet – and I acknowledge that with real pleasure. But if you have your proletariat we have our peasants in whom we place all our trust.[24] Your proletariat has as yet, never or almost never, revolted, whereas already on three occasions the Muscovite empire has been shaken by the immense revolts of our peasants; they were crushed – but they will not always be crushed. Last of all we have something that you do not have – enlightened youth. Not as enlightened as yours, but able to dedicate themselves to the popular cause, able to conspire and revolt.

So, Germans win prizes, even when it comes to servile obedience. And as for thinking, all thinking that is reactionary, obscurantist, despotic and destructive for the people and for liberty, all this is now being incubated in the ruling circles in Berlin, in the heart of that bugbear Emperor and in the powerful brain of the first chancellor of the Empire – neither citizen Karl Marx himself, nor any reasonable person in his party, can have any doubts on that score. How then can they seek to find the centre, the head of European reaction in Russia and not in Germany, in St Petersburg and not in Berlin?

We have seen that Russia's power is weaker in material terms: less rich, less well organised and with less knowledge of science as compared with the formidable power of the German Empire. Recent events have shown us the reality of its transcendent corruption; and Mr Bismarck's diplomacy leaves Russian diplomacy in the shade. We see, do we not, that those projects that most menace European liberty and independence emerge spontaneously on [Prussian] soil in Brandenburg and Pomerania. We see the great mass of Germany's people, apart from the urban proletariat, waiting only for a signal from Berlin to join a frenetic, patriotic stampede on whatever area of Europe may be indicated. So, really, why should the head and the brains of reactionary thinking be sought in Russia rather than in Germany, emanating from St Petersburg rather than from Berlin?

Such a view would exaggerate beyond any reasonable measure the intellectual capacity of Russian statesmen and would greatly underestimate the capacity of Mr Bismarck, who, in comparison with them, is a true giant. It would be an impossible assertion, an absurdity, a fantasy, a ghost, a mystical monstrosity. Political mysticism – when it has for its author someone like Citizen K. Marx, someone whose spirit is so severely rational – without doubt can only be either mystification, or a bad joke.

It was certainly a mystification and no mere joke on his part. It is his German patriotism that gives rise to his reasoning, but that is no excuse. Relying no doubt on workers' ignorance he sought to arouse among them thinking that was erroneous, but served particular German purposes: he sought to aggrandise the Russian danger beyond its real measure, to turn the attention of the good public away from the ambitious projects of his homeland. He worked to promote acceptance of Germany's conquests in the East and in the North as so many services rendered to humanity. He sought to procure from the European proletariat, if not their active cooperation, at least their sympathy for Germany's projects. If one omits personal feelings, which no doubt may also and at the same time have worked on him, this was the patriotic goal that he sought to realise. While he devoted his own life to serving the International and had been its chief promoter, he was in turn not displeased to use the IWA as an instrument for the grandeur and future power of Germany.

Something which seemed incomprehensible to me at first, was that German patriots of the International, not content with wishing to put a stop to Russia's threatening expansion to the west, also wanted to prevent its extension to the east. Indeed is it not remarkable that before even mentioning Poland, the paragraph of the *Address* just cited bitterly reproaches Russia for '*seizing as prey the mountain-fortresses of the Caucasus*'. In setting out this criticism citizen Karl Marx seems to disregard the inherent tendency of every great state to expand, spread and fortify its frontiers, to the detriment of its smaller neighbours. What else was at stake in the recent war against Denmark [of 1864]?[25] We have seen that to reach the Baltic, Germany did exactly the same thing to the detriment of the Poles and Slavs who certainly – as far as civilisation is concerned – were worth as much as the Circassian peoples. Why then should the Germans be allowed what is forbidden to the Russians? What a sample of German justice!

I would have nothing to say if Germans once and for all, without reticence, wanted to condemn outright the principle of conquest – in every instance – whatever nation was doing the conquering or whatever people were being conquered. In that case I would gladly sign with both hands every curse and condemnation that was cast against the conquests of the Russian Empire. I would have no difficulty in doing so, as conquest is a facet inherent in the state principle, and, like you dear comrades and friends, I am an enemy of [every] state, be it Russian or non-Russian. But the German patriots of the International do not share at all our hatred for the State principle; and being partisans of the State, they do not categorically reject conquest, rather they want to allow it only as the exclusive right of nations that represent modern civilisation, i.e. bourgeois civilisation (there is nothing else as yet, either in Europe or beyond).

Civilised nations' conquest of barbarous peoples: that is their principle. It is the application of Darwin's law [of evolution] to international politics. As a consequence of natural law, civilised nations, being ordinarily the stronger, must either exterminate barbarous people, or dominate them to exploit them, or, so to say, civilise them. So, in such a way, permission was given for North Americans to gradually exterminate Indians, for Britons to exploit Indians of the East, for the French to conquer Algeria and lastly for the Germans to civilise Slavs – willingly or not, in ways we are well aware of. But it should be expressly forbidden to the Russians that they should 'acquire as prey the mountain-fortresses of the Caucasus.' [...][26]

So, again, why should the German patriots of the International concern themselves with the conquest of Bukhara, Khiva [Central Asia] and a part of China by the Russians, having no patriotic interest to pursue beyond the Urals on the central Asian plateau? Ah! It is because they wish to arouse British patriotism – to consider the threat to its hitherto unchallenged domination of the Indian subcontinent – to drag them into making common cause with their anti-Slav and anti-Russian campaign.[27] In this they act patriotically no doubt, but in so doing directly contrary to the principle of justice which should inspire the International. They seek to present all this to European workers, if not as one of the final objects, then at least as one of the main aims, one which the great Association is called on to accomplish immediately.

Thus this protest against Russian power and its invasions in Asia, which, had it sprung from a general condemnation of all conquests, whoever the authors or victims might be, and had it been addressed at the same time against every state, would have been perfectly legitimate, became profoundly unjust from the moment it was directed against Russia only. Complacently, silently it passed over the crimes of other powers. This protest, I say, had as its ostensible object the cementing, within the International itself, of a particular and intimate alliance between German and British patriotism.

This emerges in the recent evidence of the discussion of this matter at the first congress of the International, held in Geneva in September 1866. The official report[28] on the session is so short that I can reproduce it in its entirety:

Eleventh question:[29] *Of the necessity of annihilating the influence of Russian despotism in Europe through the application of the principle of the rights of peoples to decide things for themselves and of the reconstitution of Poland on a social and democratic basis.*

The French delegation expressed the opinion that no vote should be taken on the matter; that congress should limit itself to a declaration that opposed all forms of despotism in every land; that discussion of such complicated matters as nationality should not be entered into. Emancipation in Russia is to be welcomed (and desired) as much as in Poland; old politics[a] – opposing one people to another – is to be rejected.[b]

British delegates expressed themselves in favour of the Polish cause, a cause that had always had the sympathies of the intelligent and democratic part of the British people. They added that the initial unity of British and French workers for common action came about when they demonstrated their feelings against Polish oppression, and this was also the first step towards the foundation of the IWA.

Nevertheless the feelings of the congress majority swung visibly towards the French proposition.

Mr Becker (the German delegate) spoke next. He regretted that congress had decided nothing on this matter. The Russian Empire is a permanent threat to Europe's civilised society,[30] and Poland would be a

a The politics of States. MB
b One can see that the report does not reproduce the speeches of each country's speakers on each matter, but only their general conclusions. On the Russian-Polish question an exception was made only for the speech of Citizen Becker. But French delegates – among whom are some of those who took an active and honourable part in recent revolutionary movements in France, in both Lyons and Paris, amongst them I will name just the most eminent member of the Paris Commune, our friend Varlin,* shot by the troops of Versailles – the French delegates I say published soon after the Geneva a collective memoir, in which their thinking was much better presented on all matters addressed by this congress. (It appeared in Brussels under the title: *Congrès de Geneva – Mémoire des Délégués Français* (Bruxelles – Parent et Fils, Editeurs - 17. Montagne de Sion. 1866). They plainly expressed their ongoing sympathy for Polish independence and freedom, and their wishes for its future emancipation on the basis of a real and complete social, political and economic emancipation – for both urban workers and for peasants. But they refused to cast out Russia as a whole, government and nation from Europe, as British and German delegates proposed. They did not believe it needful to identify the Russian Empire with the Russian people, rightly thinking that if this was done for Russia, then it should be done so equally for every other European land, which would not have turned to the advantage of the French people, governed still at the time by Napoleon III, as it is now by Versailles,* nor to the advantage of the German people above all. This was the meaning of their negative vote on this question. Mazzini, who evidently had read neither this *Memoire*, nor the official report on Geneva, took the opportunity to accuse French delegates of having refused to vote in favour of Poland. Once again this proves that he has brought into his judgements targeting the International much shallowness and bad faith. MB

barrier against it. There had been a vote to suppress permanent armies, but it would be impossible to suppress them so long as Poland was not reconstituted. He added that this Polish question was a European question, but *it was of special interest for Germany and it might be called – in some respects – a German question.* So he proposed[31] a declaration only in this sense,[32] signed by German members and others who shared these opinions, and that this should be added to the [congress] report.

The French delegation's proposition and the amendment of Mr Becker were agreed.

So it in this way the Geneva congress buried the Germans' first attempt to give the International an essentially Germanic orientation. The very manner in which this question had been posed translated this goal. If the General Council had been less preoccupied by the particular and political interests of Germany, and had had in view only human justice, only international justice, the same for all nations – which can become reality only on condition that it is applied equally to civilised peoples, as well as to those whom, from the great heights of a very bourgeois civilisation, one is pleased to call barbaric peoples – this eleventh question, which it believed should be submitted to the first congress of the International, should at least have been presented in the following manner:

Considering the necessity of destroying every European despotism, recognising that each people, large or small, powerful or weak, civilised or not civilised, has the right to decide for itself and to organise spontaneously, from bottom to top, using complete freedom, beyond all forms of influence and every diplomatic and political pretension, independently of every type of State, imposed from top to bottom by any authority at all, be it collective, or individual, be it foreign or indigenous, [it resolves and] it accepts as law and as a basis only the principles of socialist democracy, justice and international solidarity.

No doubt it would be longer, but it would be clear and just, and would have entirely excluded all equivocation. It would have been a truly international declaration of principles, not patriotic, but human; and Citizen Jean Philippe Becker, one of the founders of our great Association, would have had no need to come and declare, and avow, that this was a question that 'interested Germany especially'.

If the General Council had wished to be even more explicit, calling things by their real names, if it had wished to address the international question honestly considering its real and immediate consequences, it might have submitted the following proposal for discussion in the Geneva congress:

> [*To resolve to work*] for the abolition of States through the entirely free organisation and federation of communes and autonomous labour associations; for the necessity of destroying and abolishing European despotism in its every legal and political institution; [a despotism] which has for its perfect ideal the principle of authority and which has as its real source economic exploitation.

This, I believe, would have been the programme of the Paris Commune, and, at the same time your own, dear brothers and comrades. But in restricting the matter and in imprinting it with an exclusively Germanic tendency, the General Council of London prepared the way for an inevitable fiasco. The first congress of our great Association had to repel this bizarre proposition of the General Council, or face betraying its international character, placing itself in flagrant opposition to those principles of human justice and morality which formed the very basis of the IWA programme.[33]

The French delegates, with the lively instinct that characterises their nation, noted first the Germanic features proposed by the General Council among its cosmopolitan and philanthropic phrases. They rejected and had others reject that proposal, after which citizen J. Phil. Becker, the intimate confidante of the Germanic tendencies within the International, came to affirm their logic declaring that – in the form this matter had been posed by the General Council in London – this question was: '*of special interest for Germany and it might be called – in some respects – a German question.*' [...][34]

As for those powers and means which German patriots pretend to believe in – things which might force Germanised Prussia or rather Prussianised Germany to turn precisely against Russia, promote European civilisation and contrariwise which might prevent it from turning against socialist, democratic, liberal Europe, for the profit of heavy fisted military and bureaucratic Knouto-Germanism – German patriots have always failed to show us just what these things are. Before 1871 the Russian Empire was the leading light [of that brutalism] in Europe, whereas today it is only in its second string. The first place, the place of honour, the leading role in every reactionary initiative against western Europe belongs now, without doubt, to Prussified Germany.

It is these powers and means that the socialist-patriots of Germany lack. But they dream. Later I will speak of that lovely means of activity and propaganda that they have invented and which they call *legal political agitation*. It fills an important office in the academic economy of the new Empire: that of a safety valve. And they hope for miracles. So far they have achieved a few lovely, sterile speeches in the desert, delivered by two or three socialist deputies in the swamp of the massively bourgeois national parliament. In all this time pan-Slavist Russia and pan-German Prussia, tenderly united in a reactionary embrace, have spoken little, but acted much.

Let it not be said that, being a Russian patriot myself, I in turn strive to draw the attention of western European workers towards the harmful and ambitious activities of the new German Empire as it promotes bourgeois civilisation with the sole aim of turning it away from the very real and serious danger posed by despotic, Tsarist barbarism that today evidently threatens the cause of human emancipation and this burgeoning human civilisation of the popular masses, which is the only one which I can reasonably defer to, but which the bourgeoisie calls *revolutionary barbarism* – the foolishly and audaciously revolting mass.

Such is not my intention at all. Moreover it would be to deny myself. From my first step in public life, i.e. from 1842 to today, during thirty year of incessant activity for revolutionary socialism, I have let no occasion pass without protesting with every strength of my heart and spirit against that Russian power, against that Muscovite empire. I have been unmasking its every turpitude and brutality, be it internal or external, presenting them always in conformity with historic truth, not as the arbitrary or accidental acts of this or that person – Tsar, minister, or some other great or small state functionary (clerical, civil or military) – but as the fatal consequence of an entire system, as an inherent necessity and as the very principle of that monstrous empire. At the first Slav congress held in Prague in June 1848, in which I was honoured to take part, and in a pamphlet published in October, when Vienna was besieged by Prince Windisch-Graetz – the man who shelled Prague – I did everything I could to make Austria's Slavs understand that, infallibly, they would ruin their very just cause if they attempted to make the powers in Moscow their ally, and that its cause – that of the real emancipation of their popular masses, united in demands for national autonomy, had no more determined, more ferocious, more dangerous enemy than the Russian empire. [...] [35]

Bakunin goes on to ask how emancipation could be best facilitated.[36]

When one wishes to organise one's forces one must first carefully establish one's aims, because the fashion and form of one's organisation arises from and flows as a consequence from the nature of one's aims! And this is where we separate ourselves completely from the Socialist-Democrats of Germany. Being above all Socialist patriots and politicians they seek, through the hands of the German people, to create a great, new state, one that is called popular, republican and Germanic, which means, according to us, that they propose to establish a new prison for the German people, a fortress threatening the freedom of all neighbouring peoples. And we seek the destruction of all fortress prisons, the disappearance of all political homelands in a fraternal unity, in a free federation of peoples liberated from the yoke of states. We oppose our negative politics, calling for the liquidation of states, to their positive politics.

Given that we have such different aims, the means that we propose to the working masses must be essentially different to theirs. Wishing not the abolition but the transformation of the state, pursuing a goal that is positively political, they have to ally themselves to the *political classes*, naturally the most advanced, but bourgeois. And, on every occasion, whenever workers' associations ally themselves with the politics of the bourgeoisie, they can only become, willingly or unwillingly, their instrument. Thus it is that groupings of sections of the International in Geneva and in Zurich, which have adopted, as we know, the programme of the German Socialist-Democrats, have become conspicuous instruments of bourgeois radicalism.

We believe that this is a deplorable misdirection. We believe that the proletariat whose principle enemy – one might say single enemy – is bourgeois exploitation, the state itself, with all its force for compression and repression and *whatever form it may take*, is nothing but, at one and the same time, the consequence and the guarantor of that exploitation. We believe that the proletariat must seek every element of its strength exclusively within itself and that it must organise wholly beyond the bourgeoisie, working against both the bourgeoisie and against the state, which the bourgeoisie consider quite correctly as the last and most powerful means of their salvation.

Abolition of the state – this then is the political aim of the International, and its achievement is the *precondition* and necessary concomitant of the economic emancipation of the proletariat. But this will not be achieved all at once, because in history, as in all physical nature, nothing happens all at once. Even the most sudden revolutions, those that are most unexpected and radical, have been prepared always by a long process of decomposition and recomposition, a process that is visible or going on underground, but never interrupted and always increasing. So to, for the International, what is on the agenda is not the destruction from one day to the next of every state. To endeavour to achieve all that, just to dream of it, would be madness.

§

In another text, written at much the same time,[37] Bakunin commented on theories of German state communism. He speculated on future developments in Switzerland. He criticises Wilhelm Liebknecht for his views on the Slavs, and he regarded pan-Germanism and pan-Slavism as a pair:

> The entire history of Germany is really a struggle against the Slav race. Prussia, the keystone of the Germany's current power, is nothing but a cemetery for Slav peoples. All Germans believe instinctively that it is their mission to civilise, that is to say to germanise Slavs; an illusion that may entail bitter consequences. Despite every horror that it has committed against Slav peoples, Germany has not managed to destroy them and today this is no longer possible. The hatred that Germans have stirred in every Slav heart makes for the unity and strength of Slav peoples, and has given birth to pan-Slavism. Because pan-Slavism is nothing other than a negative product of pan-Germanism. Pan-Germanism and pan-Slavism are equally detestable, but – turn and turn again – each produces the other, they are as great enemies, and as inseparable as church and state. To destroy pan-Germanism and pan-Slavism only one means will do: to drown them both, simultaneously, in humanity as a whole through the abolition of the state. [...]
>
> Do you know how this hatred and systematic disrespect is propagated currently by leaders of the Socialist-Democratic Party among Germany's proletariat? To gather as much one has only to open an issue of *Volksstaat*, the official organ of the party, edited (under Marx's direct inspiration) by Liebknecht. In 1869 and 1870 he published a series of articles in which the following thinking was developed: that the Slavs are an essentially agricultural people, and in consequence reactionary and retrograde. We should exclude them from the International, because they remain strangers to modern civilization based on capitalist production. Having never been able to develop a bourgeoisie among themselves, they have remained outside the economic movement with its concentration of private capital in the hands of the bourgeoisie. In consequence their industry, whatever it might be, is not big industry commissioned by and producing for the world market; it is a primitive barbarous industry barely out of the fields. First of all it must take the path of bourgeois monopoly, and only in such a way could it create large scale industry – which is the agent of modern revolution – in the towns and its proletariat. There are no workers amongst them, just peasants, and we know what to do with them. We would be quite insane to embrace another one hundred million Slav peasants.

The International, in the mind of German authoritarian communists, tends evidently towards the creation of a dominant class, and in consequence a new bourgeoisie: one that might appear as a fictional collective leader, as a state, for the millions who cultivate the land, holding a new political power, that of workers in urban manufacturing industry imposing themselves as a governing class – although it would not be so in reality. I say all this would be fictional and unreal, because it is obvious that in a big state, one that is skilfully centralised, politically organised and directed, it will never be the mass of urban workers, but only their leaders who will govern the state. The state, above this new bourgeoisie or dominant class of urban workers, will in consequence be exploitative, and will engender a bourgeoisie, one less numerous but even more privileged, of directors, representatives and functionaries of a so-called popular state.

This tendency of urban workers to form an aristocracy, a new political or dominant class, is unfortunately inherent in all countries of Western Europe. It has developed over centuries, through the separation that has been made successively throughout history between the relatively more rapid development in the towns, and the relative stagnation of rural areas. It grew through the influence exerted by the bourgeoisie everywhere on the urban proletariat, and through the direct participation of the latter in every bourgeois politics up to the present day. One result has been some apparent antagonism of interest between the workers of town and country. No real antagonism has ever existed, and it exists only between aristocratic landlords and the wealthy bourgeoisie. In most countries of Western Europe the semblance of antagonism has grown through urban workers' insane, bourgeois vanity, the urban workers imagining – from the height of their grand education – that they have the right to despise peasant ignorance.

Anyone whose heart beats for the victory of the Social Revolution must deplore the harmful separation that exists between the proletariat of the towns and the proletariat of the countryside. Their every effort must work to destroy it, because we must all be aware of this: *so long as workers on the land do not give a hand to workers in the cities, for common revolutionary action, every effort of the urban revolutionaries will be condemned to inevitable fiasco.* The entire revolutionary question lies here, one must resolve it or perish.

LETTER TO CELSO CERETTI[1]

In the 1860s Italy was coming together as a new national state, reaching almost its modern borders. The kingdom replaced a patchwork of older states and destroyed the secular power of the Pope as a ruler of lands in central Italy. Only a small proportion of men had the vote.

Mazzini* had won a huge following as a proponent of Italian unity. In his view workers were: 'Sons of God and brothers all ... called upon to form one family. In that family there will always be the inequalities intended by nature ...'

Bakunin lived in Florence and Naples between 1865 and 1868 and attracted a small network of friends.[2] After the Basel congress he moved to the Ticino, not far from the Swiss-Italian border.

He criticised Mazzini's theological/political thinking[3] in *A Reply of an Internationalist to Mazzini*, he wrote: 'Where, in the plain light of day, were the atheists and the materialists yesterday? In the Paris Commune. And the idealists, and those who believe in God? In the National Assembly at Versailles. What did the men of Paris want? Through the emancipation of labour the definitive liberation of humanity. And what does the triumphant Assembly of Versailles now seek? Its final degradation under the double yoke of the spiritual and temporal force.'[4] Mazzini had portrayed the recently defeated Paris Commune as an irreligious abomination.[5] Bakunin accused Mazzini of caring not a jot that tens of thousands of working people had been massacred;[6] in various texts[7] and in *Mazzini's Political Theology and the International*, he noted that there could be no surprise that Mazzini was bitter and rancorous – through his current attitude he had lost the position of leadership in the revolutionary movement that he had enjoyed for over thirty years.[8] Bakunin was also in dispute with Engels, who asserted that he was a political heretic with his own narrow sectarian programme.[9]

Parts of a circular letter from Bakunin[10] to his friends were edited and published in November 1871 as a socialist manifesto for a national congress of Mazzini's party under the title *Agli Operai delegati al Congresso di Roma* (To the worker delegates of the Rome congress). Mazzini's proposals were accepted by most congress participants, but were rejected by Carlo Cafiero* for the IWA section in Girgenti (Sicily), by Alberto Tucci for the Naples IWA and by a delegate from Livorno, De Montel.

Bakunin wrote that Mazzini wanted changes that preserved the power of the bourgeoisie: 'the mass of the proletariat, especially the country people, were to be excluded because they would bring with them into this [Mazzini's] ideal system the barbarity of real and rude passions that might disconcert the small ideas of youth that was generous, but bourgeois from head to foot.'[11] Mazzini, wrote Bakunin, was attempting 'a coup d'état to achieve, not a revolutionary attack on the system that governs Italy today, but rather a reactionary coup against new aspirations and new ideas, which, since the fruitful and glorious insurrection of the Paris Commune, have begun to visibly agitate the youth and proletariat of Italy.'[12] Mazzini's congress was convened to reject and condemn the workers of the Commune and their insurrection.[13] Workers would be transformed into the blind and passive instruments carrying out the will of their prophet.[14] 'What Mazzini wants is to harness the proletariat to the political carriage of the bourgeoisie, something we do not want in any way.'[15] Bakunin summed up Mazzini's aims:[16]

> Let us sum up the propositions that are being put to Italy's workers:
> 1. He proposes that they should dishonour and isolate themselves from the entire world, separating themselves from revolution, issuing a solemn anathema against the Paris Commune and against the International. By way of compensation, note, they are not even to be allowed to call for a Republic, and this ambiguous phrase is to be imposed on them: 'they are not to take sides over any of the grand moral or political questions that are agitating the land'.
> 2. He proposes to workers of Italy that they should annihilate themselves abandoning their lives and thinking in favour of a Central Commission, which would be led by Mazzini exclusively. So, the consequence would be that:
> a) The Rome congress would dishonour Italy and throw it into the reactionary camp.
> b) It would create an abyss between the advanced revolutionary youth and proletariat of Italy to the great detriment of both.
> c) It would paralyse every movement – in thinking and in action –

every manifestation of spontaneous life among the working masses, given that life and motion is possible only where there is the fullest autonomy of local associations; and because the homeland organisation that Mazzini proposes has obviously no other purpose than to destroy that autonomy, to create a monstrous dictatorial power, concentrated in his own hands in Rome. Henceforth a local association would be unable to attempt any discussion, any proposition, any thinking without the permission of that heinous central authority. It would not even have the right to suggest propositions to the centre, because that right would be restricted to the thirty members of the vigilance committee alone. Still less would it have the right to express sympathy with labour associations in other countries, and not at all the right to enter into direct and immediate relations with them – given that this right would exist only for the Executive Committee, and because the International would have been stamped with an anathema by the Rome congress. What would local associations be left with? Insignificance, a void, corruption, death. They might well – as in past times – entertain themselves with some small-scale practice of mutual assistance, or with essays in producer or consumer cooperation ending up with the alienation of their organisation.

d) But by way of compensation they would be creating in Mazzini a great power, at least for one moment, since the congress has as a principle aim to transform Italy's working masses into a blind and passive instruments, for the use of the Mazzini party and to scare away free-thinking and revolutionary activity from Italian youth. This is the last word of that congress.

So now I have to ask myself – will Italian youth allow this to happen? No, it cannot do so – not without turning traitor, becoming stupid and cowardly not without condemning itself to the most ridiculous and shameful impotence, without becoming an accomplice of – at least – the criminal betrayal of home and humanity.

Cafiero sent the text of *Agli Operai* to Engels, the General Council's corresponding secretary for Italy. Engels congratulated Cafiero for writing such a useful polemic. Cafiero replied from Naples, on 29 November 1871: 'but it is Bakunin that you should congratulate and not me...'[17] By the summer of 1872, largely through Bakunin's inspiration, the IWA had thousands of new members, organised in over fifty sections.[18] Bakunin also refuted attacks that alleged he and other socialists were against the family. He replied that he was against the judicial and legal family, and for real families. 'We are also opposed to the patriarchal and legal authority of husbands over wives, of parents over children, because history teaches us that despotism in the family is the germ of political despotism in the State.'[19]

Bakunin drafted the letter below[20] in Locarno, after the death of Mazzini on 10 March 1872. It was addressed to Celso Ceretti,* a man who had collaborated with Garibaldi* and fought for the Commune. Such was the sympathy for the Commune that Andrea Costa later declared: 'Before the Paris Commune one might say that ... the International did not exist in Italy.'[21] This was an exaggeration: sections had been formed, papers published – *L'Eguaglianza*, *L'Internazionale* – strikes organised and the government had moved to arrest activists. But the statement does point to the substantial impact of this controversy and the resulting growth of the IWA. Bakunin condemned both Mazzini, and Marx and Engels, in his view they: 'always confound uniformity with unity; formal governmental and dogmatic unity with real living unity, the [latter] can result only from the completely free development of every person and every collective.'[22] Almost all of the Italian IWA would line up with Bakunin against the General Council.[23]

***

My dear friend, I received your letter at the same time as the great, sad news that Mazzini was dead.[24]

Italy has lost one of its greatest children. There can be no doubt, can there, among us all, that Mazzini, with Garibaldi, was one of the greatest Italian personalities, the second hero of the age. Intelligent, eminent, ardent of heart, indomitable of spirit, constant in his dedication, sublime: these are certainly qualities which no one would dare challenge; this is what great men are made of. And yet, at the end of this long and magnificent career, we were his convinced and irreconcilable opponents. We fought him, not in joy, but in sadness of spirit, because *our duty, our religion* – humanity's religion, one opposed to divine religion – forced us to take on the struggle.

The theological ideas of Mazzini, being armed with a freedom-killing power which is common to all divine abstraction, transformed him, in the last days of his life, into an implacable enemy of revolution and overcame revolutionary temperament and his fully Italianate and liberal nature.

He issued curses against every one of revolution's greatest current manifestations: the Paris Commune, its programme (destructive of the political State and its centralisation), its revolt and its martyred heroism which inaugurated a new era of history. Also targeted was the International, that magnificent organisation, born of the very depths of the living European proletariat, which without doubt has now become the most powerful if not the only instrument of its coming emancipation; and also free thought – its alter ego – its ideal expression, inseparable from the material emancipation of the human race; also positive science – that humane sun which is now rising and replacing the equivocal light of divine suns. Lastly, and also targeted, was that fruitful and generous alliance, based only on human solidarity and justice, that was made between the most lively and intelligent part of your youth and the Italian proletariat. Mazzini attacked everything dear and sacred to us; he sought to impose on us ideas and institutions which we detest from the bottom of our heart and with every breath in our body. We would have been cowardly traitors if we had failed to combat them with all our energy.

Despite the deep sense of sympathetic respect, of piety, which we have never ceased to feel for this sincere and sublime retrograde, this painful and unhappy struggle was forced on us, and we could not withdraw, not without betraying our cause, the cause of the final victory of the proletariat through social and economic emancipation, the great cause of humanity over divinity, over every bestiality. Mazzini, the new Joshua, struggled to stop the course of the sun. He failed. At last his great, tired and tortured soul found the rest that it failed to find in life. The great mystic patriot, the last prophet of God on earth, died, and with the last religion he took God himself to his tomb – and one hopes there will be no resurrection on this occasion.

The party of Mazzini is insufficiently strong to continue its propaganda in the future. It will be impossible for it to do so, finding no living base in the real instincts of the Italian nation – it was sustained only by the power of his retrograde genius. Undoubtedly very honourable men remain within the party: Saffo, Campanella and above all the old Quadrio, the most noble and the purest of all men that I have ever met, an old man whom I adore and who is probably damning me – and others besides, whose names I do not know. But none of them are of sufficient strength to take on the legacy of Mazzini. Such is the practical and theoretical constitution of this party, so authoritarian is it, that it needs a master to exist. With its master gone, it must dissolve. Not all at once; on the contrary, it is more likely that for a time, galvanised by the catastrophe that has just struck them, they will make another huge effort to come together. But once this hour has passed, given that there is no real link between them all, and given that their party has developed no roots in popular life, the Mazzinians cannot fail to divide up into so many small churches, which, governed by different leaders, will become little forums for political intrigue, most often opposed to one another. Many – no doubt the most lively, most sincere and the youngest – will wish to join us. No doubt you will receive them with fraternal feelings, but have a care, do not allow them to overwhelm you, and do not let them introduce their small political passions, or their deceiving and authoritarian ambitions into your compact body. Open doors wide to them, *but receive them only on condition that they accept honestly the entire programme of the IWA*.

Allow a friend to warn you of another danger. Every feeling and thinking part of Italy, seized by immense sadness, will today, in some fashion, be united in its feelings of adoration for Mazzini. Were there no other proofs than this, this alone this would suffice to show how much Italy still remains a great and living nation in the middle of general European decadence. Italy affirms and honours itself, in the value it places on one its greatest sons, one who served it with passionate devotion. What could be more natural than that in this moment of sadness and huge enthusiasm, Mazzinians and IWA supporters in Italy, bourgeois revolutionaries and socialist revolutionaries, should for a moment forget their past differences and embrace each other. But have a care; notwithstanding this patriotic reconciliation do not forget the abyss that separates your programme from that of the Mazzinians. They are sure to try, but do not let them carry you away, into plans and patterns of activity that suit their programme rather than yours, into some common practical project. Call on them to join you on your own ground, but do not follow them onto their terrain, which you could not tolerate or accept, without sacrificing and betraying that great cause – of the proletariat – that has become your own. Do not forget that there is an abyss between the bourgeois revolution that they dream about, and the social revolution that you are called on to serve today; not only in terms of goals, which are essentially different, but also in terms of means which must necessarily be in conformity with those goals. Were you to accept their plans of action not only would you ruin your socialist campaign entirely, but you would separate your country from the revolutionary solidarity that unites it today with the whole of Europe, and you would also condemn yourselves, and everyone that might follow you into this new and disastrous course, to certain defeat, to a fiasco both bloody and complete.

Always, without exception, every expedition properly planned or undertaken by Mazzini failed, that is a fact. And yet who would dare say that these attempts were not useful? Considered all together, as a system of applied practical education for Italian youth, they had an immense effect. They revived, formed, inspired and built up this patriotic youth, and made them into the true germ of Italian resurrection. This was Mazzini's great work, his immortal achievement, he shaped its youth, and thereby he created Italy *as it now is, yes, but only as it now is*: an Italy that is civilised, literate and bourgeois; political-Italy, Italy-the-state, but not social Italy, not living and popular Italy.

Mazzini's politics and ideals lacked endorsement by the people; what was missing was not the superficial or artificial endorsement that is obtained through the political suffrage, that lie and abstraction that goes by the name of universal suffrage, but rather that wider and fruitful endorsement that may be obtained only through real participation and through the spontaneous activity of living people. Mazzini's entire achievement was outside and beyond the real life of the masses. And this is why this huge activity accomplished by the greatest man of his century and achieved by two generations of Italian heroes and martyrs, seems to have been stillborn, resembling more a corpse, than an active and living body; and all that despite the transcendental idealism of the ideas that inspired it. So today the political unity that Mazzini created is more than half-dead; it has become an El Dorado for parasites and vile, preying beasts. However great a man's genius, though it may well think and reflect, though it may also inspire hundreds of youths, it cannot create life, nor life force. Life never comes from abstract thinking; the latter on the contrary always emerges out of the former, and is never more than its incomplete expression. It is only in society, in people that the secret and strength of life is found. And so long as the people have not given their sanction to the so-called national project, this project will be neither really alive, nor really national. The Italy created by Mazzini ended up fatally with the Italy of the likes of Lanza, Bonghi, Correnti and Visconti-Venosta, the Italy of Crispi, Mordini and Nicotera, and so on.[25] This result was no unhappy accident, but rather a fatal and logical necessary consequence.

No one felt this less than Mazzini. You will find the term 'people' in all his writings; it is even the second word in his famous formula 'Dio e Popolo' [God and the people] and Mazzini always declared that he would consider his work fully accomplished only when it was sanctioned by the people. But the people that Mazzini spoke of were not real people – whom one might meet in actual and living reality. His 'people' was a construct, an abstraction, one might say something theological. The popular masses, as met in living, real, natural existence, constituted in his eyes only a multitude; and for this multitude to become a people it had first to accept God's law, God's thinking, as revealed by the prophets, by men of genius crowned by virtue. So this thinking, which had the virtue of transforming a multitude into a people, is not at all an expression of the real life of that multitude. Such thinking is born outside itself, it is in consequence brought to it, and imposed on it from the outside. This is the real significance of the formula 'Dio e Popolo'. Dio [God] is thinking that is dogmatic, aristocratic, extra-popular, and in consequence against the people, something that must be imposed by full force on the multitude so that the latter, through some semblance of a spontaneous vote, should sanction it, and thereby constitute itself as a people. The people of Mazzini is a magnetised multitude, sacrificed and falsely represented in councils and constituent assemblies by men who take their inspiration not from mass interests, not from the real life of the masses, but from some political-theological abstraction, which is entirely alien to the masses.

Our principles are entirely opposed to all this. As you know, beyond positive science we recognise no source of moral truth except the real life of the people. Positive [social] science itself is nothing but the considered and methodical summary of immense historical and popular experimentation. Society – taken in the wider sense of the word – people, the *vile* multitude, the mass of workers, all these give life not only its vitality but also every part of modern thinking. Thinking that is not inspired within the people, and which is not a faithful expression of popular instinct, is, in my view, thinking that is born dead. I draw the conclusion from all this, that the role of educated and dedicated youth is not to be prophets, instructors, or doctors; nor to be creators, but only to be midwives for thinking that is nurtured by the very life of the people. And so young men who wish to serve the people should look for inspiration within the people, and not beyond them; giving a clearly expressed form to things that they carry within themselves – both unconscious and powerful aspirations.

It is material and economic emancipation that undoubtedly comes first today in popular thinking, in the hopes of the masses in every country.

The Mazzinians, from the height of their transcendental and extra-popular idealism, greatly disdain this tendency, and if they have been forced to make certain concessions lately, they do so only with a measure of disdainful condescension for the *vile brutality* of masses incapable of forgetting their stomachs, unable to live in the contemplation of the ideal. Their disdainful socialism is a snare for the masses: its beauty cannot be reached.

The Mazzinians see only a brutal expression of brutish appetites in popular aspirations. They are blinded by their own political and theological ideas; ideas which at bottom present only so many old or new chains for the people. They have not understood that if only in naïve and unconscious forms such aspirations contain this century's highest and most liberating ideals. All these desires – as they are destroyed as abstractions, fictions, or as a political, legal, poetic or theological symbols – are forcibly transformed into living and popular realities, with the ideals of truth, justice, liberty, equality, solidarity, fraternity and humanity. All such magnificent things, so long as they are remain in the form of legal, political, poetic and theological verities, serve only to consecrate and disguise the hardest and most brutal oppression and exploitation in the real life of the people; they express nothing but condemnation of the masses to eternal servitude and misery.

Throughout history, the real base and at the same time the final consequence of all these splendid abstractions, has been for the masses the exploitation of forced labour for the benefit of the privileged minorities called classes, has it not? And, since the first years of its official existence, that is to say since the [reign] of the emperor Constantine the Great, hasn't the Catholic Church been the best example of the principle of exploitation, has it not been, the most rapacious and grasping institution? And so it goes on everywhere else. Every splendour of Christian civilisation, church, state, the material prosperity of nations, science, art, poetry, and all such things – have they not been made into pretty statues for the slavery, servitude, and the misery of those millions of workers who form the true people?

What then is the people doing, when it poses this terrible economic question? It attacks the foundations, the entire civilisation that has enslaved it for so long. It compels eternal idealist thinking – be it political or theological – to fall from the sky to the ground of real life, there to be transformed into a realities that are alive and productive for the people. So, the people, as it demands daily bread, the full product of its labour, demands for itself science, justice, liberty, equality, solidarity, fraternity and in a word humanity. The consequence of all this is that the materialism that it so despised by the Mazzinians is the highest expression of real and practical idealism. This is what the Mazzinians will never understand, so long as they remain faithful to the religious and political doctrines of their master. Differences of means and revolutionary practice arise inevitably out of different precepts and goals.

The Mazzinians, infatuated as they are by ideas that come from beyond real life and popular aspirations, imagine that it is enough for them to form little conspiratorial centres in every one of Italy's principal cities – to the extent of some dozens in each of them, drawing towards them at the most a few hundred workers – for simultaneous risings to break out without warning, and for the masses to follow them. But, in the first place they have never known how to organise simultaneous risings; and furthermore the masses have always remained deaf and indifferent to their appeals, so that Mazzinian expeditions have invariably been bloody, and occasionally ridiculous. But this sequence of terrible and painful abortions and this real experience has taught them nothing, because the Mazzinians are incorrigible doctrinaires, systematically unhearing, and deaf to the cruel lessons of life. Each spring, they begin again, attributing past defeat not to the vice that is inherent in their system of thinking, but rather to some secondary circumstance, to unfavourable accidents, accidents found in every such enterprise in known history, accidents that have been overcome only in revolts that emanate out of the depths of real life.

Have Mazzinians today become more practical or clear sighted? Not at all: for proof consider that if Mazzini was not dead, they would have tried again and would have been condemned to the same outcome. They are forever destined to sterility, they are incorrigible, and they will die incorrigible.

Despite their repeated fatal outcome these ever-failing expeditions made some sense so long as there was a question of awakening and shaping the patriotism of Italian youth. This was, as I have said already, Mazzini's glorious enterprise. But once this work was accomplished, a new project was needed, failing which it would be corrupted or destroyed. The old system of Mazzini, while excellent for creating valiant youth, was no use at all when it came to producing a great and triumphant revolution. Mazzini had believed that his abstract thinking, the doctrinal enthusiasms that excited him, were sufficient to arouse the masses. Being himself dominated always by patriotic, political, poetical, theological abstract thinking; from another viewpoint being able to share, only with a more or less diminishing number of young people, his disciples, he never understood that the masses are set in motion only when they are pushed to do by forces – both interests and principles – that emanate from their own lives, and that abstractions born outside their lives can never achieve this effect. Misguided throughout his life by constant delusion, he believed to the last moment that revolutions could be made by surprise attacks, and that if some hundreds of young people spontaneously took up arms and spread into little bands all over the country that would be enough to arouse the nation.

The uprising that he planned for this spring – organised, calculated and prepared for in the same way as before – would inevitably have met the fate of previous expeditions. The consequences might maybe have been yet more cruel, because, as I see things, Italy is placed in one of those situations that are critical, one in which any error might be fatal. The revolution should neither allow itself to be dishonoured by some foolish action, nor allow that the idea of a revolutionary uprising should be made ridiculous.

What can and must save Italy from the ruinous and degraded state of prostration to which it is now descended, what must be prepared and organised so it seems to me, is not a ridiculous uprising of heroic but blind young people, but rather a *great popular revolution*. For that it is not enough if a few hundred young people take up arms, nor would it suffice to arouse the urban proletariat – what is needed is a rising of your rural areas and your twenty million peasants.

One might say that throughout Italy's social and political life, since Italy began its historic existence, since ancient Roman times even, since the middle ages, changing civilisation has been concentrated in the towns. From a moral and political viewpoint your rural areas have formed a great, silent, arid desert in the midst of which your towns and cities, exuberant with intelligence, rich with activity and vigour, had the splendour of brilliant oases. This non-participation of the countryside in the prodigious life of your urban areas was one of the principal causes of your country's decadence. In this century, the glorious resurrection of Italy was the exclusive product of your cities, and rural areas were almost entirely excluded. So until this moment your peasants, roughly twenty million Italians, have remained outside the historic life of Italy or have participated only as victims or serfs.

This is the great danger. The entire future of your country depends on which side your peasants will support in the coming revolution. Up to now they have remained passive and have suffered almost without resistance the fate and the governmental forms that cities were so good as to impose on them. And, as you know better than me, your peasants, as those elsewhere and maybe even more than elsewhere, dislike the town. Cities having been, more or less, politically revolutionary, the peasants have been of necessity reactionary, not so much indeed because of the malicious influence that priests exert over them, but rather because of their hatred against the town, something quite natural and, let us say it, quite legitimately nourished both by historical tradition and by the sequence of their more recent experience. Peasants detest the bourgeoisie.

Now that the city proletariat awakens and organises in revolutionary fashion in Italy, as elsewhere throughout Europe, the countryside, the compact mass of peasants, has become reaction's sole lever and means of salvation. So long as it is not removed from the hands of reaction, so formidable is this lever that it will always ensure our defeat. So then, the entire question of the triumph of the revolution reduces itself to this: *how to arouse, how to revolutionise the peasants?*

My friends, is it not clear to you, as much as to me, that Mazzini's magical and mystical formulas, which have lost whatever power that they might previously have had on the youth of Italy, are today insufficient to excite a rising not only of the peasants but also of the urban proletariat? Both rural and city people thirst for emancipation. But in reality what is called *political freedom* liberates only the bourgeoisie. And this sort of freedom – if it were organised in a great centralised State, even if it were a republican state such as the one that Mazzini desired, and which Mazzinians still desire, such freedom would be very costly. State spending falls in the last analysis on working people, so it follows that political freedom puts a new straw on the camel's back of the people, overburdened, and unable to carry more, as General Garibaldi has said very well. This is so-called political liberty, as it is dubbed by the Mazzinians; and despite so many cruel deceptions, they still do not refrain from using it to arouse the popular masses, without whose powerful cooperation no revolution would be possible. So this political liberty means nothing but new servitude, new misery for these masses.

Real emancipation can be won for the people only by social revolution. And, as with everything that is active and alive, this revolution necessarily will have two sides: a positive and a negative. On the negative side is the destruction of things as they are, of all that ruins and oppresses popular life; the popular camel will have the particular task of ridding itself of the ever increasing burden, one which has been weighing it down for centuries. And this burden itself has a dual nature: on the one side, it has fiscal and political aspects which inhibit the spontaneous development, the free movement of the masses, and, on the other it features excessive burdens and ruinous taxation – the burden of the state. Another part of the burden, is the economic exploitation of the labour of the people by a capital that is monopolised and is in the hands of the very high and very rich bourgeoisie. At bottom both parts of this burden are inseparable, because the state, being necessarily hostile, conquers and breaks up human solidarity on the outside, whilst on the inside it seeks only to consecrate, legitimate and regularise the exploitation of the labour of the people for the benefit of the privileged classes.

So then the negative task of the social revolution is the overthrow of the state and of current financial monopolies. How far will this revolution go? In theory, through its logic, it will advance a very long way. But practice always lags behind theory, because it is subjected to a host of social circumstances, which all together constitute the real situation of a country, and of necessity they influence every really popular revolution. It is the duty of leaders not to impose their own fantasies on the masses, but to go as far as one may, as permitted and commanded by popular wishes and instincts. The positive objective of social revolution is the [re]organisation of the new – more or less emancipated – society.

And in this area too, the ideal is clearly put on the agenda by theory. As a political organisation, there is the spontaneous and thoroughly *Free Federation of Communes and Workers' Organisations.* As social organisation, there is the *collective appropriation of capital and land by organised workers.* In practice, so long as it is the real desire of the population that decides things and not leaders' arbitrary will, or their fantasies and aversions, it will be for each section, each province, each Commune and each Workers' Organisation to see what it can [do] and what it wants [to do].

To my mind one of the greatest concerns of those who today find themselves at the head of the revolutionary socialist movement in Italy should be finding and settling, as much as one can do today, at least the principal lines of the plan and above all of the programme of the coming revolutionary rising, without losing sight of our ideals, which will guide us, much as the pole star guides sailors – towards forming a possible and practical programme. By ideals I understand justice, complete freedom, the most complete social and economic equality, universal solidarity and human fraternity. Of necessity one must keep in mind the different circumstances of each of your provinces, as well as the place in society of some of your classes, but not of all of them.

You would inevitably achieve nothing if you sought the satisfaction of all your classes. The interests of the governmental and upper classes are too opposed to those of the lower layers to allow any possibility of conciliation between them. So, I believe, all those classes which directly or indirectly are interested in the preservation of the current State should be sacrificed without pity; so the entire nobility and all the great commercial, financial and industrial bourgeoisie, all the great owners of land and capital, and in large part also the middling bourgeoisie: those whose children today fill up the ranks of the army and bureaucracy as officers and functionaries. In Italy as elsewhere, this middling bourgeoisie is a stupid and cowardly class, supporting every form of corruption, every iniquity and despotism.

There are four social layers in Italy to be considered in my opinion. Above all there are two principal and most numerous layers which form the real basis of every nation: the proletariat of the urban and the rural areas. It is they who will largely shape things and they who will define the real tendencies of the coming revolution. Do I need to say that both are by necessity, eminently and instinctively socialist?

Irrefutable evidence for this is seen everywhere, each new day the eagerness of your urban workers to promote the International and gather beneath its banner, wherever there are a few people of good will, proves as much. Even the Mazzinians have to acknowledge this. Today, with much leftish rhetoric no doubt, we see them putting on a show of badly adulterated socialism. But being idealists, they can never be serious. The socialist spirit that has taken hold of the working masses is too powerful to be further disregarded. This broad ideal, as I have just defined it, has already become the goal of a strong tendency within the urban proletarian masses. The ideal is very explicit and might advance a good long way, even if it relied on itself alone: what most inspires it is the passion for justice and equality. It desires that all should work equally, in the same social and economic conditions; that the world should become a world of workers, that there will be no more 'gentlemen'; that in the future none should grow fat on the labour of others. It looks forward to each person enjoying the complete product of their particular labour.

Mazzini himself, in his last writings, recognised the legitimacy of this demand, one first inscribed in the programme of the International. But do you know what this demand means? Nothing less than the appropriation – one way or another – of every form of capital by workers' organisations. Because, so long as capital is monopolised, and remains personal property in the hands of individuals, and for the same reason as long as workers' organisation are deprived of capital, nothing can prevent capitalists from first taking a share for their own profit, a part – always the greater part – of the product of this labour. The interest of capital, every premium that it accumulates through various industrial, commercial and financial speculations, all these add up to iniquitous deductions, because in the end, however many [forms of] capital you might join together, no children will result. The moment that workers' organisations are delivered from subjugation to capital, which means that they themselves will own capital, they will have no need to pay for the services of foreign capital; the latter will no longer earn interest, and their current owners will have to eat them up pretty quick. The emancipation of labour cannot mean anything other than the expropriation of capitalists and the transformation of every necessary capital into the collective property of workers' organisations.

As for the political ideals that are today contained in the instincts of the urban proletariat, they seem to me to be divided into two trends, trends that are opposed and somewhat contradictory. On the one hand, urban workers, however uneducated they may be, easily understand the universal solidarity of workers, being by virtue of their trades detached from the local spirit that imprints the culture of rural areas. They find their home in their particular trade rather than in the land in which they are born. Urban workers are more or less cosmopolitan. On the other hand, doubtless under the influence of the bourgeois doctrines that they have been subjected to for so many years, they are not so opposed to state centralisation. Today British and German workers dream of centralisation in a big state, but they add a proviso, that this should be a very popular state, a state of workers; for me this constitutes a utopia, because every state and every centralist government necessarily implies aristocracy and exploitation even if of the governing class alone. Never forget that 'State' means domination, and that human nature is so established that all forms of domination always and inevitably transform themselves into exploitation.

The mass of peasants, in contrast, are naturally federalist. Peasants are passionately attached to land. They detest from the bottom of their hearts the domination of the city and of every form of exterior government that imposes its will and thinking. In Britain and Germany, the coming revolution necessarily takes the form of an urban revolution, tending to a new domination of town over country. The resulting danger for the revolution will not be so great in Britain, except for Ireland,[26] because a class of peasants does not really exist. Rural workers are all wage-earners, paid by the day much like urban workers. Things are very different in Germany, where there is a mass of peasants, many of them peasant landowners like those in France. This immense mass is today the great fortress of reaction, the formidable axis on which Mr Bismarck's lever can turn, a menace to the liberty of all of Europe; and this came about through the fault of the bourgeoisie, which on three different occasions repelled and repressed the spontaneous uprising of German peasants – firstly in 1520, then in 1830, then in 1848. So a dangerous and formidable opponent will confront this abstract German socialism.

You will not fall into the same error as the Germans. You will not be content to build urban socialism; you will not neglect your rural proletariat's natural and weighty spirits and aspirations, those of twenty million peasants. You will not condemn your revolution to certain defeat. Should I tell you my entire thinking? Well, I believe that you have a much more real and powerful revolutionary element in the country than in the town. Doubtless there is more education among the workers of the town. Ignorance sadly is very widespread amongst you. But it is much greater in the country than in the town. There is more thinking, more revolutionary conscience in the town, but in the country there is a more natural power.

Despite priests, who have only a superficial influence, your country people are naturally revolutionary. And, on this point I have to say what I think of propaganda in favour of free-thinking [atheism]. Such propaganda is excellent having in mind your more or less educated youth and for the reorientation of its spirit and practical tendencies. But it has no effect on the people as a whole. Popular religion is not so much the effect of theoretical abstraction, but rather a practical protest against the narrow limits imposed on popular life, against its misery and servitude.

Your peasants are socialists of necessity. From a revolutionary viewpoint, one might say that they are in the most excellent position – I mean that they are in detestable economic circumstances. Perhaps with the exception of Tuscany, where share-cropping is widespread (I do not know of the economic situation for peasants in the Romagna) – the peasants in Piedmont, Lombardy and the whole of the old kingdom of Naples are weighed down by such misery, their existence has become so impossible, that to me it appears that a revolution starting in rural areas is inevitable; even if it is not directed by anyone. Two years ago, didn't the peasants rise up by themselves on account of the law 'del macinato'?[27] Note how sensible their instincts were. In many places, in Parma for example, they burnt their mortal enemy, official records. The auto-da-fé of every paper – civil, criminal, officious and official – seems to me to be one of the most honourable means of a frankly socialist revolution. It is much more human and much more radical than the Jacobin fashion of cutting off heads.

Imagine if the cry echoed throughout the Italian countryside: 'peace for the cottages, war on the mansions and castles' as in the great peasant uprising in Germany in 1520; and the more explicit: 'Land to the peasants, to all – and only to all – who work it with their own hands!' Do you think that there are many Italian peasants who would stay quiet? And with burning a lot of records you would have a social revolution done and dusted.

Thus, expropriation of the owner of capital, transformation of capital into collective property of workers' organisations, and organisation of universal solidarity – this is the ideal of the urban proletariat. Complete local freedom and the takeover of all land by rural workers is the ideal of the country proletariat.

These two ideals might reconciled very well by the principle of a Free Federation of Communes and Workers' Organisations, boldly proclaimed by the Paris Commune one year ago. One could trace an outline programme of revolution quite quickly if only two social layers were concerned.

But there are two other layers that you should keep in mind – firstly because their circumstances are becoming more and more miserable but also because they are becoming forcibly more revolutionary and being both very numerous they exert real influence on the people – these are the small bourgeoisie in the towns and the class of very small landowners in the country. Being both completely disorientated these two classes have no real programme. Through social vanity and tradition they are somewhat attached to the privileged classes, but being more and more menaced and sacrificed in their real lives and circumstances they are by instinct shifting towards the proletariat. Nonetheless they still retain some interests which might suffer if socialist principles – extricated as may be from the aspirations of the masses – are applied with too much logic or determination. What is needed today is the reconciliation of interests with aspirations, without sacrificing the latter.

Federalism and socialism – these are the two principle elements of the coming revolution. This is the absolute opposite of the Mazzini programme. Is it not clear that any conciliation between the two parties, on the terrain of the Mazzini party, is impossible? You cannot take part in their expeditions: firstly because they are always fatally condemned to fail, secondly and above all because your goals and your means are absolutely different. You want the definitive and complete emancipation of Italian society, with a new organisation, or reorganisation on the basis of work, work that is both free and collective, from the bottom to the top, through the path of federation and natural organisation. They, on the contrary, dream of a new round of subjection for this society, yoked to a grand unitary state. You want to prepare and organise a mighty popular rising, one that will sweep away everything opposed to it, breaking everything that resists it, even making resistance impossible. And being incapable of organising, or even of dreaming of such an uprising, these Mazzinians will continue to fritter themselves away in ridiculous expeditions.

[The next few paragraphs, omitted here, discuss Agostino Bertani and prospects for the leadership of the Mazzini party.]

If, as I presume Bertani becomes the head and the secret director of the enterprises of the Mazzini party, what is the position that you revolutionary socialists – serious partisans of proletarian emancipation – should adopt in relation to it? It would be an error to disregard it, it would also be an error to make an ally of it – and in my view a greater one. You are not utopian theorists. You wish to organise a powerful and active party, one capable of transforming your beautiful Italy into a country of honour for all, with happiness, justice, equality and liberty, in as brief a time as possible. You will organise for action, in consequence you will not be allowed to disregard any of the elements which constitute current reality. You need to recognise easily those erroneous [proposals] that you have to combat, and also those elements who, without being entirely with you, are forced to become, up to a point, and through a period of transition, in some ways your allies, your friends; since [you both] have to fight the same enemies. The Mazzini party, although in different fashion, and for reasons that are not your own, are bitter enemies of this government, a government which fears you much more than them. It is beginning to persecute you throughout Italy, and soon, I believe, it will persecute you with even greater vigour. Up to a point, you will be forced to march in parallel with them, to keep them informed of all your activities, and not only to let them act, but on occasion, on rare occasions doubtless, observing the greatest prudence, to indirectly support them, to the extent that as you do so, you hope to weaken and demoralise the current government, henceforth your most disagreeable, powerful and bitter enemy. In every struggle of the Bertani or Mazzini party – of the bourgeois republicans – against the government, you will no doubt abstain most often and as much as you may do, without morally and materially killing yourselves; but whenever you are forced to abandon this apparent passivity, you will do so, it hardly needs saying, only to take their part against the government.

You will therefore be forced to organise and march in parallel with them, to be able to take advantage of every one of their movements to promote and achieve your own aims. But you will, will you not, carefully guard against allying yourselves with them to the point of becoming mixed together. You will never allow them to penetrate your organisation. They would want to enter it only to corrupt it, only to make it shy away from its goal, only to paralyse it or dissolve it – they might not have such [deliberate] intentions, and they might work indirectly for their goals, but by so much is their nature the opposite of yours. So to me it appears absolutely necessary that all your organisations – be they public or secret – should remain entirely outside those of Bertani or Mazzini.

***

And now a word about your organisation in the Romagna, and about IWA sections in Italy in general. Do you believe that it could hold out and resist, as a public and legal organisation, in the face of persecution by your government? The persecution of the International is international and universal – one can no longer doubt that, nor expect anything else after the defeat of socialist and republican France. Imperial Germany, Bismarck's Germany is of course tenderly united with Russia's Tsarist knout, at the head of the [forces of] reaction. Bismarck seems to do little himself, but he gets others to act. He often [directs] the internal politics of other governments, without them being aware of it; and there is no doubt that there is a positive entente against the International among all of them. In Europe today the International is the most powerful and one might say, the sole representative of revolution. In France, Italy, Belgium, Germany they are raging against it. If things continue as now Switzerland will soon go the same way. In the first place it is too weak to resist long the power and imperious pressure of the major states surrounding it and they would happily divide it up between them. It should also be said that the so-called radical bourgeoisie, which now governs in greater part the cantons of Switzerland, will not be put out if the diplomatic pressure of the great states forces it to [join] this rage against the International. In Europe today it is only Britain that can provide a refuge for the IWA. An aristocratic revolution, a reversal of the constitution, would be needed to chase it away. And workers' organisations already form some real power, to the point that political parties – Tories, Whigs and Radicals – are forced to compound with them. But the avowed and public existence of the IWA is under terrible threat in every other country of continental Europe. Nowhere has it achieved a concentration of force sufficient to allow it to become a threat in its own right. I speak not of tomorrow – I am certain that tomorrow belongs to us – but of today – everywhere, except perhaps in Spain.

The letters that I receive from many places in that country, tell me in effect that socialist workers in Spain[28] are very seriously organised. And not just [urban] workers; socialist ideas are happily widely spread among the peasants of Andalucía too. They are ready to take a very active part in the coming revolution with the firm intention of giving it a frankly socialist character, on this occasion giving a hand to political parties, but without dissolving themselves into these parties. All of us are anxiously awaiting the outcome of these anticipated key events. All of southern France is organising, even Paris, despite every law that is voted by the rurals [the government of country reaction] in Versailles. And this organisation is accomplished by our allies, rather than by people acting for London,[29] whose preaching and propaganda in reality adds up to nothing.

If revolution triumphs in Spain, it will naturally form a mighty platform for European revolution. If it fails the reaction that menaces us everywhere will be even stronger. But revolution, even if it does triumph in Spain will doubtless have consequences in other European countries; there will be a reactionary revival in France, Belgium, Germany, Italy and in Switzerland (as a consequence of the centralising reform which threatens to kill the cantonal liberties of the country). And even if the Versailles government is not capable of repressing revolution in the south of France itself, it should not be forgotten that Bismarck's army still occupies north-eastern

France. I do not doubt that an entente between Bismarck and your Italian government is already in place and in the last round of negotiations the possible success of the revolution in Spain was not forgotten, and not least because all this directly interests your reigning dynasty.[30]

Finally, throughout Europe and above all in Italy I foresee socialists and every IWA organisation suffering severe persecution. Recent events in Milan prove this. The *Martello*[31] is basically a journal that never permitted any eccentricity. On the contrary it very deliberately chose a very prudent and moderate form. There is a campaign against the International, this is proved by your governments' systematic confiscations [of its editions], by orders for the arrest of its editor and its director, by menaces issued against the young people who are members of the 'Circolo operaio' [Workers' Circle] and by threats of 'domicilio coatto'.[32] I believe such actions will not be restricted to Lombardy alone, their application to the whole of Italy is already planned. I do not doubt that soon very arbitrary and energetic measures will be taken to dissolve and annihilate your *fascio operaio* [Workers' association]. So how will you act? A rising? It would be magnificent if you could hope for it to succeed. But can you hope as much? Are you well prepared, and solidly organised for all this? Are you certain that the whole of the Romagna – the peasantry included – will be with you? If yes, take up the gauntlet that has been thrown down. But if you are not confident – I am speaking not of illusions, but of confidence based on positive facts – then have a care, have the strength to restrain your indignation; avoid a battle which would only end in your defeat. Remember that a new defeat would be fatal, not only for you, but for the whole of Europe. I believe one must wait for the outcome of movements in Spain, and in due course, when the movement there takes on a wider and more frankly revolutionary character, then it will be time for a general rising, not just in the Romagna, but in every part of Italy that is ready for a revolutionary movement.

And whilst waiting, what should be done if your public organisation is forcibly dissolved? It must be transformed into a secret body, one with a character and a programme that is more revolutionary than the one you have been able to give it hitherto...

No doubt it is very desirable that you should seek to preserve a public and legal organisation for the sections of the Romagna, and for others that constitute the *fascio operaio*. But if governmental persecution forces the dissolution of these labour bodies, as political organisations, you will be forced to transform them into secret organisations, or condemn yourselves – both yourselves, your friends and your cause – to wholesale destruction. For anyone who knows you, as I have begun to know you, such thinking is inadmissible. I would go further, even in the case that you managed to safeguard the existence of your public sections through crafty and energetic effort, I believe that sooner or later you would have to realise the necessity of creating nuclei within them: those who are most energetic and most intelligent, in a word the most intimate. Such nuclei, linked intimately amongst themselves, and linked with their kindred that might organise now or in the future in other parts of Italy, would have a dual mission. Firstly they would form the lively and inspirational soul of that immense body called, in Italy and elsewhere, the International Workers' Association, further they would take in hand matters that cannot be discussed in public. They would form the essential bridge between propaganda for socialist theory and revolutionary practice. I believe I have said enough for persons as intelligent as you and your friends.[33]

It is out of concern for this intimate organisation, and for the whole of Italy, that I have greatly wished that the congress of Italian democracy, which you and your illustrious General [Garibaldi] had called for, should meet as soon as possible. For all socialist democrats, for all revolutionary socialists of Italy, it would be the most magnificent occasion, [and an opportunity] to allow the most serious [activists] to get to know each other and to build an alliance on the basis of a common programme. Naturally this secret alliance would accept into its ranks only a small number of the surest, most devoted, intelligent and best persons, because it is quality, not quantity that is needed. Your revolutionary practice should, in my view, be distinguished from that of the Mazzini party, by this: you have no need to recruit soldiers to form little secret armies, capable of undertaking small and sudden actions. The Mazzini party have to act so, because they wish and believe it possible to make revolutions without the people. You want only a popular revolution, and in consequence you have no need to recruit an army: your army is the people. What you should form is a staff [état-majors], a well organised and inspired network of leaders of popular movements. And for this it is not at all necessary to have a large number of individuals initiated into secret organisations.

So one might say I was very annoyed to see the General [Garibaldi], tired by differences of democratic and socialist opinion in Italy, conclude that he should renounce taking part in the congress, or postpone it for an indefinite period, until such time as there might be a meeting of minds. I believe that if you were to wait so, you would wait a long time, for ever, and you might all die before that absolute harmony was achieved. My dear friend, let me say that such harmony is unachievable and even undesirable. Harmony means the absence of struggle, the lack of life, death. In politics it means despotism.

Consider all history and convince yourself that in every era, and in every place, wherever there is lively development and exuberance, in thought, in free and creative action, there is dissension, social and intellectual struggle, the struggle of political parties, and that it is precisely in the midst of struggles and by grace of them that nations have become happier and greater in the human sense of the word. Such struggle existed barely or not at all in the great Asian monarchies – but then there was also a complete absence of human development. Consider on the one side the Persian monarchy, with its innumerable disciplined troops and on the other side free Greece, barely federated, continually tormented by struggles of parties, peoples and ideas. Who won? Greece! What was the most fertile period in Roman history? The time of the struggle between the aristocrats and plebs. What brought about the glory and grandeur of Italy in the middle-ages? It was certainly neither the empire nor the papacy. It was the era of municipal freedom, of internal struggles of opinions and parties. Napoleon III ended up by putting internal struggles in France to sleep, and thereby killing them off. Let the destiny of your great homeland preserve you from times where everyone is calm and in agreement – such times are deathly.

Consider how varied opinions may be. Many Italian democrats are frightened by the divisions which have arisen over the last two years within the Democratic Party and see therein the signs of that party's decadence. I, on the contrary, see signs of resurrection in all this, a guarantee of its vital and fertile power. The 'consorteria'[34] is not divided, but does that make it more alive? So long as it was still divided into certain [illegible word] it preserved signs of life. But today, now that some sort of touching unity has been established within its circles, now that agreement has taken over the left parliamentary party, now that it is only divided by personal ambition and interest, do you not feel that this official Italy is completely dead? Well, a few years ago, Italian democracy, with everyone asleep, with everyone in harmony [illegible word] was also at death's door. Socialism brought it back to life and thereby aroused within it an immense development of thinking, of diverse trends, and in consequence of internal struggle, that great and creative educative force ...

Uniformity is death – and I will never tire of repeating it. Diversity is life. Disciplined unity kills nations, within whatever circles it may be established; it comes only with effects that are detrimental to life and creative spontaneous thinking. What we all want is living unity, one that is really powerful, one that is created by freedom, through free expression, in lively diversity; expressing itself in struggles, as every living force looks for harmony and equilibrium. I can understand how a General of a regular army division adores the deathly silence that discipline imposes on a crowd. Your Generals, our Generals, the people's Generals have no need for the silence of slavery; being used to living and leading in the midst of squalls they are never so tall as when they face those squalls. Popular life, as it loses its shackles, is punctuated by squalls – only they can blow away the established world of inequality. We can never do enough to free up such lively passions.

To return to the congress of Italian democracy, I have to confess that I have neither hoped nor even desired that it might produce conciliation, or an impossible harmony between sincere revolutionary socialists and opinions of those who believe that they are 'advanced', or call themselves so, between freemasons: Campanella, Stefanoni, Filopanti and their like. Such a conciliation, were it ever to be accomplished, would in my opinion be the greatest disaster that could affect Italy, because, according to the eternal rules of logic, $+1$ and $-1 = 0$. Such an arrangement would annihilate the living cause of the people, for the benefit of a few bourgeois alone – doctrinaire talkers with empty phrases. Your congress would be, like all congresses, a Tower of Babel, but it would allow you the opportunity of recognising your own – the revolutionary socialists of all Italy – of organising a serious minority, well organised and powerful by themselves, because as they express aspirations and popular interest in this congress they alone would represent the people.

Dear friend, now that I have expressed most sincerely my idea of the only Italian revolution that appears desirable and possible, I shall respond to your other questions:

1. I believe, I am firmly convinced that the General is wrong to doubt the political honesty of that poor Terzaghi.[35] I believe I have already given my opinion on the matter. His mind is overheated, his heart is a little vain and light. [A passage on particular persons is omitted].

2. I greatly regret that the General should have placed *Campana* of Naples alongside *Proletario* of Turin. *Campana* is a much more serious journal. [A passage on *Campana* and politics in southern Italy is omitted].

3. Lastly, I come to the third question, which concerns me personally. The attacks of the Germanic-Hebrew sect[36] are nothing new to me. Since 1848, in German journals, they have attacked me publically in the most despicable manner, alleging that Herzen and I were in the pay of some pan-Slavist and Tsarist committee. Herzen and I fought the Tsar throughout our lives. As for me, since the beginning of my career I have seen it as my special duty to combat pan-Slavism – and no one knows this better than these German Jews. But slander is something normal for them. Hitherto I

disdained to reply.³⁷ It seems that they want to force me to break my silence, I will do so but very grudgingly, because I find it very repugnant to introduce personal matters into our great cause, and to me nothing is so disgusting as to make people concern themselves with my own person. I have done all that I could to prevent my name³⁸ intervening in the polemic about the International between Italian journals. For this reason I stopped the publication of my writings against the Mazzini party, and when Mr Engels attacked me indirectly, in the reply to Mazzini, I still kept silent... Now, they attack me with vile slander. At the same moment that I received your letter, I received another from Milan and a third from Naples telling me the same thing more or less. I then conceived the idea of publishing in the Italian papers a letter of defiance, addressed to the plotters on the General Council. I will do so if my patience expires. But before doing so, since it is a matter of personalities and not of principles, I want to try conciliation one last time. I will first of all address a private letter to the General Council, and I will send you a copy. And if they do not send me a satisfactory answer, then I will force them to explain themselves in public.

In the meantime I will send you the speech I made in Bern on Russia, and I will give you a correct idea of what they call my pan-Slavism. As for you, dear friend, I shake your hand fraternally, I thank you for your intelligent and noble confidence, and it is with complete sincerity that I reply to that confidence
Your devoted,
B

(À propos the lovely resolutions of your last conference, a misunderstanding has occurred. Naturally, in the third [resolution] concerning the distinction that exists between the General Council and the Committee of the Bernese Jura, the latter never thought of setting itself up as an alternative to the General Council. Its status is the same as that of your Bologna Consolato. It has never pretended to be more than a committee of the Jura region, and it has no pretension to impose its authority on any other region. It itself recognises the General Council, but only within the strict limits of its attributes, as established by general statutes.)³⁹

LETTER TO TÓMAS GONZÁLEZ MORAGO

[Second half of a letter dated 21 May 1872, in Locarno.¹]

This letter was written to Tómas González Morago,* an active promoter and leader of the Spanish IWA, also involved in the Alianza de la Democracia Socialista,*² a small group of revolutionary socialists inspired by Bakunin and by the Geneva Alliance.*

The text below, the second half of the letter, considers the relationship between a mass organisation, based on workplace solidarity, and another narrower revolutionary socialist organisation, based on ideas and intimacy between friends or brothers.

In the first half of this letter Bakunin sets out his views on a revolutionary socialist organisation and its development. He argued that it should be small and select. New members should be accepted only if there was unanimous agreement that they were serious, seeking neither career nor glory. An organisation like this should promote collective action and intelligence, and develop some potent solidarity. It needed complete transparency and honesty – in matters both political and personal and it would avoid gossip. Bakunin believed that there was some power in imagination. In a letter to Becker* he wrote 'You know better than me that some imagined beings are very useful, and should not by any means be disdained'. The 'idea' of a revolutionary body had some impact – even if it had in fact only a quarter of reality.³

When Bakunin speaks of the 'Alliance' he is thinking of an organisational *type*: a non-public organisation. Given the widespread lack of basic political rights in these times, public organisation often meant either a servile organisation that took some care not to offend the state or an organisation that was easily repressed. Non-public organisation was a necessity to help protect activists, and to provide a space where radical alternatives could be elaborated.

The IWA attempted to organise in public, but in much of Europe even basic trade-union rights were lacking. The Spanish IWA Federation was banned in January 1872. In April 1872, the Federation's congress in

Saragossa declared: 'Social war, war between rich and poor, between lords and slaves has been declared by the current government, representing the Spanish bourgeoisie. Workers, let us organise, form ranks, ready arms and prepare for a struggle that will come, in the near or not so near future.'

The Spanish IWA was portrayed as an instrument of a Swiss-based Alliance.[4] In July 1872 Engels threatened the council of the Spanish IWA: if it failed to denounce the Alliance and promptly submit to the General Council's demands, it would itself be denounced as having betrayed the International in the interests of a secret society which was both foreign and hostile to the IWA. The Spanish council replied that it was accountable to its membership.

These times saw wider and narrower forms of labour organisation and each might encounter openings or repression. The relationship between these forms might vary depending on circumstance. René Berthier asks what the difference in these forms might be in a libertarian and in a Marxist perspective and suggests this essential difference: 'in the Social-Democratic relationship type, the division of labour between mass organisation and political organisation is arrived at by the subordination of the latter to the former, only the political organisation having the competence to develop strategies and a programme; the mass organisation is considered to be like a "school" in which future member of the party are formed. The Alliance, in contrast, saw itself as an organic extension of the mass organisation and expressed only its implicit programme; between the two there was only a difference of degree, this is what Bakunin meant when he wrote that "the programme of the Alliance is the elaboration of the programme of the International. The objective of Social-democracy was the conquest of political power by the party, whilst preserving this division of labour."'[5]

Bakunin sought influence, and sometimes worked for and through secret organisations. These narrower forms might seek a leadership of ideas, but not one that allowed or worked for any form of privileged status in a new society. Rather the opposite – members of a revolutionary socialist organisation were to foreswear any role that gave them privilege.

Questions remained: how were narrower forms of political organisation to be made accountable? And to whom should they be accountable? No definitive answer is obvious.

The practice of the Alliance in Geneva might suggest one means of reconciling differences between rival ideological tendencies working in a broader organisation: a public discussion of differences.[6] Bakunin describes public mass discussion in Geneva in preparation for the Basel congress in 1869. (No such public discussion appears to have ever occurred in the London IWA.) Bakunin accused his enemies of preferring intrigue in committees, rather than public discussion; in contrast the Spanish IWA was a thoroughly democratic organisation.

***

The Alliance and the International are in no way enemies, as the Marxian synagogue of London would have everyone believe. The Alliance is, on the contrary, the necessary compliment of the International. Without this compliment the whole International would be transformed – as the Marxian coterie now evidently intends – into some sort of monstrous international state, with a very authoritarian government, with the dictatorship of Marx, becoming a docile instrument to promote their projects and ambitions, and consequently something very much in opposition to the real liberation of the popular masses.

But the Alliance and the International, although they both seek the same final goals, follow, at one and the same time, different paths. One has a mission to bring together the labour masses – millions of workers – [reaching] across differences of trades or lands, across the frontier of every state into one single compact and immense body. The other, the Alliance, has a mission to give a really revolutionary direction to these masses. The programmes of the one and the other, without in any way being opposed, are different, in keeping with the extent of the development of each. That of the International, if it is taken seriously contains in germ – but only in germ – the whole programme of the Alliance. The programme of the Alliance is the elaboration of the programme of the International.

If the founders of the International had given this great Association a particular positive doctrine – [be it] philosophical, political, or socialist – they would have committed a great error. They would have founded a very small association, a sect, but not an armed camp for the proletariat of the entire world [set] against the exploiting and dominant classes. Today, is there one philosophical, political, socialist idea that might have some capacity to unite proletarians of every country in their millions under its banner? One might at best, unite a few thousand with one positive doctrine – and then what? When Mazzini* said: 'interest divide, but ideas unite,' he was entirely correct. Yes, interests do divide the bourgeoisie, but ideas do not bring them much in the way of unity. Things are otherwise with the proletariat, it is interests, or rather one great interest – bread and emancipation, the same in every country whatever the degree of its civilisation or moral or intellectual development – which has the capacity to bring about one compact mass. There are exceptional moments – those very rare moments of history when the masses are enlivened by the bubbling up of revolutionary passions – then they rise to reach ideas, [but otherwise], as for ideas themselves – that is to say in terms of the development of theories – let us recognise [reality] my dear, that in their everyday lives, everyday worries bare down on the masses; they are weighed down by privation, compulsory work and, I say, if they are not hostile towards ideas, they are quite indifferent. There is no need to reproach them, they are kept in a crass ignorance that is cultivated systematically by every government for the interest of the privileged. They are crushed by brutalising work and hunger. I think that the profound indifference they display towards ideas – [be they] philosophical or political – and their sole preoccupation with what bourgeois idealists call *vile material interests* – for a full stomach and for bodies comfortably coddled – all these urgent preoccupations, and all their indifference now preponderant among the masses, are far from being matters that should incite criticism. They should on the contrary be considered as a proof of their natural good sense and sensible instincts, because indeed *economic and material liberation* is the greater foundation, the sole and primary basis for every other emancipation.

It was the great merit of the founders of the International, and of the Geneva congress (of September 1866), that they understood this, and made it the foundation of the entire programme of our great Association. If in this programme they had set out atheism or materialism, they would assuredly have excluded from the International millions of perfectly serious workers – persons very oppressed and miserable. It isn't that the people are really religious, I happily observe that on the contrary they are less so every day, and in every land. What they call, or believe their religion to be, is on the one hand the product of a tradition that has become a routine, a bad habit of collective thinking, and more than that an instinctive, elemental protest, and a very practical one against the narrow misery of their current existence. Let the Social Revolution open a vast earthly horizon for them and they will cease to think of heaven. The masses are not really religious, but they imagine that they are, and atheism – explicitly stated – terrifies their imagination. It is the same with reactionary socialist political ideas, which still dominate popular imagination. The proletariat detests authority and the State instinctively; it hates them in their every possible form – but just attack the State or the Church and it would not understand. Often indeed it would rise up against you – it holds by rote to ideas that are contrary to its own instinct. People often have the habit of authority, from the State or from the Church, an authority which always makes a victim of them, but one they love, and it is the same in many households where the husband provides the punches for the wife. It is a slavish habit and unfortunately the masses preserve quite a few vestiges of such detestable habits.

There is only one means to heal them – Social Revolution – the real unshackling of the masses. Only then will the masses understand the germs of every idea that slumbers now in their instincts. And then – they will embrace with passion, as the faithful expression of their own aspirations, the entire programme of the Alliance. But if one imposed the programme of the Alliance on the International, the International would be able to count on barely two or three thousand members in the whole of Europe. True, indeed, these would be very precious members, those most developed, the most energetic, and the most sincere socialist-revolutionaries in Europe. But what are three thousand men in the face of the concerted power of the State and the richer classes? Absolute powerlessness! Exploitation and reaction, that formidable coalition, can be broken only by the organised power of the masses, by proletarians in their millions – and it is certain that these millions will not accept the philosophical and political programme of the Alliance today.

And they will not accept the Marxian programme either, which, in addition to its abstract and scientific clothing also offers the terrible inconvenience of working to found new *Popular States*, that is new tutors and new prisons for the people – that much more oppressive because this oppression will be carried through in the name of the sovereign will of the people. This *Authoritarian Communist* programme, this idea of equality, justice and mass emancipation organised by the state nevertheless seems to be more or less accepted by the British,[7] the Americans, above all by the Germans – all too frequently it embraces their pan-Germanic aspirations. On the other hand, it is energetically rejected by the revolutionary instinct of Latin peoples: the French, Belgians, Spanish and Italians, as well as by all Slav peoples, who seem to have found a common banner in the revolutionary events of the Commune ... What then is to be done? Should two Internationals be established – one Germanic, the other Latino-Slav? That would be a great misfortune and a certain triumph for the bourgeoisie of every race and land. It would signify the disorganisation of the proletariat, the introduction of an internal civil war – all for the profit of the bourgeoisie.

Is there any possibility of reconciling the Marxian programme and our own? No, they contradict each other. Compromise is therefore impossible. So, finally, for the love of peace and to preserve the unity of the International, should one of these programmes be sacrificed to the other? And since it is the Germans who tend towards domination, rather than the Latins or the Slavs, should the latter submit to the yoke of Germanic ideas – a yoke that would only result in the servitude of the Slav and Latin peoples and in degeneracy – or some terrible racial war? Asking the question is enough to resolve it – a thoroughly negative reply arises from us all. So, neither reconciliation, because that is impossible, nor submission because that would be revolting and fatal, nor division because the unity of the International is the prime condition for the victory of the proletariat in its struggle against the bourgeoisie.

What is to be done then? One should seek out this unity where it can be found, and not where it cannot. It is not to be sought for in theories – be they philosophical or political – but rather in the aspirations of the proletariat of every country for solidarity, for material and economic liberation – *on the terrain of everyday practical economic struggle of labour against capital*. I will never cease to repeat this: this is the goal, the only object of organisation, and the single programme of the International. It is entirely positive. It is so simple and positive that no proletarian could fail to understand it and or choose not to embrace it very enthusiastically – however little their development, or however much they may be imbued with political and religious prejudices of one sort or another.

All proletarians – apart from some bourgeois workers who, rightly or wrongly, hope to lift themselves above the mass, whether through their work or through politics, to become in turn exploiters or bosses – all serious workers must curse the conditions of their existence, and aspire for liberation. They must detest their oppressors and exploiters. If they do not manifest this hope and hatred it is [only] because they feel powerless to satisfy the latter or to achieve the former. Show them that they can become a power, through building solidarity with all their comrades in slavery and misery, and they will throw themselves passionately into the economic struggle that it is precisely the mission of the International to organise.

Moreover, no one is required by our general statutes to declare their politics or religion. They ask each person just one thing: in workers' economic struggle against exploiters will you commit yourselves to observing solidarity, whatever the consequences may be? If a person says yes – they become in effect a member of the International, which I repeat has no mission other that of organising this struggle, of bringing together the solidarity and the federal organisation of strikes and funds for resistance – across different trades and across the frontiers of each state.

This is the serious positive side – the only one that is truly a must for the International; everything else – all those questions on the political and social organisation of the future that are discussed in our congresses, such as fully comprehensive education, the abolition of States, or the liberation of the proletariat by the state, women's liberation, collective property, the abolition of rights of inheritance, atheism, materialism or deism – all these no doubt constitute questions that are of great interest, their discussion is very useful for the moral and intellectual development of the proletariat – but congresses have neither the capacity nor the power to resolve them in any absolute manner, nor the ability to impose their resolutions as articles of some compulsory programme on sections or on individual members. Congresses can neither desire such things, nor achieve them, because in so doing they would be declaring absolute truths and so much nonsense; they would be imposing a fake majority through artificial means, a majority that would inevitably be transient; an *official truth*, a monstrosity.

The day-by-day, practical organisation of labour's international economic struggle against capital – this then is the single explicit aim, the one and only supreme and obligatory law of the International. Whoever is unwilling to submit themselves to the practical consequences of this solidarity in this struggle should leave the International, or be expelled, while whoever accepts and observe these is by right a member. This solidarity is entirely independent of the different philosophical and political currents followed by the labouring masses in various lands. For example, if German workers go on strike, if they revolt against the exploiting bourgeoisie, you would not ask them if they believe in God, or not; or if they are for or against the State? You would support them as much as your strength allows, because they are workers, rising against their exploiters. Let German workers act likewise for you – without asking first what your religious or political credo might be – and the unity of the International would be established. Because unity is based neither on philosophical nor on political solidarity, but solely on economic solidarity across every land,

To those who would tell me that I am restricting the character of the International – reducing its object and compulsory programme to that of a purely economic struggle – I would reply that what would destroy it, and kill it, would be the attempt to introduce into it one uniform and compulsory-for-all philosophical or socialist political policy. Because I challenge you to formulate even a single clear doctrine which might bring together millions under its banner; not even that, I should say tens of thousands of workers! And, unless the beliefs of one sect are imposed on all the others one would end up with the creation of a multitude of sects, or one might say, the organisation of a veritable anarchy within the proletariat, for the greater benefit of the exploiting classes.

And do you think that building mass solidarity in economic struggles is a small matter of little consequence? Already, even now, this solidarity brings immense results. Firstly it excavates a chasm between the bourgeoisie and the proletariat, and in so doing it pushes the proletariat towards revolution. In the second place, through the practice of collective action and struggle, it gives the proletariat things not drizzled onto it in small doses from on high – but rather strength, deliberation, will, socialist instruction and education; all developed logically, generously, in the midst of the masses themselves, lit up by collective reflection and passion ... through daily experience, through thinking about justice, equality, the broadest popular freedom – incompatible with the authority of any tutor or doctor. This is what our great Association accomplishes – it prepares the way for the international social revolution.

On this broad terrain, all forms of ideas, every doctrine should have the greatest freedom to develop – the authoritarian theories of Marx as much as our anarchistic theories, provided only that none should have the folly or the odious pretension to impose themselves as an *official truth*, and none should infringe on this practical proletarian solidarity in economic struggles in various lands. This is what we – supporters of the Alliance – support today and have always supported, against the dictatorial, official, authoritarian/bureaucratic pretensions of the General Council of London – dominated more and more by the Marxian coterie.

On the terrain of the International, with our explicitly revolutionary programme, we organise for revolution. We impose our programme on no one, but we propagate it freely, being certain that it is the only one that will accomplish full proletarian emancipation – which is as much social as political and economic. Furthermore, being aware that the organisation of popular power cannot be achieved only through theoretical propaganda, and knowing that an alliance and organisation of persons and revolutionary will, constituting some sort of revolutionary headquarters is required, we have formed our secret Alliance within the International itself. The London conference [1871] prepared and directed by Marx has issued a fulminating anathema against secret societies. It is a hypocritical anathema. The Marxians know very well – as well as us – that the public International, the International properly said, is excellent when it comes to agitation, to revolutionising the masses; but by itself it is incapable of organising popular power – that last instance of all social struggle – and for this a secret organisation is needed. But since they serve principles and work for goals directly opposed to ours, in the International they want a secret society quite opposed to ours, whose direction remains entirely in their own hands.[8] That society has existed since 1847 and even more so since 1848, the [society of] *German Communists* founded by Marx and Engels which has never ceased to promote its secret propaganda in the International. The one aim of the resolutions of the London conference was to deliver the government of the International into [the hands of] its hierarchically organised committees.

***

Bakunin was not averse to allowing some authority some freedom to act in certain conditions. It might be necessary, in an emergency – such as might then be the case in Spain – to allow 'some sort of dictatorial power for a very short period to a group of men known very well to them', but accounts would need to be rendered and such practices were dangerous. Bakunin wrote:

> We believe and have expressed our firm conviction that the thinking, the life and the revolutionary power of the International is not on high, but below; not in the committees, but in the people of each section – and the committees should be only administrative bureaux, always *transparent* towards the people and they should always be obeying its law. The law that in the end *international unity* – the great goal of our Association, independent from any centralised direction, which would only disorganise and paralyse it – resides [not] in the General Council, but rather in the real identity of needs, interests and aspirations of the proletariat of all lands, and in consequence that the organisation of the revolutionary activity and power of workers in Europe and *the world, cannot* be the work of some central government but only of a perfectly free Federation of autonomous sections.
>
> You can clearly see that between the Marxian party and ours there is an abyss. And when I speak of *our* party I beg you to believe that this is not *my* party ...[9]

THE PROGRAMME OF THE SLAV SECTION IN ZURICH

[Programme de la section slave de Zurich, 14-15 August 1872][1]

In the summer of 1872 Bakunin spent some time in Zurich meeting with scores of Serbs and Russians, many of them students.[2] Many Russian women sought a university education in Switzerland that they could not obtain in Russia. There were also Slav refugees from the Paris Commune.

A Slav section of the IWA was formed and joined the Jura Federation. It protested actively against the arrest and extradition of Nechaev,* despite having political differences with him. In March 1873 it sent a 50 franc donation to the Jura Federation, and took out a subscription to its *Bulletin*. The Zurich group had only a short collective life and soon broke up.[3] The programme below was dated August 1872. Bakunin's thinking appears to have aroused considerable influence in Russia.[4]

***

1. The Slav section, fully accepting the general statutes of the IWA, as agreed at the first congress of the Association held in Geneva in September 1866, takes on itself, as its particular task, propaganda for the principles of revolutionary socialism and the organisation of popular forces in Slav lands.
2. It will struggle with equal energy against all manifestations and tendencies of pan-Slavism, that is to say the so-called deliverance of Slav peoples through the power of the Russian Empire, and also against pan-Germanism, that is to say a so-called emancipation through political action as imposed by bourgeois German civilisation, which today is seeking to organise itself as a great and so-called popular state.
3. Being partisans of the anarchist revolutionary programme which, in our view, alone contains the conditions for a true and full liberation of the popular masses, we want the abolition of every state, being convinced that the existence of the state, of every state, is as

incompatible with proletarian freedom as it is opposed to the human and international fraternity of peoples. For Slav peoples especially this abolition is a question of life and death, and at the same time the only means of reconciliation between peoples of foreign races, be they German, Hungarian or Turkish.

4. Along with the state everything denominated as a legal [juridical] right should be supressed: every so called legal regulation of popular life, working from top to bottom through the means of governmental or legislative regulation, such things have never had any purpose except that of creating and systematising the exploitation of the labouring, popular masses for the benefit of the governing classes.

5. The abolition of the state and of juridical law will have as necessary consequences the abolition of individual hereditary property and of the legal family based on that property, both the one and the other contrary to the progress of human justice.

6. Only through the abolition of the state, law, property and the legal family does it become possible to [re]organise popular life, from bottom to top, on the basis of work and collective property, which become – through their own dynamic energy – accessible and necessary for everyone, through the path of a fully free federation of individuals, in groupings of productive associations, either in autonomous communes, or over and above communes in other particular associations: provincial, national; or in large homogenous associations linked by a commonality of interests or social tendency; or of communes within nations, or of nations within humanity.

7. The Slav section being atheist and materialist, will struggle against all cults and Churches, be they official or unofficial, and, whilst professing and practicing the most profound and sincere respect for the freedom of conscience of all, and whilst [being] for the sacred right of all to propagate their ideas, it will attack the divine idea in its every manifestation – religious, metaphysical, political and juridical – being convinced that these unhealthy ideas have sanctified every form of slavery.

8. It professes the greatest respect for positive science, and it demands for the proletariat every form of scientific education – equal for all, male or female – and being the enemy of all government it rejects with horror any government of scientists and academics, which, in its false pride and action, would be the worst of all governments.

9. The Slav section demands for women,[5] as well as for men, the most complete freedom and equality of rights and duties.

10. The Slav section, whilst it sets itself the particular task of promoting the emancipation of peoples of Slav race, in no way strives for the organisation of a separate Slav world, or one that might be hostile to others, or merely a stranger to other peoples of a different race. On the contrary it will have as its main aim to promote the inclusion of the Slav peoples in the greater human family which the International Workers' Association is committed to constitute on the basis of liberty, equality and universal fraternity.
11. Being convinced that to fulfil its lofty mission the IWA must make its practice and theory conform with the aims that it has set itself, that is to say with the real emancipation of the popular masses from all tutelage and from every government, the Slav section does not recognise that there should be within the greater IWA any authoritarian or governmental power at all, and in consequence recognises no organisation other than that which should arise out of the free federation of autonomous sections.
12. The Slav section recognises neither official truth, nor the need for one uniform political programme to be imposed, either by the General Council, or even by a General Congress. It recognises no law, other than the law of most complete solidarity – of all, individuals, sections and federations – in the struggle against its exploiters. The Slav section takes on itself the particular task of drawing in the proletariat of Slav lands into the practical necessities of this universal, economic solidarity, this being the sole basis of the IWA's unity.
13. The Slav section recommends to sections in every land: a) absolute freedom of social and philosophical propaganda; b) freedom to follow whatever politics they might wish to, so long as this politics does not limit the freedom and equal rights of every other section and federation; c) freedom to organise itself in the fashion that it prefers, having in mind [the promotion of] a popular revolution; d) the freedom to come together in a federation, beyond the frontiers of their own particular country, with whatever sections and federations it may find as most like-minded.
14. The Slav section of Zurich has requested its admission to the Jura Federation because it is there that these principles have been solemnly proclaimed and sincerely practiced.

***

Bakunin also wrote a Programme for a Serbian Socialist Party with the following points on gender and education:[6]

The cultural development and education of children is the responsibility of Communes – given that sexual relations are established between men and women without formal preconditions other than the ongoing reciprocal love that unites them forever or for a time, without a family being constituted. The culture and education of children as well as public education should be the same for both sexes, because these are the basis of every sort of activity, an artisan's apprenticeship being varied only in accordance with [the needs] of particular trades. That all should be brought up, taught and educated, in a word that all should be perfectly prepared to become a member of a producers' association, and that none should live as dependents of others.

***

Bakunin had written about labour politics in the Austro-Hungarian Empire* in June 1869.[7] He referred to a recent report from the journal *Volksstimme* (People's Voice), of a public meeting in Vienna attended by some 20,000 workers. He repeated the argument that so long as workers thought of themselves by nationality, as Germans, Hungarians, Italians or Czechs their exploitation would continue. He argued: 'To really unite workers of every nation in the Austrian Empire under the same banner, shouldn't they [Social Democrats] recognise that every nation must have the same rights? [Yes] they must therefore both destroy the Empire and abolish all domination throughout its territories.' Political organisational forms would give way to new (economic) forms of organisation, coming together, on the basis of local bodies, to form broader networks.

WRITINGS AGAINST MARX

[Fragment formant une suite de *L'Empire Knouto-Germanique,*
November-December, 1872]¹

On 24 August 1872 Andrea Costa wrote to the Jura Federation on behalf of the correspondence commission of the Italian IWA Federation:

> To conclude, the General Council is not the International, and if we have broken with it, we for our part also once again affirm our economic solidarity with the workers of the world. And we will go forward. When on its path, the revolution meets its Bastille, an explosion of popular anger will be enough to overthrow it. Greetings and fraternal wishes.²

The Italian IWA resolved to break with the General Council before the Congress in The Hague. On 4 October 1872, shortly after that congress concluded, Bakunin's Russian friends in Geneva and Zurich replied to its resolutions expelling Bakunin and Guillaume as follows:

> They have dared to throw accusations of fraud and swindling against our friend Michael Bakunin. We believe it is neither necessary nor opportune to discuss the alleged facts on the basis of which it was thought possible to lay weird charges against our friend and compatriot. The facts are well known to us, down to the smallest detail and, as soon as possible, we will make it our duty to set out the truth. We are prevented from so doing at present by the unhappy situation of another compatriot³ who is not our friend, but whose persecution by the Russian government renders him – at this moment – sacred to us. The skills of Mr. Marx we do not wish to contest, but on this occasion at least he has calculated matters very badly. In all lands honest hearts will doubtless only feel indignation and disgust towards such a shameful conspiracy and such a flagrant violation of the most basic principles of justice. As for Russia, we can assure Mr. Marx that all his manoeuvres will inevitably be in vain. Bakunin is too well known and esteemed there for calumny to touch

him. Signed: Nicholas Ogarev*, Bartholomy Zaitsev, Vladimir Ozerov, Armand Ross*, Vladimir Holstein, Zemphiry Ralli-Arbore, Alexander Oelsnitz, Valerian Smirnov.

Marx and Engels maintained control of the General Council, and had it relocated to New York, while hoping to rally the mass of the IWA behind them. They soon found they were generals without an army. Little or no money was coming in. They continued to publish polemics against Bakunin and the Alliance but had to rely on funds from Engels' private fortune to do so. The mass of the IWA continued without them. This was the context in which Bakunin wrote this polemic against Marx and Engels.

***

As there is solidarity among the bourgeoisie, so there must also be solidarity in the struggle against it. The sole objective of the International is the organisation of militant solidarity between the workers of the whole world. This is the objective, expressed so well and so simply, in our original general statutes.[4] They, and only they, are legitimate. They are compulsory for every member, section and federation of the International. It was under their banner that in the space of barely eight years the Association gathered together over a million members and made of them a real power. Even the most powerful monarchs of this earth have had to consider that power.

But every power attracts the ambitious, and Messrs Marx and Company imagined that they could use the IWA as a stepping-stone, an instrument to achieve their political pretensions. It would appear that they never recognised the nature or source of the energy of the International – youthful energy and prodigious power. Mr Marx had been one of the main initiators of the International – that is a glorious title that no one can dispute. And it was he who, almost alone, for eight long years constituted the whole of the General Council. He – he more than anyone – should have understood things better – things that no eye could fail to see, two points that only blindness brought on by vain ambition could have made him misunderstand:

Firstly that the International was able to develop and spread in such a marvellous fashion only because all philosophical and political questions were eliminated from its *official and compulsory* programme; and secondly the International was able to do so because, being based mainly on the freedom [of action] of sections and federations, it was unaffected by all the '*benefits*' of centralising government, benefits which, so to speak, were capable of preventing and paralysing its development. Up to 1870, precisely in the period of the Association's greatest development, the General Council was something of an ineffective or phantom monarch, resolving things only after they had happened. If things were so it was not because there was a lack of ambition in the General Council but rather because of its powerlessness – and because no one was listening to it. So it was dragged along, behind the spontaneous movement of Belgian, French, Swiss, Spanish and Italian workers.

As for the political question, everyone knows that if this was eliminated from the programme of the International, it was not the fault of Mr Marx. As one might expect from the author of the famous programme of German Communists that he and his friend, accomplice and confidant Mr Engels published in 1848, this point was not omitted from the key issues considered in the *Inaugural Address* published in 1864 by the provisional General Council in London, (written solely by Mr Marx). In this circular or proclamation addressed to the workers of all nations, the head of Germany's authoritarian communists did not fail to declare that the *conquest of political power* was workers' first duty. He went so far as to prick his *pan-German* ear, adding that for the present the main aim of the IWA should be combatting the Empire of all the Russias. This was an aim that doubtless was very noble and legitimate – and one which I, as a friend of the Russian people, subscribe to with all my heart, persuaded as I am that so long as that Empire exists this people will never cease to be miserable slaves. But this was an aim which, firstly, could not become the aim of the IWA without completely undermining its object and character; and which, in the second place, if it was to be set out in a proper fashion – one that is fair, serious and useful for the workers' cause – needed to be considered in quite another fashion.

If Mr Marx had declared war on every State, or at least on every monarchical, despotic, militarist state, such as Prussia, Austria, Napoleonic France or even the current [French] republic, and if he had placed that model state, the Empire of all the Russias in the first rank amongst them, then at least no one could have accused him of pan-Germanism. But in glossing over German despotism, a very insolent, brutal, gluttonous despotism, one that is a huge menace for neighbouring peoples, as anyone can see today, in attempting to turn the indignation of workers of every nation against Russian despotism, to the exclusion of others, in pretending even that this was the sole cause of the despotism that has never ceased to prevail in Germany since it first came into being, and lastly in rejecting every shameful act and every political crime of this land [Germany] – this land of science and of proverbial obedience, [supposedly] under the inspiration of Russian diplomacy – Mr Marx has shown himself firstly to be a very bad and very untruthful historian, and secondly not an international socialist revolutionary but rather an ardent patriot of the greater Bismarckian nation.

Just how the Congress of the International held in Geneva in 1866 responded astutely to every patriotic[5] and political suggestion that arose from the person who today advances himself as the dictator our great Association is well known. None of these suggestions remained, either in the statutes voted by the Congress or in the programme[6] which thereafter constituted the basis of the International. Take the trouble to re-read the magnificent 'Considering clauses' which head up our general statutes, there you will find these words only concerning political questions:

> Considering: that the emancipation of the working classes must be the work of working-people themselves; that the struggles of working people to achieve their emancipation should create not new privileges, but should establish the same rights and duties for all;
> That the subjection of labour to capital is the source of all [forms of] servitude material, moral and *political*;
> That for this reason *the economic emancipation of working people is the great end to which every political movement ought to be subordinated*, etc.

This is the decisive phrase in the entire IWA programme. If I may use the memorable words of de Sieyès, it *cut the cable*, it broke the chains that shackled the proletariat with bourgeois politics. Recognising this truth, a truth that grows greater by the day, the proletariat resolutely turned its back on the bourgeoisie. With each step forward the abyss between them grows greater.

The Alliance, an IWA section in Geneva, translated and made the following commentary on the 'considering paragraphs:' 'The Alliance rejects *all forms of political action which fail to have, as their immediate and direct goal, the victory of workers against capital*', as a consequence it sets out, as its aim, the abolition of the State, of every State, and the organisation 'through freedom, of a universal association, out of all local associations'.

In contrast, the party of Socialist-Democracy of German workers, [Social Democratic Workers' Party] founded the same year (1869),[7] by Messrs' Liebknecht and Bebel, under the auspices of Mr Marx, announced in its programme that *the conquest of political power was the precondition for the economic emancipation of the proletariat*, and in consequence the immediate object of that party should be the organisation of large scale legal agitation for the conquest of universal suffrage and of all other political rights; its final goal was the establishment of a great Pan-German, a so-called popular, state.[8]

Obviously there exists between these two tendencies the same difference, the same abyss, as that which separates the proletariat from the bourgeoisie. And after all this, should one be surprised that in the IWA they should meet each other as an irreconcilable adversary, and that each should continue to fight each other, in every form and on every possible occasion, even today? The Alliance taking the programme of the International seriously, had rejected with disdain any dealings with the politics of the bourgeoisie, whatever the colour of their radicalism, or however much they might endeavour to appear socialist. It recommended to the proletariat, as its single path to real emancipation, as the single form of politics which would be truly salutary for its own purposes: a politics that was exclusively *negative* – as a necessary consequence – organising internationally the scattered forces of the proletariat into a revolutionary power directed against every power constituted by the bourgeoisie and demolishing political institutions, power, government in general, the State.

German Social-Democrats recommended quite the opposite to those workers who had the misfortune to hear them: that they should adopt as the immediate aim of their association agitation within the law, winning preliminary political rights. Thereby they have subordinated the movement for economic emancipation to a movement that was in the first place exclusively political, and through this obvious reversal of the entire programme of the International, in just one move, they bridged the abyss that the IWA had opened between the proletariat and the bourgeoisie. They did more than this. They allowed the proletariat to be placed in tow behind the bourgeoisie, because obviously all political movements promoted by Germany's socialists, since they must precede the economic revolution, would be directed by the bourgeoisie alone, or, and this is even worse, *by workers who, through ambition and vanity, have become bourgeois.* In reality this process, as with all previous movements would pass over the heads of the proletariat. Such movements can do nothing but condemn them once again, making the proletariat into a blind instrument [victim], to be unerringly sacrificed by bourgeois parties as they struggle between themselves for the conquest of political power, i.e. the right and the power to dominate and exploit the masses. We can show what is going on today in Germany to anyone who might doubt this. There the organs of socialist democracy sing joyous hymns as they see a congress of bourgeois professors of political economy recommend the high and paternal protection of the state to the German proletariat.[9] In those parts of Switzerland where the Marxist programme prevails, in Geneva, Zurich and Basel, the International has fallen low, to the point of being nothing more than some sort of electoral post-box serving the radical bourgeoisie. To me such indisputable facts are more eloquent than speeches. They are so real and so logical, in the sense that they flow inevitably from the success of Marxian propaganda. And it is on account of this that we combat Marxian theories implacably. We are convinced that if they prevailed in the entire International, they would everywhere kill off at least its spirit, as they have done already in those places that I have cited above.

Doubtless [in the past] we have much deplored and today we continue to profoundly deplore the immense disturbance and demoralisation that these pan-Germanic ideas have thrown into the so beautiful, so marvellous and so naturally triumphant development of the International. But none of us has ever thought of prohibiting either Mr Marx or his all too fanatical disciples from propagating such ideas within our great Association. Had we done so, we would be neglecting its basic principle, which is that of *the most absolute freedom of ideas, be they philosophical or political*.

The International admits neither censorship nor some official truth in the name of which censorship might be exerted. It does not allow such things because thus far it has never behaved as a Church or State. And it is precisely because it has not acted in such ways that it has been able to astonish the world with the unbelievable rapidity of its expansion and development.

The congress of Geneva – being better inspired than Mr Marx – understood this. It fostered the energy of the IWA, through the elimination from its programme of all philosophical and political principles as *compulsory* principles, but it left these questions [open] for discussion and study. It is true that at the second congress of the International, held in Lausanne in 1867, some hapless friends,[10] not adversaries, but not yet fully understanding the true nature of the IWA's vitality, had attempted to put the political question on the agenda. But very happily they achieved only a platonic declaration: that *the political question is inseparable from the economic question*, a declaration that all of us can support,[11] because it is obvious that politics – the institution and mutual relations of States – has no other object except that of ensuring that the ruling classes can legally exploit the proletariat. So in consequence, the moment the proletariat wishes to free itself, it is forced to consider politics – to fight it and overcome it. Our enemies do not understand things so; what they wanted, and what they want, is positive politics, state politics. But not having found an easy terrain in Lausanne, they wisely held back.[12] A year later, at the Brussels Congress, they were inspired by this same sense – but Belgium being, as a consequence of its history, anti-centralist, anti-authoritarian and communalist, offered them no chance of progress, and once again, they wisely held back.

Three years of defeat! For the impatient and ambitious Mr Marx this was too much. He had better hopes for the Basel Congress (1869); he ordered his troops to launch a direct assault – and out they went. In Germany the Social-Democrats[13] had had time to organise, under the direction of Messrs Liebknecht and Bebel their links had spread into German Switzerland, (Zurich, Basel, and the German IWA branch of Geneva). This was the first time that delegates from Germany were present in larger numbers at an International Congress.[14] The plan of campaign, approved by the leading army General Mr Marx, mobilised Mr Liebknecht as head of the German detachment, and Messrs Bürkli* and Greulich*, as heads of the Swiss detachment. Into their ranks, as voluntary auxiliaries, came Messrs Amand Goegg and J. Philippe Becker*, and a German advocate of plebiscites, Rittinghausen – an inventor of direct popular voting for laws and constitutions. They also had on their side a few German members of the General Council (Mr Marx's vassals in matters of politics), and some Britons from the same Council (wholly ignorant of such matters but through bad habit accustomed to voting with the Marxians – something they now appear to have overcome).[15]

So with their organisation set, the Marxians went into battle – and lost. Mr Bürkli set out the question of direct popular legislation[16] against us. Mr Liebknecht defended it with much heat and insolence. Mr Amand Goegg used heroic emphasis. Mr Philippe Becker – he who always refrains from expressing a clear opinion until he knows which way the wind blows – acted with great diplomatic reticence. They were [all] buried [and the matter] was eliminated from the Congress programme.[17] It was a memorable defeat for Mr Marx, something he would not forgive.

Great was his anger! Today we know the consequence. It was after September 1869 that the General Council (or rather Mr Marx, whose threatening words[18] calmed or excited the waves of that poor Council) embraced active politics, abandoning the torpor that had been forced on him, a torpor that had been nothing but healthy for the International. We know now how things started. Anyone who dared fight him suffered a torrent of diverse, odious slanders and ignoble insults. They were peddled in German journals, by letters that were sent to confidants in other countries, by confidential circulars, and by all sorts of agents – won over by one means or another to the cause of Mr Marx. Then, in September 1871, came the London Conference. It had been long prepared by Mr Marx and it voted whatever he wanted:[19] the politics question, conquest of power by the proletariat regarded as a compulsory programme for the International, the dictatorship of the General Council, i.e. of Mr Marx in person, and in consequence the transformation of the International into an immense and monstrous State, with him as leader. When its legitimacy was challenged[20] Mr Marx – with easy political sleight-of-hand, intent on proving to the world that even without rifles or canons, the masses could be governed through lies, slanders and intrigue – organised *his* Congress in The Hague.

Barely two months have passed since that congress.[21] Throughout Europe – excepting Germany, where editors are enmeshed with lies, where workers are systematically blinkered by their leaders and journals, in all the free federations of Belgium, the Netherlands, Britain, America, France, Spain, Italy, and not forgetting our excellent Jura Federation, there are cries of indignation and disdain for the cynical comedy which dared to dress itself up and call itself a congress of the International. The congress was nothing but a travesty of honesty, good sense and justice. In the name of a manipulated majority – composed almost entirely of members of the General Council, of Germans disciplined in the Prussian manner, and French Blanquists, ridiculously played and used by Mr Marx – everything was falsified, brutalised and violated. Without pity, shamelessly the honour of the International was made into a burnt offering, its very life was put in doubt, the better to lay a foundation for the dictatorial power of Mr Marx. This was not just a crime, it was insanity. And Mr Marx, one who considers himself as the father of the International, one of its main founders as none may contest, allowed all this![22] This is what becomes of personal vanity, self-adoration and above all political ambition. In his very dramatic and lively demonstration of these deplorable facts and acts – in all that he has initiated and moved – Mr Marx has at least done the International a great service, showing that if one thing can kill it, it is the introduction of politicking into its programme.

The IWA, as I have said, was able to grow so profusely only because it had eliminated from its compulsory programme all philosophical and political questions. So clear is this, that it is astonishing that there should be any need to prove it. I do not believe that there is any need to demonstrate that for the International to become and to remain a power, it needs to be able to draw into itself, to embrace and to organise the immense majority of the proletariat of every part of Europe and America. But what is the philosophical or political programme that can flatter itself [as being capable of attracting] millions to come together under its banner? Only a programme that is excessively general, i.e. vague and imprecise, can do so, because any theoretical precision would correspond fatally with an exclusion, with some practical limitation.

Today, for example, only *atheism* can be a serious philosophical starting point, not as a positive one, but as a *negative* one that has become historically necessary, as a negation of theological and metaphysical absurdity. But can anyone believe that the Association would have been able to bring together even some hundred thousand members if that simple word 'atheism' had been inscribed on the banner of the International? Everyone knows no – not because the people really are religious, but because they believe themselves to be so – and they will go on believing so, until a social revolution opens the way for them to achieve all their aspirations here below. It is a certainty that had the International placed atheism as a compulsory principle in its programme, it would have excluded the *flower of the proletariat*. (I understand that word not as the Marxians do, as the upper, the most easy and civilised layer of the world of workers, that quasi-bourgeois layer of workers which they seek to use, constituting it as their *fourth governmental class*. Truly, it is capable of becoming such, if no order is placed amongst the great mass of the proletariat, because with its relative and quasi-bourgeois well-being, it is unhappily only too thoroughly penetrated by social and political prejudice and the narrow-minded pretensions and aspirations of the bourgeoisie. One might say that this layer is the least socialist and the most individualist of the entire proletariat.)

By *flower of the proletariat*, I mean above all the great mass, the millions of uncivilised, disinherited, miserable illiterates that Mr Engels and Mr Marx would like to submit to the paternal regime of a *very strong government*,[23] no doubt for their own salvation – for, as all know, all governments are established only in the masses own interest. By flower of the proletariat I mean precisely that fodder of eternal government, that *mass of popular rascals*,[24] which, being more or less virgins as far as all bourgeois civilisation is concerned, carries within itself, through every necessity and misery of its collective position, the passions, instincts, aspirations and every germ of future socialism. Today this mass alone is sufficiently powerful to inaugurate the social revolution and make it succeed.

So, in almost every land, these rascals would refuse to join the International as a mass if it had the word *atheism* on its banner as an official motto. And that would be a great shame, because if it did, this mass would turn its back on the International and all the strength of our great Association would diminished.

It is the same with every political principle. First of all there is not a single political principle left today – Messrs Marx and Engels may protest in vain (they would be unable to change facts that are patent everywhere). There is not even a single political principle, I say, capable of stirring up the masses. They would fail, even after several years, even in Germany. What the masses want everywhere is their immediate economic emancipation; for them this is a question of humanity and freedom, life and death. If today there is one ideal that attracts the passionate adoration of the masses it is the question of *economic equality*. And the masses are a thousand times right. For them, so long as the current regime is not replaced by economic equality, everything else, everything that constitutes the valour and dignity of human life – liberty, science, love, intelligent action and fraternal solidarity – will remain nothing but vile deception.

The masses instinctive passion for economic equality is so great that if they could hope to receive it from the hands of despotism, they would succumb – without doubt, without much reflection, as they have often done before. Happily historic experience has been of some use to the masses. Everywhere today they have begun to understand that despotism has neither the will, nor the power, to deliver. On this point the programme of the International is happily most explicit: *workers' emancipation can only arise out of their own effort*. Is it not astonishing? Mr Marx believed that he could graft his *scientific socialism*, the organisation and the government of a new society by socialist scholars, the worst of all despotic governments, onto that declaration – one moreover that was so precise, so clear and which he probably drafted himself!

Mr Marx's scholarly socialism[25] will remain forever as some kind of Marxian reverie. The great and lovely rabble will move by its own volition, pushed on by instincts that are as invincible as they are just, opposing the governmental fancies of that small minority of labour that is already disciplined and properly organised to become an accomplice of a new despotism. Society will be spared such a new experience, perhaps one that might be more distressful than all past experience, because the proletariat in general is everywhere excited by a profound distrust of politics as it now is, and against the politicians of the world, whatever their colour. All of them have misled, oppressed and exploited them – the reddest republicans as much as the most absolute monarchists.

Given such current conditions among the masses, how can one hope to attract them with any political programme? Let us suppose, as indeed is the case today, that they let themselves be brought into the International by some other enticement, how could one hope that the proletariat of every land, situated in conditions that are so different – in temperament, culture and economic development – could be yoked to one uniform programme political programme? It is only with some patent insanity that one could imagine such things. Well, Mr Marx was not only inclined to imagine, he wanted to set such things into motion. Despotically tearing up the pact of the International, he desired, and still today he has the pretension to impose one uniform political programme, *his own programme,* on every federation of the International, i.e., on the proletariat of every land!

Within the International great discord resulted. Without doubt, its greater unity was placed in question. And I repeat, this was so only because of the action of the Marxian party, which, by means of the congress of The Hague, attempted to impose its thinking, its will and its leader's policy on the whole International. Had this been serious and genuine thinking, if the resolutions of the congress of The Hague had been considered as the last word of the International, evidently our great and wonderful Association would have no choice other than to dissolve. Because one would have to be truly insane to imagine that workers – of Britain, the Netherlands, Belgium, France, the Jura, Italy, Spain, and America, not to speak of Slav workers – would agree to submit to Marxian discipline.

And yet, if one believed with the politicians of the International of all sorts – revolutionary Jacobins, Blanquists, republican democrats, not to forget socialist and Marxian democrats – that the political question should form an integral part of the programme of the International, one would have to admit that Mr Marx was right. The International could become a power only as a single unit; it was absolutely necessary that it should have just one political programme, the same for everyone, otherwise there would be as many Internationals as there were different programmes. But as it is obviously impossible for all workers of so many different lands to freely and spontaneously unite around one single political programme, the International being today the necessary instrument for the emancipation of the proletariat, and this International being unable to preserve its unity except on condition of recognising only one political programme, that political programme would have to be imposed. To prevent the appearance of despotically imposing things through a decree of the General Council or a Marxian Council, a bodged Marxian congress was needed – a congress which, in the name of the free will of all, would decree the slavery of all (thereby giving a very novel demonstration of what truth there is in universal suffrage and in the representative system). This is what was really achieved by the congress of The Hague.

This was like the battle and the surrender at Sedan for the International:[26] the victorious invasion of a Pan-Germanism, not of Bismarck, but of Marx, the imposition of the political programme of authoritarian communists, or of the Socialist Democrats of Germany, and the dictatorship of their leader over the proletariat of all other lands of Europe and America. The better to hide his game, and to sweeten the pill a little, this memorable congress sent a simulacrum of a General Council off to America – one picked and chosen by Mr Marx himself. The council, always obeying his hidden direction, would fully take on the appearance, worry and responsibility of power, whilst Mr Marx would assume the real exercise of its power in the protection of its shadow.

So, however disgusting such games may appear to a delicate and timorous soul, I declare that they were absolutely necessary from the moment it was determined that the political question should be set out in the programme of the International. Since unity in political action was recognised as necessary, and since there was no hope that it might arise freely, from a spontaneous entente between the sections and federations of various lands, it would have to be imposed. Only in such unique fashion could that political unity – so much desired and sermonised – be created; but slavery was created at the same time.

I summarise the matter: in introducing the political question into the compulsory programme of the International, our Association was placed in a terrible dilemma, the two terms of this being: *either unity with slavery,* or *freedom with division and dissolution.*

How could one escape? Simply by returning to our original General Statutes which properly gloss over political questions, leaving to sections and federations the freedom to develop. So then, won't each section and federation pursue the political direction that it pleases? No doubt. But then, won't the International be transformed into a Tower of Babel? On the contrary, only thus can real unity be built up, at first in the workplace, necessarily political thereafter. And in due time the greater politics of the International will be created, no doubt not all at once, not as the emanation from one isolated, ambitious, very scholarly head, and not from one brain – one nonetheless incapable of embracing the multiple needs of the proletariat, however well-endowed it might be[27] – but rather from activity that is thoroughly free and spontaneous, and that is developing simultaneously from workers of every land.

The basis for this greater unity will not be found through vain searches amongst current philosophical or political ideas. It is to be found readily formed in the suffering, [common] interests and needs, in developing solidarity, and in the real aspirations of the proletariat throughout the world. This solidarity exists in reality, it does not need creating. It is formed in the world of work, in daily experience and real life. *It is there in the solidarity of workplace demands* – and all that remains to be done is to develop its awareness and to help it organise consciously. To my mind, it was this understanding that was the unique, and at the same time the great merit of the first founders of our Association, amongst whom, I always like to recall, Mr Marx played a useful and influential role, barring some of his whims (very German and politicking) which the congress of Geneva wisely deleted from the programme that he had presented.[28]

I have always avoided naming Mr Marx and his many collaborators as the 'founders' of the International, because I am really convinced that the International was not their creation but rather was properly the work of the proletariat itself. I do not wish to diminish his merit out of meanness, I am on the contrary greatly pleased to do him justice. After a fashion he and they were midwives, but not authors. The major author was the proletariat, acting unconsciously as authors of great things often do, represented by some hundreds of anonymous workers – French, British, Belgian, Swiss and German. It was workers' deep and lively instinct, tried and tested by the oppression and suffering inherent in their situation that made them discover the true principles and aims of the International: the solidarity of want as a real foundation and *the international organisation of labour's economic struggle against capital* as the true object of the Association. As they gave it this object and foundation, they established, in one moment, the strength and all the power of the International. The door was opened wide to the millions of this society's exploited and oppressed, whatever their beliefs, their level of culture or their nationality. Because to conceive the desire, to have the right to join the International, only the following conditions were needed and are still needed today, in conformity with its original statutes:

1. Being a serious worker: i.e. having experienced the suffering that today afflicts the proletariat, or at least, if one is born in one or another privileged class, to desire frankly the full emancipation of the world of labour, without reticence and without ambitious self-interest;
2. Understanding that this emancipation is not an individual matter, nor one that is local, nor an exceptional affliction of one or another craft; that it can be achieved only on condition that it should embrace workers of all trades in active solidarity – from industry, commerce and agriculture; the proletariat of every commune, province, land and continent. And in consequence it should form a real, strong organisation for an international solidarity that embraces the exploited workers of the whole world against the systematic, legalised exploitation of every proprietor and capitalist;
3. Understanding that the governing, owning, exploiting classes will

never make voluntary concessions to the proletariat, out of justice or generosity, however weak they may be, or however urgent things may seem, because that would be against nature, and more precisely their particular nature, such that there has been no such example in history; no dominant class has ever made such a sacrifice of its own free will. Even little concessions are conceded by the privileged only when their existence is beset and menaced, and only then are they forced by the rising power of the proletariat to give away more important concessions. So, in consequence, the proletariat has nothing to expect from the bourgeoisie, not from their intelligence, not from some sense of equity, even less from their politics; not from the bourgeois Radicals, not from bourgeois so-called Socialists, nor indeed from bourgeois scientists. *Workers' emancipation can be accomplished only and exclusively by workers themselves*, as it is set out at the head of the 'considering clauses' [of the IWA's statutes]. And this means that workers will achieve emancipation and conquer their human rights only by hard fighting, *by an organised war of the workers of the whole world against exploiters, the rich and the capitalists of the entire world*;

4. Understanding that the better to achieve victory in this international conflict, workers of every land must organise their strength and solidarity internationally, and this is the one and true aim of the IWA;

5. Understanding that since this organisation has no object other than the emancipation of workers by themselves, it can be constituted only directly and immediately by themselves, through their own spontaneous action, i.e. from bottom to top through frankly popular, free federation, beyond the political combinations of states, and not from top to bottom, in the manner of all more or less centralised, aristocratic and bourgeois governments;

6. Understanding that since burdened manual workers and proletarians represent historically the original and last of this world's slaves, their emancipation means the emancipation of everyone, their victory is the final victory of humanity. Consequently the organisation of the strength and power of the proletariat of every land by the International, and the war that it undertakes against every dominant and exploiting class, cannot have as its aim the constitution of new privilege, or a new monopoly or class, or of new masters, or of a new state, but rather the creation of freedom, equality and the fraternity of all human beings, over the ruins of every sort of privilege, of every

class, of all exploitation, of all domination, in a word over every state;
7. Lastly, one must understand that the single aim of the International is the conquest for working people of all human rights, through the organisation of militant solidarity in every land, over and above differences of trade, or political or national frontiers. *The supreme and one might say single law* that all accept when they join this wonderful and salutary Association, is to submit themselves voluntarily to the requirements of that solidarity; and likewise thereafter: to submit all their acts, voluntarily, ardently and in full knowledge of causes; and in their own interest, as well as in the interest of their comrades of all conditions and countries [to those same requirements].

These are the true principles of the International. They are so broad, so human, and at the same time so simple, that one would have to be a bourgeois quite committed to the conservation of monopoly, or one quite brutalised by bourgeois prejudice, not to understand them and not to recognise their perfect justice. One needs to be a socialist democrat of the school of Mr Marx to adulterate these principles. There are no true, serious proletarians, (however poorly cultivated or stupefied they may be, through prejudice – be it political or religious – systematically poured into their poor heads since their early infancy), who cannot be made to understand all this, through a few hours conversation, and with a little patience and good will; because already they carry all this within themselves, in their instincts and in their every aspiration, and because all this is developing further by the day through their experience and pain. When one explains these principles to them, and when one deduces their every practical application for them, one is only giving a name and a form to things they sense. If, as it organises and further develops, the International remains faithful to the original simplicity of its being and programme, this is what, insuperably, will attract the proletarian masses into the International.

No error is greater than that of demanding more than they can give from a thing, an institution or a person; demanding too much demoralises, inhibits, twists, and kills. The International produced great results in a short time. It organised the proletariat for the economic struggle, it will do so in the future with even greater vigour. Is this a reason to suppose that it might be used as an instrument in [electoral] political struggles?

Whatever hopes he may have had, Mr Marx failed to kill off the International through his criminal work at The Hague. This is a history of the goose and the golden egg. Workers from many lands gathered in their masses, responding to the call for workplace struggle, to support the banner of the International and Mr Marx imagined that the masses would remain there. What more can I say? That they would gather in still greater numbers when, as a new Moses, he inscribed ten political commandments on to the banner of the International, as its official and compulsory programme?

This is where his error lay. The masses, whatever difference there may have been in their level of language, culture, religious belief or country, understood the language of the International, when it talked to them about their suffering, misery and slavery under the yoke of exploitative property and capital. When the necessity of uniting efforts for solidarity and a greater common struggle was explained they understood. But things were different when it came to talk of a political programme – one that was very scholarly and above all very authoritarian; in the name of their salvation a dictatorial government, (no doubt a provisional one, which in the meanwhile would be wholly arbitrary, and directed by a head endowed with extraordinary brains) would have to be imposed on them, all within this very International, one which was to organise their emancipation through their own efforts.

Was it vanity, ambition, or both at once, that pushed and drove Mr Marx, which made him imagine and hope that, on such conditions, the working masses of the various countries of Europe and America could be corralled under the banner of the International? How insane was he? But didn't Mr Marx's great triumph show he was right? Didn't the congress of The Hague vote through everything it was asked to?

No one knows better than Mr Marx how little the resolutions voted through by the unhappy congress of The Hague expressed the thinking and real aspirations of the [IWA] federations of every land. The composition and the fabrication of this congress cost him such great pains that he cannot delude himself even for a minute as to their meaning or real value. And, even had he been able to delude himself for a second, what is happening today is well placed to fully enlighten him. With the exception of the party of Socialist Democracy of Germany, federations of every land – the American, British, Dutch, Belgian, French, the Jura Swiss, the Spanish and the Italian federations – are protesting against every resolution of this damaging, shameful congress, or rather this event of ignoble intrigue.

But let us leave aside the question of morality and consider the principle part of the matter. A political programme has value only when it transcends vague generalities, when quite precisely it sets out the institutions that it proposes, instead of those that it wishes to reform or overthrow. This indeed was Mr Marx's programme. It amounted to a comprehensive outline of highly centralised and very authoritarian political and economic institutions, no doubt sanctioned – as most despotic institutions of modern society are – by universal suffrage, but nevertheless deferring to a very *strong government*, if I may use the terms of Mr Engels[29] himself, the *alter ego* of Mr Marx, the confidant of that legislator.

But why precisely should *this* programme be introduced, *officially* and compulsorily into the International's statutes? Why not that of the Blanquists? Why not our own? Is because Mr Marx invented it? That is no reason. Or because it might appear that German workers have accepted it? But, with very few exceptions, a non-state [anarchique] programme is accepted by every Latin[30] federation, and the Slavs will never accept anything else. Why then should the German authoritarian programme predominate in the International, a body that was created through liberty, one that can prosper only in liberty, and through liberty? Should it be so because the German armies failed to conquer France? But that too would not be a reason; or rather and on the contrary, it would be a reason to mistrust greatly a programme coming today from Germany.[a] And it was this the

---

a The Germans have a very peculiar way of appreciating facts, matters and persons! I find by way of example the following note in number 81 (9 October 1872) of *Volksstaat*, the principle and official organ of the Party of Socialist Democratic Workers' of Germany, an organ published in Leipzig not edited, but directly and immediately inspired by Mr Marx himself.

> News: the prohibition of the International in France has been ended! Is it possible! You don't believe it? And yet it is so. The International, which has been forbidden to organise (die durch das Vereinsthor hinausgehetzt war), has triumphantly re-entered the French capital through a bookshop. A French translation of Karl Marx's *Capital* is on sale at Lachâtre in Paris. At this very moment we have before us the first magnificently printed edition of the work with a signature and portrait of the author.

Isn't that breathtaking? Isn't it so characteristic of German spirit? I ask you, could such things be printed in any other country in a journal which describes itself as democratic and socialist, an organ of the International, and which indeed pretends to represent, alas, a large and numerous workers' organisation. How can it be so! That the appearance of a book, a portrait, a signature of Mr Karl Marx, in a Paris bookshop, can be the equivalent to the triumphant return of the International to France! It is farcical and ignoble, it is the grossest insult ever thrown in the face of the International! So, one man whoever it may be, Mr Karl Marx or someone else, can weigh as much as the International! Doesn't the impudence that permits the writing of such things – for the ears of German workers who make of this journal their everyday reading matter – show how much such workers are disdained, does it not show that they are believed to be inured to every discipline and humiliation? The idolatry of persons and the cult of authority has entered deep into the habits and culture of German people; but I never imagined that they might be so depraved that a popular journal, read by at least one or two tens of thousands workers, should recklessly dare to print such things. *Volksstaat* no doubt did so with great naïveté, and no one was offended in Germany. MB

political programme – applauded by such a socialist democracy – that the congress of The Hague pretended to impose on the free federations of every land!

How is the future success of the IWA to be assured? How is its integrity to be saved? Unless one is seeking to use tyranny against the federations of many lands, employing violence or intrigue, or both at the same time to impose the political programme of a single land, or, and this is more likely, unless one is for dissolving the International, dividing it into several parties, each of which would follow its own political programme, evidently only one way out is possible – *maintaining the original exclusion of political matters from the compulsory and official programme of the IWA, a body organised not for political struggles, but only for workplace struggles, and thereby refusing absolutely to be used as a political instrument in the hand of anyone.* The IWA, if and whenever it might be used as positive political power, in the positively political struggle of different State parties, would immediately be demoralised, diminished and curtailed, and would dissolve itself as a visible entity. Fools, if they imagined they could grasp its power, would find it melting entirely away in their hands, the moment they tried to grab it.

So then, should consideration of philosophical and political questions be forbidden in the International? Should the International concern itself only with the economic question, setting aside developments in the field of thought, or with events which come together with, or follow on from political struggles, inside or outside a state? Should it work on comparative statistics; study law and wealth and its distribution and production? Should it concern itself exclusively with setting wage levels, raising strike funds [caisses de résistance], organising local, national and international strikes, building local, national and international trades' organisations, and forming cooperative and mutual credit bodies for consumption and production, whenever and wherever such things are possible?

Such a limited agenda is – we hasten to say – quite impossible. It would be the death of the proletariat, if it were preoccupied exclusively and solely with economic matters. No doubt the organisation and the defence of its interests – questions of life and death – has to form the basis of its current activity. But it would be impossible for workers to stop there, without renouncing their humanity, without depriving themselves of the moral and intellectual strength which they need to win their rights in the workplace. Doubtless just now, given current miserable circumstances and sufferings, workers have to confront the first question – of daily bread for themselves and their families – but, (and more than with the all the privileged classes) they are in the full meaning of the word, full human beings, and as such they have a thirst for dignity, justice, equality, liberty, humanity and science. And they have every intention of winning the fullest enjoyment of the entire product of their labour and everything else. So, philosophical and political questions, even if they had not been raised in the International, would inevitably be raised by the proletariat.

So, how is this apparent contradiction to be resolved: on the one side philosophical and political questions are to be excluded from the programme of the International, and on the other side discussing them is something that arises inevitably?

The problem resolves itself through freedom. No philosophical and political theory can be set out as its essential foundation, as the official, compulsory condition of the programme of the International, because, as we have just seen, any imposed theory would become – for all the IWA federations which it comprises today – either a source of slavery, or of division, or of a dissolution which would be no less disastrous. But it does not follow from this that all philosophical and political questions should not be freely discussed in the International. On the contrary, it is the existence of some official theory which would kill off the development of thinking in the world of labour, making living discussion unnecessary. What would be the use of discussion once there was some *official truth* – a truth announced and imposed on all from the height of a Marxian Mount Sinai – discovered scientifically by isolated work, through the brains of an exceptionally and why not say also *providentially* endowed big head? All that would remain would be to ensure that these New Ten Commandments were learnt by heart.

On the contrary while no one is, or can be, in possession of the [whole] truth, the search is on. Who seeks it? Everyone, above all the proletariat which thirsts for it and needs it more than anyone. Many will not want to believe in this spontaneous search for philosophical and political truth by the proletariat. I will now try to show how this search is developing within the International itself.

As I have said, workers join the International and get organised only for eminently practical reasons in the first place: to obtain collectively their full economic rights, against the oppressive exploitation of the bourgeoisie of every land. Note that through this single act – one that you might say is initially unconscious – the proletariat stands in circumstances that are very decisively and very negatively, political. On the one hand this politics destroys political frontiers and every states' international politics, insofar as the latter are founded on the sympathies, voluntary co-operation and patriotic fanaticism of the subjugated masses; and on the other hand it builds a chasm between the bourgeoisie and the proletariat, and places the latter outside the field of action and political play of every state party. Further, as it places itself beyond bourgeois politics, it necessarily turns against those politics.

So, unwittingly at first as I have said, the proletariat finds itself in this well-defined political position because of its membership of the International. This political position, it is true, is absolutely *negative*. So the great error, if not to say betrayal and crime, of the Socialist Democrats is that they have sought to transform this negative attitude; dragging the proletariat of Germany through the paths of the Marxian programme into positive cooperation with the politics of the bourgeoisie.

The International forms a new world, a world of proletarian solidarity across every land, as it sets the proletariat beyond the bourgeois world and the politics of the state. This is the world of the future. It is at one and the same time the demolisher and funeral director of all privileged, past civilisations, which are thoroughly wasting away and condemned to death and it is its legitimate legatee. In consequence it is the necessary creator of a new civilisation, one created out of the ruins of every human and divine authority, of every slavery and inequality. This is the mission, and in consequence the true and non-official programme of the International[31] – one that is implicit, and inherent in its very organisation.

Its official programme, as I will repeat a thousand times, is very simple, and in appearance very modest: it is the organisation of international solidarity for the workplace struggle of labour against capital. From this basis – one that is at first exclusively material – it must reach out to build a new world – a new moral, intellectual and social world. For this to be really so, all thinking, every tendency of every philosophical and political question of the International should be born within the very midst of the proletariat; they should begin first and mainly, if not exclusively, with the economic demand which is the very essence and the manifest goal of the International. Is all this possible?

Yes, this is how things are developing. Whoever has followed the evolution of the International over several years has been able to see how things have grown slowly, without being at all noticeable – sometimes all at once, sometimes progressively – and always by three paths that are distinct, but indissolubly united. Firstly, through the organisation and the federation of strike funds [caisses de résistance] and international strike solidarity; secondly through the organisation and the international federation of trades' organisations and unions, and lastly through the direct and spontaneous development of sociological and philosophical ideas within the International, the inevitable accompaniment and one might say forcible consequence of the first two movements.

Let us now consider the first of these three paths in its particular field of activity, each of which is different but, as I have just said, inseparable. And let us begin with the organisation of strikes and strike funds. Strike funds have as their single goal the development of reserves needed to facilitate the organisation of strikes and the costs of sustaining them. And strikes are the beginning of the proletariat's social war against the bourgeoisie, so far within the confines of the law. Strikes have a twofold value: firstly they energise the masses, revitalising their moral energy, and they revive within them feelings of deep antagonism that exist between their interests and those of the bourgeoisie, further demonstrating to them the abyss that separates them irrevocably from that class; and furthermore, they help immensely to instigate and create both awareness and the very reality of solidarity between workers of all trades, of all places and lands; a twofold action, one both positive and negative, tending to form directly the new world of the proletariat opposing the bourgeois world in a quasi-absolute way.[32]

***

Bakunin goes on to cite an instructive episode – an early case of a promise being issued to build support for the campaign of a lawyer seeking election in Geneva in 1872, the use of the IWA as a prop for a candidate, who made a promise, on behalf of the IWA, that strikes would be avoided that year, if he was elected: 'We have also seen, six or eight months ago, also in Geneva, a lawyer belonging to the Radical Party, and the International at the same time – Mr Amberny – the same person who was graciously thanked for his services to the International in Geneva by a letter from Mr Marx,[33] publicly guarantee, before his bourgeois co-citizens, that there would be no strikes that year.'

ON LASSALLE AND MARX[1]

[Extracts from *Statism and Anarchy, (Gosudarstvennost i anarkhiya)*][2]

Bakunin's collaboration with Russian and Slav exiles in Zurich resulted in the printing and publication of a book surveying prospects for Socialism: *Statism and Anarchy: the Struggle of Two Parties in the IWA, (Volume 1), A Publication of the Revolutionary Social Party*. This then was envisaged as part of a larger project, which Bakunin did not complete. The book – the only extensive text that Bakunin wrote in Russian – had some influence on the Chaikovski circle and other radical groups in Russia

Bakunin expected that poverty, misery and servitude would foster episodic rebellion. He viewed the Russian *mir* (the village assembly) as a mixed blessing; it shaped local communities but tended to isolate them, empowering elderly, male patriarchs loyal to the Tsar. Bakunin stressed the need for the people to make their own future, independent of academics and scientists, 'no one would have the capacity to give ideals to the people if they do not shape these for and through themselves'. Socialist convictions were already present and were rooted in common feelings: firstly that those who laboured on the land should own it, secondly that the entire rural community in the *mir* should manage land ownership, thirdly that there should be local autonomy.

Cooperatives – in production and in consumption – might perhaps offer a good model for a socialist future. But coops were not so useful when it came to working for a transition from the old world to a new one. 'We do not think that cooperative movement can take on any great size in Russia'. '... we do not oppose cooperative experiences, and at the same time we believe that young people should have no illusions as to the results that may be obtained.'[3] Bakunin expected revolts but feared that revolts, if they lacked common thinking, would not bring social revolution. What was needed was to root revolt in and against the *mir*, against ideals and organisations – against the Tsar and against the patriarchs who dominated the *mir*. To accomplish such things one should brake the isolation of rural communities. Literacy was limited in this era, particularly outside the urban environment; popular education was therefore an important element for building Socialist movements; it was also a subversive activity in this era, when radical literature was censored and the distribution of unauthorised books and journals banned.

Bakunin was optimistic concerning Italy. He wrote: 'nowhere perhaps, is the Social Revolution so close ...' 'In Italy, unlike many other European countries, there is no separate, upper layer of labour, in part already privileged because of high salaries, bragging of its literary learning and so impregnated with bourgeois vanity, aspirations and ideas that they are differentiated from the bourgeoisie only by circumstance but not by feelings.'[4] '[T]he tattered proletariat [lumpen-proletariat] predominates, those whom Messrs Marx and Engels and their followers and the whole school of German Socialist Democracy address with deep contempt, and most unjustly so, because it is in them, and only in them, rather than in the bourgeoisified layer of the labouring masses, that the entire force and spirit of the future Social Revolution resides.' The Italian government was quite aware of the danger that it was facing – it was on this account that 'despite the law' it closed down every genuine workers' associations – no doubt acting, wrote Bakunin, on instructions received from the German Chancellor.

As for Germany, Bakunin noted that the defeat of the peasant's revolt of 1525 had condemned it to a long period of reaction. He saw contemporary Germany as the centre of modern reaction. German influence predominated in much of Europe. He had contempt for liberals – seeing them as little more than lackeys of the state, they contributed little to progress after 1848: 'not only were they incapable of winning freedom, furthermore they did not wish for it ...' The current German state was a militarist entity – one that might say (following Voltaire) that God was always on the side of the big battalions – and it was naturally expansionist. Bakunin hated both pan-Germanism and pan-Slavism. He hoped that German workers would revolt and placed his hopes in them, *despite* fearing for the harmful effects of Social-Democratic and Marxist thinking.

Lassalle,* his co-thinkers, and the Social-Democrats had sought to promote change by sending representatives to parliament, by changing the state into a people's state, looking for it to finance workers' associations and cooperatives

This was a programme, wrote Bakunin, that had been developed in the *Communist Manifesto* of 1848 and that Marx had alluded to in 1864.[5] It implied the government of academics (men of science) over the mass of working people: because men of science knew better than the people themselves what they should want. Bakunin deplored this elitism, and the priority assigned to electoral-party-politics; he wrote that such quiet tactics would accomplish nothing and that the pioneers of this strategy would facilitate the expansion of Bismarck's Empire.[6] Bakunin did not believe that the theory of Marx and Engels had changed much as a result of the Paris Commune. As noted earlier in this volume, he thought that they had been forced – unwillingly – to adapt their politics. He did not have to hand the volumes of their *Collected Works* bequeathed to future generations by Russian publishers and others. Bakunin's judgments of Marxism are based then, not so much on an exegesis of Marx and Engels' writings, but rather on his experience of the activities of German Social-Democrats in general, including Marx and Engels.

The extract below proceeds from such arguments.

***

We have expressed our lively hostility to the theory of Lassalle and Marx on many previous occasions, a theory that recommends the foundation of a popular state to workers, if not as a supreme ideal, at least as an essential immediate goal. This, as they themselves have explained it, would be nothing but 'the proletariat organised as a dominant class'.

So, if the proletariat is to become a dominant class, one might ask: who are they to dominate? There must remain some other class, one subjected to this new ruling class, this new state, if only, for example, country people. The latter, as we know, are not esteemed by followers of Marx, and since they have the least degree of civilisation they will probably be directed by the urban or factory proletariat. Or, if one considers matter from the viewpoint of ethnicity, let us say the Slav question for the Germans – those [Slavs] who, vis-à-vis the triumphant German proletariat, and for the same reasons, might well find themselves in the same subjection and slavery, like that of the proletariat in relation to the bourgeoisie. This is why we are enemies of states: whoever speaks of state, necessarily speaks of domination and in consequence slavery; a state without overt or concealed slavery is inconceivable.

What is the meaning of the 'proletariat organised as a dominant class'? Does it mean that the entire proletariat will be directing public affairs? There are some forty million Germans. Could it be that all these forty millions will be part of the government, with the entire people governing, and so no one will be governed? So then there would be no government, no state. But if there is a government some will be governed, there will be slaves.

This dilemma is removed rather easily in Marxist theory. By popular government Marxists understand a government of the people working through a small number of representatives elected by the people through universal suffrage. The election by the whole nation of the so-called representatives of the people and of state leaders. This – the last word of Marxists and of the democratic school – is a lie that covers over the despotism of a directing minority, a lie all the more dangerous because it is presented as the supposed will of the people. So, however one approaches consideration of this question, one arrives at the same hateful result – government by a privileged minority of the immense majority of the popular masses. But, say the Marxists, this minority is composed of workers. Yes certainly, but of former workers who, once they become popular representatives or rulers, cease to be workers. They begin to regard the proletarian world from the heights of the state, they represent themselves and their pretension to govern the people, but they no longer represent the people. Whoever doubts as much does not know human nature.

But these elected persons [it will be said] are convinced socialists – and moreover people of learning. The terms 'scientific socialist' and 'scientific socialism' recur incessantly in the writings of Lassalleans and Marxists, these alone prove that the pseudo-popular-state will be nothing but a despotic government of the popular masses by a narrow new aristocracy of genuine or not so genuine scholars. The people, being without learning, will be entirely liberated from governmental concerns and all of them will be fully incorporated into the herd of the governed. What a lovely liberation!

Marxists recognise this contradiction. Whilst they admit there will be a real dictatorship with the rule of learned people, the most burdensome, despicable and vexatious form of government possible, whatever democratic forms may be adopted, yet they console themselves with the thought that it will only be temporary and endure only a short time. They pretend that its only concern, and the sole purpose that it will adopt, will be the education of the people, bringing them forward politically and economically to such a level that all government will soon become unnecessary, and the state, having lost its political characteristics, i.e. its authoritarianism, will transform itself into an entirely free organisation with common economic interests.

There is a flagrant contradiction here. If their state is effectively a popular state, what reason would there be to get rid of it? And if, moreover, its suppression is needed for the real emancipation of the people, how can it be termed a popular state? In our polemics with them we have lead them to recognise that freedom or anarchism – that is to say the free organisation of people from bottom to top – is the final goal of social evolution and that every state, including their popular state, is bondage, meaning that on the one hand it engenders despotism and on the other hand slavery.

According to them this state bondage, this dictatorship, is a necessary transitional phase leading to the total emancipation of the people; freedom or anarchy being the goal, the dictatorship or the State being the means. So then, in order to liberate the popular masses one must begin by placing them in bondage.

This contradiction is where our polemic must end for the present. The Marxists pretend that only dictatorship – of course their own – can create freedom for the people; to this we reply that no dictatorship can have any other goal but to endure as long as possible and that it is capable only of engendering slavery for the people who suffer it, and can only educate people into slavery. Liberty can be created only by liberty – that is to say by the uprising of the entire people and by the free organisation of the working masses from bottom to top.

This question, which becomes the point around which every interest in modern history crystallises, will be the object of more in-depth analysis in the second part of this work. For the moment we seek to attract the attention of the reader to one significant reality, something that is constantly replicated: whereas the social-political theory of anti-authoritarian or anarchist socialists leads them unerringly to a complete breech with all governments and all forms of bourgeois politics, leaving them with no alternative but Social Revolution, the opposite theory, the theory of authoritarian communists and of scientific authoritarianism, under the pretext of tactics attracts and enmeshes its partisans into unending compromise with governments and the various bourgeois political parties, that is to say it pushes them directly into the camp of reaction.

Lassalle is the best proof of this. No one is unaware of his relations and negotiations with Bismarck ...[7]

LETTER OF RESIGNATION FROM THE JURA FEDERATION

[Aux compagnons de la fédération jurassienne, October 1873].[1]

Bakunin wrote this letter to resign from the Jura Federation, shortly after the IWA congress of September 1873. The editors of the *Bulletin* in which it appeared commented: 'We recognise comrade Bakunin's resignation in the letter he addresses to us (the letter may be read below), a resignation motivated by his age and illness. We believe we act as the organ of every member of the Jura Federation when we assure him that he has the friendship and the esteem of Jura internationalists for all the eminent service he has rendered, and we trust that these feelings will accompany him into his retirement.'

***

Dear Comrades

I cannot leave public life without sending you a few words of sympathy and gratitude.

You have preserved your esteem for me, your friendship and your confidence, through the four and a half years or so that we have known each other, despite every machination of our common enemies, despite the infamous libels that rained down on me.

When the 'Bakuninist' label that was thrown in your face, you have never let yourselves be intimidated; rather than living with the certainty of having been unjust you preferred to allow some appearance of being [cast as] human dependents. So transparent were the perfidious intentions of our enemies that the only way that you could treat their malicious and wounding insinuations was with the most profound disdain. You always knew, perfectly well, that your tendencies, opinions and actions arose entirely consciously, in spontaneous independence.

And this is how you acted – it is precisely because you had the persistence and courage to do so that you have had such a complete triumph today, against the ambitious intrigues of the Marxists, promoting both proletarian freedom and the entire future of the IWA.

Aided by the strong support of your brothers from Italy, Spain, France, Belgium, the Netherlands, Britain and America you have re-set that great Association, the IWA, on its [proper] path; defeating Mr Marx's dictatorial attempts to divert it.

The two congresses that have just taken place in Geneva have been a decisive, triumphant demonstration of the justice and, at the same time, of the power of your cause. Your congress – a congress of freedom – brought together delegates from all the principle federations of Europe except Germany;[2] it solemnly affirmed, and fully established – or rather confirmed – the autonomy and fraternal solidarity of workers of every land.

Appearing to have had nothing but disgust for freedom, the authoritarian or Marxist congress, composed only of Swiss and German workers, vainly attempted to reassemble the broken and much ridiculed dictatorship of Mr Marx. Having cast its many insults right and left, as if to bear witness that they were for the most part from Geneva and Germany, they produced a [new] hybrid, no longer the complete authority as dreamed of by Mr Marx,[3] but something that represents freedom even less. They retired profoundly discouraged and dissatisfied with themselves. This congress was a funeral.

So your victory is complete: a victory for the International and for freedom against authoritarian intrigue. Yesterday, when it might have appeared uncertain – although I for my part never had any doubts – yesterday, I say, no one would have been permitted to abandon your ranks. But today, when this victory has become an accomplished fact, freedom of action – in accordance with personal preferences – is returned to each person. So, dear comrades, I take the opportunity to ask you to accept my resignation as a member of the Jura Federation and as a member of the International.

I have many reasons for acting so. Do not believe that it is mainly on account of personal disgust – in recent years I have had my fill of them – that I act. I will not say that I am entirely insensitive; yet I feel I would have sufficient strength to resist, if I thought that my further participation in your work and struggles might be of use for the success of the proletarian cause. But I do not think so.

Through birth and personal situation I am only a bourgeois, although my tendencies and sympathies are different. As such, I can only do theoretical and propaganda work for you. Well, I have this conviction –

that the moment for great theoretical discussion, written or spoken, has past. Within the International there have been developed over the last nine years more ideas than are needed to save the world, if ideas alone could save it, and I defy anyone to invent something new. Now is no longer the time for ideas – but for facts and deeds. What matters above all today is the organisation of the forces of the proletariat. This organisation should be the work of the proletariat itself. If I was young I would go to some place of workers, and with my brothers I would do my bit in a life of labour. I would equally take part in the great work of [building] this indispensable organisation. But neither my age, nor my health allow me to do so. On the contrary – they command me rest and solitude. For me every effort, every single journey, becomes a very serious business. My moral strength is quite good, but physically I tire quickly, I feel myself lacking in the strength needed for struggle. In the proletarian camp I would be an embarrassment rather than a help. You see dear comrades that everything forces me to retire. Living at some distance from you, and far away from everyone, what use could I be for the International in general or for the Jura Federation in particular? Your great, handsome Association, being very militant and practical for the future, must allow within it neither honorary positions nor sinecures.

So dear comrades I retire full of respect for you, full of sympathy for your great and holy cause, the cause of humanity. I shall continue to follow with fraternal concern your every step, and I will salute with happiness your every success. I will be yours till death.

But, before I leave you, allow me to address one last bit of fraternal advice. My friends, the centre of international reaction today is not in that poor France, with its burlesque dedication to the Sacred Heart, but in Germany, in Berlin, and it is represented as much in the socialism of Mr Marx as in the diplomacy of Mr von Bismarck. This reaction which envisages as it final goal the pan-Germanisation of Europe, now threatens to swallow and pervert everything. It has declared a war to the death with the International – today represented only in free and autonomous federations. Although you still live in a free republic, you, as much as proletarians of every other land, are compelled to fight it, because it has placed itself between you and your final goal, the emancipation of the proletariat of the entire world. The struggle that you will have to sustain will be terrible. But do not let yourselves be discouraged. Know, that despite the immense material strength of your enemies, your final victory is certain, so long as you faithfully respect two conditions:

1. Hold firmly to your principle of wide and ample popular freedom,

without which solidarity and equality would be so many lies.

2. Organise ever more firmly a practical, militant, international solidarity amongst workers of all trades and lands, and remember that however infinitely feeble you may be as individuals, as local communities or as isolated countries, you will find immense, irresistible strength in that universal association. Farewell.

Your brother,
Michel Bakounine

LETTER TO ÉLISÉE RECLUS

[15 February 1875, from Bakunin in Lugano]¹

Bakunin reflects on prospects in Europe: he had looked for revolution in Italy and Spain, but in both countries the IWA had been disorganised and uprisings had met with defeat. Bakunin appears to be replying to a letter he had just received² from Élisée Reclus.*

***

Very dear friend,
Thank you so much for your kind words. I have never doubted your friendship, a feeling that has always been mutual, and I measure yours by mine. Yes you are right, for the moment revolution has gone back to bed.³ We are falling back into a time of evolution – that is to say of revolutions that are invisible, subterranean and often even imperceptible. The changes that are happening today are very dangerous, if not for humanity at least for certain nations. This is the last incarnation of an exhausted class, playing its last card, protected by the military dictatorship of MacMahon-Bonapartism in France, or of Bismarck in the rest of Europe.

When you say that the revolutionary moment has past, I agree with you: not because of terrible disasters that we have witnessed, nor because of the terrible defeats of which we have been the more or less culpable victims, but because, to my great despair I have observed – and continue to observe again from one day to another – that revolutionary passion, hope and thinking are quite lacking amongst the masses, and when these are absent it is vain to complain, nothing can be done. I admire the patience and heroic perseverance of the Belgians and the Jurassians – these are the last Mohicans of the International – and despite every difficulty and every obstacle, in the midst of general indifference – they put up an obstinate front, they continue working calmly, as they did before catastrophe struck, when the general movement was on the rise, and when the least effort created a powerful effect. This work is all the more praiseworthy insofar as they may not see the benefit of it. But they can be sure that their effort will not be wasted– nothing is wasted in this world – and drops of water, though they may be invisible may go on to form an ocean.

As for me, my dear, I have become too old, too infirm, too weary, and I should say to you too disappointed, to feel the desire or sufficient strength to share in this work. I have very deliberately retired from the fray and I will spend the rest of my days in a contemplation that will not be idle, but on the contrary very active intellectually and I hope that something of use will come of it. Immense curiosity is one of the passions that now dominates me. Having had to recognise that bad things had won out, that I was unable to prevent them, I put myself to work to study change and development with a quasi-scientific passion, and complete *objectivity*.

What a scene presents itself! And what actors are at work! At the root of the entire situation in Europe are Emperor Wilhelm and Bismarck at the head of a great population of lackeys. Up against them are the Pope with his Jesuits and the whole Roman Catholic Church – with riches by the million. Through women, through the ignorance of the masses, through the incomparably skilled manoeuvring of their innumerable allies, and with their hands and eyes everywhere, they are dominating a large part of the world. The third actor, French civilisation, is incarnated by MacMahon, Dupanloup and Broglie – tightening the screws on a great, but fallen people. Then, around them Spain, Italy, Austria, Russia, each one of them making occasional grimaces; further away Britain, unable to decide what it should do and further off the model republic of the USA cosying up to military dictatorship.

Poor humanity!

Evidently it can escape from this cesspit only through some immense social revolution. But how will it make this revolution? Never has international reaction in Europe been so formidably armed against every popular movement. Repression has been made into a new science – taught systematically to every lieutenant by the military training schools of every nation. And what do we have, to attack these impregnable fortresses? Unorganised masses. And how should they be organised, when they lack even the energy to look after themselves, when they do not know what they should want, and when they do not want the only things that might save them.

What remains is propaganda, such as is made by the Belgians and the Jurassians. That is no doubt something, but really not so much, a few drops of water in the ocean; and if there were no other means of salvation, humanity would have occasion to rot ten times before being saved. One other hope remains universal war. Sooner or later these huge military states will surely destroy and devour each other. But what a prospect! *[Manuscript ends.]*

NOTES

Introduction

1. Several writers see Bakunin as developing fully as a revolutionary socialist only after he joined the IWA, e.g. Franck Mintz, 'Bakounine et notre militantisme', and René Berthier, 'Théorie politique et méthode d'analyse dans la pensée de Bakounine', both in Philippe Pelletier, Ed, *Actualité de Bakounine 1814-2014, Bicentenaire de Michel Bakounine*, Paris: Le Monde Libertaire, 2014, p. 31, 41.
2. Jacques Freymond, *La première internationale*, Vol. 2, Geneva: Droz, 1962, pp. 108-9.
3. The motion was presented towards the end of the congress. A variety of discordant opinions were voiced as it was discussed, but time was lacking, differences were not pressed, and the motion was agreed.
4. From a letter to the Jura comrades, 'Aux Compagnons de la Fédération des Sections internationales de Jura', February-March, 1872; a further extract is presented below.
5. Circular from the Congress of Sonvilier, 12 November 1871; in Freymond, op. cit., 2, 265. Emphasis added.
6. 30 May 1870, letter to Carlo Gambuzzi.
7. 'The Chartist Movement', *New York Tribune*, 25 August 1852. Emphasis added.
8. James Guillaume comments that nothing socialist was ever heard from those IWA members who were elected to local government positions. (There has never yet been a Social-Democratic majority government in Switzerland.)
9. Letter to Albert Richard, 1 April 1870. http://www.fondation-besnard.org/spip.php?article755
10. 'Les Endormeurs', (The Sedators), *L'Égalité*,10 July 1869. *Mémoire présenté par la Fédération jurassienne de l'Association internationale des Travailleurs à toutes les Fédérations de l'Internationale*, Sonvilier: Fédération jurassienne, 1873, p. 75.
11. 'Les Endormeurs', (The Sedators), *L'Égalité*, 24 July 1869. *Mémoire présenté*, op. cit. p. 85.
12. Bakunin, although he worked harmoniously with Jewish comrades, used anti-Semitic epithets in his condemnation of Marx and others. Anselmo Lorenzo condemned such language as contrary to basic internationalist principles. Anselmo Lorenzo: *El proletariado militante*, Vol. 1, p. 214. (available online).
13. Sometimes political conflicts are presented in terms of (subsequent) industrial development. Suffice it to say that at this time few workers in large scale

industries had joined the IWA. All over Europe the typical IWA member was more likely to be a skilled worker or artisan rather than a factory worker or miner.

14 Very few German Social-Democrats were affiliated to the IWA. Bakunin says that this journal was the 'official' organ of the Marxian clique that dominated proceedings on the General Council. He also remarked that the General Council attempted to use agents to win influence in Italy and Spain.

15 Marx had written to Engels, 20 July 1870: 'The French need a thrashing. If the Prussians win, the centralisation of the state power will be useful for the centralisation of the German working class. German predominance would also transfer the centre of gravity of the workers' movement in Western Europe from France to Germany, and *one has only to compare the movement in the two countries from 1866 till now to see that the German working class is superior to the French both theoretically and organisationally.* Their predominance over the French on the world stage would also mean the predominance of our theory over Proudhon's, etc. From: *Collected Works*, 50 Volumes, London: Lawrence & Wishart, 1977-2004; Vol. 44, p. 3. The editors of *Volkstaat* adapted these sentences.

16 'Statism and Anarchy', *Oeuvres complètes*, Amsterdam: IISG, 2000, CD.

17 Golo Mann commented: 'In the 19th century there was much talk of a Russian danger, of a French one, of a revolutionary one, but never of a German one.' Golo Mann, *The History of Germany since 1789*, Harmondsworth: Penguin, 1987, p. 287.

18 Bakunin stresses the influence of militarism in German as compared with elsewhere: the greater professionalism of the officer class and its power over recruits. See 'Statism and Anarchy'.

19 Michel Bakounine, Oeuvres, 6 volumes, Paris: La bibliotheque sociologique/ P-V Stock, 1907, p. 399.

20 Bakunin wrote: 'If ... one wanted to judge it [Germany] in terms of the facts and the acts of its bourgeoisie, one would have to consider that it was predestined to accomplish the ideal of voluntary slavery.' 'L'Empire Knouto-Germanique', p. 455. Marx had written in contrast: 'I am firmly convinced that, although the first blow will come from France, Germany is far riper for a social movement.' To Engels, 12 February 1870, *Collected Works*, 43, 429.

21 22-28 December 1871, 'Italy and the General Council of the IWA', *Oeuvres complètes*, CD.

22 Letter to Tómas González Morago, 21 May 1872.

23 In *Oeuvres complètes*, CD. French title: *La Théologie Politique de Mazzini et l'Internationale*, Neuchatel: G. Guillaume, 1871, p. 19.

24 Ibid, pp. 20-21.

25 Letter to Albert Richard, 7 February 1870.

26 'L'Empire Knouto-Germanique', p. 291.

27 'L'Empire Knouto-Germanique', p. 344.

28 'Italy and the General Council of the IWA', 22-28 December, 1871,

29 'Les Endormeurs' (The Sedators), L'*Égalité*, 17 July 1869. *Mémoire présenté*, op. cit. p. 82.

30 Letter to Celso Ceretti, 15 December 1871.
31 'Circular letter to my Italian friends', op. cit., p. 323.
32 Ibid, pp. 326-7.
33 Letter to Ludovico Nabruzzi and other IWA members in the Romagna, 23-26 January 1872.
34 'L'Empire Knouto-Germanique', p. 335.
35 'Circular letter to my Italian friends', October 1871, in Michel Bakounine, *Oeuvres*, op. cit., 6, 344.
36 Appendix A, *Statism and Anarchy*, (*Gosudarstvennost i anarkhiya*) in *Oeuvres complètes*, Amsterdam: IISG, 2000, CD.
37 '*Statism and Anarchy*', op cit., see also the letter to Celso Ceretti of March 1872: 'the role of educated and dedicated youth is not that of prophets, instructors, or doctors; nor that of creators, but only of midwives for thinking born of the very life of the people"
38 Alias *Kommunistischer Arbeiterverein*, or *Bildungsverein*. Several members of the General Council were members including Eccarius* and Lessner. The latter was delegated by this body to the Congress in The Hague in 1872, and Maltman Barry was delegated to the Ghent Universal Congress in 1877.
39 For example see Marx's letter to Engels, 14 March 1869: 'The reply to the Genevans has been sent off. In the French text I kept the tone still icier and passablement ironique [moderately ironic]. Luckily, this was not noticed by the English, who naturally only know my English translation.' *Collected Works*, 43, 235-6. Other texts were edited at convenient times: 'the Central Council has adjourned until the Tuesday after New Year's Day, so we on the sub-committee are free to work without the cosy intervention of the English.' Marx to Engels, 17 December 1869, ibid, p. 404.
40 Names are listed here: https://www.marxists.org/francais/marx/works/1872/03/scissions.htm
41 15 June 1872.
42 *Collected Works*, vol. 21, 112; vol. 43, 332-3, 489, 492.
43 Testut lists 31 journals published in Austria, Belgium, France, Germany, Italy, Spain, Switzerland and the USA (German language). He does not differentiate between Social-Democratic papers published by bodies not affiliated to the IWA and journals sponsored by IWA federations. (Oscar Testut, *L'internationale*, Paris: E. Lachaud, 1871, pp. 57ff.) By 1872 it was mostly German language papers that supported the General Council: *Vorbote* and *Tagwacht* (Swiss), *Volksstaat* of Leipzig and *Volkswille* of Vienna. The journals *Emancipacion* and *l'Égalité* were also sympathetic to the General Council, but were largely unrepresentative of opinion in the countries where they were published (Spain and Switzerland). The Jura *Bulletin* of 1 August 1872 set out a list of other papers critical of the General Council: *l'Internationale* of Brussels, *Mirabeau* of Verviers, *Razon* of Seville, *Justicia* of Malaga, *Boletin de la Asociacion de Trabajadores* of El Ferrol, *Proletario* of Turin, *Martello* of Milan, *Fascio operaio* of Bologna and *Campana* of Naples. The most enduring and internationally influential journals appear to have been: the press of the Romande/Jura Federation the *Bulletin*, the press of the Belgian Federation (*La*

Liberté and *L'Internationale*), the Social-Democratic paper *Volksstaat*, and Becker's *Vorbote*. At the other end of the scale were journals which had a more localised circulation, or which managed to produce only a few or just a single issue (e.g. the *Sozialdemokratischen Bulletin* published in 1874, sponsored by the Jura Federation, distributed mostly in Switzerland but with a few copies being sent on to Germany).

44 Jung* and Eccarius* were also asked to contribute. James Guillaume, *L'Internationale: documents et souvenirs, 1864-78*, Book 1, Paris: Société nouvelle de librairie et d'éditions, 1905, p. 102.

45 *Collected Works*, op. cit., 43, 404. Marx: 'Bakunin had already turned the *Égalité*, central organ of the French-speaking members of the International in Switzerland, into his own organ, and had, in addition, started at Le Locle a little private journal of his own, the *Progrès*. The *Progrès* is playing this role up to the present day under the editorship of a fanatical adherent of Bakunin, a certain Guillaume...' From the secret: 'Confidential Communication', of c. 28 March 1870; *Collected Works*, op. cit., 43, 114. By March 1870 Bakunin was in the Ticino and had no easy means of contact with his friends in the Jura or Geneva, and his friends there were no longer the editors of *L'Égalité*. Marx was intent on misleading his correspondents.

46 In his letter to Ludovico Nabruzzi and others of 23-26 January 1872, Bakunin recognises that the Council had no financial resources.

47 Interestingly, in December 1869, Marx wrote to Engels that the General Council could not recognise *L'Égalité*, when the latter criticised it, but could only correspond with the Romande Federal Council: matters must go through channels.

48 James Guillaume, *L'Internationale: documents et souvenirs, 1864-78*, Book 2, Paris: Société nouvelle de librairie et d'éditions, 1907, p. 214.

49 Editorial control of the paper came into the hands of N. Utin* in 1870.

50 Annual dues payable to the General Council from Switzerland were 10 centimes per member. A daily wage might be as low as two to five francs. Bakunin suggested that a journey to London might have costs perhaps 400 francs. (Michel Bakounine, *Oeuvres*, 6, 169.) The Jura *Bulletin* of 1.8.1872 noted that of the regions likely to oppose the General Council only Belgium was close to The Hague; others from Switzerland, Southern France, Italy and Spain would have to travel and pay most and could least afford costs of representation. It was no accident that Engels offered to pay delegates' travel expenses for those likely to toe the correct line in The Hague.

51 The Jura *Bulletin* of 15 September 1872 sets out that the mandates of the majority of the congress delegates at The Hague – from France and Germany – could not be checked since there was no regional federations there.

52 The conference mentioned was called by the General Council in London in September 1871, it was formed for the most part by members of the General Council itself; it was held in semi-secret conditions, its agenda was not subjected to prior discussion. The conference discussed policies but voted no resolutions – these were edited after the event by the General Council. James Guillaume, *L'Internationale*, op. cit., pp. 192ff.

53 'On the Alliance'.

54 Letter to Nechaev, 2-9 June 1870.
55 In contrast, Engels wrote '[T]here are circumstances in which one must have the courage to sacrifice momentary success for more important things. Especially a party like ours, whose ultimate success is so absolutely certain, and which has developed so enormously in our own lifetime and under our own eyes, momentary success is by no means always and absolutely necessary.' Engels to Bebel; 20 June 1873; *Collected Works*, 44, 512ff.
56 Marx and Engels' attempts to control the IWA and purge unwanted and recalcitrant members foreshadowed Stalinism.
57 For example see: August H. Nimtz, 'Marxism Versus Anarchism: The First Encounter' in: *Science & Society,* 79:2, April 2015. The July 2016 issue is due to publish a reply by this editor.
58 In 'Statism and Anarchy' he describes 'our convictions' as socialist-revolutionary, 'and on that account we are called anarchists. We do not protest against this epithet, because we are indeed, enemies of every authority ...'
59 On occasion Bakunin appears to have considered it useful for friends to work to have themselves elected to legislatures. See for example a letter of 16 November 1870 to Carlo Gambuzzi, in which he wrote that in current times there was little danger of falling back into 'former political habits'.
60 My emphasis.
61 'Circular letter to my Italian friends', op. cit., p. 336.
62 Ibid, p. 351.
63 Developments in the later 1870s are sketched in René Berthier, *Social-democracy and Anarchism in the International Workers' Association, 1864-1877*, Merlin Press, 2015.
64 René Berthier, 'Théorie politique et méthode d'analyse dans la pensée de Bakounine', in Phillippe Pelletier, op. cit., p. 57.
65 Franz Mehring, *Karl Marx – The Story of his Life*, London: Allen & Unwin, 1939, p.
66 Marcello Musto, Ed, *Workers Unite!: The International 150 Years Later*, London: Bloomsbury, 2014, p. 51.
67 Hal Draper, 'The Death of the State in Marx and Engels' in Ralph Miliband & John Saville (Eds), *Socialist Register 1970*, London: Merlin Press, pp. 281-307.
68 *Pensiero e Voluntà*, 1 July 1926.
69 Paul Avrich, *The Russian Anarchists*, Princeton: Princeton University Press, 1967, pp. 20-21.
70 An essay by Maurizio Antonioli, 'Bakounine entre syndicalisme révolutionnaire et anarchisme' (in Philippe Pelletier, Ed, *Actualité de Bakounine*, op. cit.) discusses these controversies in the period before the First World War. Guillaume's works are listed below in Suggestions for Further Reading.
71 He re-cycled writings and used similar passages in several texts.
72 Letter to Herzen, 28 October 1869, quoted in 'Les Ours de Berne et l'Ours de Saint-Pétersbourg', Neuchâtel: G. Guillaume Fils, 1870, re-published in Michel Bakounine, *Oeuvres* 2, 8. Extracts below – 'On Real Democracy'.
73 Paul Avrich, *Anarchist Portraits*, Princeton: Princeton University Press, 1988, p. 6.
74 Introduction, Michel Bakounine, *Oeuvres*, 1, viii

Programme of the International Alliance for Social Democracy

1. *Mémoire présenté par la Fédération jurassienne de l'Association internationale des Travailleurs à toutes les Fédérations de l'Internationale*, (Pièces Justificatives), Sonvilier: Fédération jurassienne, 1873, pp. 39-40.
2. *Mémoire présenté*, p. 53.

Open Letter from the Central Bureau of the International Fraternity & Letter to James Guillaume

1. *Oeuvres complètes*, CD.
2. Its catechism is available online:http://www.connexions.org/CxLibrary/Docs/CX11019-Bakunin-National-Catechism.htm
3. Esparteros and Prim were military statesmen.
4. *Oeuvres complètes*, CD.

Articles in *L'Égalité*

1. The IWA in Switzerland was organised by region and by language; German speakers had distinct organisations in some parts of French speaking Switzerland. Smaller local sections were formed in Basel and Zurich.
2. Willy Keller, 'L'influence de la Ier Internationale ouvrière sur le mouvement syndical suisse', in *Revue syndicale Suisse*, http://dx.doi.org/10.5169/seals-3853, Vol. 56 (1964), No. 10, p. 280.
3. *Mémoire présenté*, op. cit., p. 46.
4. On Democracy and Education, second lecture to the workers of the Saint-Imier valley, in Michel Bakounine, *Oeuvres*, op. cit., 5, 330.
5. The twelve hour day was widespread. Legislation of 1877 banned night work for women and children and proscribed a maximum eleven hour working day.
6. *Schweizerische Arbeiterbewegung Dokumente zu Lage, Organisation und Kämpfen der Arbeiter von der Frühindustrialisierung bis zur Gegenwart*, Zürich: Limmat Verlag, 1975, pp. 49-50.
7. 'Up to 1870, it had scarcely done more than constituting the left wing of radicalism, ... directing all its activity towards [the system of] direct legislation, and not yet giving priority to the defence of interests of the working class alone.' C.-G. Picavet, *La Suisse: une démocratie historique*, Paris: Flammarion, 1920, p. 151. Bürkli,* from Zürich, was one of those who did participate in the IWA. A minority of Grütli members joined the IWA.
8. *Le Progrès* (Le Locle), 1 May 1869. (Fourth letter from MB).
9. James Guillaume* has a comment: 'Although this appears to have been written by [Charles] Perron* rather than Bakunin, we reproduce it here because the thoughts expressed fall in well with the scheme of ideas and the line of propaganda promoted by Bakunin in the International.'
10. Michel Bakounine, *Oeuvres*, 5, 48ff.
11. An article in the Brussels IWA journal *l'Internationale*, of 27 March 1869; it recalled a massacre of workers from the previous year, and noted the growth of local IWA sections.
12. A reference to the vote of the French National Assembly to abolish feudalism, 4 August 1789.

13 A note here refers to an assembly of the local bourgeoisie held on 31 March that had blamed recent strikes on foreign agitators, designed to compromise national independence. A counter-demonstration, comprising only workers of Swiss nationality, was held on 2 April, it rejected this assertion and concluded with a commitment to bring about radical change in the relations between labour and capital.
14 *L'Égalité*, 24 July 1869; Michel Bakounine, *Oeuvres*, 5, 96.
15 *L'Égalité*, 10 July 1869, reported on a meeting held on 30 May at Crêt-du-Locle that had unanimously condemned Coullery. That text is reproduced as an appendix to René Berthier, *Social-democracy and Anarchism*, op. cit. pp. 167-8. See also: *Political conflict in the International Workers' Association, 1864-1877*, available on monde-nouveau.net.
16 *L'Égalité*, 17 July 1869; Michel Bakounine, *Oeuvres*, 5, 84.
17 The title of this series of four articles appears to be from James Guillaume; From: Michel Bakounine, *Oeuvres*, 5, 169ff.
18 'Le Jugement de M. Coullery' ('Judgement and Mr Coullery'), *L'Égalité*, 7 August 1869.
19 [A reference to] a session of 31 July 1848. *Le Progrès* of Le Locle had published extracts from the minutes of the Constituent Assembly in an issue of 17 April 1869. JG
20 Later documents, particularly 'Prospects for Socialism', set out Bakunin's critique of the Social-Democratic programme in greater detail.
21 The chorus of a song of Pierre Lachambeaudie. JG
22 Guillaume says Bakunin had in mind workers like those of the Fabique.*
23 *Oeuvres complètes*, CD.
24 Ibid, CD; James Guillaume, *L'Internationale*, Book 1, 1905, p. 202; Jacques Freymond, *La première internationale*, op. cit., 2, 94-5.
25 Virginie Barbet was perhaps the author of an article in *L'Égalité* on inheritance that is often attributed to Bakunin; see Antje Schrupp: *Virginie Barbet, une lyonnaise dans l'Internationale*, Lyons: Atelier de création libertaire, 2009.
26 This is a phrase used by Bakunin in a text below: 'Socialism and the Paris Commune', from: *Préambule pour la seconde livraison de L'Empire Knouto-germanique*.
27 A formulation to be found in *Mémoire présenté*, op. cit. p. 78: reformers wanted to conquer the state, revolutionaries sought to destroy it.
28 James Guillaume, *L'Internationale*, Book 1, 1905, p. 200ff.
29 Report of the Fourth Annual Congress of the International Working Men's Association, held at Basel, in Switzerland, from 6 to 11 September 1869; published by the General Council, 1869; available via http://hdl.handle.net/10622/B6E656DD-15BA-4E47-A6F7-B7132F4544C3.
30 Eccarius was speaking for the General Council.
31 The French language congress report carries reports of discussions in the commissions of the General Council and in various federations and sections. Compte-rendu du IVe Congrès tenu à Bâle en septembre 1869, Brussels, Imprimerie Désirée Brismée, 1869. Available online: on http://books.google.co.uk/

On Real Democracy

1. *Les Ours de Berne et l'Ours de Saint-Pétersbourg*, first published by G. Guillaume Fils, Neuchâtel in May 1870; re-published in Michel Bakounine, *Oeuvres*, 2, 36ff.
2. Swiss national institutions are called 'federal' bodies.
3. 'La situation politique en France', (Letter to Palix) Lyons, 29 September-early October 1870. Bakounine, *Oeuvres*, 4, 195.
4. Engels also asserted: 'Every victory by the bourgeoisie over reaction on the other hand is at the same time in one sense a victory for the workers, [it] contributes to the final downfall of capitalist rule and brings the moment closer when the workers will defeat the bourgeoisie.' (*The Prussian Military Question and the German Workers' Party*, 1865.) In chapter four of the *Communist Manifesto* Marx and Engels had written: 'In Switzerland, they [communists] support the Radicals, without losing sight of the fact that this party consists of antagonistic elements, partly of Democratic Socialists, in the French sense, partly of radical bourgeois.'
5. Nechaev was eventually betrayed to the authorities by a police spy and arrested in August 1872. He died in prison in Russia some ten years later.
6. *Oeuvres*, Vol. 2, p. 57
7. Basel was divided into two half-cantons – city and country – as a result of this conflict.
8. Bakunin refers to a conflict between two parties over the validity of an election. Shots were fired, three persons killed and others wounded. Swiss federal troops had a presence in the city for a six month period. Several Radical Party members were imprisoned.
9. Bakunin might have remarked that the electorate was restricted to male citizens.
10. In Switzerland the basic administrative area is called a Commune – corresponding to a rural village or an urban ward.
11. Political practice varied from canton to canton: in most cantons executive bodies were nominated by a legislature, two cantons elected executives directly, while in a few rural cantons politics was conducted through assemblies (*Landsgemeinde*).
12. In using the word 'delegates' Bakunin has in mind members of the lower house of the national legislature, a house directly elected by the people, in which the representation of each canton was proportional to population.
13. The Council of States was composed of two members for each canton, irrespective of the size of their population. In a certain number of cantons these members are elected today by the people themselves and no longer in the [cantonal] legislatures. But for all that things are no better. JG
14. The Princess, who had separated from her husband, was deprived of the custody of her children; with the local police force handing them over to the father.
15. Bélisaire Limousin was a French postal official in Mennetou-sur-Cher, condemned to six months imprisonment for offences relating to letters in her charge; and handed over to French authorities. *Le Confédéré* (Sion, Valais), 23 June 1870.

16 Jakob Dubs, head of the Swiss Federal Council, had requested searches for Nechaev.

Prospects for Socialism

1 Our title. An extract from 'Lettres à un français sur la crise actuelle, (suite)', written circa 3 September 1870, in Michel Bakounine, *Oeuvres*, 4, 22ff. (Lettre à un Français: Conséquences du triomphe prussien pour le socialisme. August-September 1870); also quoted texts published on 20 August, and written on 25-26 August, from *Oeuvres Complètes*, CD.
2 Letter to Marija Kasparovna Reichel-Ern, 11 August, 1870 in *Oeuvres Complètes*, CD.
3 20 August, in *Oeuvres Complètes*, CD.
4 Letter of 2 September, *Oeuvres*, 2, 257-8.
5 See text below 'On Discipline'.
6 Signed: H. Bachruch, B. Malon*, and E. Varlin*.
7 An armistice was agreed in January 1871 and a peace treaty some four months later.
8 Bismarck subsequently facilitated the repression of the Paris Commune releasing captured French troops.
9 A rump Papal State had been maintained under the protection of the French army. The Franco-Prussian War was the occasion for this army to be withdrawn, leaving the way open for the area to be incorporated into the Kingdom of Italy against the will of the papacy.
10 Bakunin notes Great Britain might be an exception, because it no longer had a substantial peasantry.
11 *Oeuvres*, 4, 17.
12 Ibid. p. 18.
13 Napoleon's (First) Empire lasted from 1804 until his defeats in 1814-15, when the French monarchy was restored.
14 In June 1848 in Paris, the French army was used to put down workers protesting for jobs and unemployment relief; some 10,000 were killed.
15 Bakunin's foresight was pretty accurate. The labour movement revived when the General Confederation or Labour (CGT) organised, circa 1900.
16 Read the characteristic and insolent letter of Colonel de Holstein to M. Emile de Girardin. MB
17 One can see that Bakunin had illusions in respect of German Socialist Democracy and its readiness to join with a revolutionary movement that might begin in France. JG
18 Cavaignac had been France's dictator in 1848 and had organised the repression of the June revolts.
19 Robert Macaire was a cartoon character used to lampoon Napoleon III.
20 New Caledonia was chosen as the destination for rebels.
21 In 1800 Cardinal Ruffo had raised an army in Calabria against the French Empire.
22 Unitary organisation is not defined here. One may surmise that Bakunin had a contrasting federalist model of organisation in mind – he drafted rules for

the operation of the Romande Federation of the IWA that were agreed by the regional congress held in Geneva in January 1869. These specified, that within norms, sections of that body were fully autonomous organisations and had every right to decide policy for their own area.

23   In 1869 'Germany' implied a patchwork of large and small states. 'Federal' referred to a North German confederation. After the Franco-Prussian war, German unity was achieved as southern German states joined their northern neighbours in a new German Empire.

24   A year earlier, in September 1869, at the International [IWA] congress in Basel, Bakunin had spoken for an *international state*, as he called it, in opposition to the traditional concept of a necessarily national state. He had demanded 'the destruction of every national and territorial state, and on their ruins the constitution of an international state of workers in their millions; the International [Workers' Association] would have a role in creating such a state.' In his words a demand for the constitution of an international State on the ruins of [all] national states was the equivalent to a demand for the destruction of the state. JG

25   There were differing perspectives among German radicals as to the shape of a new, modern state. Liebknecht hoped for greater Germany, in which Prussia would not be dominant; 'I start from the viewpoint that the fall of Prussia equals the victory of the German revolution.' (11 December 1867, quoted in R.P. Morgan, *The German Social Democrats and the First International*, Cambridge University Press, 1965, p. 19.) Lassalle looked for a progressive Prussian state, on one occasion writing to Bismarck to call not for a popular republican state – a Volksstaat – but rather a *Volkskönigtum*, a popular Prussian-led *monarchy*. (Hermann Beck, 'Working-Class Politics at the Crossroads of Conservatism, Liberalism, and Socialism' in David E. Barclay & Eric D. Weitz, *Between Reform, Reaction and Revolution*, Oxford: Berghahn, 1997, p. 70.) Engels – as we have noted elsewhere – believed that Bismarck was 'clearing the ground for us'.

26   As one must be honest before all else I have to note that in Germany many organs of bourgeois democracy, and most of all Berlin's *Die Zukunft* [The Future], protested with nobility and energy against the furies of the German-bourgeoisie. They understood from the way in which the question was posed between Bismarck and Napoleon III, that either the victory or the defeat of the armies of Germany would bring only horrible distress to the latter. In the first case the cost that would be enormous in money and in men, and there would be indigenous – Prussian, Bismarckian – slavery, subjection of the German nation to the claws of a victorious, military monarchy, 'By the grace of God', and subjection to all sorts of Pomeranian military insolence; in the second case, foreign domination, pillage and the dismembering of Germany. But what would be the use of protesting, if one had the glory of being a part of a great triumphant nation and of being imprisoned by the insoluble dilemma of state and freedom? MB

27   I have not translated a section in which Bakunin goes on to review Bismarck's record over recent years. In the next few pages he probes questions as to Ger-

man identity asking what respect there might be for other peoples: Poles, Moravians, Czechs, etc., who do not wish to be Germanised? The next sentences begin on page 57 of the published text, a text which Bakunin never completed. Michel Bakounine, *Oeuvres*, 4.

Letters to Nikolai Ogarev, the Red Poster and On Discipline

1 Letter to A. Richard,* 12 March 1870.
2 On events in Lyons see: 'La Première Internationale à Lyon' [2 parts], http://www.commune-rougerie.fr/la-premiere-internationale,fr,8,72.cfm4 http://www.commune-rougerie.fr/la-premiere-internationale_1,fr,8,73.cfm
3 Bakunin refers to texts published as 'Letters to a Frenchman', (Lettres à un français sur la crise actuelle) – extracts of which are translated above, under the title 'Prospects for Socialism'.
4 Bakunin had written to Ogarev a month earlier: 'You are [a] Russian [revolutionary] only, whereas I am an internationalist and the events now happening in Europe have brought me to a fever pitch.' Bakunin was evidently thinking that if the revolution progressed in France it would return the favour and the Russian revolution would benefit too.
5 From *Oeuvres completes*, Amsterdam: IISG, 2000.
6 From Michel Dragomanov (Edited & translated by), *Correspondance de Michel Bakounine: Lettres à Herzen et à Ogareff (1860-1874)*, Paris: Didier Perrin, 1896, pp. 341-2.
7 Beloche, perhaps. (Dragomanov's note.)
8 As Paris was occupied by German troops the offices of the French Government were relocated to Tours
9 Our title.
10 From: 'L'Empire Knouto-Germanique et la révolution sociale: révolution sociale ou dictature militaire', in Michel Bakounine, *Oeuvres*, 2, 297-8. First published with an earlier title on an inside page: *La Révolution sociale, ou la dictature militaire*, in 1871.

On Democracy and Education

1 Our title: Michel Bakounine, *Oeuvres*, 5, 323-331.
2 Since 1871 matters are much changed in the Saint-Imier valley. The watch and clock making industry has entered a phase of large scale production; most male and female watchmakers now work in plants or factories and wages are much diminished. JG

Socialism and the Paris Commune

1 *Oeuvres*, 4, 248-64; written in Locarno and first published seven year later, in Geneva, in 1878, by Élisée Reclus.*
2 'Lettres à un français sur la crise actuelle, (appendice)', in Michel Bakounine, *Oeuvres*, 2, 226, 228.
3 James Guillaume, *L'Internationale*, op. cit., Vol. 2, book 2, 143ff.
4 Jean-Christophe Angaut in *Marx, Bakounine, et la guerre franco-allemande*, available online: 2005/02 http://www.sens-public.org/spip.php?article131

Angaut surveys and contrasts Bakunin and Marx's writings.
5   Letter to the editor of *Gazzettino Rosa*, 1-2 January 1872.
6   'Circular letter to my Italian friends, in Michel Bakounine, *Oeuvres*, 6, 354.
7   Bakunin goes on to examine the role of religion in motivating and energising reaction.
8   René Berthier writes that 'science' had a different meaning when the term was used by radicals and others in Germany in the early 19th century: it had the meaning of philosophy. At that time the hard or natural sciences were barely developed. See his: 'Théorie politique et méthode d'analyse dans la pensée de Bakounine', in Philippe Pelletier, Ed, *Actualité de Bakounine 1814-2014*, op. cit., p. 45.
9   It is equally accepted, and will be accepted more so, by the essentially non-political instincts of Slav peoples. MB
10 See his letter to Littré in the *Progrès* of Lyons. MB
11 Letter to *La Liberté*, Brussels, 5 October 1872. In *Oeuvres*, 4, 387.

On Leaders and Politics

1   Michel Bakounine, *Oeuvres*, 6, pp. 3ff and pp. 15ff; Bakunin left this text incomplete. Excerpts were first published in *Almanach du Peuple* (1872) and in the *Mémoire de la Fédération jurassienne* (1872-1873) op. cit. This title is ours.
2   Utin's letters affirmed his intention to carry out instructions sent from London.
3   Jean Maitron, *Le mouvement anarchiste en France*, Vol. 1, Paris: Gallimard, 1992, pp. 57-8; emphasis added.
4   9 April 1870, quoted in *Mémoire présenté*, op. cit., p. 143.
5   Membership records were very poor. Many IWA bodies paid dues irregularly or not at all. The General Council was able to use non-payment of dues as grounds for de-recognition.
6   Jung replying to Guillaume's letter of 30 May 1870, quoted in *Mémoire présenté*, op. cit., pp. 134-6.
7   See also *Mémoire présenté*, op. cit., pp. 65ff.
8   See letter to Ludovico Nabruzzi* and others, 23-26 January 1872.
9   Jung's letter of 30 May 1870, quoted in *Mémoire présenté*, p. 138.
10 *Oeuvres*, 6, 274.
11 Letter, Marx to Paul Lafargue, 19 April 1870, *Collected Works*, op. cit., 43, 493.
12 The Romande Federal committee represented the Romande Federation; IWA organisations in Geneva formed only a part of that federation. The Romande Federal committee was elected for one year by the congress of the Romande Federation and had its seat in Geneva for the year 1869. JG
13 This comment is rather pointed. The General Council refused to recognise the rights of the majority of the Romande Federation congress which appointed a new Federal Committee after the regional congress of April 1870. It chose to ignore the new Federal Committee and continued to correspond with its predecessor.
14 Bakunin refers to a reference that appears to have been made in a part of the text now lost. JG

15 Here again Bakunin appears to refer to a part of the text that has been lost.
16 It was not the congress which chose Brosset as its president, it was the Federal Committee which chose him, from amongst its members, to carry out the role of president. JG
17 As will be shown below, Bakunin was addressing workers of the Jura mountains. JG
18 Bakunin has in mind Henri Perret* and Grosselin.* In reality Henri Perret alone was the delegate for the Fabrique sections. Grosselin, along with Brosset and Heng,* had been elected as a delegates by a vote of Geneva sections as a whole. JG
19 On this discussion see the text: 'Summary and extracts of the report of the opening day's discussion, on the Congress agenda and on state politics', Basel, 1869, in René Berthier, *Socialism and Anarchism in the International Workers' Association, 1864-1877*, op. cit, pp. 169-172.
20 On that programme see above: 'Prospects for Socialism'.
21 At the Basel Congress Liebknecht condemned as reactionaries those who opposed discussion of the tactic of electoral-party-political activity.
22 There were many arrests and imprisonments following a large scale demonstration in Vienna in December 1869.
23 German and Swiss-German IWA members in Geneva had set themselves up with a distinct administration and organisation completely separate from that of the Geneva Central Committee and the Federal Committee of Romande Switzerland. (Bakunin's note.)
24 The history of the electoral campaign of the Party of Socialist Democracy in the autumn of 1868 in Geneva, and of Catalan's journal, *Liberté,* which served as the party's organ, is told in my *L'Internationale, Documents et Souvenirs,* Vol. 1. JG
25 In the Jura region of canton of Neuchâtel. JG
26 Paragraphs have been omitted here, the translation resumes from page 55. Bakunin describes proposals to create strike funds under the control of members' assemblies, with a committee formed of recallable members – an attack on the oligarchic forms that prevailed in Geneva.
27 Marx was not involved in the initial negotiations between leaders of trades' bodies from England and France which resulted in the formation of the IWA. He was involved later drafting IWA documents; some of these were modified and adopted by the IWA's initial congress.
28 The correspondence of Marx, Engels and Becker with Sorge,* [first] published in 1906, clearly justifies Bakunin's judgement. JG
29 A few paragraphs on circumstances in and around 1864-6 have been omitted, and the translation resumes from page 65.

On the Alliance

1 'Rapport sur l'alliance', August 1871; Michel Bakounine, *Oeuvres,* Vol. 6, Paris: Stock, 1913, pp. 171ff. The title above is the editor's.
2 Such events contradict accusations that Bakunin was some sort of dictator, e.g. Marx to Engels, 27 July, 1869: 'This Russian obviously wishes to become

the dictator of the European workers' movement.'; Marx & Engels, *Collected Works*, op. cit., 43, 332-3; repeated elsewhere – e.g. in a letter to De Paepe* (24 January 1870) and in a 'Confidential Communication' to contacts in Germany (March 1870).

3   Letter from Malon and Lefrançais to Verrycken: 'Despite the freedom enjoyed by these Geneva people, despite all the means at their disposal – a free press, freedom of assembly and of association, the International here has no real intellectual existence: neither meetings, nor conferences, nor discussions of principles. Most members are absolutely ignorant of the International's principles and goals. Each is content to say: "I am a member of the International." But again nothing serious; the intelligent, the disgusted, draw away or are excluded by the committees that alone, govern and direct sections, and which meet once a month at best!' See: K. Steven Vincent, *Between Marxism, and Anarchism: Benoît Malon and French Reformist Socialism*, University of Chicago Press, 1992, p. 45.

4   At a meeting on 2 December 1871; *Le Mouvement social*, No. 51, April-June 1965. http://gallica.bnf.fr/ark:/12148/bpt6k5622756d/texteBrut

5   *Mémoire présenté*, op. cit.

6   I have not translated every one of Guillaume's notes on these differences.

7   Guillaume writes: 'the question addressed here then concerned – as will be seen – the causes that had provoked the hostility of Fabrique and of leaders of the Fabrique sections' committees towards the Alliance section.'

8   The International Circle, the common HQ of the sections of the International in Geneva. In 1868 its meeting place was at the *Brasserie des Quatre-Saisons*, in the Grottes area; in March 1869 it relocated to the Temple-Unique, the former masonic Temple.

9   See: James Guillaume, *L'Internationale, Documents et Souvenirs*, op. cit., I, 92. The address, which Bakunin drafted, was dated 21 October 1868. JG

10 i.e. on the official recognition of the group, as a section of the International, by the London General Council. JG

11 The provisional Central Bureau of the Alliance for Socialist Democracy was intended to serve as a link between the groups of that international organisation, corresponding with national bureaux that were to be constituted in various lands. The founding members of the Alliance had decided that the Central Bureau should be located in Geneva and should have seven members, nominated by themselves and named in the text above. These seven were all – at the same time – members of the International. Their national origins were as follows: three from France and one each from Geneva, Germany, Poland and Russia. JG

12 Bakunin was probably wrong to suppose that Becker did not write to London at all, or wrote in a manner at odds with what he was saying to the Central Bureau of the Alliance. It appears that Becker was truly keen on the Alliance for a time. In the 'Confidential Communication' of March 1870 to his friends in Germany (which Bakunin never knew) [see https://www.marxists.org/archive/marx/works/1870/03/28.htm], Marx reprimands Becker and portrays him as having been, at first, Bakunin's dupe. He says – as he talks of the first steps of

the Alliance in Geneva: 'J.-Ph. Becker, who lost his head sometimes when the zeal of the propagandist affected him, was pushed to the fore.' Moreover, if Becker had not acted in good faith at the time, one cannot understand – when [at first] the General Council refused to accept the membership application of the Alliance – was made so angry, as will be narrated further on in the text. JG

13 Bakunin had himself been involved in discussions with London. Marx, having been made aware of the Alliance's programme, had written in the second half of December to Alexander Serno-Soloviévitch,* a young Russian socialist based in Geneva, raising [the point of] an incorrect expression – class equalisation – which appeared in that programme. Serno showed Marx's letter to Bakunin, and the latter immediately wrote the following letter to Marx published in *Neue Zeit*, 6 October 1900:

'Geneva, 22 December 1868.

My old friend Serno told me about that part of your letter that related to me. You asked him if I was still a friend of yours. Yes, and more than ever, dear Marx, because better than before I have come to understand how much you were in the right in taking the greater road of economic revolution, and in inviting us to do likewise. Also in criticising those amongst us who would lose our way in other national or exclusively political by-ways. What I am doing now is what you began to do over twenty year ago. After the solemn and public farewells I addressed to the bourgeoisie at the Congress in Bern, [of the League for Peace and Justice] I know no other world than the world of workers. My homeland now is the International of which you are one of the principal founders. So you see, dear friend that I am your disciple, and proud to be so. So there you have all that is needed to explain my relations and personal feelings.' (Bakunin went on to comment on the concept of equalisation [levelling] of individuals and classes; he mentioned sending speeches that he had made in Bern, and spoke of his separation from Herzen,* which date from 1863. He then continued ...) 'I am sending you the programme of the Alliance which we founded with Becker and many French, Italian and Polish friends. We have much to say about this subject. Presently I will send you a copy of a long letter I have written on this matter to friend César De Paepe*...'Greet Engels for me, if he hasn't died again – you know that he was buried once. I also ask you to give him a copy of my speeches, and to Mssrs Eccarius and Jung also.

'Your most devoted, M. Bakunin.

'Remember me please to Mrs Marx.' JG

14 This text was not inserted in Bakunin's manuscript: the reference in brackets to 'Pièce justificative n° 5', should be located here. (The words 'n° 5' tell us that in the first pages of this lost manuscript, that there were references to four other justificatory texts.) The document was printed in the *Mémoire [présenté]*, and was also included in Marx's brochure 'Fictitious Splits in the International' [https://www.marxists.org/archive/marx/works/1872/03/fictitious-splits.htm]. We reproduce it in the text. These resolutions were 'communicated confidentially to the central councils (of the International) of various countries.' (Letter of Marx to Hermann Jung, of 28 December 1868). In this way a copy of the resolutions was sent to Carlo Gambuzzi* in Naples,

on 20 January 1869, by Eugène Dupont, a member of the General Council in London, who had represented Naples workers' sections at the Brussels congress of 1868. It was this copy that was communicated to Bakunin from Naples, and which he received before the decision of the General Council was passed, officially, on to the Central Bureau of the Alliance; it was found by Max Nettlau, who inserted it in his biography of Bakunin. JG

15 Although these resolutions were perfectly logical they were not adopted unanimously. Three delegates, César De Paepe,* Charles Perron* and Adolphe Catalan, had voted against them. Other delegates, absent when the vote was taken, were, at the time far from thinking that the existence of the League for Peace* was useless; among them was Charles Longuet* who in the following year, 1869, continued to take part in the League. He attended its Lausanne congress in that year. Furthermore members of the second Paris commission of the IWA, detained in Sainte-Pélagie [Paris] following their condemnation to three months imprisonment, thought it necessary to protest against the 'invitation of members the Brussels [IWA] congress sent to the League for Peace inviting the latter to dissolve itself', and sent an address to members of the Bern congress [of the League for Peace] containing their protest; this address was signed by Combault, Mollin, Granjon, Malon,* Varlin,* Humbert and Landrin. JG

16 To my knowledge only one of those persons who subsequently formed part of the 'initiating group' had voted for the Brussels resolutions: J.-Ph. Becker.* But, after the minority of the Bern congress delegates left the League to create the Alliance, Becker judged that this new organisation, being part of the International, had its own raison d'être. JG

17 Earlier, when members of the minority at the Bern congress were separating themselves from the League for Peace, Bakunin had expressed the same opinion: 'The French and Italians ... wanted the Alliance to organise quite independently of the IWA, and would have been content if individuals were members of the IWA. Bakunin opposed this, for the reason that this new international organisation would in some fashion place itself as an undesirable rival vis-à-vis the IWA. The result of these discussions was that it was decided to create a public association named the International Alliance for Socialist Democracy and to announce that it was to be an integral part of the IWA, whose programme was recognised as being compulsory for every member of the Alliance.' [JG cites texts on the International published in Zurich in 1873, under the title *Istoritcheskoé razvitié Internatsionala*.] Nevertheless given that the General Council of the IWA had found that – insofar as it had a particular Central Bureau and international organisation – the Alliance could not be a member of the IWA, it is no cause for astonishment that Bakunin, in conformity with his wish to avoid everything that might give the Alliance any appearance of 'a rivalry that was not wanted at all vis-à-vis a workers' organisation', and declaring that the regulations of the Alliance should be modified in line with the comments of the General Council. JG

18 The draft of Perron's letter was found in Geneva by Max Nettlau, and he inserted it in his biography of Bakunin:

Geneva, 26 February 1869.

The Central Bureau of the International Alliance of Socialist Democracy to the General Council of the IWA,

Citizens, we have received after some time the letter that you sent to us on 28 December 1868. We will not examine the interpretation which you thought you should give to our regulations, an interpretation which – we hope and believe inadvertently – was erroneous on many points. To get to the point:

If we have not replied to you earlier it is because we had to consult our national committees. So now this then is our reply:

We would only propose to all our sections to dissolve our organisation after you had made known your opinion to us:

1. If the principles announced in the programme appended here are, *yes* or *no*, contrary to the principles that the IWA might admit?

2. If the various groups who promote these principles may, *yes* or *no*, be affiliated to the IWA, it being understood that these said groups each declare that they accept the regulations and statutes of the said IWA?

3. If in consequence the groups that have come together through the Alliance might, *yes* or *no*, be recognised as sections of the IWA in the event that – after having taken the advice of our national committees and of every section of our International Alliance of Socialist Democracy – we announce its dissolution?

On the first question, if your reply is NO,

On the second and third questions, if your reply is YES,

We declare:

To avoid division in the forces of labour, we would work as hard as we can, to obtain from those that it concerns, the dissolution of our Alliance, which moreover has already born excellent fruit in Switzerland and especially in France, Spain and Italy, where the IWA has not been able to take root in any serious fashion, and where a radical programme like ours appears to us suited to promote the attraction of a large mass of workers. And so, we add, we hope to see the proposals that we are making achieve this desired outcome.

But we also wish to declare to you equally, that if against our hopes, you might reply yes to our first question and negatively to the other two, we decline responsibility for the division that your resolution of 22 December last might infallibly tend to produce and we will preserve our International Alliance of Socialist Democracy. Being unable to sacrifice our programme, that is to say our convictions, we would have the satisfaction of having fulfilled our duty in proposing the sacrifice of our organisation once again to promote the unity of workers – whatever the opinions they may adhere to.

So citizens, we leave to you the responsibility of deciding our existence, and declaring whether in your opinion the IWA can admit into itself groups that profess and propagate the ideas that are contained in our programme. Given the gravity of this matter, we hope, citizens, that you will not delay a reply, and that a reply will be in keeping with the spirit of reasonableness in which this letter was written.

Receive, citizens, our fraternal greetings,

In the name of the Central Bureau of the International Alliance of Socialist Democracy, the general secretary:

Ch. Perron. JG

19 At the congress of the Romande Federation in Chaux-de-Fonds, of 4 April 1870, Guétat* spoke as follows: 'Guétat declared that he withdrew from the Alliance, because there were secret committees within it, whose members were tending to set up nothing less than a dictatorship. He himself had been a part of these secret committees, as had Henri Perret*, Duval* and other members of the Federal Committee likewise; but later he had left them, as his colleagues did also ... He said the ladies who were members of the Alliance were never on these secret committees, because the superior committee was against it, and that when the matter was discussed, Bakunin and his allies used foul language which he did not want to repeat. He called on Duval to corroborate his testimony.' Henri Perret* and Duval spoke of the secret committee: 'Henri Perret spoke of several details concerning the former secret Alliance committee ... Duval said that he was still a member of the Alliance; he recognised that women had never been accepted as committee members; but he contradicted the other statements made by Guétat, Perret, etc.' (*Solidarité*, No. 1, 11 April 1870.) JG

20 Bakunin was prone to making hostile comments about the Jewish identity of political enemies. Herzen replied to one such letter on 21 October 1869 – 'your letter did not please me. Why do you speak so much of races, of Jews?'

21 Bakunin left Geneva after the Basel congress to live in the Ticino. He had no easy contact with developments in Geneva thereafter. Utin* attended some public meetings of the Alliance. Becker and others supported changes to the programme of the Alliance. Bakunin perhaps saw Utin's hand at work here. He was able to muster sufficient support to reverse these changes. Becker participated in meetings of the Alliance before the split in the Romande Federation at La Chaux-de-Fonds, but thereafter appears to have resigned.

22 See note 19 above. JG

23 In the *Mémoire présenté*, the two passages of Bakunin' manuscript immediately following have been deleted and replaced by the following lines: 'I have not found in my papers the copy of the reply from London to our request from Geneva. Happily this reply of these Marxist gentlemen dated 20 March 1869, is printed entirely in the private circular (of 5 March 1872); it is from there that I take the text, and so, in this way the authenticity cannot be challenged.' [There follows the text of the resolution of the General Council of 9 March 1869, a text sent on to Geneva in a letter dated 20 March.] JG

24 The full text of this reply, and other texts – are reproduced in *Fictitious Splits in the International* (Les prétendues scissions), which can be found online: https://www.marxists.org/archive/marx/works/1872/03/fictitious-splits.htm. One of the points of the reply made in 1869 to the Alliance noted 'Consequently, it belongs not to the function of the General Council to subject the program of the Alliance to a critical examination. We have not to inquire whether, yes or no, it be a true scientific expression of the working-class movement. All we have to ask is whether its general tendency does not run against the general tendency of the International Working Men's Association, viz., the complete emancipation of the working class?' (General Council 9 March 1869.) Guillaume adds that the draft of this resolution – in French – and in

Marx's hand was published as an appendix to a book by Gustav Jaeckh, *Die Internationale*, (Leipzig, 1904) and that there were some minor differences between the draft and the final text. Guillaume suggests that the General Council correspondent for Switzerland had attempted (unsuccessfully) to improve the French of the Master's writing. So the text, as revised by Jung,* still contained the ultra-Germanic phrase: 'There is a phrase of your programme which is from this viewpoint defective', which should probably be translated by the words: 'which from this perspective is badly expressed'.

25 The word *published* is not correct, because no *publicity* was given to the resolutions of 22 December 1869. JG

26 These lines, and those above, separated in the manuscript, by dashes from what precedes and what follows, are omitted from the *Mémoire* [*présenté*]. But the content of the first of these two paragraphs were placed in the text of the *Mémoire*, p. 55; and the phrase: 'The Madrid Section was transformed into a section of the International, whilst preserving the programme of the Alliance', gave way to a correction on p. 244, expressed as follows: 'When we wrote the words [above], we did not know exactly in what fashion the certain Spanish internationalists had become members of the Alliance – whether they were so as members of existing sections in Spain or as members of the section in Geneva. We were never clear on this point: all the Spaniards who belonged to the Alliance of Socialist Democracy, a public body affiliated to the International, were simple members of the section of Geneva. There never was, in Madrid, an Alliance section; the section of the International [there] was created directly, when Fanelli* made his journey there.' JG

27 Some of the extracts from the minutes of the Geneva Alliance as published by Max Nettlau in his biography of Bakunin show that these terms, as used here by Bakunin, should not be taken as being exact. For example, the discussion on the new Alliance section's regulations began on 17 April and ended only on 24 April. Furthermore, there were several occasions again, in May and June, when there was further discussion of one point or another in the programme and it was only on 26 June that the section was properly constituted. JG

28 Article 24 lists only three reasons for expulsion: 1. Cowardly or shameful behaviour; 2. Flagrant violation of the programme or of the fundamental articles of the regulations; 3. Betrayal of workers' solidarity. MB

29 These words show the spirit that impelled Bakunin and some of the 'collectivist' delegates at the Basel Congress to support an increase of the powers of the General Council. JG

30 An earlier rendition of this text referred to how ridiculous was the accusation that the Alliance sought to undermine or destroy the work of the General Council. JG

31 One should not look to Bakunin to find exact indications or a rigorously exact chronology. He was writing two years after these events and lacked access to the minutes of the Alliance section. Perron's letter was dated 22 June; the meeting at which the Geneva Alliance section was finally constituted was on 26 June; and, already at a section meeting of 12 June, Bakunin had announced that the regulations would be sent to London for the 19 June so that the section might be admitted into the International (Extracts of the minutes published by Max Nettlau). JG

32 Why was this letter written by Perron? Evidently because previously he had functioned as the secretary of the Central Bureau of the Alliance. He was not the secretary of the Alliance section of Geneva, since he had refused to be elected as a member of the section Committee; rather it was Fritz Heng who was nominated as secretary on 1 May. But, insofar as everything was still 'provisional', no doubt members of the Alliance considered it was better that Perron should continue, temporarily, to correspond with the General Council. Moreover in this letter there are phrases in which Perron speaks as the former secretary of the Central Bureau, those in which he says 'we submitted the matter of dissolution … As we informed various Alliance groups of this decision we invited them …' etc. JG

33 Note, that with almost the only change being the one noted above (concerning the words *equalisation of classes*), it was the entire programme of the old Alliance [that was noted] and that the first article of this programme began with the words: The *Alliance declares itself atheist*. MB

34 Here again there are errors in the chronology. The Alliance section had existed definitively from 26 June onwards. Its committee was designated on 1 May. It was in the committee meeting of 17 July that it was decided to send dues to London (10 francs 40 for 104 members). And it was only in a section meeting of 31 July that Eccarius's letter was read out. JG

35 Note that members of a section might be persons who had lived only temporarily in an area (e.g. Geneva), and who now lived elsewhere. Sections might appoint persons from other sections as their congress delegates, persons who could afford costs of travel. Attendance at congresses also reflected distance from the congress location.

36 This decision preceded the arrival of the letter from Eccarius. In the minutes of the Alliance section committee after 17 July, the question was raised of asking the Cantonal Committee of Geneva sections to admit the Alliance section into the federation. On 30 July Bakunin read a draft letter to the committee of the Alliance section to the Cantonal Committee and this was agreed. JG

37 The number of members, sixty, corresponding with the presence of thirty sections, is exaggerated. At the time of the Brussels General Congress of September 1868, there were 24 sections in the Canton Geneva (report of delegate Graglia); at the time of the foundation of the Romande Federation, in January 1869, the number of Geneva sections was 23 (report of the Romande Federal Committee to the congress of La Chaux-de-Fonds, April 1870, *L'Égalité* of 30 April 1870); in October 1869 it was 26 (cf. *L'Internationale, Documents et Souvenirs*, 1, 230). Lastly, according to a text in *L'Égalité* of 28 April 1870, the Geneva sections, at the time of the congress of La Chaux-de-Fonds, were 28. JG

38 Skilled workers defended their competitive advantages. For example, a regional meeting of Romande and Savoyarde typographers of May 1870 resolved to work for the expansion of their organisation to places where it was as yet unorganised; to increase rates of pay; to prevent low-pay competition between typographers; to regulate apprenticeships and to create a strike fund.

39 A reference to Étienne Cabet, whose book *Voyage en Icarie*, (Travels to Icaria) published in 1842 described an imaginary utopian socialist society.

40   In Geneva, members of the Conseil d'État, i.e. the cantonal government, were elected directly by the people. JG
41   Article (No. 52) said: 'Each year the [Romande] congress will fix the price and programme of its journal.' However another article (No. 42), relating to the powers of the Federal committee set out that: 'It will be responsible for exercising a moral overview of the association's journal.' JG
42   As is said above, Bakunin exaggerates the number of sections that existed in Geneva. JG
43   The split in the Romande Federation might be traced back to this confrontation and to the resentment of Fabrique politicians seeing their priorities disregarded.
44   There were seven Fabrique sections that chose Henri Perret as their delegate: watch and clock makers, jewellers, sheath-makers, turners, engravers, parts-makers, music box makers: Report of Henri Perret, in *Compte-rendu du 4e Congress international, tenu à Bâle*, p. 49. JG
45   Bakunin is in error when he says that these three were elected as delegates by the building workers together with cutters and shoemakers: they were delegates of the entire Geneva Federation. After Fabrique sections had decided that they should have themselves represented by a special delegate, Henri Perret, the general assembly, meeting on the 17 August, decided that there should be a collective delegation of three members elected by all sections. *L'Égalité* of 21 August contains the following article on this subject:
'There was a general assembly of all Geneva sections on Tuesday 17 August. There it was decided that three delegates should be sent to Basel representing all the French language sections of Geneva. Every member or group was able to propose candidates whose names would be written up on a board. The vote would be by secret ballot, each member placing three names on a list. To be allowed to vote, one had to prove, by presenting membership documents that each member [and their dues] were in compliance with their section. The ballot would be open:
On Saturday 21 August, from 8 till 10 in the evening; on Sunday 22 from 8am till 4pm; and on Monday 23 from 8 to 10pm.'
At the Basel congress, Heng, Brosset and Grosselin were admitted as 'delegates of the Geneva international sections', Henri Perret as a 'delegate of the Fabrique sections of watch and clock makers, jewellers and music-box makers in Geneva.' JG
46   The contradiction between the assertion of Bakunin that Grosselin and his two colleagues were delegates of the building workers, and the facts as attested by *L'Égalité*, that the three delegates were elected to represent 'all the French language sections of Geneva' (since there were also in Geneva German [language] sections which were represented at the Basel congress by Becker), may be resolved thus: the general assembly had indeed decided that all the French language sections should be invited to take part in the election of three common delegates; but the seven sections of the Fabrique, having already named their particular delegate, abstained; in the voting of 21, 22 and 23 August the only participants were members of sections of building workers and some intermediary sections (cutters, shoemakers and typesetters), such

that in effect, if this explication is correct, as I believe it to be, Grosselin although a watchmaker, found himself elected by building workers. JG

47 This confirms what was said in the note above. The Fabrique sections, having Henri Perret as their particular delegate, did not contribute funds for the common delegation of the Geneva sections. JG

48 At the Basel congress, it was Grosselin who delivered the administrative report for the Geneva sections. When he had finished reading it he added a personal observation about his mandate: 'He finished,' says the *Compte-rendu du Congress*, 'saying that the Central Committee had allowed him complete latitude on the questions of property and inheritance, contrary to what has been done for his colleagues.' But Brosset protested at once: he said that Grosselin, just like himself, and like Heng, had received a firm mandate to vote in favour of collective property and the abolition of inheritance, and that seventeen sections had given him this mandate. (*Compte-rendu*, op. cit., p. 60). Obviously the seventeen sections were those which had taken part in the voting on 21, 22 and 23 August. If one adds to these seventeen sections the seven Fabrique sections, which had Henri Perret as their delegate, one comes to 24. It should also be noted that the society of makers of musical pieces were not part of the 'grouping of sections of Geneva and of the Romande Federation.' (Report of Henri Perret, *Compte-rendu*, p. 50). JG

49 I have forgotten to say that on this occasion Perron was not absent, he supported us energetically in general assemblies. He was eloquent, logical, and captivating, he contributed greatly to our success. MB

50 The rest of the text discusses developments in Geneva and in the Alliance after the Basel congress, when Bakunin was living at some distance away from Geneva. He considers the roles and impact of local comrades and enemies.

Letter to the Jura Comrades

1 'Aux Compagnons de la Fédération des Sections internationales de Jura', February-March, 1872; in Arthur Lehning, Ed., Bakounine; *Les conflits dans l'Internationale: 1872*, Antony (France), Ed. Tops-H. Trinquier, 2003, pp. 53ff.

2 Engels, some twenty year earlier, had viewed war in terms of peoples (rather than classes) and as facilitating progress: 'the question is not that of a fraternal union of all European peoples under a single republican flag, but of an alliance of the revolutionary peoples against the counter-revolutionary peoples, an alliance which comes into being not on *paper*, but only on the *battlefield*.' Engels, *Neue Rheinische Zeitung*, 14 February 1849.

3 Marx wrote in a letter to Engels of 16 September 1868 of: 'Belgian nonsense that it was necessary to strike against war…' He was perhaps suggesting that such action was impractical. *Collected Works*, London: Lawrence & Wishart, 1987, 43, 101.

4 Bakunin writes of the General Council's 'Manifesto', referring to the *Inaugural Address*. Although widely quoted since, it was never brought to or approved by an IWA congress. Indeed, as Bakunin shows, Marx's views on Russia were not endorsed by the first congresses of the IWA. https://www.marxists.org/archive/marx/works/1864/10/27.htm

5   Marx wrote of: '... the mountain fortresses of the Caucasus falling a prey to, and heroic Poland being assassinated, by Russia: the immense and unresisted encroachments of that barbarous power, whose head is in St. Petersburg, and whose hands are in every cabinet of Europe ...'
6   'Aux Compagnons', op. cit. p. 49.
7   October 1871, 'Circular letter to my Italian friends', in Michel Bakounine, *Oeuvres*, op. cit. 6, 403.
8   I earnestly do justice to the leaders of the party of Socialist Democracy, and to its leading committee, to the Bebels, Liebknechts and many others...' Michel Bakounine, *Oeuvres*, 2, 405.
9   An interesting review of Engels' and Bakunin's ideas on national identity is presented in: Roman Rosdolsky, 'Engels and the "Nonhistoric" Peoples: the National Question in the Revolution of 1848', *Critique*, 18-19, Glasgow, 1986.
10 *Tribune* (New York), 7 April 1853. https://www.marxists.org/archive/marx/works/subject/russia/crimean-war.htm. Marx, in his letter to Engels of 16 September 1868, cited above, viewed the prospect of a civil war in Europe – between France and Germany – as a war that would profit Russia.
11 Engels, in a letter to Marx in London of 15 August 1870, set out that a new united Germany was a step forward for working people. 'Bismarck, as in 1866, is at present doing a bit of our work *for us*, in his own way and without meaning to, but all the same he is doing it. He is clearing the ground *for us* better than before.' Our emphasis. http://www.marxists.org/archive/marx/works/1870/letters/70_08_15.htm; see also a letter dated 31 July, Marx & Engels, *Collected Works*, 44, 18. Bakunin knew these perspectives from extracts published in the Social-Democractic press. He read similar perspectives in a letter from Engels to Cafiero. (See 'Fragment formant une suite', in *Oeuvres*, 4, 456. For a perspective stressing Marx and Engels' internationalism see: Hal Draper & E. Haberkern, *Karl Marx's Theory of Revolution*, Volume 5, New York: Monthly Review Press, 2010, pp. 126ff.
12 A secession or withdrawal should not provide an opportunity for a new alliance to be formed with another power to facilitate the curtailing of the freedom or destruction of the independence in the body from which a sesession takes place. 'Lettres à un français sur la crise actuelle', continuation, on consequences for Socialism of a Prussian victory, *Oeuvres Complètes*, CD.
13 'Aux Compagnons', op. cit., p. 57.
14 'Aux Compagnons', op. cit., p. 44.
15 In *Ouevres complètes*, CD. French title: *La Théologie Politique de Mazzini et l'Internationale*, Neuchatel: G. Guillaume, 1871, p. 94.
16 Ibid, p. 95.
17 Ibid, p. 95-6.
18 'Statism and Anarchy', *Oeuvres completes*, CD.
19 See the final paragraphs of 'Writings against Marx', below.
20 'Aux Compagnons', op. cit., p. 28.
21 *La Théologie Politique de Mazzini*, op. cit, p. 110-1.
22 See for example *Neue Rheinische Zeitung*, 20 August 1848, in Marx-Engels, *Collected Works*: 7, 352-353; and a call for a European war against Russia:

http://marxengels.public-archive.net/en/ME1724en.html

23   Part of the manuscript reviewing texts written on Polish freedom in 1863 is omitted here. Another discussion of the politics of the labour movement concerning Polish issues is set out below.

24   Bakunin hoped that the rural collective village peasant bodies that already existed in part in Russia, if they had greater freedom to develop, might form cells of a new federated society. See Michaël Confino, 'Bakunin et Nechaev [Les débuts de la rupture: Introduction à deux lettres inédites de Michel Bakunin – 2 et 9 juin 1870', in: *Cahiers du monde russe et soviétique*. Vol. 7, No. 4. October-December 1966, p. 655; doi: 10.3406/cmr.1966.1686 http://www.persee.fr/web/revues/home/prescript/article/cmr_0008-0160_1966_num_7_4_1686

25   Schleswig-Holstein was annexed by Prussia two years later. A plebiscite was promised, it was not held at the time, but only after the First World War, and resulted in North Schleswig being returned to Denmark.

26   Four paragraphs of polemic against Borkheim are omitted, and the extract resumes from the following page, p. 58.

27   Maltman Barry served briefly as the chairperson of the IWA. Marx worked closely with him and described him as his factotum. Barry stood for election to parliament as an anti-Russian conservative.

28   *Congrès ouvrier de l'Association Internationale des Travailleurs tenu à Geneva du 3 au 8 septembre 1866*, Geneva, Imprimerie J.C. Ducommun et G. Oettinger, route de Carouge, 1866. MB

29   It was the General Council in London of which citizen K. Marx was then, as now, a very influential member, which drew up the questions discussed by congress. MB

30   Bakunin asks: I would very much like to know what citizen Becker makes today of the German empire's civilising mission?

31   No doubt to disguise an honourable retreat. MB

32   i.e. in the sense of exclusively Germanic nationality on this question. MB

33   Bakunin refers to the IWA statutes and their commitment that all IWA societies and individuals should acknowledge truth, justice, and morality as the basis of their conduct.

34   Two pages concerning J. P. Becker are omitted here; the text resumes from p. 63.

35   Some pages omitted here reproduce a speech made by Bakunin to the League for Peace and Freedom,* in Bern, in September 1868. Bakunin went on to ask questions about minorities and ethnically mixed areas – e.g. how would Polish speaking areas currently in the German Empire be treated in the future? Would Germans refrain from trying to Germanise regions peopled by Danes, Czechs, Moravians, Silesians? He called for rights of secession for associations and communes, provinces and nations. 'Aux Compagnons', in *Les conflits*, pp. 70-3.

36   This translation resumes from pp. 74 onwards.

37   Paragraphs extracted from 'L'Allemagne et le communisme d'état', in Arthur Lehning, Ed., Bakounine; *Les conflits*, pp. 116, 118.

Letter to Celso Ceretti

1. Arthur Lehning, Ed, *Michel Bakounine et l'Italie*, Leiden: E. J. Brill, (Two volumes), Vol. 2, 1963; and *Oeuvres complètes*, CD.
2. See the chapter by Gaetano Manfredonia on Bakunin in Italy (1864-1867) in Philippe Pelletier, Ed, *Actualité de Bakounine 1814-2014, Bicentenaire de Michel Bakounine*, Paris: Le Monde Libertaire, 2014.
3. *Mazzini e l'Internazionale* is available online on www.liberliber.it
4. Published by *Gazzettino Rosa*, of Milan, October 1871; by *La Liberté*, of Brussels, and by *La Federación*, of Barcelona; Michel Bakounine, *Oeuvres*, op. cit., 6, 109ff, (120).
5. 13 July 1871, *La Roma del Popolo*.
6. Ibid, p. 124.
7. Max Nettlau, *Bakunin e l'Internazionale in Italia*, Geneva: Edizione del Risveglio, 1928, pp. 444ff. Available online: http://www.liberliber.it/mediateca/libri/n/nettlau/bakunin_e_l_internazionale_in_italia/pdf/nettlau_bakunin_e_l_internazionale_in_italia.pdf
8. In *Oeuvres complètes*, CD. French title: *La Théologie Politique de Mazzini et l'Internationale*, Neuchatel: G. Guillaume, 1871, p. 6; also published by the *Gazzettino Rosa*, and by *La Liberté*; Arthur Lehning, Ed, *Michel Bakounine et l'Italie*, op. cit., 2, p. 1.
9. Letter to *La Roma del Popolo*, 21 December 1871.
10. October 1871, 'Circular letter to my Italian friends, *Oeuvres*, 6, 305ff.
11. Ibid, p. 348.
12. Ibid, p. 313.
13. Ibid, p. 318.
14. Ibid, p. 333.
15. Ibid, p. 336.
16. Ibid, p. 339-42.
17. *Bakunin e l'Internazionale in Italia*, op. cit., p. 461. Cafiero criticised Engels' strong-arm tactics, repudiated the politics of the authors of the *Communist Manifesto*, and chose to work with Bakunin. The new-born Italian IWA federation broke all solidarity with the General Council.
18. Nunzio Pernicone, *Italian Anarchism, 1864-1892*, Oakland & Edinburgh: PM Press, p. 44.
19. Letter to the editors of *Proletario Italiano*, 16-28 November 1871.
20. For the circumstances of this letter see chapter XXI of Max Nettlau, *Bakunin*, op. cit.
21. At the IWA congress of September 1873. Max Nettlau, op. cit., p. 337.
22. Letter to Celso Ceretti, 15 December 1871.
23. 'The influence of the General Council and of its secretary for Italy was minimal or non-existent…' Ibid, p. 438. See also pp. 559-560.
24. Mazzini died on 10 March 1872.
25. Political figures.
26. Bakunin refers to England when he might have referred to Britain and Ireland.
27. A tax on milling grains, imposed in 1869, designed to raise funds to repair the state's insolvency. It caused mass revolts. Many peasants were killed.

28 Illegible word.
29 By 'London' Bakunin refers to the leaders of the General Council of the IWA.
30 A reference to Amadeo, the second son of the King of Italy, King of Spain 1870 to 1873.
31 Only four issues of this Milan weekly were published in February-March 1872. Three were seized by the authorities, and its associates were arrested. Its editor, Vincenzo Pezza, was imprisoned for five months.
32 'Domicilio coatto' was a form of internal exile and open arrest: victims were directed to live in locations chosen by the government – sometimes remote islands – and were subjected to police surveillance.
33 F. Vyncke comments that this tactic of Bakunin 'resulted in him having a reputation as a dangerous and perfidious conspirator. The documents do not confirm this imputation, which seems to have been adroitly disseminated by German Marxist circles. Considering Bakuninist ideology in its entirety, such secret cells would have been, it seems to us, nothing more than an appropriate means for leaders to collectively prepare revolutionary action.' F. Vyncke, 'L'influence idéologique de Bakounine en italie', *Philosophica*, 2, 1964.
34 The privileged rich group.
35 Carlo Terzaghi was a police spy.
36 Bakunin was embittered by repeated attacks. He often used such derogatory phrases in his comments about Marx and his allies.
37 Bakunin drafted several replies but few were ever published.
38 Many of Bakunin's writings were published anonymously, or pseudonymously.
39 Bakunin has in mind passages of the General Statutes of the IWA – as agreed at its first congress – that set out that each IWA organisation had a right to an independent existence.

Letter to Tómas González Morago

1 *Oeuvres complètes*, Amsterdam: IISG, 2000, CD.
2 The programme of the Spanish Alliance is reproduced by Max Nettlau, *Miguel Bakunin, la Internacional y la Alianza en España (1868-1873)*, New York, Iberama Publishing Company, 1971, p. 33. Available online: https://docs.google.com/file/d/0B14Synwe1mHzVGxuUE91Z1c1RVE/edit?pref=2&pli=1
3 Letter from Bakunin, 4 December 1869. (A sentiment that may have been shared by the author of the words: 'A spectre is haunting Europe....'?)
4 Paul Lafargue wrote that the Alliance was centred in Switzerland and its orders emanated from the mystery Pope in Locarno. Lafargue was told: 'The joke was a bit much: in reality the Alliance, in Switzerland was just an IWA section with its seat and members in Geneva; the section was recognised by the London General Council and sent a delegate to the Basel Congress; all its acts were public; and since soon it will have been dissolved for over a year, it could have had absolutely no influence on the Zaragozza Congress.' Jura Federation, *Bulletin*, 15 June 1872.
5 See the chapter on Key Questions in René Berthier, *Social-Democracy and Anarchism in the International Workers' Association, 1864-1877*, London: Merlin Press, 2015, pp. 60-61.

6   See the text above: 'On the Alliance'.
7   Bakunin uses the word English where British would be more apt.
8   Bakunin was guessing perhaps – but correctly: see for example a letter of Marx to Engels of 11 September 1867: 'when the next revolution comes, and that will perhaps be sooner than might appear, we (i.e. you and I) will have this *mighty instrument in our hands*.' (*Collected Works*, 42, 424, emphasis added.) For some twenty years before his retirement Engels was a manager and partner in a textile business in Manchester (and a member of the Cheshire hunt). Over many years Marx confided IWA secrets to him. Although he was Marx's personal friend he was also an employer, and as such a person not eligible for membership of the IWA. Critics of Marx and Engels might see their correspondence as conspiracy. Conspiracy is a political crime defined by those hostile to the purposes of the conspirators. When Marx and Engels accused Bakunin of conspiring to be a dictator in the IWA they were sadly lacking in even-handedness.
9   Letter to Anselmo Lorenzo*, 10 May 1872 (the first of two texts on the *Oeuvres complètes*, CD).

The Programme of the Slav section in Zurich

1   Later published as an Appendix B of *Gosoudarstvennost i Anarkhia / Statism and Anarchy*. From: *Oeuvres complètes*, Amsterdam: IISG, 2000, CD.
2   Guillaume writes that there were also Serb members in this group. Some texts were sent by the group to Serbia. Some Serbian socialists were calling for the dissolution of existing states in the region, and the construction beyond the influence of Austria-Hungary, Ottoman-Turkey and Russia, of new polities of Balkan peoples, organised between themselves in a new federation.
3   James Guillaume says the group broke up in 1873 as a result of conflicts between Russian members. In part these were personal conflicts, but there were also political differences with Peter Lavrov, another influential group member. Bakunin wanted a somewhat more lively form of propaganda and activity whilst Lavrov advocated a slower approach. Bakunin's closest collaborators were Zamfirij Konstantinovitch Ralli-Arbore and Armand Ross (Michel Sazhin*). Ralli printed a collection of socialist essays *The Historical Development of the International* (*Istoritcheskoé razvitié Internatsionala*), including one – on the Alliance – by Bakunin. Later these two fell out with each other. Kropotkin developed contacts with the Jura Federation in this period but never met Bakunin, perhaps symptomatic of Bakunin's retirement from active politics.
4   See: Graham John Gamblin, *Russian Populism and its relations with Anarchism 1870-1881*, Thesis, Centre for Russian and East European Studies, University of Birmingham, 1999.
5   Vera Figner was a medical student member of the group. There were many women students from Russia in Zurich, attracted to radical ideas and living in poverty.
6   5 August 1872, Zurich. *Oeuvres complètes*, CD.
7   *Égalité*, 19 June 1869.

Writings Against Marx

1. This text – 'Fragment formant une suite de l'Empire Knouto-Germanique' ('Fragment forming a continuation of On the Knouto-Germanic Empire'), is in *Oeuvres,* op. cit., 4, 395-439. The title 'Writings against Marx' is from Arthur Lehning, Ed., Bakounine; *Les conflits dans l'Internationale*: 1872, Antony (France): Ed. Tops-H. Trinquier, 2003, pp. 169-93. The first two pages of the Mss. are lost. Before the opening paragraph above there is an incomplete sentence in the Mss: '[for] exploitation and necessarily also for a solidarity's compression across every national frontier, and despite the political differences that actually exist between many states.'
2. Jura Federation, *Bulletin,* 1 September 1872.
3. A reference to Nechaev.
4. James Guillaume has a note that refers to the statutes voted by the first General Congress of the International, in Geneva, (September 1866), as against the text Marx suggested. See *Mémoire présenté,* op. cit., pp. 206ff, and the appendix 'July 1872, Jura Federation – Polemic against the General Council.' in René Berthier, *Social Democracy and Anarchism in the First International,* London: Merlin Press, 2015.
5. Bakunin refers to debates at the first IWA congress, see above: 'To the Jura Comrades'.
6. The programme of the IWA as defined by the 'Considering clauses' agreed as statutes at its first congress.
7. Bakunin is a year out: the Alliance was founded in 1868. JG
8. Bakunin exaggerates, but gets to the heart of the matter: Marx and Engels were very slow to criticise German Social-democracy *publicly*.
9. Bakunin in his manuscript placed a memo here, to add a note, but forgot to insert it. The congress 'of professors bourgeois political economy' of which he spoke was a congress held in Eisenach in 1872, by a group of economists slightly tainted with socialism and called in Germany 'cathedral-socialists' (Katheder-Sozialisten). What was meant thereby was the professorial chair rather than the ecclesiastical chair. JG
10. Charles Perron*, Jules Monchal, and other Geneva delegates. In asking the congress to comment on matters of political liberties, they wished simply to be assured that some of the Parisian delegates were not agents of Bonaparte [Napoleon III] – as was alleged by supporters of Blanqui. JG.
11. Bakunin forgets that the declaration contained two clauses; the first was indeed limited, saying: 'That workers' social emancipation is inseparable from their political emancipation'; but the second added: 'that establishing political liberties is a first and absolutely necessary measure'. The declaration was voted unanimously; but amongst the voting delegates there were many – and I was one of these — who as yet had only very confused ideas about the programme of the International and the relationship between politics and the emancipation of the proletariat. JG.
12. Bakunin wishes to say that they refrained from presenting a positive political programme, proposing the 'conquest of political power' to the proletariat. JG
13. Bakunin writes of the party of Socialist Democracy – 'la democratie socialiste'.

14 There were three [German delegates] at the Congress in Geneva (1866), six in Lausanne (1867), four in Brussels (1868) and (including two Austrian delegates) eleven in Basel. JG
15 The British delegates had recently voted against the Marxists at the Congress of The Hague (1872).
16 In some Swiss cantons new laws came to be proposed (or ratified) through popular votes, in other small cantons popular assemblies voted laws.
17 Five items were set by the General Council for the Congress agenda and discussed in IWA bodies. A discussion on participation in bourgeois politics was suggested as an additional item, without prior discussion. Congress decided that it might be discussed, but only after the five items that had been previously announced. Since time was lacking no further discussion on the matter took place. Extracts from the discussion are set out in an appendix to René Berthier, *Social Democracy and Anarchism*, op. cit.
18 'Quos ego'.
19 The conference held discussions but did not approve resolutions, resolutions were edited after the event.
20 A reference to the Sonvilier circular drafted by critics of the General Council on 12 November 1871.
https://firstinternational.files.wordpress.com/.../the-sonvillier-circular.pdf
21 This text was written in November 1872. JG
22 He did not just allow things to happen, he himself was in the thick of making things happen. JG
23 These are terms used by Mr Engels in a very instructive letter addressed to our friend Cafiero (Bakunin's note). On the correspondence of Engels with Cafiero in 1871 and the spring of 1872, see James Guillaume, *L'Internationale, Documents et Souvenirs*, Vol. 2, p. 280. JG
24 Messrs Marx and Engels habitually used the picturesque and disdainful term lumpen-proletariat, to designate paupers, the rag-bag proletariat. MB
25 'socialisme savant'.
26 A decisive battle in the Franco-Prussian war, resulting in German victory and the collapse of the Napoleonic regime.
27 A reference to words of [Friedrich] Sorge*, an American delegate, at the congress of The Hague, who said: 'Partisans of autonomy say that our Association needs no head. We on the contrary think one is needed and one with a good brain.' JG [Sorge became for some time the chief actor of the General Council in New York.]
28 Bakunin's information was not exact. The congress of Geneva [1866] had nothing to 'eliminate' from a 'programme presented by Marx'. The congress adopted without change, the text of the 'considering clauses' of the provisional statutes, wherein are exposed in their general terms the principles on the base of which the International came together. As for the Manifesto [*Inaugural Address*] of 1864, in which Marx formulated the idea that 'the conquest of political power is the first duty of the proletariat', before 1872 *Marx never submitted this to the approbation of any congress of the International, and it remained only an expression of the personal opinions of its editor and of its co-signatories.* JG

29 Bakunin refers to Carlo Cafiero*, who had received a letter from Engels using this term. Cafiero broke with Engels in a letter dated 12 June 1872, accusing Engels and Marx of wishing to impose a strong, centralised government; foisting a strategy on to the IWA that they had elaborated some two decades earlier, in the *Communist Manifesto*. He rejected a perspective that would 'teach illiterates how to read, fighting the Camorra and brigands', using agricultural and industrial armies. Jacques Freymond, *La première internationale*, Vol. 3, Geneva: IUHEI, 1971, pp. 298ff.
30 Bakunin had in mind the federations of Belgium, France, Italy, the Jura and Spain.
31 Let every Christian and pagan God and paradise protect us from that [an official programme]. MB
32 Guillaume noted that at this point there began an extensive digression discussing the politics of Mazzini, not reproduced here.
33 Declaration of the General Council of the International Working Men's Association, *The Eastern Post*, 24 February 1872; Marx & Engels, *Collected Works*, op. cit., 23, 77. https://www.marxists.org/archive/marx/iwma/documents/1872/russia.htm

On Lassalle and Marx

1 Our Title.
2 Written between January and August 1873 in Locarno. An edition edited by Marshall Shatz was published by Cambridge University Press in 1990. The texts below are our translations from the text in *Ouevres complètes*, Amsterdam: IISG, 2000, (CD).
3 Bakunin commented on cooperatives' potential to facilitate change in the Appendix A of this book: he did not oppose coop projects but saw them as a drop of water in a desert.
4 See comments of Bakunin on privileged sectors of the labour movement such as those in Geneva in the Fabrique.*
5 Bakunin refers to the *Inaugural Address*.*
6 Letter of 22-28 December 1871 on Italy, the General Council and the IWA.
7 Bakunin goes on to discuss the development of proletarian, bourgeois and 'democratic' party politics.

Letter of Resignation from the Jura Federation

1 From *Bulletin de la Federation jurassienne*, (Supplement), No. 27, 12 October 1873.
2 No dues-paying IWA federation was ever organised in Germany; the Social-democratic party noted its sympathy, but it affiliated only as far as the 'law allowed'.
3 No official report of the 'Marxist' Geneva congress of 1873 was ever published. There were disagreements over the powers and the location of the General Council. Bakunin no doubt heard reports of its internal division and conflict.

Letter To Élisée Reclus

1. From *Ouevres complètes*, Amsterdam: IISG, 2000, (CD).
2. Written by Élisée Reclus from La Tour de Peilz, (Canton Vaud), 8 February 1875. http://kropot.free.fr/Reclus-corr-T2.htm#Nettlau
3. This phrase appears in Élisée Reclus's letter.

PEOPLE, PLACES, ORGANISATIONS, EVENTS

Alliance for Socialist Democracy: founded in October 1868 as an International body. It largest section was in Geneva, this section was admitted into the IWA by the General Council and was dissolved in 1871. It had non-resident members: Bakunin in the Ticino and others in France, Italy and Spain

Alianza de la Democracia Socialista: founded in the spring of 1870 by Farga Pellicer and Sentiñón and others with sections in Barcelona and Madrid.

Austria: more properly the Austro-Hungarian Empire, a dual state in which some German and Hungarians had more privilege as compared with other peoples: Czechs, Poles, Rumanians, Ruthenians, Serbs, Slovenes and others.

Bakunin, Mikhail: (Mikhail Alexandrovich, 1814-1876) Russian, married Antonia Kwiatkowska; lead a socialist current in the League for Peace and Freedom; President of the Geneva Alliance group, in 1869 a co-editor of *L'Égalité*; attended Basel congress of the IWA and then moved to the Italian speaking part of Switzerland and developed contacts with the Italian IWA, a distant member of the Jura Federation, expelled from the central section of the Geneva IWA in August 1870, expelled from IWA at The Hague, attended St Imier congress in 1872.

Bebel, August: a long-lived political organiser, active in Lassalle's organisation, the Saxon People's Party and Social-Democratic parties until his death in 1913.

Becker, Johann Philipp: a veteran of German revolution of 1848, a member of the Communist League, a friend of Marx and Engels, once a friend, later a bitter enemy of Bakunin. Becker played a leading part in setting up German language IWA sections and published a newspaper *Der Vorbote* in Geneva that circulated as far as Germany and America. His network collapsed when Social-Democratic party organisation began in 1869. He was vice-president of the 'Bakuninist' Alliance in Geneva, but broke with it shortly before the split in the Swiss Romande IWA Federation. He organised the 'authoritarian' congress of the IWA in Geneva in September 1873.

Bismarck, Otto von: Prussian political leader, later Chancellor of Germany.

Blanqui, Louis Auguste: (1805-81), French socialist, participated in several insurrections, and was frequently imprisoned.

Borkheim, Sigismund: participated in the insurrection in Baden in 1848-9, a personal friend of Marx. Encouraged by the latter he published attacks on Bakunin, as a pan-Slavist.

Brosset, François: Savoyard workers leader in Geneva. First president of the Romande Federation.

Bürkli, Karl: Swiss, influential supporter of co-op and socialist movements in Zurich.

Cafiero, Carlo: Italian, worked for a time with Engels but later broke with him; attended St Imier congress in 1872, helped finance Bakunin's home in the Ticino, died 1892.

Ceretti, Celso: Italian, worked with Garibaldi, then Bakunin, imprisoned in 1873; a socialist in later life.

Coullery, Pierre: Swiss, a doctor in Canton Neuchâtel, with a reputation for generosity. His first paper *Voix de l'Avenir*, was for some time recognised as the local IWA journal. He made an alliance with local conservatives to further his local government ambitions.

December days: The coup d'état of December 1851 which lead to the establishment of the Empire of Napoleon III.

Delescluze, Louis-Charles: French radical, died in 1871 fighting for the Paris Commune.

Duval, Theodor: at one time a member of the Central Bureau of the Geneva Alliance, later a bitter critic of Bakunin.

Eccarius, Johann Georg: German tailor, a member of the Communist League circa 1848, IWA general secretary in London; attended several IWA congresses including the one in Geneva in 1873, died 1889.

L'Égalité: journal of the IWA in Geneva. Before the split in the Romande Federation largely influenced by Bakunin and his co-thinkers; thereafter edited by his enemy Utin, q.v.

Fabrique: a set luxury trades in Geneva; their IWA sections worked for an alliance with the local Radical Party.

Fanelli, Giuseppe: Italian, worked with Garibaldi, then with Bakunin; his journey to Barcelona inspired the formation of IWA in Spain, elected as a deputy for Torchiara in December 1870, attended St Imier congress in 1872, died 1877.

Federal Committee (or Regional Committee, or General Committee): the committee of an IWA regional federation (e.g. Belgian, Romande, Spanish).

Friscia, Saverio: Sicilian medical doctor, worked in the League for Peace and Freedom, at one time close to Mazzini, then Bakunin; attended the Rimini congress of the IWA in 1872. He was first elected to parliament in Sciacca in 1862 and was re-elected several times thereafter. Died 1886.

Gambetta, Léon: French lawyer and politician, helped establish a republic to replace state of Napoleon III, died 1882.

Gambuzzi, Carlo: worked with Garibaldi, then with Bakunin.

Garibaldi, Giuseppe: His red-shirted irregular army fought for a united Italy. He participated in the League for Peace and Freedom in 1867, died 1882.

Goegg, Amand: Active in the German democratic movement in 1848-9, and later in Switzerland, participated in League for Peace and Freedom, attended IWA congress in Basel 1869, died 1897.

Greulich, Hermann: German, worked in the League for Peace and Freedom, active for many years in the Swiss labour movement. Editor of *Tagwacht*.

Grosselin, Jacques: Swiss watchmaker, later a Radical Party deputy.

Grütli: A nationalist workers' association, created in 1838, membership was restricted to Swiss nationals.

Guétat, at one time a member of the Central Bureau of the Geneva Alliance, later a bitter critic of Bakunin.

Guillaume, James: Swiss, teacher, printer and editor; expelled from IWA at The Hague, attended St Imier congress in 1872 and later IWA congresses up to 1877. Edited the Jura Federation journals: *Le Progrès*, *Solidarité* and the *Bulletin*. Later edited a six volume anthology of Bakunin's writings and a three volume documentary history of the IWA. Died 1916.

Heng, Fritz: Engraver, activist in the Alliance and IWA, attended Basel congress 1869 and successive congresses of the Romande and Jura IWA Federation between 1870 and 1874.

Herzen, Alexander: Russian exile and dissident, published *Kolokol*; died 1870. Gave money to support Bakunin.

Inaugural Address: a statement written by Marx and sanctioned by the IWA General Council. James Guillaume comments that it might be seen as the personal view of its editor and of those members of the General Council who had approved it, but it was neither submitted to, nor adopted by the first IWA congress.

IWA: International Workers' Association.

Jacobin: the centralising radical party around Robespierre and St Just that took the leadership of post-revolutionary France in 1793 and was ousted from power in 1794.

June days (1848, Paris): the French army killed some 10,000 workers protesting for jobs and unemployment relief.

Joukovsky, Nikolaï Ivanovitch: Russian, worked in the League for Peace, the Alliance, the IWA; close to Bakunin; supporter of the Jura Federation, expelled from the central section of the Geneva IWA in August 1870, attended congresses of the IWA in 1873 and 1876.

Jung, Hermann: Swiss, member of the General Council for many years, later critical of Marx.

Kolokol, (The Bell), journal, see Herzen.

Lassalle, Ferdinand: a member of the Communist League circa 1848, the founding leader of the General Association of German Workers', (Allgemeiner Deutscher Arbeiterverein, ADAV), held secret talks with Bismarck 1863, died 1864.

League for Peace and Freedom: founded after the wars of 1866, members included Bakunin, Louis Blanc, Garibaldi, Herzen, Victor Hugo, John Stuart Mill, the Reclus brothers.

Lefrançais, Gustave: active in the Paris Commune then in exile in the Jura IWA, attended St Imier congress in 1872.

Liebknecht, Wilhelm: a member of the Communist League circa 1848, German Social-Democrat, reprimanded at the Basel congress for libel against Bakunin; editor of *Volkstaat*, died 1900.

Longuet, Charles: married Marx's daughter Jenny.

Lorenzo, Anselmo: long-lived Spanish libertarian activist and organiser, died 1915.

Malon, Benoît: active in the Paris Commune, in exile in Switzerland up to to 1880.

Mazzini, Giuseppe, Catholic radical, campaigner for Italian unity, died 1872. In 1869, under pressure from Italy, the Swiss canton of Ticino, bordering on Italy ordered him to leave its territory. Died 1872.

Meuron, Constant: 1804-72, veteran Swiss revolutionary. In 1869 he lost his employment as a consequence of the conflict in the Le Locle IWA between radicals and supporters of Coullery.

Morago, Tómas González: engraver, activist in Madrid and in the Spanish IWA and in the Alianza, attended congresses of The Hague, St Imier, Verviers and Ghent, died in prison in 1885.

Nabruzzi, Ludovico: journalist, leading figure in the Italian IWA, spent many years in exile, attended St Imier congress in 1872.

Nechaev, Sergey: Russian radical, fled abroad, captivated Bakunin, arrested in Zurich in 1872, extradited to Russia, died in prison 1882.

Ogarev, Nicholas: close friend of Herzen, a Russian radical active in the League for Peace. In October 1872, signed a letter rejecting the Bakunin's expulsion from the IWA, died 1877.

Ostyn, Charles: Communard, in exile in Switzerland up to 1880; born Paris 1823, died 1912.

Palix, Louis: French tailor, active in the Lyons IWA, a delegate to the Lausanne and Basel IWA congresses, died 1871(?).

Paepe, César De: Belgian, influenced by Proudhon, later a socialist, attended congresses of the IWA up to 1876.

Peoples' Democratic Party (Volkspartei) South German liberals.

Perret, Henri: Swiss, one time secretary of the Geneva Central Section committee, and of the Romande federal committee; later took up a career with the police.

Perron, Charles: Swiss, painter, cartographer, member of the Central Bureau of the Alliance, co-editor of *L'Égalité*, attended Basel congress in 1869, supporter of the Jura Federation, expelled from the central section of the Geneva IWA in August 1870.

Pindy, Jean-Louis: a carpenter, sentenced to death for supporting the Paris Commune, attended St Imier congress in 1872, lived the rest of his life in exile, in Switzerland.

***Le Progrès*,** journal published in Le Locle supported by the Romande (Jura) IWA Federation, succeeded by *Solidarité*.

Proudhon, Pierre-Joseph, French, 1809-1865, his writings influenced many members of the IWA. He was elected to the Constituent Assembly in 1848, and was imprisoned between 1849 and 1852 for insulting the future emperor, Napoleon III. He lived much of the rest of his life in exile in Belgium.

Reclus, Élisée & Élie: brothers, French, academic geographers, IWA members, active in League for Peace and Freedom, Communards, exiled from France for many years. Died 1905 and 1904.

Richard, Albert: weaver, Lyons IWA activist, Alliance supporter; later sided with Bonapartist party, died 1925.

Robin, Paul: French, teacher, sometime co-editor of *L'Égalité*; briefly a member of the General Council in London, expelled from that body after opposing the procedure and decisions of the London Conference of September 1871. Died 1912.

Romande: French-speaking Switzerland.

Sazhin, Michael, (**Ross, Armand**), Russian anarchist, active in Zurich in 1870-76; printer/publisher.

von Schweitzer, Johann Baptist: became president of the German General Worker's Association after the death of Ferdinand Lassalle in 1864; resigned 1871.

SDWP: Socialist-Democratic Workers' Party, see below.

Second Empire: the regime of Napoleon III 1852-1870.

Serno-Soloviévitch, Alexander: Russian radical, lived in exile in Geneva, joined IWA, supported a short-lived Social-Democratic party. Committed suicide in 1869.

Socialist-Democratic Workers' Party, (SDWP) German party formed of dissidents from Lassalle's General Workers Association and other democrats at Eisenach in 1869, sometimes referred to as the Eisenacher party. Journal: *Volksstaat*.

Solidarité: the journal of the Romande (Jura) IWA Federation, banned in September 1870 and succeeded by the *Bulletin*.

Sorge, Friedrich: German radical, sentenced to death for his part in rising of 1849-9; settled in USA, a Marx loyalist; the General Council in New York co-opted him to act as its General Secretary in 1872, died 1906.

Temple-Unique: a (masonic) meeting hall in Geneva used for large public meetin gs.

Tolain, Henri Louis: French, signed the manifesto of the sixty in 1864. An IWA activist, he was elected a mayor and a deputy in 1871 and denounced the Commune. On this account he was expelled from the IWA. Died 1897.

Utin, Nikolai Isaakovich: Russian revolutionary active in the Geneva IWA. He returned to Russia in 1878, and was licensed to supply vodka, died 1883.

Varlin, Eugène, activist in the IWA and in the Commune; captured, tortured and shot in May 1871.

Versailles Government: The French Third Republic was proclaimed in September 1870. From Versailles, it organised forces for the suppression of the Commune

Voix de l'Avenir: Journal published by Coullery, q.v.

Volksstaat: the principle organ of the Socialist-democratic Workers' Party of Germany, published in Leipzig.

Vorbote, Der: Journal published by Becker, q.v.

Zagorski, Jan: Polish secretary of the Central Bureau of the Alliance, previously active in the League for Peace and Freedom.

SUGGESTIONS FOR FURTHER READING

Bakunin: In French: a six volume collection of his *Oeuvres*, edited by James Guillaume and published in Paris by P. V. Stock (Available online, e.g. http://fr.wikisource.org/wiki/Bakounine/%C5%92uvres); and *Ouevres complètes*, Amsterdam: IISG, 2000 – presented on a CD – which is much more comprehensive.

René Berthier, *Social-democracy and Anarchism in the International Workers' Association, 1864-1877*, Merlin Press, 2015.

James Guillaume, *L'Internationale: documents et souvenirs 1864-78*, (Four books, 1905, 1907, 1909 and 1910). Books 1 and 2 are available online in one volume (Paris, Société nouvelle de librairie et d'éditions, 1905); books 3 and 4 are available online in a second volume (Paris, Stock, 1909). http://fr.wikisource.org/wiki/Auteur:James_Guillaume

Mathieu Léonard, *L'émancipation des travailleurs*, Paris: La Fabrique, 2011.

Franz Mehring, *Karl Marx – The Story of his Life*, London, Allen & Unwin, 1939. (Available online). The *Marxists* website (http://www.marxists.org/) has this and many other texts.

Philippe Pelletier, Ed, *Actualité de Bakounine 1814-2014, Bicentenaire de Michel Bakounine*, Paris: Le Monde Libertaire, 2014.

Web Sites

On Bakunin:

http://atelierdecreationlibertaire.com/blogs/bakounine/

Michail Aleksandrovič Bakunin. Michail Aleksandrovič Bakunin Papers. Internationaal Instituut voor Sociale Geschiedenis, Amsterdam. http://hdl.handle.net/10622/ARCH00018

On congresses of the International Working Men's Association:

Resolutions of the Congress of Geneva, 1866 and the Congress of Brussels, 1868.

http://archive.org/stream/resolutionsofcon00inte/resolutionsofcon00inte_djvu.txt;

Report of the Fourth Annual Congress of the International Working Men's Association, held at Basel, in Switzerland, from the 6th to the 11th September, 1869; Published by the General Council, 1869; available via http://hdl.handle.net/10622/B6E656DD-15BA-4E47-A6F7-B7132F4544C3

Much more complete is the Compte-rendu du IVe Congrès tenu à Bâle en septembre 1869, Brussels, Imprimerie Désirée Brismée, 1869. Available online: on http://books.google.co.uk/ mRegards

SOURCES

1868
October: **Programme of the International Alliance for Socialist Democracy**, 33-4.

1869
March: **Open Letter from the Central Bureau of the [International] Fraternity**, 35-7.
21 April: **Letter to James Guillaume**, 38.
April, June and August-September: **Articles in L'Égalité**: 'Organisation and the General Strike'; 'The Politics of the International', 39-56.
1 May: **Letter in Le Progrès** (Le Locle), 40.
August-September: **Draft resolution on inheritance; On Inheritance, speeches at the Basel congress of the IWA**, 56-7.

1870
7 February: **Letter to Albert Richard**, 11.
12 March: **Letter to Albert Richard**, 90.
1 April: **Letter to Albert Richard**, 6.
April-May: **On Real Democracy**, *Les Ours de Berne et l'Ours de Saint-Pétersbourg;* (The Bears of Bern and the Bear of St Petersburg), 62-70.
30 May, **Letter to Carlo Gambuzzi**, 6.
2-9 June, **Letter to Nechaev**, 21.
August-September: **Prospects for Socialism**, *Lettres à un Français & suites);* (Letters to a Frenchman & continuations), 71-89; 101.
September-October: **Letters to Nikolai Ogarev**, 90-4.
26 September: **The Red Poster,** Lyons, 92-3.
September-October: **Letter to Palix**, *La situation politique en France;* (The Political situation in France.), 61.

1871
Winter: **On Discipline**, *L'Empire Knouto-Germanique et la révolution sociale: révolution sociale ou dictature militaire;* (The Germanic-militarist Empire and the Social Revolution, first part.), 95.
May: **On Democracy and Education**, second lecture to the workers of the Saint-Imier valley, 97-101.
June: **Socialism and the Paris Commune**, *Préambule pour la seconde livraison de L'Empire Knouto-germanique;* (*Preface to the second delivery of The Germanic-militarist Empire and the Social Revolution.*) 103-112.

July: **On Leaders and politics**, *Protestation de l'alliance*; (*The Alliance Protests.*), 103-111.
July/August: **On the Alliance**, *Rapport sur l'alliance*; (*The Alliance reports back*), 117-141.
September-October: **A Reply of an Internationalist to Mazzini**, *Risposta d'un Internationale a Mazzini*, 184.
October: **Circular letter to my Italian friends.** Excerpts were published as *Agli Operai delegati al Congresso di Roma* (To the delegates of the Rome congress), 12, 14, 22, 170, 185-6.
August-November: **La Théologie Politique de Mazzini et l'Internationale;** (Mazzini's Political Theology and the International), 10, 171, 254n.
16-28 November: **Letter to the editors of Proletario Italiano**, 186-7.
15 December: **Letter to Celso Ceretti**, 12-3.
22-28 December: **Italy and the General Council of the IWA**, 8-9.

1872
February-March: **Letter to the Jura Comrades**, *Aux Compagnons de la Fédération des Sections internationales de Jura*, 172-183.
March: **Germany and State Communism**, *L'Allemagne et le communisme d'état*, 183-4.
10 May 1872, **Letter to Anselmo Lorenzo**, 216.
21 May: **Letter to Tómas González Morago**, 9, 208-216.
12 June: **Letter to the Jura Bulletin** (responding to 'Fictional Splits in the IWA'), 16.
5 August: **Programme for a Serbian Socialist Party**, 220.
14-15 August: **The Programme of the Slav section of Zurich**, 217-20.
October: **Letter to La Liberté** (Brussels), 111-2.
November-December: **Writings against Marx**, *Fragment formant une suite de L'Empire Knouto-Germanique; Fragment forming a continuation of The Germanic-militarist Empire and the Social Revolution*, 221-241.

1873
January-August: **Statism and Anarchy**, *Gosudarstvennost i anarkhiya*, 14-5, 242-6.
October: **Letter of resignation from the Jura Federation**, 247-50.

1875
15 February: **Letter to Élisée Reclus**, 251-2.

SUBJECTS DISCUSSED BY BAKUNIN

Authority and discipline, 10-12, 21, 63, 91, 95, 101, 105, 120, 211, 216, 246

Conspiracy, 7, 21, 24, 152-3

Co-operatives, 131-2, 242

Democratic process in labour organisations, 7, 21, 204-6

Education, 97-99

Electoral politics, 22, 60-70, 99-100, 166, 225-6

Federalism, 21-2

Gender, 23, 90, 153, 186-7, 219-220

Internationalism, 59, 84-5, 129, 130, 167, 170-2, 176-80

Marxism, 13-4, 221-241

Paris Commune, 102-112, 179, 184, 199, 244

Politics, 5, 14, 22, 23, 86, 117, 128-9, 228, 233

Press, the, 17, 61, 68

Programme of the IWA, 43-5, 52-6, 210-213, 222, 224, 228-33

Revolution, 7, 11-14, 21, 36, 39, 45, 47, 52-5, 72, 65-6, 73-4, 79-80, 95, 96, 101, 110, 185, 191, 195-6, 204 (*see also Paris Commune*)

Rural conflict, 73, 182, 198-9

Solidarity, 8, 9, 11-3, 20, 34, 44, 47-9, 77, 85, 104, 106, 129, 133-6, 139-41, 156, 213-5, 222, 233-5

State, the, 6, 13, 14, 22, 36, 40, 46, 56, 59, 73, 84, 86-9, 93, 97-8, 106, 109-111, 128-9, 139, 181, 217-8

Unity, 12-3, 43, 90, 132-3, 140, 187-190, 204, 205, 213-6, 231-2

Urban workers, 116-20, 132-4

GENERAL INDEX

Abstentionism, see *Electoral politics*
Alianza de la Democracia Socialista, 208
Allgemeiner deutscher Arbeiter-Verein; see *General German Workers' Union*
Almanach du people, 17
Alliance for Socialist Democracy, 9, 19, 33-4, 113-7, 142-7, 208-10, 225, 226, 269-272n, 278n, 280n
Amberny, Jean-Antoine, 241
American (USA) Labour and IWA, 105, 212, 228, 236, 281n
Anarchists & Anarchism, 2, 22, 26, 102, 215, 217, 245, 246
Angaut, Jean-Christophe, 263-4n
Austria-Hungary, 6, 42, 61, 129-30, 179, 182, 220, 265n
Authority, 3, 105, 110
Avrich, Paul, 26

Barry, Maltman, 255n, 276n
Bastelica, André, 4, 92, 93
Bazaine, General, 75
Bebel, August, 170, 227
Becker, Johann Philip, 16, 33, 115, 131, 148, 151, 152, 155, 158, 161, 177-9, 208, 227, 266-7n
Belgian Labour and IWA, 4, 20, 39, 40, 228, 251, 252
Bertani, Agostino, 200-1
Berthier, René, 24, 209, 253n, 257n, 259n, 278n, 281n,
Bismarck, Otto von, 5, 71, 73, 74, 76, 77, 86, 129, 174, 2002, 203, 246, 249, 251, 252
Blanc, Gaspard, 92, 93
Blanquists, 228, 231, 237

British labour movement and IWA, 5, 116, 171, 177, 202, 228, 281n
Broglie, 252
Brosset, François, 124-5, 148, 159, 162, 165, 167-9 *passim*, 265
Bulletin de la Fédération Jurassienne, 16, 17, 217, 247
Bürkli, Karl, 227

Cafiero, Carlo, 185, 186, 282n
Cambessédès, 165, 168
Campana, 206
Campanella, Federico, 188, 206
Catalan, Adolphe, 131, 265n, 268n
Cavaignac, General, 76, 261n
Ceretti, Celso, 12-3, 184, 187, 255n; Letter to 184-207
Chartism, 5
Combe, 93
Costa, Andrea, 187, 21
Coullery, Pierre, 42, 114, 131, 164
Crosset, 159, 16, 161, 166, 168

Delescluze, Louis-Charles, 107
Draper, Hal, 24
Dupleix, 163, 166
Dupanloup, 252
Dupont, Eugène, 72, 268n
Dutch Labour and IWA, 228
Duval, 148, 152, 154, 158, 161, 162, 163

Eccarius, Johann Georg, 16, 58, 151, 153, 158, 255n, 256n, 259n
L'Egalité, 17, 18, 39, 113, 114, 116, 121, 122, 125, 148, 159, 160, 165, 255n; Bakunin's articles in 40-57
L'Eguaglianza, 17, 187

Electoral politics, 83-4, 253n
Engels, Friedrich, 16, 19, 22, 60, 114, 135, 170, 184, 187, 207, 209, 215, 222, 237, 243, 274n, 275n
Espartero, Prince, 36
Esquiroce, 93

Fabrique, 114-6, 122-6, 130-1, 142, 143-7, 160-9 *passim*
Fanelli, Giuseppe, 4, 35, 147
Fazy, 165
La Federación, 17
Federalism, 3, 38, 102
Federation of Free Producer Association: 2, 3, 46, 102, 104, 111, 136, 139, 164, 199
Filopanti, Quirico (alias of Giuseppe Barilli), 206
French Labour and IWA, 4, 53, 72-80, 90-3, 106, 154, 177-9, 202, 228 *see also Lyons, Paris Commune*
Friscia, Saverio, 35, 147

Gambetta, Léon, 75, 107
Gambuzzi, Carlo, 28, 147, 253n, 257n, 267n
Garibaldi, Giuseppe, 11, 187, 195, 204, 206
Garleret, 165
Il Gazzettino Rosa, 17, 264n, 277n
General Council of the IWA, 8, 15-21 *passim*, 57-8, 115, 142, 149-158, 171, 178-9, 186-7, 207, 209, 216, 221, 227, 228, 231
General German Workers' Union, 80, 81
Geneva Labour and IWA, 7, 39, 66, 113-4, 119-126, 143-151, 159, 160-9, 209, 241 *see also Fabrique*
German Communist Workers Association (London), 15
German Labour Movement, 16, 71, 75, 80-2, 135, 179, 254n; *see also Social-Democrats (German)*
German People's Party – *see People's Party*

Goegg, Amand, 227
Greulich, Hermann, 227
Grosselin, Jacques, 161, 164-9 *passim*
Grütli, 39, 40, 258n
Guétat, L, 148, 152, 154, 158, 161, 162, 163, 165, 166, 168
Guillaume, James, 13, 18, 19, 26, 27, 38, 61, 72, 91, 92, 102, 115, 117, 142, 143; on federalism, 102

Heng, Fritz, 143, 158, 159, 162, 168
Herzen, Alexander, 90, 206, 257n, 267n, 270n
Holstein, Vladimir, 222

Ideas-based organisation, 9, 20, 23, 24, 215; *see also Alianza de la Democracia Socialista, Alliance, International Fraternity*
International Fraternity, 35-7
International Workers' Association (IWA), 2, 10, 12-3, 15-9, 115, 142, 212, 221-3, 290; IWA statutes, 16, 33, 35, 44, 48, 52, 55, 56, 147, 151, 155, 156, 167, *see also Regions; General Council; IWA Congresses and Conferences*
IWA International Congresses and Conferences: 281n
1866, (Geneva Congress), 9, 176-9, 211, 280-1n
1867, (Lausanne Congress), 226
1868, (Brussels Congress), 150, 159, 160, 170, 226
1869, (Basel Congress), 3, 20, 56-9, 115, 125, 127, 158, 165, 265n, 281n
1871, (London Conference), 8, 15, 18, 20, 143, 216, 227, 256n
1872, (The Hague Congress), 13, 20, 221, 228, 231, 235-6, 238
1872, (St. Imier Congress), 31
1873, (Geneva Congresses), Federalist, 20, 248; Marxist, 248
1874, (Brussels Congress), 32
1876, (Bern Congress), 32
1877, (Verviers Congress), 26, 32

L'Internationale, 17, 40
L'Internazionale, 187
Italian Labour and IWA, 79-9, 154, 186, 194-9, 201-4, 221, 228, 243, 251

Jacobins, Jacobinism, 5, 21, 42, 103, 107-9, 199
Joukovsky, Nikolai, 35, 115, 287
Jung, Hermann, 115, 136, 151, 153, 158, 256n, 267n, 287
Jura IWA Federation, 3, 17-20, 96-100, 103, 114, 115, 142, 143, 170, 217, 228, 247-50, 251-2

Kolokol, 90
Kropotkin, Pierre, 26

Lassalle, Ferdinand, 14, 80-1, 242-6
Lavrov, Peter, 279n
League for Peace & Liberty, 33, 51, 52, 87, 127, 150, 160, 267n, 268n
Lefrançais, Gustave 142, 266n.
Lehning, Arthur, 27
Léo, Mrs André, 42
La Liberté (Brussels), 17, 255-6n, 264n, 277; 111-2
La Liberté (Geneva), 265n
Lessner, Friedrich, 136, 255n
Liebknecht, Wilhelm, 82, 170, 182, 227, 262n
Limousin, A, 136
Limousin, Mrs, 68-70
Lindecker, 91
Lorenzo, Anselmo, 253, Letter to, 216
Lyons, 4, 72, 90-3

MacMahon, General, 75, 251, 252
Malatesta, Errico, 25-6
Malon, Benoït, 4, 19, 35, 142, 261n, 266n
Martello, 203
Marx, Karl, 59, 13, 16, 19, 22, 114, 117, 135, 170, 174-5, 187, 215, 221-3, 227-8, 230, 237, 241, 243; *Communist Manifesto*, 243, 260n, 277n, 282n; *Fictional Splits*, 16, 267n, 270n; *Inaugural Address*, 170, 175, 223, 224, 274n, 281n, 282n
Marxism, 225-6, 230, 243-5
Marxists. 24, 111-2, 246, 248
Mass labour assemblies, 144, 166-7, 209
Mazzini, Giuseppe, 8, 12-3, 23, 61, 68, 70, 78, 103, 177, 184-207, 210; Insurrectionism, 192-3; Youth, 190; Letters on, 10, 171
Mehring, Franz, 24
Meuron, Constant, 38
Mirabeau, 17
Montagne, 42
Montel, de, 185
Morago, Tómas González, 23, 208-216
Musto, Marcello, 24

Nabruzzi, Ludovico, Letter to 116, 255n, 256n, 288
Napoleon III, 1, 4, 7, 11, 71, 74, 76, 86, 173, 177
Nechaev, Sergey, 21, 61, 68, 217, 257n, 260n, 276
Netherlands – see *Dutch Labour*
Nettlau, Max, 26, 268n, 271n, 277n

Obolensky, Princess, 68
Odger, George, 150
Oelsnitz, Alexander, 222
Ogarev, Nikolai, 90-3, 222
Ostyn, Charles, 142
Ozerov, Vladimir, 222

Paepe, César de, 266n, 267n, 268n, 288
Paillard (brothers), 166, 168
Palix, Louis, 91, 92, 93, 260n, 288; Letter to 61
Pan-Germanism, 74, 81, 127, 129, 171, 175, 181, 182, 217, 243
Pan-Slavism, 172, 179, 182, 207, 217, 243
Paris Commune, 4, 92, 95, 101, 103-112, 115, 130, 142, 184, 187, 199
Patru, 166, 168
Peasants, *see Workers, Rural*

People's Party (Volkspartei), 82, 127, 129, 130
Perrachon, 136
Perrare, Antoine, 142
Perret, Henri, 148, 149, 152, 158, 160, 161, 162, 163, 165, 168, 169
Perron, Charles, 35, 115, 131, 147, 149, 151, 155, 156, 157, 159, 160, 161, 164, 288
Pindy, Jean-Louis, 2, 103, 288
Pius IX, Pope, 103, 184, 252
Prim, General, 36
Le Progrès, 17, 18, 41, 61, 121, 148
Proletario, 206, 255n, 277n
Proudhon, Perre-Josephe. 51, 102, 254n
Proudhonists (Mutualists), 38, 57, 106

Quadrio, Maurizio, 188

Racism, 176, 254n, 270n
Radicals & Radical Party, 7, 8, 39, 40, 42, 60, 62, 64-9, 114, 125-6, 131, 164, 166, 168, 234, 241, 260n; *see also* People's Party
Rajon, 93
Ralli-Arbore, (Rally) Zamfirij Konstantinovitch, 222
Reclus, Elié, 35, 103
Reclus, Elisée, 35, 103, 251
Reichel-Ern, Marija Kasparovna, Letter to 71, 261n
La Révolution Sociale, 17
Reymond, 166
Richard, Albert, 4, 72, 92, 93, 289; l letters to, 6, 11, 90
Rittinghausen, Moritz, 227
Robin, Paul, 19, 166-169 *passim*
Romande Federation, 6, 19, 113, 114, 116, 121, 122, 125, 143, 149, 156, 158, 159, 161, 163-5, 169, 256n, 272-3n
Ross, Armand (Michel Sazhin), 222
Rossetti, 168
Rousseau, Jean-Jacques, 104
Ruffo, Cardinal, 79
Russia, 11, 21, 42, 61, 72, 74, 90, 170-177, 217, 221, 242

Saffo, 188
Saignes, E-B, 93
Sazhin, Michel, *see Ross, Armand*
Schweitzer, Johann Baptist von, 129, 289
Sentiñon, Gaspard, 158
Serno-Solovievitch, Alexander, 131, 159, 267n, 289
Shaw, R, 150
Slav lands and peoples, 6, 28, 30, 85, 171, 182, 244
Slav section of the IWA, 217-220
Smirnov, Valerian, 222
Social Democrats (German), 5, 7. 16, 23, 75, 80-9, 126-30, 138, 170-1, 182-3, 224-6, 240, 243, 244; *see also: German labour movement, General German Workers' Union, Marxists, Social-Democracy*
Social-Democracy, 23-4, 62, 73, 105, 181, 212, 220, 235-6
Solidarité, 3, 5, 21, 102, 114, 116
Sonvilier Circular, 3, 253n, 281n
Spanish Labour and IWA, 23, 154, 202, 203, 208-9, 228, 251, 271n
Specific organisation, *see Ideas-based organisation*
Stalinism, 257n
Stefanoni, Luigi, 206
Strikes and strike funds, 2, 10, 40-1, 87, 241
Sutherland, Henry, 91, 115
Swiss Labour and IWA, 6, 40, 63, 80, 181; *see also Fabrique, Geneva, Grütli, Jura, Olten, Romande*
Syndicalism, 26

Terzaghi, Carlo, 206
Tolain, Henri-Louis, 38, 136, 290
Tucci, Alberto, 185

Utin, Nicholai, 114, 116, 153, 158, 163, 256n, 270n

Valence, 93
Varlin, Eugène, 4, 92, 107, 109-110, 177, 261n
Vautier, 165
Volksstaat, 7, 80, 128, 182, 237, 254n, 255n 256n
Volksstimme, 220, 255n
Vorbote, 16, 255n, 256n, 284

Waehry, Joeseph and. P (brothers), 160, 161, 166, 168
War, 1, 71, 72, 74, 78, 170-2, 175, 261n, 287
Weyermann, 161, 165, 166
Windisch-Graetz, Prince, 179

Workers, Rural, 4, 11, 57-9, 64, 73, 76, 79-80, 96, 172, 174, 177, 182, 182, 194-203, 243
Workers, Urban, 10, 45, 213, 234, 243; Building, 29, 39, 119, 122-4, 143-6, 148, 160-2, 164-9; Child, 98, 258n; Intermediate,123; Quasi-bourgeois, 7, 213, 229, 243 *see also Fabrique*; Precarious, 47, 114, 116; Tattered (Lumpen), 229, 243, 281n; Textile, 1, 6, 90.

Zagorski, 148
Zaitsev, Bartholomy, 222
Zhoukovsky, Nikolai *see Joukovsky, Nikolai*

ALSO AVAILABLE FROM THE MERLIN PRESS

René Berthier
**Social-Democracy & Anarchism
in the International Workers' Association, 1864-1877**

This book explores the conflicts that took place in the First International. Social and economic conditions varied greatly in Europe in the 1860s and 1870s. The strategies adopted by the various federations and sections of the International Workers' Association, or IWA, reflected this diversity.

Although Marx and Engels have been seen as the leaders of the International, there were many who rejected their leadership. In September 1872 an extraordinary congress took place in Saint-Imier (Switzerland) which rejected the decisions taken at The Hague congress by Marx and his friends. A year later six IWA federations met in a regular congress in Geneva and reasserted the principle that political organising should be subordinate to workplace – economic – organisation. The great aim of the IWA was for working people to liberate themselves.

The ongoing IWA disregarded edicts of expulsion issued by the New York based General Council, at the instigation of Marx and Engels. The latter discovered they were generals without an army, isolated and at odds with the bulk of the organised labour movement.

René Berthier reviews the historiography of this conflict. Much of the ongoing IWA were inspired by Bakunin. He argued for the priority of labour solidarity. But it was not an anarchist International that was created in 1872. Anarchism was born some five years later, when Bakunin was dead. Rather, the adoption of anarchism by the remnants of the IWA marked a breach with Bakuninism.

ISBN. 978-0-85036-719-5   223 pages   paperback

www.merlinpress.co.uk